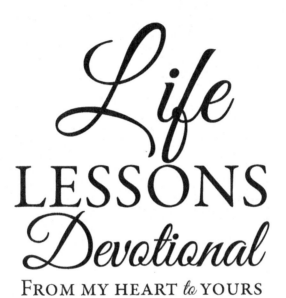

Life
LESSONS
Devotional
FROM MY HEART *to* YOURS

JIM BRACELIN

xulon PRESS

MONTH OF
January

Is Your All on the Altar? – January 1

We begin a New Year today! Today marks a new beginning for people around the world. Every morning we wake up marks a new opportunity for a new beginning for the believer. What are we going to do with this day we have been given? The Old Testament book of Leviticus speaks about the kind of sacrifice we ought to bring to our God. "*Ye shall not offer unto the LORD that which is bruised, or crushed, or broken, or cut; neither shall ye make any offering thereof in your land*" (Leviticus 22:24). Paul urged us in the New Testament book of Romans to present our bodies as a living sacrifice to God on a daily basis.

Elisha A. Hoffman wrote a song entitled, "Is Your All on the Altar?" Consider the words he wrote in thinking about these verses today:

Verse 1: *You have longed for sweet peace, and for faith to increase, and have earnestly, fervently prayed; but you cannot have rest, or be perfectly blest until all on the altar is laid.*

Verse 2: *Would you walk with the Lord, in the light of His Word, and have peace and contentment alway, you must do His sweet will, to be free from all ill, on the altar your all you must lay.*

Verse 3: *Oh, we never can know what the Lord will bestow of the blessings for which we have prayed, till our body and soul He doth fully control, and our all on the altar is laid.*

Verse 4: *Who can tell all the love He will send from above, and how happy our hearts will be made, of the fellowship sweet we shall share at His feet, when our all on the altar is laid.*

CHORUS: *Is your all on the altar of sacrifice laid? Your heart, does the Spirit control? You can only be blest and have peace and sweet rest, as you yield Him your body and soul.*

You have control over your own life today. Take responsibility for it and surrender yourself as a living sacrifice to God today to begin the New Year. Don't selfishly hold on to your dreams and plans for this day. Give up all you have to the God Who is so deserving of being the Captain of your life. Many will fight with God today for ownership of their life. Don't be one of them. Surrender, and place yourself on the altar of God today. He will use you in ways you could never imagine! He will provide in ways you could never imagine! Your part is to place your all on the altar today. Do it now!

Abba Father – January 2

A little over thirty-three years ago I became a father. I remember the day very well. Having our first child was quite an adventure for us. We attended all the child-birth classes, and did all the exercises. We fixed a room in our apartment for our new arrival. We discussed names and were very excited to see if God was going to give us a little girl, or a little boy. When the day finally arrived, it was one of the most impressive entrances I can remember. When our little girl was born and the nurse placed her in the arms of my wife, all the two of us could do was cry. We were amazed that God had allowed us to become a Mom and Dad for this little girl.

I remember praying over this precious little girl right there in the delivery room of the hospital. We asked God to give us the wisdom we would need to raise her and for His protection on her life all the way through. It was such a blessing to wrap that little girl up and take her home a few days later. During her lifetime she has brought us incredible joy. She learned to talk and walk, ride a bike, and color inside the lines, and many other things. She and her husband have now given us three beautiful grandchildren.

One of the greatest things she ever did (and still does) is call me "*Dad*." I always love to hear her and our other children say, "*I love you Dad*." God enjoys the same thing. There is a title in our Bible for our God that conveys the same feeling and emotion. It is not a title so much as it is a term of endearment (deep intimacy ... love). Paul wrote, "*For ye have not received the spirit of bondage again to fear; but ye have received the Spirit of adoption, whereby we cry, **Abba**, **Father**"* (Romans 8:15).

I am sure that when you speak to God with this kind of love in your voice, it makes Him smile and He remembers why He made you. How often do you run to God and talk to Him with these words of deep affection and love? Have you fallen into the trap of "throwing" spiritual words at God and thinking that these are what impress Him? When you pray to Him, does your love for Him shine through, or are you using words that will impress those who are listening to you? God is looking for His children to look into His eyes as our loving Daddy and tell Him how much we love Him. When was the last time as His adopted child that you stopped all you were doing and told Him that He means the world to you? When was the last time you snuggled up close to Him to let Him know you cannot imagine going through life for one second without Him? When was the last time you bragged to someone else about your Abba Father? He is worthy of your love and adoration today. Let Him know you love Him!

The LORD is His Name! – January 3

Monday night is "family night" with our kids and grandkids. As they are leaving, I walk the family outside. The last two Monday evenings, I have looked into the sky to admire the beauty of the universe my God has made. I was never very good at remembering the different patterns the stars make, or the names of them, but their splendor always amazes me.

Amos wrote about this in trying to describe how awesome our God is. He wrote, "*Seek Him that maketh the seven stars of Orion, and turneth the shadow of death into morning, and maketh the day dark with night: that calleth for the waters of the sea, and poureth them out upon the face of the earth: the LORD is His name*" (Amos 5:8). Using the expanse of the star cluster of Orion, Amos shows us what we really should be admiring.

Too often we make ourselves the "center of our universe," when in reality, there is nothing we have done that is worth anything apart from the might and power of God. The God Who breathed the stars into existence; Who turns night into day; Who put the waters into the seas which cover our earth. This is the One Who deserves our praise and attention. Take a moment today to praise God for Who He is and all He has done for you.

Not only should we praise this great God, but we should also depend upon Him for the guidance that our world so desperately needs today. God spoke to each of us through the words of Psalm 32:8, and said, "*I will instruct thee and teach thee in the way which thou shalt go: I will guide thee with Mine eye.*" What a great thought … today, wherever I will go, God has already been! The challenge for me today is not to plow a new row in my life, but to make sure that I am going in the direction God's eye is leading me.

He is worthy of this trust … after all, He placed each star that I see at night exactly in the right place. He has made the oceans to fill the places He decided they should be. He has the ability to move mountains if He desires. I want to walk in the center of His plan for my life today. I want the guidance of His eye, the leadership of His Holy Spirit in my life today. I want to make sure that I do everything I can to "*seek Him,*" and to allow Him to "*guide*" me with His eye. I want that because, simply stated, "*…the LORD is His name.*" He is worthy of my trust for this day in front of me.

"*Faith, mighty faith, the promise sees and looks to God alone, laughs at impossibilities, and cries, 'It shall be done'.*" – Charles Wesley

Open My Eyes – January 4

"My son, attend to My words; incline thine ear unto My sayings. Let them not depart from thine eyes; keep them in the midst of thine heart. For they are life unto those that find them, and health to all their flesh. Keep thy heart with all diligence; for out of it are the issues of life" (Proverbs 4:20-23).

Clara H. Scott wrote a beautiful song that has been sung in many churches over and over again. There is a reason it has been sung again and again. It speaks to a desire that we all ought to have for following the Word of God. There is something about reading the Word of God with not only our eyes being opened, but our ears, and our hearts as well. After we have heard the words of this Book we then need to tell someone else about what it has taught us, and what we have learned through it. Consider the words he wrote in thinking about these verses today:

Verse 1: *Open my eyes, that I may see glimpses of truth Thou hast for me; place in my hands the wonderful key that shall unclasp and set me free. Silently now I wait for Thee, ready my God, Thy will to see; open my eyes illumine me, Spirit divine!*

Verse 2: *Open my ears, that I may hear voices of truth Thou sendest clear; and while the wave-notes fall on my ear, everything false will disappear. Silently now I wait for Thee, ready my God, Thy will to see; open my ears, illumine me. Spirit Divine!*

Verse 3: *Open my mouth, and let me bear gladly the warm truth everywhere; open my heart, and let me prepare love with Thy children thus to share. Silently now I wait for Thee, ready my God, Thy will to see; open my heart, illumine me. Spirit divine!*

Let's start this day by asking God to open our eyes. I want eyes that are open to the truths of Scripture, but I also want eyes that are open to the hurting people that will cross my path today. I want open eyes to the opportunities for service to the King of all kings today. I want to have eyes that see the open doors of opportunity that God has planned for me today. One of the things I pray each morning is that I will accomplish all God desired for me for this day when He gave me the breath to enjoy it. That means even though I might not like the places, people and things God leads me into today, I want to have eyes that are open to see the potential God saw in those things for me. I want to have my eyes wide open today to all that God is going to do! I don't want to miss a thing!

Cry Out to Him ... He is Listening – January 5

This thirty-fourth chapter of Psalms has been a favorite of mine for the past thirty-plus years. It contains the verse that my precious wife and I used to begin to build our family upon. Psalm 34:3 says, *"Oh magnify the LORD with me, and let us exalt His name together."* This has been the cry of our heart for more than thirty years.

God has been so faithful to our family. I wish I could tell you we were equally as faithful to Him, but that is not humanly possible. I am sad to say our sinfulness, frailties, and weaknesses in our flesh have kept us from always magnifying Him. There have been times over these years that we have magnified our own desires at the expense of His will for our lives. I wish I could tell you we have always exalted His name together. There have been times we have promoted ourselves and our own glory rather than maintaining a humility that would reflect the glory of God in us.

Having said all that, there is another verse later in that same chapter which really touched my heart as I read it this morning. *"This poor man cried, and the LORD heard him, and saved him out of all his troubles"* (Psalm 34:6). I want to tell you that *"this poor man"* (a very appropriate description of me, and possibly you too), has had to cry to the Lord more than once.

What I want to encourage you with here today is that every time I recognized my "poor" condition before my God and humbled myself to cry out to Him ... He heard my cry *"... and saved* [me] *out of all* [my] *troubles."* What an incredible God He is! His mercy is endless ... praise God for that! His grace is always sufficient for every one of my weaknesses ... praise God for that! His love is without boundaries toward me ... praise God for that! His forgiveness is never-ending, and He promises to forget my sin and remember them no more ... praise God for that!

What I am trying to say is, for each of us reading this, we must all confess we all have failed to live righteously and magnify our God every day. We have not exalted His name in every moment of our lives as Christians. Please do not despair ... God knows we are all *"poor men"* that will need to cry out. I am writing to encourage you to cry out to the One Who can make a difference in your life! The lies of the Devil are not true. God will hear and forgive the humble earnest prayer of His children!

"Grace grows best in the winter. When you have nothing left but God, then you become aware that God is enough." – Maude Royden

Amen – January 6

"And unto the angel of the church of the Laodiceans write; These things saith the __Amen__, the faithful and true witness, the beginning of the creation of God" (Revelation 3:14).

If this word "Amen" was used in the beginning of a statement, it meant that whatever was to follow was truth. If it was spoken after a statement had been made, it meant that those saying, "Amen," had taken that truth to be their own – they would obey it. Today we use this word in the same way. When someone says, "Amen" in church, or even outside of church, it means that they agree with what has been said – they believe it to be truth.

When Jesus used this term as a title for Himself, He was speaking to a church that had issues of not taking a stand for the truth. He told them they were not hot, but they were not cold. He described them as being *"luke-warm."* We also must battle this condition in our spiritual lives every day. I have asked God to bring Bible truths alive in a fresh new way. We can easily become creatures of habit in that when we repeat any action again and again we lose the freshness of it. You too can fall into a rut of reading these devotionals and not allowing the Holy Spirit to do His work in your heart.

When the Word of God says something, there should never be a half-hearted approach to it as though we need to give our stamp of approval for it to be true. We ought to simply say, "Amen" to whatever we read – accept it as absolute truth! Jesus is absolute Truth. Whatever He taught ... however He lived ... the words He spoke ... the places He went ... the people He reached out to ... even the way He accepted the cross and died for us – all these are truths we ought to copy in our lives, and follow Him!

He is absolute truth! If Jesus made a statement; that statement is truth. If Jesus demonstrated an action; we ought to mimic that action in our lives. His title of "Amen" is one that tells us we ought simply to agree with Him, and follow in the footsteps He left us. The cults of our day have caused millions to question the truth of Jesus Christ. This is not something that we should be shocked to hear, or discouraged with in any way. Jesus told us this would happen. Rather than be disgusted with how the world looks at Jesus, I think we ought to have a stronger determination that we will follow Him more determinedly. We will stand and be counted for our Savior in these days we are living. We will determine not to be lukewarm, because we are following the great "Amen."

Ancient of Days – January 7

*"I beheld till the thrones were cast down, and the **Ancient of days** did sit, whose garment was white as snow, and the hair of His head like the pure wool: His throne was like the fiery flame, and His wheels as burning fire"* (Daniel 7:9).

The title, *"Ancient of days"* refers to God as being eternal. What a great thing to know that our God was not made out of a piece of wood, or stone by the hands of a man as most gods were made. He is a God that has no creator, because HE is the Creator! He is a God that had no birthday ... He has always been! He also is a God Who will have no funeral service! He has always been, and He will always be! The psalmist said He was *"from everlasting to everlasting."*

This is the God we serve today. He has seen it all, and He knows all the answers! There is nothing that God cannot do; there is nothing that has happened that God does not already know the answer to. There is nothing that could possibly enter your life today that would be a surprise to God. He has always been and will always be here.

What exactly does it mean to you that you serve the Ancient of days? It is extremely comforting that our Heavenly Father has power over everything we see happening around us today. We sometimes think the times we are living in are the toughest times in the history of mankind. God was on the throne during all the toughest times in history, and He remained God. He can handle anything that will come across my path today. We must simply yield to Him.

I never had the privilege of having a grandfather. Both my father and mothers dads died long before I was born. I have always been amazed at how well balanced my own father was in the art of being a father. His dad died in a car accident when my dad was only a year old. How did my father know how a dad was supposed to act? How did he know the balance of loving discipline and a hug around the shoulder? He knew because he was introduced to the "Ancient of days" as a boy. He knew the ultimate example.

You will be tempted to think you must have all the answers to life's challenges. Don't believe that lie. If you are a child of God, you have the ultimate authority behind you in the "Ancient of days." He has seen it all, and has all the answers. Don't try to manufacture His will, simply walk with Him daily and surrender to His plan for your life.

Love Strong – January 8

In our lifetime there has been an amazing cyclist named, Lance Armstrong. Lance started a foundation called, "Livestrong" that was designed to raise money for fighting the disease of cancer. Many people purchased bracelets that had those words, "Livestrong" embedded in them. It was a reminder to them of the battle to fight against cancer every time they saw the bracelet.

Peter gave a very strong challenge to us to "Love strong." He said, *"But the end of all things is at hand: be ye therefore sober, and watch unto prayer. And above all things have fervent charity among yourselves; for charity shall cover the multitude of sins"* (I Peter 4:7-8).

We hear a good deal today about the "end of the world," and while I don't think the world is coming to an end, I do believe the open door of opportunity we have enjoyed is closing. Because of that, I believe we Christians need to wake up and serve God now while we have the time. Peter reminds us of this very thought in this verse. It is time to be serious about our service to God, and to stop planning to do something, and actually do whatever it is God touches our heart to do.

There should be an urgency in our Christian lives! However, balancing that urgency are five clear words of direction … *"have fervent charity among yourselves."* As we realize the importance of the days we are living in, we ought to love each other more. I'm not talking about a romantic love; I am talking about the charity that is described in I Corinthians 13. The kind of love that is patient and kind; that does not envy and is filled with jealousy; a love where a person does not exalt themselves, but others instead; a love that behaves wisely; a love that does not look to satisfy selfish desires, but lives for others; a love that is not easily upset, or holds grudges; a love that thinks the best of others rather than the worst; a love that rejoices in truth, not sin; a love that puts up with a lot, believes strongly in others, demonstrates hope, and continues.

"Fervent charity" will demonstrate itself in these qualities. Will you plan to love others this way today? Will you continue to live selfishly, thinking only of yourself and your desires? Find someone who feels unloved, and make a huge difference in their life today.

"We are not here to COMPETE with each other, but to COMPLETE each other." – Bill McCartney

How Great Thou Art – January 9

"The lofty looks of man shall be humbled, and the haughtiness of men shall be bowed down, and the LORD alone shall be exalted in that day" (Isaiah 2:11). There is a great truth taught here. Every last human being on the earth needs to hear and understand. Man is not the most important personality in the universe! God is the Person that everything else revolves around. Have you ever really looked at the detail in nature that many people never see?

I can remember when I was training for the track season the spring of my senior year in High School. We have a Bird Sanctuary near where I grew up. There were trails all over the hills on the property of that Sanctuary. I loved to go there and run, because the air was clear and there were no people around to see how horrible I looked while I was running. One day I had about finished my workout and I collapsed under some young pine trees. One of the branches hung near my face, and as I sat there gasping for breath; I examined one of the tiny evergreen leaves. The detailed veins on that leaf made a beautiful pattern. Each of the other leaves on that tree was just at intricately designed.

I was overwhelmed with my insignificance. I might have been the only person in the world who had seen these particular leaves, but they were not made for me. They were made to declare the glory of God! They were doing their job. I wonder, am I doing my job of declaring the glory of God?

Verse 1: *Oh Lord my God! When I in awesome wonder consider all the worlds Thy hands have made, I see the stars, I hear the rolling thunder, Thy power throughout the universe displayed …*

Verse 2: *When through the woods and forest glade I wander and hear the birds sing sweetly in the trees; When I look down from lofty mountain grandeur and hear the brook and feel the gentle breeze …*

Verse 3: *And when I think that God, His Son not sparing, sent Him to die, I scarce can take it in; That on the cross my burden gladly bearing, He bled and died, to take away my sin …*

Verse 4: *When Christ shall come with shout of acclamation, and take me home, what joy shall fill my heart! Then I shall bow in humble adoration and there proclaim, 'My God, how great Thou art!'*

Chorus: *Then sings my soul, my Savior God to Thee; how great Thou art, how great Thou art!*

Author of our Faith – January 10

*"Wherefore seeing we also are compassed about with so great a cloud of witnesses, let us lay aside every weight, and the sin which doth so easily beset us, and let us run with patience the race that is set before us, looking unto Jesus the **Author** and Finisher of our faith; who for the joy that was set before Him endured the cross, despising the shame, and is set down at the right hand of the throne of God"* (Hebrews 12:1-2).

The word, "Author," in this verse carries the idea of a person who takes the lead in something; a person who sets the example; a person who is a pioneer. Jesus Christ left the glories of heaven to come to this sin-cursed earth to live for thirty-three years. He was the first and only of His kind. He was born of a virgin, without sin. He lived thirty-three years without sinning, and He died in the place of others having done nothing wrong Himself. There never has been anyone else like him in the past, and there will never be anyone like him in the future. He is the Author of our faith. It was in his mind that our faith was created and in his life it was made possible.

This word *"author"* has taken on a new meaning for me in recent years. For the past several years I have been writing this devotional each morning. I have tried to stay away from reading other devotionals, because I would like this to be a unique and fresh approach to the Word of God as it touches my heart. As the author of this devotional I have opened my heart and placed the words I have seen there on this paper. This is very personal to me, and they are the things that have touched my heart which I write about. What you see written on these pages may not seem that important or impressive to you. They're not meant to impress you, they are simply the things God has impressed upon me.

Jesus Christ is the *"Author"* of our faith – He did not depend upon someone else for how he would begin our faith; this faith is His idea. When others argue that there should be many ways to heaven, they are not considering the *"Author."* Over the years I have read hundreds of books but I have never had any author so powerfully impact my life as Jesus Christ has impacted my life. I am so thankful that Jesus Christ wrote the book on faith. What we believe today is not based on man's opinions, but has come from the heart of God. When I was a six-year-old boy I met Jesus Christ face-to-face for the first time. He has been an incredible leader in my life ever since. I can trust His judgment; I can trust His leadership; and I can live by the example He set for my life. As the 'Author" of my faith I can think of no greater example to follow! I thank God for the *"Author"* of my faith!

Beginning – January 11

*"And He said unto me, 'It is done. I am the Alpha and Omega, the **Beginning** and the End. I will give unto him that is athirst of the fountain of the water of life freely"* (Revelation 21:6).

In the last book of our Bible, in the second to last chapter of the book of Revelation, Jesus, from the throne of Heaven, made sure we know He is the *"Beginning."* In the book that closes out our Bible, Jesus wants us to be sure we know He is the one Who began everything. The eternality of God is a very difficult concept for us to understand with our limited abilities. I have a hard time understanding I am as old as I am. In my mind, I am still a very young man. My body tells me a different story. Things I did before cannot be done today. Places I never had pain before are beginning to have aches and pains now. To imagine our God never having a beginning date is hard to fully understand.

Moses asked God (at the burning bush), by what authority should he tell the Israelites had sent him. God's reply was to tell them "I AM" had sent him. "I AM" is present tense. That is because God has always been! When it is stated here that Jesus is the *"Beginning,"* it reminds us nothing in the history of man has surprised Him. He has seen it all take place. I have heard people say there is "nothing new under the sun." For Jesus Christ, that is absolute truth.

He has already seen the challenges you will face today. The things you think will be impossible … He already has the answer waiting. He is the *"Beginning."* He spoke and light appeared. He separated the water from the land. He created every animal, fish and bird you see today. He formed the first man out of the dust of the ground. He was there when Adam and Eve ate the fruit … He made the first clothing out of animal skins.

As you begin today, rather than worrying about how you will face the day, be more concerned with staying close to the One Who has seen it all take place? The One Who was there in the beginning and is the *"Beginning."* He ought to be the first Person you turn to when you face the challenges of this day. He should be the Person you run to for advice and help to face these challenging days. He is not only the *"Beginning,"* but He is also the *"End."* It would be good to start today out with some time alone with Him, and watch Him orchestrate your day for His honor and glory. Don't arbitrarily wander through a day. Make sure you start at the *"Beginning"* and go forward from Him!

Ivory Palaces (Heaven) – January 12

As a small boy I can remember my aunt and my mother singing many duets in church. One of their favorite songs was a song called "Ivory Palaces." The song speaks about the time when Jesus Christ left the Ivory Palaces (Heaven) and made His way to this sin-cursed earth. I can still see them singing of Him coming here to rescue sinners like you and me. They sang about Him paying the ultimate price for our redemption. It made me realize if He had not left Heaven for me I would have had no opportunity at all to meet God face to face as my Heavenly Father. The only position He could have rightfully held with me would have been that of a Judge.

This song becomes even more meaningful to me in that both my aunt and my mother are there in the Ivory Palaces waiting for me to come. This is a wonderful hymn that described Jesus coming for us this way ...

Verse 1: *My Lord has garments so wondrous fine, and myrrh their texture fills; its fragrance reached to this heart of mine, with joy my being thrills.*

Verse 2: *His life had also its sorrows sore, for aloes had a part; and when I think of the cross He bore, my eyes with teardrops start.*

Verse 3: *His garments too were in cassia dipped, with healing in a touch; each time my feet in some sin have slipped, He took me from its clutch.*

Verse 4: *In garments glorious He will come, to open wide the door; and I shall enter my heavenly home, to dwell forevermore.*

Chorus: *Out of the ivory palaces into a world of woe, only His great eternal love ...made my Savior go.*

I believe the song Ivory Palaces came from this passage in Psalm 45. *"Thy throne, O God, is forever and ever: the scepter of Thy kingdom is a right scepter. Thou lovest righteousness, and hatest wickedness: therefore God, thy God, hath anointed thee with oil of gladness above thy fellows. All thy garments smell of myrrh, and aloes, and cassia, out of the ivory palaces, whereby they have made thee glad"* (Psalm 45:6-8). Heaven is a very real place. If you have doubts about whether or not you will see it someday, please put those doubts aside. God sent His perfect Son to die as payment for your sins on Calvary's cross. If you will recognize your sin (stop making excuses for them); understand Jesus is the only One Who could pay for your sin; believe that His death and resurrection are the only thing that can fulfill the demand for righteousness of God; and receive that gift for yourself; your sins will be forgiven! Do it now, don't wait! Pray through this simple progression and find Heaven as your home today!

What the World Needs Now is Love – January 13

There is one thing human beings cannot manufacture by themselves. That one thing is love. It is important for us to realize you and I are basically selfish beings. If we had our way, everyone would agree with our opinions; every restaurant would serve our favorite food; our favorite sports team would always win; everyone else would wake up at the time we think is best and go to sleep when we thought it best. We are basically selfish people.

In order to love, we must be taught. I John chapter four is a great chapter to understand real love and where it comes from. Check out these verses: *"He that loveth not knoweth not love; for God is love"* (I John 4:8). There it is! The only way for us to really love is to know God, because God is love. The only way a basically selfish human being can truly love someone else, is to completely surrender to God ... because we can only truly love when we know Him.

"Beloved, if God so love us, we ought also to love one another" (I John 4:11). I love the power of the simplicity of the Word of God. It makes total sense to me that if we are following God, we will love others like He does. Consider a few questions here ... when was the last time your heart was broken for a friend, family member, co-worker or neighbor who was struggling with a health issue? When was the last time you were moved to tears over the soul of someone you know who is not saved? When was the last time you loved someone without expecting any payment in return? If God loves us this way, we should also love others that same way.

"We love Him, because He first loved us" (I John 4:19). Notice the progression of this chapter with me quickly. We know what love is when we meet God and He gets a hold on our lives. Knowing God is love and He loves others motivates us to love as well in obedience to Him. And now we realize that in loving others, we are simply carrying on the ministry of Christ following His ascension into Heaven. I am reminded as I read these verses that Jesus told His disciples, *"By this shall all men know that ye are my disciples, if ye have love one to another"* (John 13:35). Does your love for God show in your love for other people? If we are truly His disciples, we will have love that sets us apart from the rest of this world. Look for those people today that others have missed, and love them like God has taught us to love. It will bring a smile to the heart of God!

"Don't love things ... love people." – Dr. Ted Camp

Holy, Holy, Holy – January 14

There will be a day when those who have met Jesus on the road to Hell, and trusted His death, burial and resurrection for their forgiveness of sin will step into the courts of Heaven! Isaiah got a quick glimpse of what that might be like for us. We often wish we could pull back the curtain of Heaven and take a look inside.

There is not a great deal written about Heaven in the Bible, but when Isaiah got his chance he wrote; *"And one cried unto another, and said, 'Holy, holy, holy, is the LORD of hosts: the whole earth is full of His glory'"* (Isaiah 6:3). Can you just imagine that chorus of angels singing to each other about the holiness of God? You will notice this verse says they cried one to another. I know the word "holy" is only repeated three times, but I have a feeling there is a never-ending song of "holy, holy, holy, holy, holy, holy ... and this song will continue for eternity.

After reading this passage, I read in the psalms, *"God is gone up with a shout, the LORD with the sound of a trumpet. Sing praises to God, sing praises; sing praises unto our King, sing praises"* (Psalm 47:5-6). I get the idea God enjoys hearing us sing to Him about His holiness and what it means to us. Prayerfully read the words to the great and famous hymn, "Holy, Holy, Holy." Don't just pray these words, but take the time to read them out loud in praise to your God today. Reginald Heber wrote:

Verse 1: *Holy, holy, holy! Lord God Almighty! Early in the morning our song shall rise to Thee; holy, holy, holy. Merciful and Mighty! God in Three Persons, blessed Trinity!*

Verse 2: *Holy, holy, holy! All the saints adore Thee, casting down their golden crowns upon the glassy sea; cherubim and seraphim falling down before Thee, which wert* [was], *and art* [is now], *and evermore shall be.*

Verse 3: *Holy, holy, holy! Though the darkness hide Thee, though the eye of sinful man Thy glory may not see, only Thou art holy; there is none beside Thee perfect in power, in love and purity.*

Verse 4: *Holy, holy, holy! Lord God Almighty! All Thy works shall praise Thy name, in earth, and sky, and sea; holy, holy, holy! Merciful and Mighty! God in Three Persons, blessed Trinity!*

I am thankful I serve a holy God today. Our God is nothing like the substitute idols of our world today. Honor Him with a holy life of your own today. He is worthy of the effort it will take from you.

Lean Into Your Master – January 15

"Life is tough." "There are traps and "pit-falls" everywhere I turn." "The challenges I will face today will be far more than I can handle." "Where do I turn when I am faced with a fork in the road?" "I don't have the strength or wisdom for the problems I am going to face today."

You may have said some of these things in the past week, and you were being honest about what was in front of you. We are living in a very challenging time in the history of the world. Things we once thought were sure, have crumbled and failed. Companies we thought would always be in business have become bankrupt and are gone. Governments we once thought strong have shown signs of weakening and some have fallen. Where is the strength coming from today?

The psalmist wrote these words many years ago about the nation of Israel, but they hold the answer to the questions we have for our own future. *"For they got not the land in possession by their own sword, neither did their own arm save them: but Thy right hand, and Thine arm, and the light of Thy countenance, because Thou hadst a favor unto them"* (Psalm 44:3).

There is a place of peace and security close to the heart of God. This world we are living in will constantly pull at you to draw closer to it, but I want to encourage you today to realize the strength you are looking for in the challenges of life, is found in an intimate relationship with God and Him alone. Your money will not be able to meet the needs you will have in the future. Your health is not guaranteed. Your retirement plan is not necessarily going to be around by the time you retire.

The strength you are looking for cannot be provided by someone else. It is only found in a vibrant relationship with our living God! He was the One that opened the door for Israel to go into the Promised Land. He was the One responsible for defeating giants like Goliath. He was the One that parted the Red Sea. He is the One Who will fight for you as you walk with Him today.

There will certainly be challenges ahead of you today that are outside your ability to provide. Be sure, those challenges are not too big for God. Lean into Him and allow Him to show Himself powerful on your behalf. He is ready and willing to work for you. You must surrender all you have! You will not regret it for one second.

"When God guides – God provides." – Adrian Rogers

Bridegroom – January 16

"And while they went to buy, the **Bridegroom** *came; and they that were ready went in with Him to the marriage: and the door was shut. Watch therefore, for ye know neither the day nor the hour wherein the Son of Man cometh"* (Matthew 25:10, 13).

The New Testament uses the illustration of a bride and a bridegroom to picture the relationship between the repentant sinner and Jesus Christ. Jesus told a parable about those waiting to meet and marry the Bridegroom with their lamps. Some of the ladies waiting did not come prepared and needed to leave to fill their lamps with oil. While they were gone, the bridegroom appeared and they missed their opportunity. Verse 13 tells us we ought to be anticipating the return of Jesus Christ, and it should affect our lives.

We ought to be paying attention to the details that will enable us to meet Him face-to-face with joy, and not miss His coming. There is a day coming when Jesus Christ will split the eastern sky. He will come in the clouds to call the dead in Christ to Himself first. Those who are believers and are still alive will then meet Him in the air and go to Heaven. We will begin the Marriage Supper of the Lamb at that point, and will eat for seven years in celebration. This is going to be a wonderful union that will last for eternity!

I vividly remember the night my bride stepped through the back doors of the church where we were married. I don't think I have ever had a moment of more sheer excitement in my whole life. Every ounce of my being was waiting for that moment when she would become my bride. We did not have our ceremony until seven o'clock in the evening. I have never had such a long day in my life! I washed my car ... my parent's car ... my best-man's car ... I could not wait for the time when my fiancée would become my wife!

I am also excited about the union I will have with Jesus Christ! I cannot wait to thank Him face-to-face for dying for me. He has been preparing a place for me for many years, and I cannot wait to see what it looks like! I want to fall on my face and thank Him and thank Him and thank Him for all He has done for me. I cannot wait to see my *"Bridegroom!"* There's an old hymn that says it well ... "What a day that will be when my Jesus I shall see; when I look upon His face, the One Who saved me by His grace. When He takes me by the hand and leads me through the Promised Land. What a day; glorious day that will be!" Don't be caught off guard when the *"Bridegroom"* appears. Be ready; be excited; our Lord is coming soon!

God is Still God! – January 17

In a time when nothing seems to be stable and dependable, I am thankful that God is God. I am grateful that regardless of how my health is ... God is still God. I am thankful that whether the value of the dollar goes up or down ... God is still God! I am relieved to know that regardless of who is in the position of political power ... God is still God! I am thankful that no matter what challenge is waiting for me today ... God will still be God!

I would recommend that each of you read the entire chapter of Psalm 46. It is an amazing collection of encouraging verses for times just like we are living in. The last verse of the chapter is what captured my attention today. *"The LORD of hosts is with us; the God of Jacob is our refuge. Selah"* (Psalm 46:11). Think a little bit with me about how strong God showed Himself to Jacob and the nation of Israel.

God allowed Jacob to have a blessing and birthright he did not earn or deserve. God has given us many blessings in spite of how many times we have turned our back to Him. God allowed Joseph, Jacob's son, to be taken into captivity in order to save Jacob and his other sons and their families during a famine. God has provided for each of us repeatedly in ways we cannot explain, or fully understand. God provided a heritage for Jacob that continues today with the twelve tribes of Israel.

Just as you can look at the life of Jacob in the Bible, you can see in your own life how God has blessed you beyond what you deserve too. I am thankful God has always been the place that I could run to hide when I feel troubles closing in around me. I am thankful that, when I am facing a challenge which is far beyond my wisdom, I can lean on His Word He has given me for knowledge. I am grateful when my heart rejoices to overflowing and I don't have words to speak, He can understand the language of my heart.

I am thankful *"God is our refuge and strength, a very present help in trouble"* (Psalm 46:1). When troubles come and we take the roll, God is never absent! When I need strength to make it through a day ... there He is. When you need a place to hide today, run to Him ... God is still God! What a wonderful thought for the remainder of this day! God is still God!

"Did it ever occur to you that nothing ever occurred to God?" –
Curtis Hutson

There is a Fountain – January 18

I find we often try to make ourselves look much better than we know we really are. The Bible has a way of helping us to see ourselves the way God sees us. The reality is, we are wretched sinners even at our best. We fail God in multiple ways every day that we live. Our human nature helps us to rationalize it and to explain it away in many different ways. The reality is that we are still an offense to a holy and righteous God. The prophet Jeremiah described our hearts at one point as deceitful and desperately wicked. David said it this way, *"Have mercy upon me, O God, according to Thy lovingkindness: according unto the multitude of Thy tender mercies blot out my transgressions. Wash me thoroughly from mine iniquity, and cleanse me from my sin. For I acknowledge my transgressions: and my sin is ever before me. Against Thee, and Thee only, have I sinned, and done this evil in Thy sight: that Thou mightest be justified when Thou speakest, and be clear when Thou judgest"* (Psalm 51:1-4).

The truth is, we all have this sin problem … and there is only one solution that will take care of this problem. William Cowper wrote one of my favorite hymns about the subject of the forgiveness of our sins.

Verse 1: *There is a fountain filled with blood drawn from Immanuel's veins; and sinners, plunged beneath that blood, lose all their guilty stains.*

Verse 2: *The dying thief rejoiced to see that fountain in his day; and there may I, though vile as he, wash all my sins away.*

Verse 3: *Dear dying Lamb, Thy precious blood shall never lose its power, till all the ransomed Church of God be saved, to sin no more.*

Verse 4: *E'er since, by faith, I saw the stream Thy flowing wounds supply, redeeming love has been my theme, and shall be till I die.*

Verse 5: *Then in a nobler, sweeter song, I'll sing Thy power to saved, when this poor lisping, stammering tongue lies silent in the grave.*

If you're reading this today and you have any doubt at all about whether you will be in Heaven when you die, take a moment and tell God you know you have sinned. Tell Him you realize Jesus came here to pay the price for your sin when He died in your place on the cross. Tell Him you believe Jesus rose from the dead and that He is the only way into Heaven. He will forgive your sin debt and you can be sure of Heaven. If you prayed something like this today, would you let me know? I want to give you some verses that will help you to understand it more clearly.

Jesus is the Sweetest Name I Know – January 19

There are certain names, that as soon as you hear them, your mind automatically recognizes them for either good or bad. Babe Ruth is considered one of the greatest baseball players in the history of the game. John F. Kennedy is one of the most famous presidents in American history. D.L. Moody is a name that most Christians would identify as a great preacher. Tiger Woods is known as a great golfer, and not so great father/husband.

There is one name everyone on this earth should know, deserves to know ... that name is the name of Jesus Christ. We know that there will be a time when every knee is going to bow to the name of Jesus. We know there will be a time when every voice will announce Jesus Christ is the Lord to the glory of God the Father. David wrote about this in the Old Testament when he said, *"I will praise Thee forever, because Thou hast done it: and I will wait on Thy name; for it is good before Thy saints"* (Psalm 52:9). We ought to praise the name of Jesus Christ today because it is worthy to be praised. There has never been a sweeter name to you if you have trusted Him as your Savior. Look at this great old hymn that was written by Lela Long about that very issue.

Verse 1: *There have been names that I have loved to hear, but never has there been a name so dear to this heart of mine, as the name divine, the precious, precious name of Jesus.*

Verse 2: *There is no name in earth or heaven above, that we should give such honor and such love as the blessed name, let us all acclaim, that wondrous, glorious name of Jesus.*

Verse 3: *And someday I shall see Him face to face to thank and praise Him for His wondrous grace, which He gave to me, when He made me free, the blessed Son of God called Jesus.*

Chorus: *Jesus is the sweetest name I know, and He's just the same as His lovely name, and that's the reason why I love Him so; Oh, Jesus is the sweetest name I know.*

Buddha, Mohammed, Allah, the Virgin Mary, Billy Graham, Benny Hinn, etc., cannot forgive your sins. Only Jesus Christ lived without sin here on the earth and died as a substitute for your sins and mine. The great joy is that He died for the sins of the whole world. It is a great thrill to know there is no person you will meet that is beyond the grace of God!

Christ the Lord – January 20

"For unto you is born this day in the city of David a Savior, which is ***Christ*** *the* ***Lord"*** (Luke 2:11).

It touches my heart that the Angels made this announcement to such a humble group of shepherds. The announcement could have been made to the royalty of the nearby kingdom. It could have been made to the rich people who lived in the town of Bethlehem. It interests me that God chose to make it to the humble shepherds. Look at that announcement: *"For unto you is born this day in the city of David a Savior, which is* ***Christ the Lord.***" That announcement said unto YOU is born this day a Savior, which is Christ the Lord.

This Savior came for every person on this earth. This Savior came not for the wealthy and the powerful only, but also for the common, ordinary man. His title is one of royalty. The title *"Christ,"* means the anointed one. It points directly to the fact that Jesus Christ is the Messiah. The second part of this title showed He is not only the Messiah, but deserves to be the ruler of each person's life. The term *"Lord"* carried the meaning of being the supreme, and eternal. This title showed that He is the rightful Ruler of all the heavens and the earth.

Jesus Christ earned this title. The question is, has He earned this position in your heart? Is He the master of your decisions? If you read something in the Bible today that you don't like, are you willing to obey it anyway? Do you feel the principles of Scriptures are open for debate? When your pastor preaches a message that convicts you, do you try to rationalize improper behavior, or do you accept this message as coming from *"Christ the Lord?"*

Before making decisions for your day today, stop at the feet of Jesus and ask for his guidance. It would be a great thing to start this day by telling Jesus Christ you know he is your Lord. It is amusing to me that we human beings rebel against this thought that God ought to have some control in our lives. We allow many other things to control our lives including bad habits, other people, the opinions of our friends, and even people we have never met that appear on our televisions. Why is it so difficult for us to surrender the controls of our lives to *"Christ the Lord?"*

Today is a brand new opportunity for you and me to serve the King of all Kings. It is an opportunity for us to show our submission to the Lord of our lives. Don't take a step today without considering what *"Christ the Lord"* wants you to do along the path you walk today. You will not regret it.

Work, for the Night is Coming – January 21

"If you're going to do a job, then take the time to do it right." These words ring in my ears. They are words my father said over and over to me while I was growing up. He drilled that thought into my mind so much that I have never forgotten it. He drilled them into my mind so deeply that even when I am tempted to "cut a corner" in my work, I remember I am to do everything I can to do the job right. I was helping a friend with a landscaping business a few years ago. I know I am crazy, but I love to cut grass, so on my days off, I would help him cut lawns. We were in some of the most beautiful neighborhoods cutting grass. There were some places on some of the bigger properties where no one was probably going to go to check out the work. I still tried to cut every blade of grass the best it could be cut because of how I was raised from a boy.

There is a far more important work than cutting grass that we each should be involved in today. That work is to do the will of our Heavenly Father, and to do it right! Matthew wrote Jesus' response to the faithful Christian doing the will of His Father: "*His lord said unto him, 'Well done, thou good and faithful servant: thou hast been faithful over a few things, I will make thee ruler over many things: enter thou into the joy of the lord'*" (Matthew 25:21).

I believe that Jesus Christ could return at any moment. I believe my life could end in an accident or an unexpected disease very quickly. I don't want to waste any time in serving the Lord with all my heart! Look at the words to this song and ask God to help you to continue to work until He comes! Anna Coghill wrote …

Verse 1: *Work, for the night is coming, work through the morning hours; work while the dew is sparkling, work 'mid springing flowers; work when the day grows brighter, work in the glowing sun; work, for the night is coming, when man's work is done.*

Verse 2: *Work, for the night is coming, work through the sunny noon; fill brightest hours with labor, rest comes sure and soon. Give every flying minute, something to keep in store; work, for the night is coming, when man works no more.*

Verse 3: *Work, for the night is coming, under the sunset skies; while their bright tints are glowing, work, for the daylight flies. Work till the last beam fadeth, fadeth to shine no more; work, while the night is darkening, when man's work is o'er.*

Commander – January 22

"Incline your ear, and come unto Me: hear, and your soul shall live; and I will make an everlasting covenant with you, even the sure mercies of David. Behold, I have given Him for a witness to the people, a Leader and Commander to the people." (Isaiah 55:4).

The title *"Commander,"* immediately brings the meaning of a person who is in charge, and a person to whom I am to submit my will. When the Holy Spirit inspired this title to be given to Jesus, He had a very important picture in mind for us. Christ is to be the *"Commander"* in our everyday lives. We ought to run to our *"Commander"* every morning to get instructions for the day. Before making a move on the battlefields of life, we should make sure we have a clear plan of action from our *"Commander."*

Just as any good soldier completely commits to the commands that come from their superiors, we ought to yield our hearts to the desires of Christ. There are many times in a day when we make decisions that will affect the outcome of that day, and we don't even stop to think about what our *"Commander"* would like us to do. This could be considered a refusal to obey orders! We need to run to our *"Commander"* on a consistent basis.

There is something else about a *"Commander"* I think is important for us to consider. I have noticed that a person is not given the position of a *"Commander"* quickly. That is a title that is earned through experience and skill demonstrated on the battlefield. Jesus Christ is the ultimate example of a seasoned *"Commander."* He has been on the battlefield that we walk through (we call it "life"). He has safely negotiated all the way through this battlefield where landmines of sin wait at every step. He has experienced the things that we experience; but He has done it perfectly, without sin!

What an incredible *"Commander"* we serve! He is not a *"Commander"* Who simply points and tells us where to go and what to do. No; He is a *"Commander"* Who has already been down that path and has conquered everything that could potentially wound and kill us. He is a trusted leader! He is a capable strategist! He is a man we can follow all the way through the journey we find ourselves on in this life!

Today it would be good to go to our *"Commander"* in prayer and ask for the orders for the day. We do not naturally like to take orders, but when facing the challenges that are ahead of us today, it is wonderful to know we have a *"Commander"* that has "been there ... done that ..." yet, without sin. He is to be trusted today. Praise God for the victories that will come!

Consolation of Israel – January 23

"And, behold, there was a man in Jerusalem, whose name was Simeon; and the same man was just and devout, waiting for the Consolation of Israel: and the Holy Ghost was upon him" (Luke 2:25).

We use the word "console" when someone we know dies, or has a very sad situation they are facing. Mankind had been in a horrible situation until Jesus Christ stepped on the scene. He is not only the *"Consolation of Israel,"* but He is the *"Consolation"* for every sinner that has ever lived on the earth! From the time Adam and Eve ate the fruit of the tree of the knowledge of good and evil, we all have been under the curse of sin. There is not one person reading this today who can truthfully say they have never sinned. Only Jesus, Himself can make that claim.

I grew up in a wonderful home. It was not perfect, but it was centered on the message of Jesus Christ. I was taught songs about the Bible and Jesus from before I could walk or talk. I was encouraged to memorize Scripture from before the time I can remember. I was in church three times every Sunday of the year. We went to Wednesday night Prayer Meeting every week too. I noticed that everyone in the car I road to and from church with was a sinner ... including me.

When I was six-years-old I realized for the first time in my life that I was a liar. I also had been taught well enough to know lying was a sin. Not long after that realization came to me of being a sinner, I heard a preacher explain the Gospel of Jesus Christ. I promise you, I had heard that simple message at least 100 times before, but this time it sounded like it was just for me. That was the day I recognized Jesus was my *"Consolation."* He was able to apply the healing balm of His precious death, burial and resurrection to my need.

You see, Jesus was the answer for the problems of this young man who was a guilty liar, and Jesus is still the answer for the problems you might bring Him today. What a wonderful message we have to proclaim today! We have the chance to tell the world there is a Savior Who can console, comfort, and ease their eternal aching soul if they will simply turn to Him. He was available to me, but I had to make a choice and receive what He was offering for it to become my own.

Ever since that wonderful day over fifty years ago, I have known the daily comfort of the *"Consolation of Israel."* I can honestly tell you He has never failed to bring comfort to me in my deepest needs! I love Him!

Consuming Fire – January 24

*"For the LORD thy God is a **Consuming Fire**, even a jealous God"* (Deuteronomy 4:24). *"For our God is a **Consuming Fire**"* (Hebrews 12:29).

I was awakened by a knock on the door in the middle of the night. I answered the door and found our youngest daughter telling me there was a tree on fire! We were in a Deaf Camp for children in Ukraine. Our daughter was fearful for the spread of fire and the danger it posed to the Deaf children for which we were responsible. Thankfully, the tree that was on fire was the only thing that was consumed by the fire. In the morning, after watching the powerful display of the fire the night before, we all went out to see the charred remains of that tree. There was not much left to see, except the burned trunk of the tree.

What an appropriate title for God. He is *"consuming."* Once that fire began at the base of that tree in Ukraine, it spread without slowing or stopping until it had completely engulfed the entire tree. When God comes into a life, His desire is to completely take over that life. The goal of every believer should be to have God completely control their life. The question is, are you allowing God access to all areas of your life, or are you struggling to maintain control. There is a part of us that thinks we have more knowledge of what is good for us, and of what we need than God.

Allow your *"Consuming Fire"* to have access to all of you today. Allow Him to engulf your schedule today. Allow God to take over what you do and when you do it all day today. Allow Him to engulf your mind. Surrender all the thoughts that pass through your mind to His will today. Allow Him to remove any improper thought today. Allow Him to engulf your plans today. Don't try to follow the will of God when it fits something you "like" to do. Allow Him to engulf your dreams for tomorrow. Today, tell God you are willing to do anything; go anywhere; and try to become all He has planned for you.

God is a *"Consuming Fire."* Don't try to hold anything back from Him today. Life is so exciting when you yield to His control! If you will leave your comfort zone and step out by faith, you will watch the evidence of the *"Consuming Fire"* as He moves across the lives of others that God places in your path. He can do what you could only dream about doing. He can change lives of people you thought would never change. The key to it all is for us to yield to the *"Consuming Fire"* daily.

Hope in Your Storm – January 25

Have you ever had a time when a bad storm knocked out your electricity? You searched all the cabinets and drawers in your house desperately searching for that flashlight you know is there somewhere ... only to discover after finding it that the batteries are so old they are corroding the switch to turn it on! You are in trouble without a light. It is then that you discover an old pack of matches (or lighter if you are the younger generation). You light that single candle in your kitchen and peace seems to filter into the room along with the light. As long as you have even one candle lit, things just seem to be better.

That picture of light in your Bible always refers to hope for our darkening world. It seems we are in the middle of a storm as Christians all over the world today. Don't fear ... we have the Light within us. Here is the way the Old Testament prophet Micah saw it: *"Rejoice not against me, O mine enemy: when I fall, I shall arise; when I sit in darkness, the LORD shall be a light unto me"* (Micah 7:9).

What a great thought for you and I to hold close to our hearts for this day. The LORD will be a light for you in the middle of the storms life brings your way. I know when our children were living at home and a storm was predicted they would begin to gather the candles. We all were hoping (in a weird way) we would lose power, because when the darkness would engulf our house, the light of the candles made our home seem even warmer than normal.

You know what your enemy means for evil, your God can change to good! Just ask Joseph after being sold into slavery in Egypt and then placed in the position of second in charge. Or, ask Saul of Tarsus after being blinded on the road to Damascus and then becoming the missionary to the Gentiles. Or, ask any one of the eleven disciples on the fourth day after Jesus' crucifixion. I think you get my point. All of the things mentioned above could seem to be bad, or that the enemy had triumphed.

Just remember when you are sitting in this dark world, and it seems your enemies are winning the battles of life, you have a God of light that is nearer than you think. He will always make a way for you to shine brightly if you will yield to Him. Don't struggle today, light the candle!

"God may not still your storm, but He can still you in the storm." –
Dr. Ted Camp

Counselor – January 26

*"For unto us a child is born, unto us a son is given: and the govern-
ment shall be upon his shoulder: and his name shall be called Wonderful,
Counsellor, The mighty God, The everlasting Father, The Prince of Peace"*
(Isaiah 9:6).

This title speaks about a person who has a standing of honor. It was
used for a person who deserves to stand near a prince or king and give them
advice. This describes a person who has great wisdom. That wisdom gives
this person the qualification to give guidance and direction to the king.
Long before the birth of Jesus, He was given this title of *"Counselor."* He
is a Person that can be trusted to give wise counsel and guidance for the
things you will be facing in your life. When you are facing a situation you
are unsure about, search your memory for a time when Jesus might have
faced a similar situation. It is a wonderful source of *"counsel"* to see the
example of Jesus and follow in His steps.

If you are a husband concerned about loving your wife today; follow
the example Jesus gave us. Give yourself and your desires up for the good
of your wife. If you are wondering how to treat the little children that
might sometimes annoy you; remember what Jesus said, and welcome
them. Remember you must be like a child if you want to see Heaven. If
you know a person who is saying half-truths about you today; look at how
Jesus acted when people were offering false testimonies against Him. If you
are tempted to worry about what the future will hold for you; think about
what Jesus said about sparrows that fall, and lilies in the fields. Remember
your Heavenly Father notices everything and cares for you. I could go on
and on with these examples, but I think you get the picture.

I find Jesus' *"counsel"* not only in the things He did, but also in the
things He said to us. I praise God for His Word today. Jesus spoke volumes
in just a few words on the pages of our Bibles. I believe it was John Mark
who wrote that if they were to include all Jesus said while on the earth, there
would not be enough books on the earth to hold the words. That means the
very few words we do have in our Bible that Jesus spoke are extremely
important! Our Bible contains the words of Jesus that God thought were the
absolute, most important words He said. If God thinks they are the absolute
most important words He spoke, we ought to give them more time and a
place of greater importance in our own lives. Jesus is a great *"Counselor"*…
are you listening to His counsel today? He has all the answers the world is
searching for … run to Him today!

The Haven of Rest – January 27

I have noticed, I want to be a man of faith, but as soon as God gives me an opportunity to trust Him I quickly panic and wonder how I am going to survive! Maybe you have faced similar situations. Too many times I rely on my eyes before I will trust God. I have asked just as the disciples did, for the Lord to help my unbelief! One of the most vivid pictures of the struggle between walking by faith and walking by sight is given to us in the Old Testament. God told Moses to separate a choice man from each of the tribes of Israel to go into the land of promise and to see what it was like. These men decided to step out by sight, not by faith.

When they returned, ten of the twelve spies warned they should not go into the land promised to them but should stay out. Only Caleb and Joshua stood by faith. Caleb said, *"Only rebel not ye against the LORD, neither fear ye the people of the land; for they are bread for us: their defense is departed from them, and the LORD is with us; fear them not"* (Numbers 14:9). Are you ready to criticize those who walk by faith, but not willing to walk yourself? Decide to trust the Anchor for your soul. Henry L. Gilmour wrote these beautiful words:

Verse 1: *My soul in sad exile was out on life's sea, so burdened with sin and distrest, till I heard a sweet voice saying, "Make Me your choice;" and I entered the "Haven of Rest!*

Verse 2: *I yielded myself to His tender embrace, and faith taking hold of the Word, my fetters fell off, and I anchored my soul; the "Haven of Rest" is my Lord.*

Verse 3: *The song of my soul since the Lord made me while, has been the old story so blest, of Jesus, Who'll save whosoever will have a home in the "Haven of Rest."*

Verse 4: *How precious the thought that we all may recline, like John the beloved and blest, on Jesus' strong arm, where no tempest can harm, secure in the "Haven of Rest."*

Verse 5: *Oh, come to the Savior, He patiently waits to save by His power divine; come, anchor your soul in the "Haven of Rest," and say, "My Beloved is mine."*

Chorus: *I've anchored my soul in the "Haven of Rest," I'll sail the wide seas no more; the tempest may sweep o'er the wild stormy deep, in Jesus I'm safe evermore.*

Help is on its Way – January 28

Discouraged? Thinking there is no hope or help for you or the world? Don't lose heart, there is still a God in Heaven. There is still a God Who is actively working for you, and He has not forgotten what you need the most. We might ask God for money, or success in business, or for good health; but the things we need the most are His mercy and His truth. Here is a great promise for you to hold on to today. *"He shall send from heaven, and save me from the reproach of him that would swallow me up, Selah. God shall send forth His mercy and His truth"* (Psalm 57:3).

There are certainly plenty of people around today who would threaten to "swallow us up." There is a sin nature within us that threatens to "swallow us up." There are plenty of temptations for us to yield to in our everyday lives. Don't look at them. Don't focus on the troubles, but focus on the answer to each of them. Look to Heaven where your help comes from! We are not alone in this struggle for holiness. We are not alone when we stand for what is right and true. We are not in the minority when we stand where God wants us to stand!

David faced Goliath with no fear after asking the question, *"Is there not a cause?"* I ask the same question for today … is there not a reason for us to attempt to live godly lives in our world today? The resounding answer to David's question was "yes!" The answer to my question is also "yes!" This verse from Psalm 57 should give you encouragement that help is never far away when you stand for God in a world that seems to be godless. There is a cause … there is a reason to stand for God today … there are people depending on your testimony to remain strong and solid in the face of the enemy today.

I want to stress today that just about the time you think there is no hope, you need to realize God is standing with you every minute of every day you live as a Christian. He has with Him an endless supply of mercy and truth! When you come to the end of your resources, He will always be there with His mercy and truth to take care of you. When you have read everything you can read, and you still don't have the wisdom you need, He will be there with mercy and truth. When you have come to the end of your wealth of advice, and there is still counsel needed, trust Him to come along with mercy and truth. He never fails! He is always on time! Help is on its way!

"You should not meddle with the charts, compass, or the day, but simply trust the Captain … because He knows the way" – Dr. Ted Camp

I Will Stand For/With God – January 29

What a feeling of peace and comfort, knowing God not only saved me, but He also keeps me. I know there are some who will tell you that you can become "unsaved" after trusting Christ as Savior. Don't believe them for one second! The word, *"everlasting"* means exactly what it says. *"Forever"* means that it will never end. You will always have a choice to make ... will you trust your wisdom, or will you trust the promises of the Word of God? My wisdom has proven to be so insufficient so many times that I have decided to trust the Word of God by faith.

Today in my daily reading, two verses, that ended two different chapters I had read, struck my heart. *"Unto Thee, O my Strength, will I sing: for God is my defense, and the God of my mercy"* (Psalm 59:17) ... *"For the great day of His wrath is come; and who shall be able to stand"* (Revelation 7:17)? There may not be much of a connection in your mind, but they are inseparably linked together in my heart. I know God because Jesus Christ has forgiven my sin and I fully trust His payment on the cross, and His resurrection from the dead to pay my sin debt before God. I am saved forever because God made the payment and His payment was absolutely all that was needed. Nothing more could be added, and praise God, when He has made the payment, nothing more could be taken away!

Knowing I am trusting God gives me a *"blessed hope"* for the day when the wrath of God will be poured out on this old world. I don't have a worry in the world for that because the God Who will be in charge of the *"pouring part"* is my Heavenly Father. He is THE ONE Who paid my debt ... Who loved me enough to give His only-begotten Son ... Who knows all my sin and has wiped clean my standing before Him through Jesus! I'm standing with the right Person! I'm standing WITH God.

There's a children's song that asks the question, *"How can I fear? Jesus is near ... He ever watches over me!"* Instead of worrying about an uncertain future today, stand FOR God in the world that desperately needs Him. We hear a great deal today about caring for your fellow-man. I believe the best way to care for other people is to tell them there is a way of escape for the upcoming disaster that is coming. I believe it is coming quickly; I believe it could come very soon. Do all you can to stand FOR God today wherever you are. He is a God of mercy, tell everyone you meet today! You will not be sorry you did ... neither will they–if they accept Him!

"You are only valuable to God when you are available to God"
– Spurgeon

34

Door – January 30

"Then said Jesus unto them again, 'Verily, verily, I say unto you, I am the Door of the sheep. All that ever came before Me are thieves and robbers: but the sheep did not hear them. I am the Door: by Me if any man enter in, he shall be saved, and shall go in and out, and find pasture. The thief cometh not, but for to steal, and to kill, and to destroy: I am come that they might have life, and that they might have it more abundantly'" (John 10:7-10).

When a shepherd brought his sheep in at night, he would make a makeshift corral for them out of branches and sticks and perhaps existing bushes. The *"Door"* for the corral was a simple opening. The shepherd, himself, would lay at that opening. He did that to assure the safety of all the sheep inside that corral. He also did it to make sure none of the sheep wandered off and were at risk of the dangers outside.

What a comforting thought for the believer today! Jesus Christ is our *"Door."* If anything destructive would try to enter our life, it would need to pass through Him to reach us. You have a *"Door"* that serves as protection for you all day today. He is the Great Shepherd Who has become the *"Door"* that serves as a protection for you today. What a joy to know we are safe behind our *"Door!"* I am thankful when I feel insecure or fearful that I can remember Jesus is there for me and is my *"Door."*

I am also thankful I cannot ever leave the presence of my Heavenly Father, because my *"Door"* will not allow me to leave the Fathers hand! He has a firm grasp on my soul, and nothing can reach me without first coming through Him! Some have doubted their eternal security because of their own sin. This picture of the *"Door"* helps us to realize just as Satan cannot overpower Jesus, my sin cannot either! I am safe inside the protection of God because Jesus is my *"Door!"*

What a joy to know Jesus as Savior! When this world presents multiple thieves looking to break through and steal, it is a blessing to know the One Who came to bring life in the place of death! I am glad for the day I stepped through the *"Door"* and entered the forgiveness God had waiting. I had to trust Christ, the *"Door,"* in order to receive the forgiveness which comes through the blood of Jesus Christ! I will be forever grateful for the *"Door"* that was opened for me to walk into the presence of God. I cannot imagine living one day without this relationship!

Help! – January 31

There is not a day that passes when I do not need to call on my Heavenly Father, not only for help, but for "extra" help. Some days we might feel we need it more than others, but the reality is that a firm dependence on God is a sign of spirituality. We have within us a sin nature that battles the influence of God's Holy Spirit within us. We live in a strange world full of enemies to our faith. We have opportunities to fall to temptations at every turn. We make multiple decisions each step of our day that can lead us to success or failure in our walk with God.

Where will we find the wisdom and help we need for this day we are in right now, and for tomorrow, and the next day? The answer (as always) is in our Bible. *"Give us help from trouble: for vain is the help of man. Through God we shall do valiantly: for He it is that shall tread down our enemies"* (Psalm 60:11).

There is a God in Heaven Who desires to guide you with His eye. He knows the right path we should take, and if we will yield to Him on a consistent and daily basis, He will make His way clear to us. There is so much in our Bible that speaks of God's desire to care for us in our normal lives. Why do you think we find it so strange the "little" things we are facing are important to our God? He has fashioned us to make a difference in this world we are living in, and the details of our lives are important to Him.

The question today is not if God is interested in what we are facing … the question is if we are willing to stop our busy scurrying about to listen to the "still small voice" that lives within every believer. He had placed His precious Holy Spirit within us. I believe the Holy Spirit spends a great deal of time just knocking on our hearts, minds and consciences to help us make the right choices throughout our days.

Please take time today to really stop what you are doing and ask God to give you the wisdom in your choices. Ask Him to give you the ability to choose well in the cross-roads of life which you will intersect today. I believe we serve a great God Who deserves to hold the steering wheel of our lives without any tugging to the side from us. He is the One Who can give you the help you so desperately need for the day. Surrender fully to His will for your life today. I know it's not easy, but it's worth it!

"This is the will of God for me. I did not choose it. I sought to escape it. But it has come. This is my task. God help me." – William E. Sangston

MONTH OF
February

Eternal God – February 1

"The Eternal God is thy refuge, and underneath are the everlasting arms: and He shall truths out the enemy from before thee; and shall say, 'Destroy them'" (Deuteronomy 33:27).

"The Eternal God" – There is no other god that can claim to this title. There have been many others who have claimed to be God or even Christ. However, there is only one *"Eternal God."* We can never ask God, *"When is your birthday?"* God has never had a birthday. He has always been, and will always be. The beauty of God's eternal reality is that it benefits us in tremendous ways. Because God is eternal, we have a blessed eternal hope.

There may be days when you feel God has forgotten you. Be assured God is always on call. Be assured God never loses sight of you. Be assured there will never be a time in your life today, or in the future, or in eternity where God is not aware of what you are facing. It is an amazing thought for me when I consider the God I pray to today for help is the same God who parted the Red Sea's for Moses. He is the same God who rescued Isaac off of the altar on Mount Moriah. He is the same God Who loved me enough to send His Son to die in my place.

It is wonderful to look back and see God's eternal reality. It is also wonderful to look forward and understand He is going to be eternal in the future. Every promise God has made in His Word is guaranteed because He is eternal. I have bought many products that had a lifetime warranty. Once in a while one of those products will fail. When I try to contact the company to have it replaced, I find the company has gone out of business. So much for my warranty! I am so thankful to know the thing I have committed to God (my eternal salvation) is totally secure in his eternal hand.

"The Eternal God" has complete control of what I am going to face today. *"The Eternal God"* is far bigger than any challenge that will come my way. I am so thankful my God is this *"Eternal God."* Because God is eternal that means His characteristics are also eternal. God will always be love. God will always be just. God will always be God! He cannot change because He is not like us. He does not have a beginning and an end like we do. I feel sorry for those who don't believe in God. I feel sorry enough for them that I want to give my life to tell them about His Son Jesus Christ. Will you join me today? Will you look for an opportunity to tell someone about Jesus today? The whole world deserves to know this wonderful God.

Everlasting Father – February 2

"For unto us a child is born, unto us a son is given: and the govern-ment shall be upon His shoulder: and His name shall be called, Wonderful, Counsellor, The Mighty God, The Everlasting Father, The Prince of Peace" (Isaiah 9:6).

This verse has many titles for Jesus! Consider the title, *"Everlasting Father."* This title has two parts that are vitally important. The first is the word *"Everlasting."* We might say the word *"Everlasting"* means always continuing. I am thankful our God will always continue to be our God! There is no worry that one day we will wake up to find our God has ceased to exist. He cannot do that, because part of His character is that He is *"Everlasting."*

The second part of this title is He is our *"Father."* This word means different things to different people. For example, some reading this have had wonderful fathers on this earth, and they smile when they read this title for God. Others, however, have not known their father at all. Still others, know their father, but were abused by him so they might wish they never had known him.

I have been blessed with an earthly father who made our *"Everlasting Father"* his model. My earthly father never knew a father. His dad was killed in a car accident when he was just over a year and a half old. His model for what a father should look like was found in his Bible. My dad is not perfect, of course; but was quick to ask for forgiveness, and move forward after falling. My earthly father is a beautiful picture of my *"Everlasting Father."* There is a major area where there is a difference. My earthly father will have a day when his life ends. My *"Everlasting Father"* is *"Everlasting!"*

If you are a father, follow the example of your *"Everlasting Father."* Let your family know He is in the driver's seat of your family, and it is not you. It was hard to argue with a rule that was established in our family because my dad always pointed us into the Word of our *"Everlasting Father."* When discipline was necessary, it was done like our *"Everlasting Father"* does it. When a knee was scrapped, there was the loving embrace from our dad that was just like the loving embraces of our *"Everlasting Father."* Realize whatever kind of earthly father you have had, you have an *"Everlasting Father"* Who is worthy of your obedience and adoration today.

Our Great Savior – February 3

"*And said unto Jeremiah the prophet, 'Let, we beseech thee, our supplication be accepted before thee, and pray for us unto the LORD thy God, even for all this remnant; (for we are left but a few of many, as thine eyes do behold us:) That the LORD thy God may show us the way wherein we may walk, and the thing that we may do*" (Jeremiah 42:2-3). The Israelite remnant found themselves in captivity. Their large number had dwindled to a very a remnant. Their hearts were crushed and they were ready to cry out for the mercy and leading of God. Their nation had taken their eyes off God, and began to trust the idols of this world instead.

It is very easy for us to replace God with the cares of this world. It would be good for all of us to take a moment and examine our hearts before God to see what sits on the throne of our heart. Each of us open our eyes in the morning and begin an inventory of what the day will hold for us. Plans are formulated, decisions made even before we step a foot out of bed. Give God that most important place of "decision-maker" for your plans today.

The people who were a part of this remnant twice said to the prophet, Jeremiah, "*the LORD **thy** God*." Where are you today? Do you need to ask someone else to pray for you? Just as a child who has gone astray from their parents, you need to repent and come back to your God today. J. Wilbur Chapman wrote an incredible hymn about the great God we serve and all the things He wants to do for us. Read these words and be comforted with all our Great Savior wants to do for us today! Take the time to praise God for all He has done for you and is doing for you!

Verse 1: *Jesus! What a Friend for sinners! Jesus! Lover of my soul; friends may fail me, foes assail me, He, my Savior, makes me whole.*

Verse 2: *Jesus! What a strength in weakness! Let me hide myself in Him; tempted, tried, and sometimes failing, He, my strength, my vict'ry wins.*

Verse 3: *Jesus! What a help in sorrow! While the billows o'er me roll, even when my heart is breaking, He, my comfort, helps my soul.*

Verse 4: *Jesus! What a guide and keeper! While the tempest still is high, storms about me, night o'er-takes me, He, my pilot, hears my cry.*

Verse 5: *Jesus! I do now receive Him, more than all in Him I find, He hath granted me forgiveness, I am His, and He is mine.*

Chorus: *Hallelujah! What a Savior! Hallelujah! What a Friend! Saving, helping, keeping, loving, He is with me to the end.*

Jesus, Savior, Pilot Me–February 4

I remember vividly as a child waking from a sleep in the middle of the night. I opened my eyes and thought I saw Frankenstein come into my bedroom. I can still see Frankenstein walking over to our bunk beds and bending over to look in at my sister. He then turned around (in case you are wondering at this point, I do not believe Frankenstein is real, but in my dream he was very real) and left our room. As soon as he left, I jumped out of bed and ran into my parents' bedroom for help and protection.

I'm older now, but I still have fears just as real as those I just described. Some of the fears I have are just as silly as the one I had then, but they are just as real! I am so thankful for a God Who is bigger than any "Frankenstein" I can concoct in my mind today. God is able to protect me and care for me when no one else can. The psalmist wrote, "*How excellent is Thy loving-kindness, O God! Therefore the children of men put their trust under the shadow of Thy wings*" (Psalm 36:7).

Frankenstein was not real, but the challenges we are facing in our world today are very real. What a comfort to know God is not sleeping or unaware of the things you are facing today. The real challenge today is that we will not try to use our own human reasoning and strength to battle these things on our own, but we will surrender our will to His and trust Him to do battle for us. I don't know what you are facing today or tomorrow, but I know the answers to your challenges are found in our God and in Him alone. This world and its fears and challenges are far more than we can handle. Edward Hopper wrote a song that gives us a great word-picture today. It is the idea of us sailing through this life with waves on every side; wind blowing strong; and no hope other than Jesus taking the controls of our lives.

Verse 1: *Jesus, Savior, pilot me over life's tempestuous sea; unknown waves before me roll, hiding rock and treacherous shoal; chart and compass came from Thee: Jesus, Savior, pilot me.*

Verse 2: *As a mother stills her child, Thou canst hush the ocean wild; boisterous waves obey Thy will when Thou say'st to them "Be still!" Wondrous Sov'reign of the sea, Jesus, Savior, pilot me.*

Verse 3: *When at last I near the shore, and the fearful breakers roar 'twixt me and the peaceful rest, then, while leaning on Thy breast, may I hear Thee say to me, "Fear not, I will pilot thee."*

In the Presence of Greatness – February 5

When I was about fifteen years old, I was asked to play my trumpet in an orchestra that was being conducted by John W. Peterson. John W. Peterson has written a multitude of hymns you would still be familiar with today (songs like, "Heaven Came Down," "Springs of Living Water," Surely Goodness and Mercy," and many more). He wrote many cantatas for church choirs, and this happened to be an Easter Cantata entitled, "No Greater Love." There was a volunteer choir of about 1,000 people from various churches around Philadelphia, a full orchestra, and people who were there to do a drama. I remember showing up the night of rehearsal and meeting John W. Peterson for the first time. I was really impressed with this man and his humility.

That was about as close as I have come to a "brush with greatness." But, it really is not … you see, I met the King of all kings when I was just six-years-old. The day I trusted Jesus Christ to forgive my sin and give me a home in Heaven, I met the Master of the universe in a very personal way. Look at the way the psalmist describes the meeting: *"Blessed is the man whom Thou choosest, and causest to approach unto Thee, that he may dwell in Thy courts: We shall be satisfied with the goodness of Thy house, even of Thy holy temple"* (Psalm 65:4).

There was a day when I recognized the hand of God waving me to approach His throne. Please be sure … I know I did not deserve that invitation. It was purely and completely the grace of God that beckoned me there. However, since that day, I have had the sweet privilege of getting to know the King of all kings. He is now my Heavenly Father. He has made His thoughts known to me in the Word of God and I have had the privilege of talking to Him every day of my life since that time I trusted His Son as my Savior! I have loved getting to know my Heavenly Father better each day.

I will tell you there have been many days when my Heavenly Father needed to get out His heavenly "wooden spoon" and chasten this rebellious heart of mine. I have not always enjoyed the discipline, but I do thank Him for the results. If you don't know God personally, turn your heart over to Him today. If you know Him, realize you are in the presence of greatness every day you walk with Him. There is "goodness" in the presence of God. Go to Him today and bask in the blessings of your relationship with Him.

"Sinners cannot find God for the same reason that criminals cannot find a policeman – They are not looking for them." – Billy Sunday

I Will Declare – February 6

"Come and hear, all ye that fear God, and I will declare what He hath done for my soul" (Psalm 66:16). When was the last time you told someone else what the Lord is doing in your life? When did you purposely give praise to God for what He has been teaching you through the Word of God? When was the last time you shared with someone else something you heard in a good sermon? Or you shared the words that drove deep into your heart from a good song? When was the last time you stood for your God (even among believers who might be caught up in all the "cute" spiritual issues of our day) and testified about the greatness of your God. When was the last time you were so thrilled with what God has been doing in you that you "had to" share it with someone else?

I feel sorry for God ... He does all these wonderful things for His children – including providing for needs; giving heavenly wisdom for earthly trials; chastening us when we step out of line; providing health and provision for us to live and succeed ... and what does He hear in return from us? Silence, many times. Today would be a good day for we who are believers to stand up wherever we are and tell people we have an incredible God!

If you haven't noticed, the world we are living in is a confused mess right now. The finances most people coveted and built their life to attain are fleeing away from them without any plans to return. Cancer, heart conditions, leukemia, etc. are on the rise, not the decline (even with all our research and discoveries). The political situations in most countries are filled with unrest and violence. The hope for most good people coming in the future is evaporating right before our eyes. What a perfect time to stand up and declare there is a God in Heaven with the answers to the deep needs in the soul of men today!

That word, *"**declare**"* means to *write down*, to *announce*, to *make known*, and to *celebrate*. When was the last time you wrote a letter to someone telling them about how great your God is? When was the last time you announced on your FaceBook page that you loved God and told what He had been doing for you? When was the last time you let everyone know you have an allegiance to the King of all kings? When was the last time you actually celebrated the fact you were a Christian and stopped trying to hide it? God is looking for Christians who will stand and declare Him to this lost and dying world. STAND AND DECLARE TODAY!

"Go all out for God, and God will go all out for you!" –
Jonathan Goforth

Firstfruits – February 7

"But now is Christ risen from the dead, and become the Firstfruits of them that slept. For since by man came death, by man came also the res- urrection of the dead. For as in Adam all die, even so in Christ shall all be made alive. But every man in his own order: Christ the Firstfruits; after- ward they that are Christ's at his coming" (I Corinthians 15:20-23).

Jesus Christ is the *"Firstfruits"* of our faith. My mind goes to my great-grandfather's house and his back yard. I can remember as a boy going to visit my great-grandfather. I remember the peach trees my great-grand- father had growing in the back yard. For a boy, there is nothing better than a fresh peach you pick off a tree and eat! When the peaches were ripened, and we visited my great-grandfathers house, I was bound to end up with a sticky face, with a big smile attached to it!

Much like those first ripened peaches, Jesus Christ coming to the earth was something that was anticipated all through the cold, winter days of the history of mankind. From the time of Adam's sin, mankind was looking for the *"Firstfruits"* of God's promised Redeemer (Genesis 3:15). They were looking for the sacrifice that would satisfy the righteous demand of their Heavenly Father. The daily/weekly/yearly sacrifices they were required to do for their sin had become stale and old to them. They were looking for God's permanent sacrifice. Jesus Christ was and is the *"Firstfruit"* God provided for them and us.

Paul pointed out in I Corinthians 15 that when Christ rose from the dead, He provided exactly what man needed. Man needed the *"Firstfruits"* to match the faith they had been holding on to since Adam and Eve left the Garden of Eden. God provided exactly what we needed and even more! You see; I believe God offered not only the sacrifice for the sins of those who would believe in Him for salvation. I also believe Jesus offered the sacrifice that would be adequate to save even those who would not believe! That's right! I believe Jesus died for the sins of the *"whole world!"*

If you have tasted the *"Firstfruits"* God has provided for you ... if you have trusted Jesus Christ as your personal Savior, tell someone else about it! Just like you would brag on the sweetest fruit you have ever tasted ... tell someone about the *"Firstfruits"* God provided you when He gave you a risen Savior! There is no greater story in all the world than this story. Jesus came to this earth to die for sinful men! Proclaim it from the housetops!

Foundation – February 8

"For other Foundation can no man lay than that is laid, which is Jesus Christ. Now if any man build upon this foundation gold, silver, precious stones, wood, hay, stubble; Every man's work shall be made manifest: for the day shall declare it, because it shall be revealed by fire; and the fire shall try every man's work of what sort it is. If any man's work abide which he hath built thereupon, he shall receive a reward" (I Corinthians 3:11-14).

More than twenty years ago I watched our home being built. I remember the first day they started building. I was sitting on the street in front of where our house would be built with my video camera in hand. The contractor showed up pulling a backhoe on a trailer. I was thrilled to watch our house being built. For the next several hours I watched as he sat on that backhoe and dug the footers. It was not as exciting as I thought it would be. It is thrilling to me today when the wind in howling; when the rains are beating down, and the snow is piled on top of our house. Our home was built on a solid foundation that has stood the testing of the past twenty-plus years.

Our faith is built upon the *"Foundation"* of the only Person that could stand the storms life brings us every day. Jesus Christ is the *"Foundation"* my life has been built on. I am thankful that since I was saved my foundation has never moved! He has remained faithful and sturdy! He has not been affected by the Hippie generation. He did not even flinch when many religions told me my salvation was not secure! He did not move an inch the day my mother breathed her last breath on this earth!

My *"Foundation"* is steadfast and sure! Where have you built your life? If you have placed your confidence in anyone, or anything other than Jesus Christ, I am sure you have faced disappointment. I know if someone had made me their foundation, they would have been highly disappointed more than once! I have not been faithful to God, family or friends like I would like to, but He has remained my solid *"Foundation"* my whole life. We Christians face so much criticism of our faith in Christ that sometimes we become weak and begin to cave. When you feel the temptation to do this in your life, remember your *"Foundation."*

Jesus Christ has not moved since before the foundation of the world! I love this verse: *"Jesus Christ the same yesterday, and to day, and for ever"* (Hebrews 13:8). Now that's a *"Foundation!"* I am so thankful for my faithful *"Foundation,"* my Rock and my Fortress. When troubles come in your day today ... run back to your *"Foundation!"*

45

God Help Me – February 9

What a great thing to know the God Who created this universe, the earth, animals, plants, oceans and land, as well as man himself! Today I listened to a song that said God created Adam from the dust of His (God's) heart. I am still amazed God has any interest in me. I do not see much value in me, how could He see anything worthwhile in me? I will not be able to answer that question. Nor will I ever understand why God has the patience He has with me. Even though I fail Him repeatedly, every time I repent and return to Him I find His mercies are new every morning.

What a joy to know when I finally come to the end of my rope, and turn back to God, He is ready to forgive and has been waiting for me to return. The psalmist said this: *"But as for me, my prayer is unto Thee, O LORD, in an acceptable time: O God, in the multitude of Thy mercy hear me, in the truth of Thy salvation"* (Psalm 69:13). I need the help of God today and every day of my life. I need His mercy ... I need the reality of His salvation. We, who are sinners by our nature, need the forgiveness only God can offer. What an honor to know the God Who paid the price for sinners. We know the One Who has the answer to the sin problem that plagues this world today.

Notice the writer of this chapter did not ask for justice, but for mercy. Each of us needs the mercy of God and each of us ought to fear the justice of God. When you begin to feel God is lucky to have you as a child, take a moment to consider the sin He had to forgive in your life just yesterday. All the evil, hate-filled thoughts you had. Every idle moment you wasted away without any thought of others, or what God wanted you to do. All the moments of selfishness, envy, vain-glory, impurity, etc. I think you get the picture.

God touched my heart with this thought as I was meditating on this verse today ... if I desire His mercy to be extended to me so much today, I ought to extend that same mercy to others whose paths I cross who need to see mercy from me. Rather than exalting yourself today, humbly crawl to Jesus and ask for His mercy and the truth of His salvation. He is ready and willing to help you. Then go on your path today and look for opportunities to extend that same kind of mercy and salvation to others who might harm you in some way. Help is available for us today ... and for them!

"Below the clouds it is dark and above the clouds it is light. Are you above or below the clouds?" – Job 37:21

Gift of God – February 10

"Jesus answered and said unto her, 'If thou knewest the Gift of God, and who it is that saith to thee, Give me to drink; thou wouldest have asked of him, and he would have given thee living water'" (John 4:10).

I know I am supposed to be older and more mature, and I am supposed to be more excited to give a gift than to receive one. But I must tell you I am always excited when a gift given to me is the biggest gift given! I'm just being honest. Jesus Christ was the *"Gift of God"* to me ... and you.

I will never forget the day I realized Jesus Christ the *"Gift of God"* for me. That day followed another very important day in my life that I have vivid memories of as well. I was just a boy trying to help his mother. I was as innocent as I could be as a six-year-old boy. I was helping my mother by breaking off some "unruly" flowers that had grown out of the ground unevenly. When my mother rounded the corner of our house and loudly called my name, I knew I was in danger of an encounter with the wooden spoon! When confronted with whether or not I had broken off my mother's flowers, I openly lied to her. This was the first time I realized I was a liar.

A few weeks later came the time when I realized Jesus Christ was the *"Gift of God"* for me. As I had heard many times before, a preacher said we were all sinners. Of course, my mind reverted to the lie I told. He then explained our sin separated us from a perfect Heaven. He then told how God sent the *"Gift of God"* in His Son, Jesus Christ. He talked about trusting Jesus' death, burial and resurrection as payment for sin ... for my sin ... for my lies.

That afternoon I knelt beside my mother's bed and received the *"Gift of God"* as my own! Jesus became MY Savior. Oh the joy that floods my soul to this day at that thought! He came for me! He rescued me from my lies, selfishness, evil thoughts, attitudes, actions and for every last sin I have or will ever commit! I need Him desperately.

This is a *"Gift"* we are encouraged to give away to others after we have received it for ourselves! How can we remain quiet about such a wonderful *"Gift?"* How can you know your sins are forgiven, and not tell that co-worker of yours they can have peace with God through Him too? How can we be so selfish as to worry about our acceptance or rejection by others when we have the *"Gift of God"* for them too? Tell someone today ... you will not be disappointed you did.

They are Precious in His Sight – February 11

On January 23rd, 2011 one of our daughters, just two days short of her third month of the pregnancy, lost a dear little baby boy named Joseph David. On that very day, I read Psalm 71 and just "happened" to read these two verses: *"For Thou art my hope, O Lord God; Thou art my trust from my youth. By Thee have I been holden up from the womb: Thou art He that took me out of my mother's bowels: my praise shall be continually of Thee"* (Psalm 71:5-6).

I was reading this chapter today and saw Joseph's name written in the column of my Bible, and the thought occurred to me that it was about this same time the infamous Roe Vs. Wade decision was made. On January 22nd, 1973 the court made the decision that it was man's decision whether or not a baby had the right to live or be killed. Abortion was legalized exactly thirty-eight years and one day before Joseph entered into the presence of our Heavenly Father. All of this led me to think about that little song we learned in Sunday School when we were just children. *"Jesus loves the little children; all the children of the world; red and yellow, black and white,* ***they are precious in His sight;*** *Jesus loves the little children of the world."*

The Bible does not lie ... life is precious in the sight of God. Now, I am not going to use this devotional today to debate when life begins (I believe Psalm 71:6 makes it clear that it begins long before we see that little baby with our eyes); and I am not going to use this devotional today to debate the issues of pro-life or pro-death. I want you to consider this thought ... your life is precious to God today; what are you using it for?

I have noticed us human beings love to point out the faults of others, while ignoring our own short-comings. I am 100% against abortion and euthanasia, and I am also 100% for using the life God gives you to its fullest potential for the glory of God. I don't want to waste one minute God has given me to use for Him. I don't want to waste one talent or ability God has given me to use for Him. I don't want to waste one opportunity God will place in front of me to represent Him. This life we have been given is far too valuable to waste a single second! Don't complain about what you cannot do today ... do what you can with all your might. Life is precious! Please don't waste away the precious time God has given you for this day!

"Jesus will judge us not only for what we did, but also for what we could have done and didn't." – George Otis

All Creatures of Our God and King – February 13

"So we Thy people and sheep of Thy pasture will give Thee thanks forever: We will show forth Thy praise to all generations" (Psalm 79:13). There seems to be an epidemic of complaining among Christians today. I have noticed when going to most church services where there is an opportunity for praise followed by prayer requests, the leader almost has to beg people to give praise for what God is doing.

We who have been saved from the brink of Hell and been placed on the sure path to Heaven have passed from death into life! We have a reason to praise Him. We were sheep wandering without a Shepherd. We were on our own to find food and shelter. We were sheep without hope of any kind of quality life until we met Jesus Christ!

I heard a prisoner give a testimony something like this: *"I thank God He allowed me to be placed in this prison. If I were not here, I would have been dead by now, and would never have heard about Jesus Christ. I am thankful I came to prison to hear about Jesus Christ and He is now my Savior!"* This man knew how to praise God! Why is it we so quickly criticize a prisoner who trusts Christ, and we assume the stuffy, arrogant, pompous person sitting next to us dressed in all the "right" clothing has a better testimony? Francis of Assisi wrote:

Verse 1: *All creatures of our God and King, lift up your voice and with us sing, "Alleluia! Alleluia!" Thou burning sun with golden beam, thou silver moon with softer gleam!*

Verse 2: *Thou rushing wind that art so strong, ye clouds that sail in heav'n along, O praise Him! Alleluia! Thou rising morn, in praise rejoice, ye lights of evening, find a voice!*

Verse 3: *And all ye men of tender heart, forgiving others, take your part, O sing ye! Alleluia! Ye who long pain and sorrow bear, praise God and on Him cast your care!*

Verse 4: *Let all things their Creator bless, and worship Him in blessedness, O praise Him! Alleluia! Praise, praise the Father, praise the Son, and praise the Spirit, Three in One!*

Verse 5: *Praise God from Whom all blessings flow, praise Him all creatures here below, Alleluia! Alleluia! Praise Him above, ye heavn'ly host, praise Father, Son and Holy Ghost.*

Chorus: *O praise Him, O praise Him! Alleluia! Alleluia! Alleluia!*

What is IN You? – February 13

Being a kid is a great thing. You get to do all the things people do before they become mature and dignified. I remember one day peeling an orange and looking at the bright orange skin, thinking to myself; "*I bet that bright orange skin would taste good.*" I then proceeded to bite off a pretty large piece of that orange peel. Just in case none of you have ever experienced the sensations that attack your mouth when eating an orange peel, I will just tell you this ... what is inside that orange peel is much sweeter than what is on the outside.

The same thing is true of you. What is inside you is far more important than the shell everyone sees. You can dress up ... comb all your hairs ... brush your teeth ... put on deodorant ... pluck those unruly eyebrows ... put lip-stick on ... and a bunch of other things I have no idea about. The reality is what is inside you is far more important than all that "paint" on the outside of the old barn.

When Israel was in the middle of captivity, God the Holy Spirit inspired the Old Testament prophet, Zechariah to pen these words: "*And many nations shall be joined to the LORD in that day, and shall be My people: and I will dwell in the midst of thee, and thou shalt know that the LORD of hosts hath sent me unto thee*" (Zechariah 2:11). What great hope for Israel ... what great hope for us today! As you wallow through this life, failing often, succeeding infrequently, be encouraged there is hope! The challenge for each believer today is to empty yourself of all those things you think are so attractive, and allow the Spirit of God to be seen in what you say, do, and think.

I am so encouraged to think the God of the universe has seen enough value in me to allow the Holy Spirit to indwell me. I am such a pitiful testimony many days of my life, but I know if I will just allow the Holy Spirit to have His way in my life, He will show this world the answer to the cries of their heart! God's plan has always been to reach "***many nations***" through Him indwelling His people! The Holy Spirit of God is in reality "*in the midst of thee*" today. The question is ... have we covered His presence with our greed, our selfish desires, our hatred/prejudices, our plans and dreams, our dreams for the future, our _____? This hurting world needs to see the fruit produced by a spirit-filled life. Can they see God's work in the midst of you today? Let His light shine out of you today!

"*The only thing God is interested in is people.*" – Jerry Falwell

God is Love – February 14

"Beloved, let us love one another: for love is of God; and every one that loveth is born of God, and knoweth God. He that loveth not knoweth not God; for God is love. In this was manifested the love of God toward us, because that God sent His only begotten Son into the world, that we might live through Him. Herein is love, not that we love God, but that He loved us, and sent His Son to be the propitiation for our sins" (I John 4:7-10).

Over and over again God has loved a group of people who have consistently turned their backs on Him. His love never wavered or ceased, but remains constant. Let me share a few very profound ideas with you about the fact that *"God is love."* You cannot do one thing to make God love you more. He has loved you as deeply as it is possible to love a person. He demonstrated this when He sent His Son to die on the cross to pay your eternal sin debt.

You cannot do anything that would make God love you any less than He already does. If it were possible for God to love you less, there would have been many times throughout your life when He could have caused your life to come to an end, but the reality is *"God is love."* The decision to love you was made long before you were born. Remember, God knew who you would be before your first breath was taken. He knew your times of rebellion against His will, and He loved you. He knew when you would listen to the advice of friends, ignoring His will, and He loved you.

Love is not something God choses to do. Love is what God is! I love this truth! God is often painted as a severe Judge Who delights in zapping people into Hell. He is blamed for every natural disaster by some. Fingers are pointed at Him when bad things happen to good people and He is sternly challenged. In spite of all these nasty reactions to Him, He remains the same, because *"God is love."* God never has to reach deep in His heart to find love for someone ... *"God is love."* He never has to think of warm and fuzzy thoughts to find love for a person ... *"God is love."*

Today is a traditional day when we tell others we love them. We buy cards, chocolates, roses, and gifts to display to our loved ones that we notice them. I think today is a good day to pause and thank God for introducing us to this concept of love! I think we ought to thank Him for loving us first, so we could love others. I think we ought to thank Him over and over again for displaying His love so vividly to us that day on the hill of Calvary. I think today is a great day to tell God we love Him!

Good Shepherd – February 15

"I am the Good Shepherd: the Good Shepherd giveth His life for His sheep. But he that is an hireling, and not the Shepherd, whose own the sheep are not, seeth the wolf coming, and leaveth the sheep, and fleeth: and the wolf catcheth them, and scattereth the sheep. The hireling fleeth, because he is an hireling, and careth not for the sheep. I am the Good Shepherd, and know My sheep, and am known of mine" (John 10:11-14).

Jesus made the point that there was a difference between someone who is filling a role that must be done (*hireling*), and the actual owner of the sheep. What an incredible thought that our Maker, became our *"Good Shepherd!"* There is no other person on the face of the earth who will love you like your *"Good Shepherd"* loves you. There is no other person willing to give up all they have for you like your *"Good Shepherd"* did.

Think for a moment about the responsibilities of a shepherd. First, this was one of the most humble ways to make a living known in the time of Jesus. It was a job no one wanted because it did not involve any kind of notoriety, or publicity. You were alone with sheep all day and night caring for their needs. Jesus humbled Himself to become our *"Good Shepherd."* He gave up the splendor of Heaven to be made a servant that went to death for His sheep. I thank God for my *"Good Shepherd."*

Secondly, the responsibilities of a *"Good Shepherd"* included risking their life for the protection of the sheep. The *"hireling"* (or paid help) turned tail and ran at the sign of a wolf. The *"Good Shepherd"* stayed and fought off the enemies of the sheep for the purpose of sparing their lives at the risk of losing his own. The greatest enemies we face are these three: sin, the Devil, and death. When Jesus died on the cross for us, and rose from the dead, He absolutely won the victory for us over all three of these.

Third, the *"Good Shepherd"* is responsible to make sure the sheep are well fed. Psalm 23 talks about the *"Good Shepherd"* leading the sheep to the green pastures. One of the most amazing things Jesus did for us to make sure we were well fed, was ascending back into Heaven. When He did that, He opened the way for the Comforter (the Holy Spirit) to come to dwell in us! He sent the Holy Spirit of God to guide us into all truth. He gave us the Holy Spirit that had breathed the words through the hearts of men and onto pages we now call our Bible!

What a *"Good Shepherd"* we have today! Don't fight against His leadership. Don't try to go wherer He does not lead. Trust Him today!

Set Yourself Apart ... Unto Holiness – February 16

There is a topic that is not discussed much in our churches today it seems. It is the old-fashioned topic of living a holy life. I think part of the reason we do not hear it taught or preached much today is because it is something all of us struggle doing ... it's not easy to be holy. In days gone by, in a nearby city, Billy Sunday would come to the Philadelphia Ice Palace and Auditorium for a week of meetings, and it was told all the bars and gamblers would be put out of business for that week as a result. You see, Billy Sunday preached on the theme of living holy lives and the conviction that set in as a result meant there was little or no traffic to these places where sin was rampant.

I read a verse that got my attention today and a specific phrase really got a good hold on my heart. When David became the second king in Israel, he decided to move the Ark of the Covenant back to Jerusalem. He did not do it as God had instructed, but sent a "new cart" for it to be transported on. One of the men driving the cart, Uzza reached out to steady it at one point and was instantly killed (I Chronicles 13). The Ark of the Covenant represented the presence of God. Not even the priests were to touch it ... God had instructed it be made with rings fastened to either side for a pole to be inserted in and carried by the poles. After Uzza was killed, David became angry and refused to move the Ark back to Jerusalem.

Later on, David realized his error, and also realized the mistake was his, not God's. He gave the following instructions upon returning to the home of Obed-Edom to get the Ark ... *"Ye are the chief of the fathers of the Levites: sanctify yourselves, both ye and your brethren, that ye may bring up the ark of the LORD God of Israel unto the place that I have prepared for it"* (I Chronicles 15:12). David had learned the lesson God is trying to teach all of us. God is holy and holy actions/attitudes among His people are expected. Your mind will quickly tell you *"No one is perfect!"* While it is true none of us is perfect, it is equally true we serve a HOLY God Who is perfect. His desire is for you and me to live holy lives while we are here on this earth. He wants you and me to represent Him and His holiness to a lost and dying world who needs something different than what they can produce. We realize we cannot be perfect, but that ought to be our goal every day we have breath. Let's not fall into the trap of making excuses in this life. Losers make excuses ... winners make adjustments. Make it your goal to live a holy life for the cause of Christ today!

"You cannot have a conquest without a challenge." – Dr. Ted Camp

Draw Me Nearer – February 17

One night I was driving home after dropping off some teens from an all-day event at a local amusement park. It was late, I was tired, and I was headed home. The roads were empty, except for one lone car coming towards me. As that lone car approached me, I recognized it as a State Police car. I looked down at my speed-o-meter. I was going ten-miles-an-hour over the speed limit. The kind police officer informed me I was going fifteen-miles-per-hour over the speed limit and gave me a nice reminder.

The officer told me I should go to court and not pay the ticket. I will never forget the feeling I had sitting in that courtroom waiting for my name to be called. I realized the depth of a position of authority, and I was very sober. The Bible says, "...*for we shall all stand before the judgment seat of Christ. For it is written, 'As I live, saith the Lord, every knee shall bow to Me, and every tongue shall confess to God.' So then every one of us shall give account of himself to God*" (Romans 14:10b-12).

There will be a day for every person who has ever lived on this earth when we will stand before God Himself. I believe this will be a very sober time for each of us as well. I don't believe one of us will be thinking about how much money we made at this point. I don't think one of us will say, "*I wish I had driven a faster car ...*" or "*I wish I had lived in a bigger house ...*" I do think we will wish we had served the Lord in more ways. I believe we will wish we had obeyed Scriptures we had read more effectively. Fanny Crosby wrote a great hymn that we ought to live by.

Verse 1: *I am Thine, O Lord, I have heard Thy voice, and it told Thy love to me; but I long to rise in the arms of faith, and be closer drawn to Thee.*
Verse 2: *Consecrate me now to Thy service, Lord, by the pow'r of grace divine; let my soul look up with a steadfast hope, and my will be lost in Thine.*
Verse 3: *Oh, the pure delight of a single hour that before Thy throne I spend, when I kneel in prayer, and with Thee, my God, I commune as friend with Friend!*
Verse 4: *There are depths of love that I cannot know till I cross the narrow sea; there are heights of joy that I may not reach till I rest in peace with Thee.*
Chorus: *Draw me nearer, nearer blessed Lord, to the cross where Thou hast died; draw me nearer blessed Lord, to Thy precious bleeding side.*

Who Are You Pleasing Today? – February 18

There is something to trying to keep your boss, or coach happy with what you are doing. I remember trying to do my best to accomplish whatever my coach wanted done when I was playing a sport. If he was impressed with showing up on time, I would be early to every practice. If he was impressed by the people who finished first in the practice drills, I did my best to finish first. If he wanted us to eat a certain diet, I would limit what I ate to his preferences. I wanted to play so badly, I would do all I could to please him. When getting a job, I always wanted to find out what my boss preferred when it came to the different things related to my job. I did not always agree with my boss and his/her choices, but I always realized the importance of doing my best to please them, or I would be planning to look for a new job.

Why should my Christian life be any different? I have a Heavenly Father Who is far better than any earthly coach or boss I have had. My Heavenly Father wants the absolute best for me and my life. He has an absolutely perfect will that is designed to bring Him ultimate glory, and me absolute peace and happiness. What is the key to me pleasing and surrendering to my Heavenly Father's desires for my life? What is it that angers my Heavenly Father in regards to me following His will?

The psalmist put it this way ... *"Therefore the LORD heard this, and was wroth; so a fire was kindled against Jacob, and anger also came up against Israel; because they believed not in God, and trusted not in His salvation"* (Psalm 78:21-22). Here is the key to pleasing our Heavenly Father. The thing that angered God throughout the history of the nation of Israel was their disbelief and their lack of trust. God loved these people like He loves us today. He had all the protection, provision and success they could ever want waiting for them in the middle of trusting and believing in Him.

There was one problem with Israel, and I fear it could be a problem with us today. We fear the disapproval of men/women around us that we can see more than we fear the disapproval of our Heavenly Father we cannot see. Don't fall into the same trap Israel fell into in the past. Trust the plan God has for you regardless of who on this earth agrees with Him or not ... follow Him! Believe what He tells you in the Word of God no matter what loud voices tell you it is wrong ... believe Him! Be brave enough today to trust the leadership of the Holy Spirit within you ... not those around you.

"The prospects are as bright as the promises of God." –
Adoniram Judson

Do Unto Others – February 19

I have heard many people say, "You know in the Bible it says, do unto others as you would have others do unto you." That is not actually a statement directly from the Bible. This phrase has been called the "Golden Rule." This principle is in the pages of our Bible, and I came across it again today in the Old Testament book of Zechariah with a slightly different ending. *"Thus speaketh the LORD of hosts, saying, "Execute true judgment, and show mercy and compassion every man to his brother"* (Zechariah 7:9).

Did you notice the difference? The difference is we are to do good to others without expecting anything in return. God is asking each of us as Christians to live a life where we show mercy and compassion whether that mercy or compassion is returned at all. We ought to be willing today to live the life Jesus showed during His thirty-three years here on earth. He gave and others took from Him without giving back. He loved and others returned His love with hatred. He forgave and others spit in His face. He promised to give life and we crucified Him. He is the ultimate example of this verse today. He shows mercy and compassion and does it to whosoever will come to Him by faith. He even offers that mercy and compassion to those who will refuse Him.

We have a very high calling today in our Savior ... we are called to show His mercy to those who need it most that we will pass today. We are called to demonstrate His Christ-like compassion to those He would single out when all others around Him would have over-looked. That is the goal for your day today. Have the heart Jesus Christ had for those around Him, for the people who He has placed around you. Mercy and compassion are not being demonstrated a great deal in our world today. Mercy and compassion do not normally flow from us toward others. We are much better at vengeance and retaliation than we are at mercy and compassion. Reverse the normal flow today. Look for chances to show Christ's mercy and compassion where you work/go to school/shop/live.

We love to talk about being "salt" and "light" in this world. There is no mystery about this. The world will know we are His disciples when we demonstrate love one for another. That is not just showing love to the lovely people we meet, but to all the people we meet. Try it today!

"Someone took time to invest in you. You need to invest in others." –
Dr. Ted Camp

Send Out Your Invitations – February 20

I can vividly remember my mother standing on the back porch of our house, ringing the bell I bought her for Christmas one year, calling my sister and me in from playing with our friends in the neighborhood. There were times I didn't like to hear that bell, especially if I was up to bat at the time. I did not like to hear the bell, but I loved the food that was waiting for me inside our home. I loved the fellowship around that kitchen table. It was the place we reviewed all that had happened throughout the day when the four of us were apart from each other. It was a time we discussed what was coming up the next day. For those of you who do not eat together on a regular basis ... you're missing out on a great time. That is not the purpose of this devotional today.

In almost the last verse in our Bible, God comes to the back porch and rings the bell. He is inviting all to come in for a time around His table. Here is the invitation to each of us, and to the whole world: *"And the Spirit and the bride say, "**Come**." And let him that heareth say, "**Come**." And let him that is athirst **come**. And whosoever will, let him take the water of life freely"* (Revelation 22:17). Do you get the idea God wants you to come in from playing in the world to sit around His banquet table there in Heaven? Perhaps we will discuss the events of our lives that led us to Him. Maybe we will review the blessings we have experienced in our lives as a result of a right relationship with Him. I'm not sure all we will do there, but I am sure He will be sitting at the "head" of the table. I would not miss coming in from this world to enjoy that time around the table.

Don't miss the first two of those invitations to come in verse 17; The Spirit and **the BRIDE** say "Come." The Holy Spirit places within each of us the desire to invite others to come to know Jesus Christ. It is our responsibility to invite as many as we can to this reunion with Jesus Christ while we have the chance. Jesus encouraged His disciples to go to the highways, and the hedges and compel people to come in. This is not some passive activity you can participate in. You and I must actively send out the invitations to this meeting with God. I want all of my friends, family, and acquaintances to be able to hear, *"Well done, thou good and faithful servant,"* and not *"Depart from Me, I never knew you."* Send out the invitations today!

"We talk of the Second Coming when half of the world has never even heard of the first." – Oswald J. Smith

Hungry? – February 21

"Hi Mom ... I'm coming home from college this weekend ... can you ask Grandmom to make her chicken and dumplings?" While at college eating "college" food (which many days meant peanut-butter bread because the food was so bad – when they served the green hot dogs it was a little more than I could handle), I could not wait to get home to "real" cooking! I can remember sitting around the tables in our college cafeteria, describing my grandmother's chicken and dumplings. I could almost taste them while I was describing them to my buddies. I always wondered why my friends always wanted to come home with me ...

Let me ask this question ... why would you settle for green hot dogs when you could eat home-made chicken and dumplings? Let me change the question slightly to a spiritual application ... why would you trust anyone, or anything other than Almighty God to take care of you? God's Word clearly says, *"There shall no strange god be in thee; neither shalt thou worship any strange god. I am the LORD thy God, which brought thee out of the land of Egypt: open thy mouth wide, and I will fill it"* (Psalm 81:9-10). Why is it we lean toward that which could never satisfy like our God? Why is it that we trust the opinions of our friends before we will trust the time proven truths of the Bible? Why is it we will follow the pattern of this world before we will live a sanctified life? Why? ... Because we are sinners by our nature and we need constant reminding.

We have a natural tendency to follow after that which could never satisfy the longing of our soul. Most of us do not have wooden figurines, or stone carvings we bow down to in our homes, but we do have cars that we polish and care for like they are our baby. We have sports teams we idolize and skip church to watch play. We have jobs we dedicate far more time and energy to than we do to our walk with God. We put effort into earthly relationships that far surpass the time/energy we put into our relationship with God. When the tough times come, we will not run to our car / sports team / job / or earthly relationship for the help we need. We will run to God. Go to God today for all you will need. Make your relationship with Him top priority today. Allow Him to feed you the things He knows you need the most. He is ready and able to fill up your open mouth, but He is waiting for you to turn your back on idols, and turn to Him. Are you hungry today? I know where the banquet table is full to overflowing!

"Hands can only be filled when they are open." – Curtis Hutson

Who Are You Looking For? – February 22

We had an international dinner during our Missions Conference at the church I pastored one year. Right in the beginning of the meal, the back door of the church opened and a homeless man named Jonathan came in. I noticed one of our Deacons approaching him and taking him through the line for a plate of food. My grandmother was sitting with some of the other older women, and they witnessed Jonathan's entry. One of the women asked (in a way that showed her displeasure), *"Who is that???"* The innocent reply of my grandmother was priceless ... and one that has given us a chuckle every time this story is told. She never looked up from her plate of food, but said, *"Don't worry about him, Jimmy attracts people like that."*

I hope that statement is true. I hope I will always care for people who are in need. The psalmist wrote, *"Defend the poor and fatherless: do justice to the afflicted and needy. Deliver the poor and needy: rid them out of the hand of the wicked"* (Psalm 82:3-4). Today is a good day to look to help someone who has not had the blessings you have had in your life. The "poor," the "fatherless," the "afflicted," and the "needy." You don't need to look very far these days. There are people like this in every town and city. But don't misunderstand ... there are people just like this in every fancy office and school too. There will be people all around you today who will fit this description. The question is not if these opportunities are there, the question will be if you will decide to step outside of your comfort zone to minister to them today?

This could be the person who lives in the biggest house in your neighborhood. This could be the person wearing the most expensive clothing, or driving the newest car, or getting straight "A's" in school. There is one thing for sure; any person without a relationship with Jesus Christ could be described as "poor, fatherless, afflicted and needy." I believe what God is trying to get us to realize is, the entire world needs a relationship with Him in order to be happy and successful. I preached in prison recently, and one of the prisoners approached me after my message and said; *"Christianity is just one beggar telling another beggar where the bread is."* What a powerful and true statement that is. The next time you begin to feel that attitude of superiority coming upon you, remember who you really are. You are nothing more than a sinner saved by the incredible grace of God. You have not earned that, you cannot pay for that, you have received it from God ... pass that along to others today.

The Old Rugged Cross – February 23

The thought of the cross has always aroused a deep emotion in my heart. I cannot get over the fact that the sinless, innocent Son of God willingly endured the agony of the cross for me! I cannot get over the thought of my sinfulness, my disregard for holiness and purity nailed Jesus Christ to the cross. I cannot get past the fact that if I had not been a sinner, none of that would have been necessary. I am a sinner ... and it was necessary.

"And I, brethren, when I came to you, came not with excellency of speech or of wisdom, declaring unto you the testimony of God. For I determined not to know any thing among you, save Jesus Christ, and Him crucified" (I Corinthians 2:1-2). I often stand behind pulpits and speak for a half-hour or more. Each time I prepare to walk to the pulpit, I am fully aware of my worthlessness. I feel unworthy because I am unworthy. I understand fully what Paul was talking about in I Corinthians 2.

Our power is not found in the illustrations we find ... in the delivery of the message ... the power of any message that is effective is how high we can exalt Jesus Christ during the message! Paul is often called one of the greatest Christians the world has ever known. He recognized clearly it was not about him, but about the crucified Savior he served! One of the most beloved hymns of the fundamental church has been this hymn today. George Bennard wrote one of my favorite hymns about this thought.

Verse 1: *On a hill far away stood an old rugged cross, the emblem of suff'ring and shame; and I love that old cross where the dearest and best for a world of lost sinners was slain.*

Verse 2: *Oh, that old rugged cross so despised by the world, has a wondrous attraction for me; for the dear Lamb of God left His glory above, to bear it to dark Calvary.*

Verse 3: *In the old rugged cross, stained with blood so divine, a wondrous beauty I see; for 'twas on that old cross Jesus suffered and died, to pardon and sanctify me.*

Verse 4: *To the old rugged cross I will ever be true, its shame and reproach gladly bear; then He'll call me some day to my home far away, where His glory forever I'll share.*

Chorus: *So I'll cherish the old rugged cross ... Till my trophies at last I lay down; I will cling to the old rugged cross ... and exchange it some day for a crown.*

There Shall Be Showers of Blessing – February 24

"I did more work than any of the people who were listed in the bulletin and MY name was not there!" *"They put him/her into the game before me and I worked harder than them all!"* When you have feelings or thoughts like these, you are missing a major truth we all need to be reminded about. Whatever it is we are talking about, we need to remember it's not about us … it should be about Him! There is a sin each of us battles on a regular basis … pride.

There have been many times when I have asked God to keep me humble. I do this because I know God gives grace to the humble and resists the proud! After praying for this humility I have found myself complaining to God when I am not given credit where I think I deserved credit! I love what Paul wrote in I Corinthians 3 on this topic: *"I have planted, Apollos watered; but God gave the increase. So then neither is he that planteth any thing, neither he that watereth; but God that giveth the increase"* (I Corinthians 3:6-7).

I realize if anything good will come out of my life, it will be a direct result of me getting out of the way, and God taking over. If I give good counsel to a person, it is because I have remembered a good Bible truth that has helped someone. If I invest my money wisely, it is because God gave me good counselors and He used them to lead me in the right direction. If I preach/teach a good message/lesson, it is completely because God taught me a truth from His Word and empowered me to pass it along to others.

The things you see God doing around you today are a blessing from Him. Stop and thank Him for the work He is doing in your life. Daniel W. Whittle wrote a simple, but great old song about where our blessings come from. It is a good reminder for us today.

Verse 1: *"There shall be showers of blessing:" This is the promise of love; there shall be seasons refreshing, sent from the Savior above.*

Verse 2: *"There shall be showers of blessing" – precious reviving again; over the hills and the valleys, sound of abundance of rain.*

Verse 3: *"There shall be showers of blessing:" Send them upon us, O Lord; grant to us now a refreshing, come, and now honor Thy Word.*

Verse 4: *"There shall be showers of blessing:" Oh, that today they might fall, now as to God we're confessing, now as on Jesus we call!*

Chorus: *Showers of blessing, showers of blessing we need: mercy-drops round us are falling, but for the showers we plead.*

Immanuel / Emmanuel – February 25

"Therefore the Lord himself shall give you a sign; Behold, a virgin shall conceive, and bear a son, and shall call his name Immanuel" (Isaiah 7:14). *"Behold, a virgin shall be with child, and shall bring forth a son, and they shall call his name Emmanuel, which being interpreted is, God with us"* (Matthew 1:23). *"God with us"* … just think about those three words! Who would have ever thought I would ever be able to speak to the One Who spoke and the stars took their places in the universe? Who would have ever thought a person like me with sins, and failures would ever have the opportunity to have an audience with the King of all kings and Lord of all lords? Who would have thought someone like me, whose name is not famous, even in my own town, would be known by God, and He would offer His only-begotten Son to die in my place? *"Emmanuel"* … God is with me! An imperfect, unimportant person … God is with me!

I'm sorry, but I must pause for a moment and consider the over-whelming truth that is contained in this simple title for Jesus! *"Emmanuel"* has always had an almost poetic quality to me. Even in Sign Language it is a beautiful name! You see, it represents the greatest humility any man could ever imagine! God literally became a man! That man lived, as God is, perfect here on earth. He faced the same challenges you and I face, but He did not sin. He vividly displayed the grace and truth of God perfectly housed in a human being. He then allowed sinful, imperfect, impure, and unrighteous men to beat Him … spit upon Him … and crucify Him! He then showed us how God deals with death … He conquered it with life! Why?

We see in Jesus' life and death the love of God. Because we have *"God with us,"* we have the opportunity to have a right and relationship with God! If God had not come among us to dwell with us, and die and rise from the dead for us we would never have the opportunity to ever be *"man with God."* He had to reach to us through His Son, because we could never reach to Him without His help. We have no hope apart from what God did for us in sending His only Son to rescue us.

Man has tried for his history to build another bridge that would reach God. Some built with riches … and failed. Some built with power … and failed. Many are building with religion even today … they will fail too. There is only one Bridge that will reach God, and that is *"Emmanuel!"* Thank God the prediction of the prophet Isaiah came true in a stable in Bethlehem! We have exactly what we need!

What a Friend We Have in Jesus – February 26

September 11, 2001 something happened in America that we will not soon forget. Many turned to God that day ... "*So foolish was I, and ignorant: I was as a beast before Thee. Nevertheless I am continually with Thee: Thou hast holden me by my right hand. Thou shalt guide me with Thy counsel, and afterward receive me to glory. Whom have I in heaven but Thee? And there is none upon earth that I desire beside Thee*" (Psalm 73:22-25). There is a little chorus we sing that immediately comes to my mind when I think about these verses. The chorus simply states, "He's all I need ... Jesus is all I need." When we heard the news of the attacks on September 11, 2001 we were all stunned, followed by some genuine fear of what was happening in the world around us. What a comfort to know we have a Friend that comes along side and holds our right hand during these times.

I have some very dear friends I know would drop everything to pray for me right now. If need be, I have friends who would drop whatever it was they were doing to come and stand with me if I needed it. I am blessed with these friends but I will tell you, they all have their limitations. I am so thankful for a limitless God! This Friend (God Himself) knows all my flaws and weaknesses and still loves me. My other friends only know a limited amount of my flaws and they love me. If they knew me like God knows me they might have second thoughts.

God, totally pure and righteous, has chosen to love me and stand with me regardless of the situations I will face. Joseph Scriven wrote one of my favorite hymns about this friendship.

Verse 1: *What a Friend we have in Jesus, all our sins and griefs to bear! What a privilege to carry ev'rything to God in prayer! O what peace we often forfeit, O what needless pain we bear, all because we do not carry ev'rything to God in prayer!*

Verse 2: *Have we trials and temptations? Is there trouble anywhere? We should never be discouraged, take it to the Lord in prayer. Can we find a friend so faithful who will all our sorrows share? Jesus knows our ev'ry weakness, take it to the Lord in prayer*

Verse 3: *Are we weak and heavy-laden, cumbered with a load of care? Precious Savior, still our refuge, take it to the Lord in prayer. Do thy friends despise forsake thee? Take it to the Lord in prayer; in His arms He'll take and shield thee, thou wilt find a solace there.*

Jehovah – February 27

"That men may know that thou, whose name alone is JEHOVAH, art the most high over all the earth" (Psalm 83:18). The title of *"JEHOVAH"* is a very powerful title for God. This word was used to speak about the uniqueness of God. It is unique because of the self-existence of God, and in reference to the fact He is eternal. This name is used throughout the Bible to speak about God with an awe that all men should have for Him. It is a title that demands an understanding of His uniqueness as God. There is no human point of reference to compare to Him.

Think about how different *"JEHOVAH"* God is to anything, or anyone else you know. For example; think of the love of God. Do you know anyone else who has loved those who mocked Him and cursed Him that they sent their very own Son to die for them? Do you know anyone who would encourage you to love your enemies? Do you know anyone who would teach you to do good to those who treat you in spiteful ways? Of course not! Only *"JEHOVAH"* God can aspire to these heights.

Think about the mercy of God. Yesterday you and I abused the offer of God's mercy. We did that by sinning again–doing the same things we had confessed before, just before returning to Him and begging for His mercy. We also do it when we sin, and we do not return to Him and ask for His mercy. Through all of this, we all know His mercies are new every morning! There they are waiting for us for this day.

Think about His long-suffering. The section of Scripture has always amused me where Peter asks Jesus how many times he ought to forgive someone. He thought seven times was overly generous; but Jesus answered Him, seven times seventy! I am sure when Peter denied the Lord three times in a matter of a few hours outside the trial of Jesus, he was grateful for the forgiving power of our God. God proved His long-suffering patience when Jesus re-commissioned Peter to "feed His sheep/lambs."

Think about the justice of God. We often see injustice in our world today. There are things we see constantly that make us question whether common sense still exists in our world. We don't need to worry about this. Our *"JEHOVAH"* God is always fair and just.

"JEHOVAH" … can we even whisper that name without respecting the incredible character of our God! Today is a good day to bow your knee in humility to Him. He is worthy of all praise and adoration we can give Him!

Jesus – February 28

"*And she shall bring forth a son, and thou shalt call His name JESUS: for He shall save His people from their sins*" (Matthew 1:21). Has there ever been so sweet a verse in all the Bible, or in all the books of the world combined? "*... Thou shalt call His name JESUS: for He shall save His people from their sins!*" What a promise! What a man "*Jesus*" is to me! I hope He is precious to you too. There is a song I loved growing up, and I still love it to this day. This song says what I feel in my heart every time I hear the name, "*Jesus*." "There have been names that I have loved to hear, but never has there been a name so dear to this heart of mine, as the name divine, the precious, precious name of Jesus. There is no name in earth or heav'n above, that we should give such honor and such love, as the blessed name, let us all proclaim, that wondrous, glorious name of Jesus. And some day I shall see Him face to face to thank and praise Him for His wondrous grace, which He gave to me, when He made me free, the blessed Son of God called Jesus. Jesus is the sweetest name I know, and He's just the same as His lovely name, and that's the reason why I love Him so; Oh, Jesus is the sweetest name I know."

His name is beautiful because He is the one and only Person Who came to die in our place. He is the one and only Person Who loved His enemies enough to give His life for us! He paid the deepest price anyone could ever pay for love! He gave His life to be the Savior of the world! He came to this earth with one purpose in His mind. That purpose was to offer Himself as a perfect sacrifice for our sins. He did just that, but He did not stop there. He also rose from the grave.

I remember the first time I realized I was a sinner. It was a horrifying thought to me. Oh, believe me, I knew other people were sinners, but it had never crossed my mind that I was a sinner before a warm summer day. It was not long after that when I heard a preacher describe the rightful eternity sinners could expect. I was filled with horror at my deserved place for eternity. The preacher followed that explanation up with the most incredible love story I have ever heard in my entire life. He told me "*Jesus*" had taken all the debt I owed for my sin, and paid it off on the cross at Calvary!

I still have a hard time fully comprehending that news! I may not understand it all, but I know one thing ... "*Jesus*" is the sweetest name I know! I love Him, and want to tell the world about Him. Will you join me?

Total Submission – February 29

Every day through almost every media outlet we are bombarded with advertisements about a political candidate who is making great promises to us about what they will do when they are in power. Most of the people I know do not trust the promises being made by many of these people because they have made promises before and not been true to their word. There are other times promises have been made, but they were not within the power or authority of the person to make them happen. Today I was reading about a King that will take authority, which will fulfill every promise He makes. The reason He will do exactly what He says is, He does have the power and authority to do all He has promised.

"And the LORD shall be King over all the earth: in that day shall there be one LORD, and His name one" (Zechariah 14:9). What a great day that will be for the entire world! That day is coming, but is not here yet. These words are prophecy of a time when Jesus will set up His millennial kingdom here on this earth. Here is the thought that touched my heart today. For those who have trusted Jesus Christ to forgive our sins and clean our account before our righteous and holy God, we already have Jesus as our King.

Our relationship to our King is affected by how much or how little we submit to Him. It is affected by how much or how little we yield to His perfect plan for our lives. When we live in obedience to Him and His commands in the Bible, He promises to bless us. When we live in rebellion against His commands and teachings in the Bible, He will chasten us to draw us back to Him. One day Jesus will rule and reign on this earth … that is going to be a great day. Today, Jesus desires to rule and reign in your heart. When we submit to Him, it is a great day. There is nothing as sweet as walking in the center of the will of God. The challenge comes when our flesh recognizes it must yield to the perfect will of God for that to happen. This submission of will is something we control. As powerful as God is, He has given us a free will to make our own choices, good or bad. Today you and I will choose either to walk with God, or against His plan for our lives. The best choice is obviously to yield to all the King of all kings would want us to do. There is happiness there and disappointment when we choose another way. Choose God's way today.

"I am willing to go anywhere, at any time, to do anything for Jesus." –
Luther Wishard

MONTH OF
March

I Know That Name! – March 1

We often are very pleased to tell people when we know someone who is thought to be famous. I have had people tell me, *"Oh, I have met _____,"* as though that was going to impress me. The Old Testament prophet Malachi said, *"'for from the rising of the sun even unto the going down of the same My name shall be great among the Gentiles; and in every place incense shall be offered unto My name, and a pure offering: for My name shall be great among the heathen,' saith the LORD of hosts"* (Malachi 1:11). The reality is every tongue is going to confess Jesus is Lord to the glory of God the Father. God's name brings very strong reactions wherever it is spoken even today. When some hear the name of God they fall on their faces in adoration. Others use His name as a curse word. Still others say His name as a common expression of their surprise, or just to say it without any thought of the magnificence of God.

There are many people alive today who are trying with all their influence to tell us there is no God. It does not matter how loudly they make their claim, there are people from the rising of the sun in the east to the going down of the sun in the west who know the name of God. Even the atheist uses God's name (although in vain), and in using His name, recognize His existence. I believe one of the driving forces in the life of every Christian ought to be to make His name known among the people we will meet every day. To many, God is simply a figment of some religious person's imagination. To the believer, it is the name of our Heavenly Father, our Abba (our Daddy).

One thing is for sure … if a person is ever going to meet God as their Heavenly Father, they must go through His only-begotten Son. There is simply no other way to know God. We need to realize that reality of the singular way into Heaven. No, we are not trying to make the way to Heaven so narrow that very few enter, but we must be in line with the Word of God. The Bible says clearly in Matthew 13 there is a "broad" way which leads to Hell and destruction, but there is a "straight" and "narrow" way which leads to life everlasting with God. Don't be shy today to tell someone you know God personally. God made every person born on this earth to want to know Him. Don't be bashful about knowing God personally. Go tell someone about what He means to you today!

"No other generation but ours can evangelize the present generation." –
John R. Mott

Total Commitment = Success – March 2

There are many things people are trying to get that they think will show they have been successful. Some people think if you earn a great deal of money, the pleasure you can get from it would mean success. Others think the more people that know who you are bring success. Some think the number of degrees you have earned in college or university means you are successful. Others think the amount of people you can call a friend equals success. As I grow older, success has changed in my mind many times. Today I read a verse which reminded me of what I think God sees as success in our lives.

We are introduced to a man in I Chronicles 13, named Obededom. In this chapter, the story is told of the children of Israel bringing the Ark of the Covenant back to Israel. Instead of carrying the Ark the way God had given instruction to carry it, a new cart was used drawn by two oxen. Uzza (one of the men driving the cart) reached out to steady the Ark when it shifted on the cart, and he was instantly killed. David then refused to bring the Ark of the Covenant back to Jerusalem, but instead placed it in the home of Obededom.

Obededom and his family experienced great blessing because of the Ark being in their home (I Chronicles 13:14). When David decided to bring it back to Jerusalem, Obededom decided to up-root his family and follow the Ark to Jerusalem (I Chronicles 16:5). He left all he had known to remain close to the presence of God. Some probably criticized his decision; some probably thought he had become some kind of radical person; some may have told him he was not needed in Jerusalem. None of that mattered to Obededom ... he wanted his family to be near the Ark of the Covenant. Because of his decision to move his family to stay with the Ark, look at what God did for him: "*All these of the sons of Obededom: they and their sons and their brethren, able men for strength for the service, were threescore and two of Obededom*" (I Chronicles 26:8). Did you catch that? Obededom's family continued to be men of strength to serve the Lord. You will also notice sixty-two of his family members were named as faithful workers. I want to have this kind of success in my life and the life of my family. It will only happen as I remain close to the presence of God. Decide today to stay in His Word and allow the Holy Spirit to change you.

"*One good father is worth more than a hundred schoolmasters.*" –
George Herbert

Produce Fruit – March 3

I can remember visiting my mother's grandfather when I was a very young boy. The thing that has remained in my memory from those visits (besides the fact my great-grandmother had about fifty cats) were the peach trees in his back yard. I can remember how excited I was to go there when the fruit had ripened and we could pick a peach right off the tree and eat it. There is something about getting to eat fruit that is that fresh. As I think about that, I wonder … *"What kind of fruit will my life produce today?"*

"Those that be planted in the house of the LORD shall flourish in the courts of our God. They shall still bring forth fruit in old age; they shall be fat and flourishing" (Psalm 92:13-14). According to this verse, there ought to be fruit being produced in our lives all throughout our years. From the time we are planted, until the time we become old and fat (sorry about the "fat" part … I didn't write it). There are some very important things mentioned here that speak to the production of fruit in our lives. First, we ought to be planted in the house of the Lord. I'm not saying this is the local church, but it certainly refers to being planted in a place where the Lord is exalted and displayed. I want to be in a place like that on a regular basis. Today we are blessed to have churches that preach and teach the Word of God. Find one and commit yourself to it.

The second thing it says here is, our fruit should be visible in the courts, or outside the house of the Lord. I want my light to so shine that men may see my good works and glorify my Father which is in Heaven (Matthew 5:16). I want to have testimony such that the fruit of my life is evident to those looking. When we went to my great-grandfather's house and it was not the season of harvest for the peaches, I remember thinking about the time the fruit would be ready and dreaming about it. I want to walk with God so closely today that God will touch my heart with things that will produce fruit for Him, even into my "old" age.

When the psalmist talked about bringing forth fruit in our old age, I believe he was saying we ought to be fruit-producers all the way through our lives. In other words, if I am breathing, I should be doing something that will count for God. Don't live your life today in a selfish way that only provides benefits for you. Live full out for God.

"I am the Vine, ye are the branches: He that abideth in Me, and I in him, the same bringeth forth much fruit: for without Me ye can do nothing." – Jesus

Don't Be Too Smart for Your Own Good – March 4

I was remembering a funny thing I saw on a television show years ago. One man was talking about going to his homeland that was very far from the United States. A friend asked, *"Do you know how far that is from here?"* To which a third man answered, *"Four-thousand, seven hundred, fifty-three miles."* Both of the first two men looked at the third man with a sense of awe, and asked how he knew that. The third man simply replied, *"You mean I'm right???"* Sometimes we get information, just to impress others, when the reality is, that information is basically useless and results in no actual benefit for our walk with Christ. As a believer, you have a responsibility to be constantly growing and becoming more and more like Jesus. If you are not careful, much learning can make you useless.

The writer of Proverbs says it so simply, yet powerfully. *"Wisdom is the principle thing; therefore get wisdom: and with all thy getting get understanding"* (Proverbs 4:7). I love that last little phrase ... *"Oh yes, and while you are gaining all that wisdom, don't forget to pick up some understanding along the way."* I have found some of the smartest people I have met in my life had the least amount of actual "book-learning." I am not in the least putting down a good education. I believe we should get all the information possible in our lives today. One of the big problems I see in our society is after a certain age, we feel we can now coast, and we do not need to continue to learn. Nothing could be farther from the truth, and I am not advocating ignorance today.

Having said that, I believe we do need a great deal more of "understanding" today. We have some incredibly "wise" people, but we are really lacking in good old fashioned understanding. Please continue to pursue knowledge and facts and details, but don't forget in all that pursuing to remember to learn as well how to apply what you are learning to real-life situations. When a person is sitting in a hospital room having just received a bad report from a doctor, they will not need to know how many gallons of water pass over Niagara Falls in an hour (sorry, just picked out a random thing). They also will not necessarily need every verse you have memorized quoted "at" them at that point. They will need someone with compassion and a working knowledge of Scripture to speak to their heart. With all your getting, get understanding today.

"Have an understanding so you don't have a misunderstanding."
– C. Blair

Give God What He Asks For – March 5

"'*Bring ye all the tithes unto the storehouse, that there may be meat in mine house, and prove me now herewith,' saith the LORD of hosts, 'if I will not open you the windows of heaven, and pour you out a blessing, that there shall not be room enough to receive it. And I will rebuke the devourer for your sakes, and he shall not destroy the fruits of your ground; neither shall your vine cast her fruit before the time in the field,' saith the LORD of hosts*" (Malachi 3:10-11).

Isn't it amazing how quickly we ask God for the things we want, but how hesitant we are to give Him what He asks of us? We run to God when we have a problem and almost demand deliverance from whatever it is we are facing. However, God makes some very simple requests of us and we have a list of arguments, or rationale that explains why we cannot do what He wants us to do. In these two verses there is an amazing promise. That promise is God will take care of us, even in the face of our enemies. The promise is our enemies will not be able to triumph over us as long as we remain faithful to our God. These are incredible promises.

The promises of verse eleven are dependent upon our obedience in verse ten. God makes a simple request ... bring 10% of what I bless you with, and give it back to Me. I don't believe this is some kind of "forced" giving, but it is to be totally voluntary, and from a thankful and loving heart. Notice the third word in verse ten ... "*ALL*." God is looking for us to bring something from ALL He has blessed us with. Think about what that means in your life personally. What things can you identify in your life that you know are absolute blessings only God could have given you? He wants you to willingly return 10% of that to Him, or to His control.

We often read this verse and think about our (precious) money. Your money is only one small speck of what God is talking about here. Your health; your family; your job; your house; your car; your abilities and talents; your time; your reading; your entertainment; your thought life; your ... I think you get the idea. Sometimes I think we get the idea God is our "genie" and we just run up a quick prayer if we want something. The reality is we need to be faithful to give God what He deserves every day. Use what God has given you to be a blessing to Him and others today. There is a great blessing in giving back to God, because He gives more.

"*There is more to life than making a living.*" – Dr. Bill Rice Sr.

Do "IT" (whatever "IT" is) – March 6

An interesting thought hit me a few years ago while we were involved in a Missions Conference. One of the other missionaries at the conference had the ministry of translating the Bible into the language of a group of tribal people. While the missionary was showing pictures of the people they were translating the Bible for, my mind wandered to this question ... *"I wonder how many Deaf there are in that tribe?"* This is my burden. I'm sure most of you reading this would not have even given a moment for that thought. That is not to criticize you, but to emphasize a point ... God made each of us different for a reason. He has given each of us a unique set of burdens, talents, interests, abilities and passions. The key to these things are two simple words I saw today in the Old Testament.

*"And David said to Solomon his son, 'Be strong and of good courage, and **DO IT**: fear not, nor be dismayed: for the LORD God, even my God, will be with thee; He will not fail thee, nor forsake thee, until thou hast finished all the work for the service of the house of the LORD'"* (I Chronicles 28:20). David was encouraging his son, Solomon, to carry on the work of building the temple for the glory of God. Within this encouragement there is some great instruction. David told Solomon to be strong – we all need to stand strong for what we believe in. He told him to be of good courage – there will be times of weakness in the battle we all face ... don't give in to cowardice when these times come. He told him not to be afraid ... because the LORD is with the child of God.

The thing I want to emphasize in all this is contained in two short words ... DO IT. What is it God has specifically touched your heart about doing for Him? I'm not talking about a profession; I'm talking about a lifestyle. I'm not talking about something you think about once-in-awhile, but something you are absolutely passionate about. I'm talking about that "one thing" God places in the heart of each of us to do. That "one thing" will be different for you than it is for any other person. Please be sure to note if God gave you that passion, He might not have given it to anyone else but you, and He is depending on you to act on it fully! When you realize what the "one thing" is, then DO IT with all your might for as long as you can do it, the best you can do it. God will stretch you to go beyond what you can do to what He can do through you.

"I have found that there are 3 stages in every great work of God; first, it is impossible, then it is difficult, then it is done." – J. Hudson Taylor

Last Adam – March 7

"And so it is written, The first man Adam was made a living soul; the **Last Adam** *was made a quickening spirit"* (I Corinthians 15:45). Think of the wonder of the world when Adam was first created! There was no sin in the world (that is enough right there). There was a canopy covering the earth so the temperature was perfect all the time. There was harmony between all the animals and man. God then created a perfect woman for Adam's wife, named Eve. They had all they could ever want! They had food, a wonderful place to live, and a relationship with God that was constant and intimate.

Think of the world Jesus was born into. There had been a period of silence for 400 years because mankind had basically ignored the warnings and teachings of the prophets of God. Rome, a pagan society, had invaded the homeland of Jesus' people, and was oppressing the Jews. Sin had been the rule of mankind (including the Jews) so much that God had already "cleaned things up" by sending a universal flood … only Noah and his family were saved. Things did not improve after Noah, but had reverted to the same idol-worship and heathen practices like sacrificing children to the gods.

And then everything changed, because the *"Last Adam"* came on the scene! Hope came where despair had reigned. Adam's Redeemer finally came into the world to bruise the head of the serpent, the Devil! Adam and his sin brought death for all men, including Jesus Christ. Jesus Christ, the *"Last Adam"* was made a *"quickening spirit."* Jesus brought life into a world filled with death. Jesus brought hope to a hopeless world and still offers hope today. Jesus, the *"Last Adam"* did what no man before Him could do, including Adam. He lived in a human body … without sinning! Our Redeemer showed up, right on time!

I want you to consider one very important word in this title for Jesus. He is called the *"**Last** Adam."* Let me end today by saying we do not need another *"Adam."* Jesus is all we need! Some have come claiming to be a brother of Jesus or another son of God in the past. I want you to be sure Jesus was and is the *"Last Adam."* There is no need to look for another redeemer. We have THE Redeemer we need in Jesus alone! He certainly is the *"**Last** Adam."* Today is a good day to thank God for sending Jesus; "the way, the truth and the life" to take our place there on the cross! He is certainly all we needed to satisfy the righteous demand of God. He is all the first Adam needed too. He waited a long time for the *"Last Adam"* to come.

Life – March 8

*"In the beginning was the Word, and the Word was with God, and the Word was God. The same was in the beginning with God. All things were made by Him; and without Him was not anything made that was made. In Him was **Life**; and the **Life** was the light of men"* (John 1:1-4).

*"Jesus saith unto him, 'I am the way, the truth, and the **Life**: no man cometh unto the Father, but by Me'"* (John 14:6).

Make no mistake about it; we could never have life ... either physical or eternal ... without the *"Life,"* Jesus Christ! It has always amazed me how often I have thought of myself as the center of the universe. Oh, please don't criticize me ... I believe we all do it more than we would like to admit. I often am amazed at why people do not always agree with me on my opinions. After all, my opinions are always right (SMILE).

The reality is Jesus Christ is the actual "center" of everything we know. Is it any wonder God places such a demanding standard on how to get to Heaven? It should be that way, regardless of what man thinks. So many times I have heard that I have a very narrow view of how to get to Heaven. I have been criticized, and the philosophy of ... *"As long as we all believe we will eventually get to Heaven."* I'm sorry, but God says Jesus Christ is the *"Life."* Without Him, there would be no life to have at all! Later John wrote, *"He that hath the Son hath life; and he that hath not the Son of God hath not life"* (I John 5:12).

I love the simplicity of the power of the Word of God! Even a child can understand that verse! Why is it so difficult for us adults to grasp that truth? The question goes back to us viewing our opinions with more weight than we trust the Word of God. The reality is, in Jesus is eternal life; without Jesus Christ there is no eternal life. Simply stated, Jesus is *"Life."* It is completely because of Him we have life at all!

It is important we understand, without the death of Jesus Christ, we could not know eternal life! Without the resurrection of Jesus Christ (the ultimate display of *"Life"*), we could never have conquered death! Jesus Christ is the pivotal point of our faith for everlasting life! As the verse so clearly states, if we have Jesus Christ then we have life. If we have refused Jesus Christ, and have not accepted Him, we are bound in the death we have earned because of our sin. Jesus faced death ... accepted the reality of it ... was buried and considered gone. Praise God this title for Him is real! He could not remain in the grave, because He is not *"Death,"* He is *"Life!"*

Little is Enough – March 9

Simple things can become great when they are placed in the absolute control of God. All throughout our Bible there are stories where the most unlikely person or thing became the center-piece for the teaching of Jesus. Jesus used little things like salt and light and bread and children as allegories to show what He was teaching. He used a lost sheep, a lost coin and a lost son to show how important each sinner is to His Heavenly Father. Today I was reading and came upon a very familiar story where Jesus used the things that were in front of Him to teach an incredibly important lesson.

As was usual, a large crowd had gathered to hear Jesus' teachings and to see some of their friends/family healed from sicknesses. As it got close to dinner time, Jesus asked the disciples to feed the people. The only food available was a small boy's lunch (five loaves and two small fishes). Jesus instructed all (5,000 men plus their families) to be seated. He then prayed for the food and they passed out enough food to feed all. When all had eaten enough to be filled up, Jesus instructed His disciples to gather what was left over. "*And they did all eat, and were filled; and they took up of the fragments that remained twelve baskets full*" (Matthew 14:20).

There are a number of applications we need to grasp today. The first is, when we simply place what we have in the control and hands of Jesus, He can make it become far more than we can if we hold onto it ourselves. Your worries, debt, health issues, abilities, finances, tests and challenges should be placed within His control. He can do more with these things than you can if you worked all day to produce something. Second; not only does Jesus make something good come out of what we give Him, but He makes it good in abundance! Remember, there were twelve baskets "*full*" left over. I'd say five loaves and two small fishes did a miraculous job of feeding the 5,000 men and their families. I'd say God was trying to tell us something by allowing there to be twelve baskets "*full*" left over.

What is it you are struggling to overcome today? What kind of things have you done to try to solve your problem? How many other people have you told about your problem, hoping they would have an answer? How about taking what you have (your five loaves and two small fishes), and placing it in the hand of the Creator of the universe. Even what's left over will be a blessing! He is able to do far more than you can imagine …

"*When God wants an oak tree, He does not transplant it …He just drops an acorn.*" – Oliver B. Greene

Making Memories – March 10

One of my favorite things to hear is our children sitting around our kitchen table and reminiscing about the things they did when they were younger. To hear each person's unique perspective of what has happened is really interesting. My wife and I have also learned about a number of things we had no idea happened when we were not around. I guess they assume because they are married the statute of limitations has expired on us disciplining them. Seriously, it is so great to hear all the things which have shaped and molded our children's lives to make them what they are today. There are sweet memories and there are some not-so-sweet memories as well.

The writer of Proverbs said, *"The memory of the just is blessed: but the name of the wicked shall rot"* (Proverbs 10:7). Memories can either be a blessing, or something that haunts us. There are certainly bad memories each of us has about our past. There are also a multitude of good memories for the person who is a child of God. We are living in a time when people are encouraged to pull up every bad memory they have ever had and blame others for negative things that have happened. They become slaves to dwelling on those things for the rest of their lives. Somehow we have been led to believe blaming someone else for all the negative things in our lives frees us from any responsibility for our actions today.

This verse is a blessing to me because when I look back over my shoulder to the things that have happened in my past, I see many wonderful memories. My dad and mom built a home out of love, respect and joy. They did that by building our home on Bible principles that created a safe environment for me to be raised. When discipline was needed, I received it (for which I am extremely grateful). When we needed to decide what we would believe, and what the standards would be for our home, we opened our Bible and tried to obey what we read. We were in no way a perfect family. We made many mistakes as a group and individuals, but we continued to use the Bible as the compass for our lives. Because of making the Bible our foundation, we were spared a great deal of "bad" memories.

I want to close today with this thought … regardless of where you or I have come from; today is a wonderful day to begin making good memories for ourselves and our families. Trust God today and follow His direction for good memories for tomorrow.

"When we have done our best, we should wait the result in peace." –
J. Lubbock

Don't Believe the Hype – March 11

"When pride cometh, then cometh shame: but with the lowly is wisdom" (Proverbs 11:2). There is always going to be someone ready to give you praise somewhere. We all love to hear praise. We all will hang around with people who give us praise and tell us how good we are, and how much we are appreciated. There is nothing wrong with this ... until we begin to believe all that is being said. There is nothing wrong with hearing praise, as long as we do not begin to trust the words of men/women who don't see what is in our heart.

The reality for each of us reading this today is, there is not one of us who is righteous. There is not one reading this who is as good as others say we are. The reality is each of us reading this today deserves an eternity that is spent separated from a holy and a righteous God. Each of us is at best a sinner that has been saved by the grace of God. Before you and I drift into believing all that is said about us in a positive light, let's remember who we are and where we came from. Before we start to list all of our wonderful qualities to God and others, let's remember we had our feet stuck in the miry clay, without hope until Jesus came to rescue us.

Each of us ought to take a few moments today to thank God for seeing value in our sorry souls. We should pause to reflect on how many times we have asked for blessings from our Heavenly Father and then walked away from Him. We should reflect on how many times we have used up all His blessings and find ourselves in one of the worlds "pig-pens," just wishing we could go back to the way it "used" to be.

The good news is we can go back! The good news is *"When pride cometh, then cometh shame: but with the lowly is wisdom."* God even uses the mistakes and failures we are going to make to mold us into the person He wants us to be. There are two keys to this as I see it today. First, we must humble ourselves on a daily basis if we expect God to be able to do anything with us. Second, we must get back up after we have failed and try to live for God again. We have a God Who can use people just like us if we will humble ourselves before Him. Don't believe all the good things said about you today. Don't believe all the bad things the Devil wants to whisper in your ear today either. There is a God in Heaven Who can handle your failures and your successes. Trust Him today and walk humbly with Him. He will use you, if you stay close to His heart.

"A failure is not someone who fails, but someone who quits." – Ted Camp

Bow the Knee– March 12

"*Whoso loveth instruction loveth knowledge: but he that hateth reproof is brutish. A good man obtaineth favor of the LORD: but a man of wicked devices will He condemn*" (Proverbs 12:1-2). No one likes to be corrected, but a wise person will deeply appreciate it when someone tries to help them improve. We are living in a time in the history of man when it seems no one wants to admit doing anything wrong. We have seen leaders excuse improper behavior away by trying to define the word, "is." We have seen athletes justify unlawful behavior by blaming others. We have seen religious leaders fall, trying to explain away their wrong actions by just saying, "*I'm sorry.*"

When coaching young men in the past, I have explained to them many times there is a correct response to instruction, and an incorrect response. The incorrect response involves any kind of excuse. The proper response is to listen and make changes. I have said it this way to my former players; "*Losers make excuses; winners make adjustments.*" According to these verses, there is a right way and a wrong way to respond to correction. We need to realize correction helps us get back on track after we have made mistakes. All of us have made mistakes. All of us will make mistakes. Our response to these times will determine whether we will grow and mature, or continue to wallow in our sin and back-slide.

The person who refuses instruction is called "*brutish*." The word literally means, *stupid*. I have been called *stupid* before, and I have acted that part before. I do not want God to look at me and call me "*stupid*." I want God to be able see when He corrects me, I respond correctly and make changes and bow my knee to Him. I want to respond well when God offers me instruction. I do not want to try to explain my actions, but I want to repent of them and accept God's plan for me.

The second verse say a man of "*wicked devices*" will be condemned. The word, "*devices*," literally means, machination. According to Webster's Dictionary, the word means ... *a scheming or crafty action or artful design intended to accomplish some usually evil end*. I do not want my life to be characterized by sneaking around, trying to fool people into believing I am spiritual. Today I want to receive correction with a godly attitude; changing areas of my life that need to be changed; accepting God's way over mine.

"*Wisdom is seeing through the eyes of God.*" – Unknown

Lord – March 13

"So after He had washed their feet, and had taken His garments, and was set down again, He said unto them, 'Know ye what I have done to you? Ye call Me Master and Lord: and ye say well: for so I am. If I then, your Lord and Master, have washed your feet; ye also ought to wash one another's feet. For I have given you an example, that ye should do as I have done to you" (John 13:12-15).

This title, *"Lord,"* is one that really touches my heart. It means the person to whom another person or thing belongs – a person who has the authority to make decisions for another. Jesus Christ is the ultimate *"Lord."* Of course, later we will talk about Jesus as the *"Lord of lords."* For now I think it is important to recognize Him as *"Lord"* as He presents it in John 13. We all have read this story about Jesus washing the feet of His disciples. Most of us have heard about this in a sermon or Sunday School lesson. The power of the lesson Jesus taught is, even the Master bowed in humility to serve others.

Jesus Christ has the authority to make decisions for us, and yet, He allows us to make our own decisions for our lives. What an incredible God we serve! He, Who has the power and authority to force us to do what He wants, gives us the privilege of making our own choices. In this passage, He shows what a loving *"Lord"* does for His people. As *"Lord,"* the rightful owner of our lives, Jesus gave an incredible picture of humility. He made the statement to the disciples present then, but carries through to us today. Just as Jesus demonstrated this humility as *"Lord,"* He is teaching us regardless of our position, or our rightful place in our family, church, work, or school, there ought to be a humility involved in our lives so we can affect others.

Let's consider one additional truth from this title. Jesus is our *"Lord,"* our Master, and He does deserve our service back to Him. We ought not to hold on to anything He has given us as our own. We need to realize all we have been given is really His to use through us. Today consider your relationship with Jesus, the *"Lord."* Are you fully surrendered to His will for your life today? Is there a genuine humility in your service for Him? Jesus is the *"Lord"* and He deserves our honest service to Him in any way He leads us. I think it is important for us to treat Jesus as *"Lord,"* and not to act as though we are the lord of our own lives. Surrender your heart to Him today and serve someone else in humility as your *"Lord "*and Master served you.

The Influence of One Person – March 14

"And the God that hath caused His name to dwell there destroy all kings and people, that shall put to their hand to alter and to destroy this house of God which is at Jerusalem. I Darius have made a decree; let it be done with speed" (Ezra 6:12).

In the middle of the captivity of Israel, Ezra was motivated to return to Jerusalem to rebuild the temple. He had the permission of leadership, and even the funding for the project. Opposition came as they started the work, as so often is the case when we are attempting to do something for God. It is important for you to understand today if you are going to serve God, there will be people lined up to oppose what you are doing. Don't be surprised by this, or allow this opposition to stop you. Keep serving God faithfully, this opposition is just a normal part of the process of standing for God. Ezra was determined to continue the work, but the opposition slowed them down. An appeal was made to King Darius. Ezra 6:12 is his quote at the end of a speech he made in support of the rebuilding of the temple.

When I read these verses this morning, I thought about the other significant time we see King Darius in the Bible. In one of the most familiar stories in our Old Testament, Daniel was thrown into a den of lions to be destroyed for praying to God rather than praying to the king. Darius was the king at that time and had been tricked into signing the law that Daniel violated. He had to follow his own command, and he had Daniel thrown into the lion's den. After throwing Daniel in the den, King Darius asked this question: *"...Daniel, O Daniel, servant of the living God, is thy God whom thou servest continually, able to deliver thee"* (Daniel 6:20)? Darius did not have faith, but God was still God and spared the life of Daniel.

When Darius returned the next morning, after a sleepless night, he found Daniel alive and well. He then made this statement: *"... In every dominion of my kingdom men tremble and fear before the God of Daniel: for He is the living God, and steadfast forever, and His kingdom that which shall not be destroyed, and His dominion shall be even unto the end"* (Daniel 6:26). The thought that hit my heart today was how God used the faithfulness of Daniel to help Ezra and the other Israelites in rebuilding the temple. What difference will your faithfulness or unfaithfulness today make on future generations? Your life is valuable. Your testimony will affect the future for someone. Use this day wisely to stand for God like Daniel did.

"Go as far as you can on the right road." – Bob Jones Sr.

Not Worthy – March 15

There have been a few times in my life when I have been in the presence of people I have highly respected. I can remember very clearly shortly after we started working with the Deaf in our local church. God had used Dr. Ted Camp to touch my heart with the need to reach out to the Deaf. Dr. Camp was only at our church for one Sunday night that year, and I never even introduced myself to him. He returned the following year and my pastor asked me to take Dr. Camp around to make visits with the Deaf in our area. I can still remember how nervous I was that my car was too dirty, or too small, or not worthy of someone like Dr. Camp. He and I drove all over our town visiting different Deaf. I was in awe of his ability to communicate with the Deaf, and wanted to be like him "when I grew up."

Solomon built a temple for God after his father, David, had gathered all the materials necessary. After the completion of the temple, Solomon asked this question: *"But will God in very deed dwell with men on the earth? Behold, heaven and the heaven of heavens cannot contain Thee; how much less this house which I have built"* (II Chronicles 6:18)? Solomon was asking, "How can I build a house for God, when Heaven is not worthy to house Him?" The thought that came to me was, God has chosen to take up His residence on earth within every believer! After you trust Christ for your salvation, the Holy Spirit of God begins to live within you! Who am I that the spectacular God of Heaven should live within me?

The answer to both Solomon and me is, neither the temple he built, nor my life are worthy of His presence. What an absolute privilege to walk with God every day. What a joy to know His Holy Spirit is willing and ready to help guide me into all the truths of the Word of God! What a thrill to know when I need to talk to God and I do not have the words to speak, the Holy Spirit will convey the feelings of my heart in words I cannot even imagine or speak. It is tough, but I thank God the Holy Spirit convicts me of sin as it happens in my daily walk and offers the road to restoration. We who are believers have the incredible privilege of housing the great I AM within us. Don't think this is something we deserve, but treasure the honor that it is. Live wisely for God today … He's watching you.

"Moses spent forty years thinking he was somebody, forty years learning he was nobody, and forty years discovering what God could do with a nobody." – D.L. Moody

God is Enough – March 16

There are problems you are facing today that make you wonder if you will be okay in the future. There are situations taking place all around you in the world that might cause you to lose some sleep at night. When you hear all about the wars that are happening, and about the wars that might happen, you have reason for worry ... but, do you really? We have a God Who spoke this world and its universe into existence in six, twenty-four hour days! He is able to stand up for you too, if you will allow Him. We need to be careful as Christians to realize when we worry, we are simply telling the world our God is NOT enough. When we trust Him, and demonstrate trust, we are telling the world our God IS enough.

Ezra thought about this very thing himself when re-building the temple. Look at what he said: "*For I was ashamed to require of the king a band of soldiers and horsemen to help us against the enemy in the way: because we had spoken unto the king, saying, 'The hand of our God is upon all them for good that seek Him; but His power and His wrath is against all them that forsake Him.' So we fasted and besought our God for this: and He was entreated of us*" (Ezra 8:22-23). Did you catch it? Ezra said he could have asked the king for help. The king had offered help, and even ordered any funds they needed for the repairs should be given to them. He had a "blank check" from the most powerful man in the area. As Ezra thought about asking for help, he knew there would be damage the testimony of God and the Jews who claimed to trust Him.

Ezra made a decision we need to make today as well. Ezra decided to trust God and prove His power to supply the things they would need. Are you willing to trust God today? In the face of the economy, will you trust God? In the face of the troubles our world is in, will you trust God? Regardless of what the doctor tells you during your visit, will you trust God? For the protection and care of your children, will you trust God? For wisdom for what you should do and where you should go in the future, will you trust God? Remember, there are people watching the way you are living to decide if you really believe in God, or if it is just some "thing" you put on once-in-awhile. If you will trust God like Ezra did, and put God to the test, God will take care of you, just like He did the children of Israel back then. God IS enough ... live in a way that shows others you trust Him!

"God's part is to put forth power. Our part is to put forth faith." –
Andrew A. Bonar

The Mark of a True Friend – March 17

I have done a good deal of reflecting on my friendships recently. When I think of the people who I consider my better friends there is one quality I notice in all of them. All of the people I call my friends have the wonderful ability to overlook my failures and see things in me they can love. I need friends like this. The Bible says, *"He that covereth a transgression seeketh love; but he that repeateth a matter separateth very friends"* (Proverbs 17:9). Each of us has the opportunity to point out the faults of our friends, or choose not to focus on them. Which are you to the people who call you friend?

We were visiting friends from out of state, and I was telling them about my best friend growing up. I explained we do not see each other as often now as we did when we were in school together. I then made the statement that if either of us needed anything, regardless of how long it had been since we had seen each other, we would do whatever it took to help the other one out. When you have a problem and a friend is needed, you need that friend to stand with you, not necessarily to give you advice, or correction. A true friend will certainly be aware of the faults and failures of their friend. A true friend, according to this verse will knowingly choose to be a friend rather than a critic.

Certainly there is a time to confront a friend with a sin, or harmful behavior that is observed, but even that is done from a position of wanting to help, not to judge. Let me encourage you to consider this truth as it relates to your friendships and relationships. It is always better to seek love than to point out each failure. When Jesus spoke with Peter on the shore after He had risen from the dead, He dealt with kindness toward Peter rather than criticism. Peter had denied he knew the Lord three times just before His crucifixion. Jesus could easily have pointed out these three times, as well as the point He had warned of this just hours before. Instead, Jesus chose to love Peter. He not only gave Peter a second opportunity to pledge his love to Him, He also gave Him a responsibility to become a leader in the early church. Jesus practiced exactly what this verse was teaching in the book of Proverbs. What kind of friend are you? Are your friends encouraged when you are around them, or do they dread your coming? Do you best to be an encouragement to your friends today.

"Toleration is the greatest gift of the mind; it requires the same effort of the brain that it takes to balance oneself on a bicycle." – Helen Keller

Don't Waste a Minute – March 18

I was raised with this mandate ... *"Anything worth doing, is worth doing right."* My parents drilled that into our way of life. Therefore, not regarding the worth of the job we were getting ready to do, we were determined to do it as well as it possibly could be done. I recall a time in my early teenage years when I went to Kentucky for a month to help with a children's summer camp. My job was to "clean" the outhouses on the property. Now, honestly, this was not the best job I have ever had, but it needed to be done properly. If you do not clean an outhouse properly, everyone will know it in just a matter of a day or two when the temperature is in the 90's. I set out to clean those outhouses as well as they had ever been cleaned in the past.

Words of wisdom from Proverbs 18 say, *"He also that is slothful in his work is brother to him that is a great waster"* (Proverbs 18:9). *"Slothful"* is not a word we use a great deal today, but it means a person is lazy. Every now and then, I like to have a "lazy" day where I do not drive myself as hard as I usually do. This kind of lazy day should not be a characteristic of my normal life. I want to be a person who is known as a hard worker. I want to have the reputation of finishing what I start. When I show up for a job, I want people to think ... "now the job will get done right."

This kind of work ethic does not come naturally to any of us. This is a learned behavior. According to this verse, if we are lazy in our work ethic, God says we are also wasters. I don't want to be guilty of wasting anything God gives me, including my time and energy. We are living in a time in the history of the world which demands we work while we have the opportunity to work. We never know how long we will be able to do the things we think are important. There are many people who have lost their jobs in the past few years. They realize now how valuable that job was to them. Don't wait too long to appreciate the work you get to do. Do it with all your might.

Be careful not to become spiritually lazy in these days we are living in. There is so little time left to do the things God wants you to do with your life. Don't waste a moment! Use the opportunities you will have today as though it is the last day you will be alive. Not working hard equals wasting time. God has given you this day ... use it wisely!

"Always render more and better service than is expected of you, no matter what your task may be" – Og Mandino

God Wants Your Obedience, Not Sacrifice – March 19

"And Solomon brought up the daughter of Pharaoh out of the city of David unto the house that he had built for her; for he said, 'My wife shall not dwell in the house of David king of Israel, because the places are holy, whereunto the ark of the LORD hath come'" (II Chronicles 8:11).

David had been a man who followed after the heart of God throughout his life. Yes, I know he made some major mistakes, but it is in the New Testament (after the mistakes had been made) when God called him a man after His own heart. When David died, God made a promise to Solomon of blessing and peace on the land for as long as he obeyed the Lord and would not turn to worshipping idols. Solomon followed the desires of his father, David, when he built a temple for worshipping God. The verse you read above is what happened very shortly after the building of that temple was completed. The remainder of this chapter explains how often Solomon offered sacrifices to God on a very regular basis.

Sacrificing to God is a good thing, but if you have invited Pharaoh's daughter to become your wife, you are also inviting all her false idols to come with her. Solomon knew this woman was not a godly woman by the description of where Solomon had her live. Notice he realized from the beginning this woman could not live in the household of his father, David, *"because the places are holy ..."* This thought hit my heart while reading it today: Regardless of how many sacrifices Solomon made, he was still going home to a sinful vice ... the daughter of Pharaoh. We all know the story of the life of Solomon. His wives (numbering about 1,000) eventually turned his heart from God and he ended his life as a spiritual failure.

I'm not writing this devotional for Solomon, but for those of us who are living now. What "things/relationships", we know are not healthy for our spiritual life, are we holding on to? What things are we hiding deep within our hearts we have not allowed God to completely master and control? It is important for each of us to realize God is not interested in the things we "do" outwardly, as much as he is concerned with what is in our heart today. Don't be so busy making sacrifices you forget to offer God a clean heart first. Don't be so consumed with what others see you doing, as with what God sees in your heart. Be a man/woman after God's own heart! God wants your heart more than your efforts without your heart.

"Delayed obedience is disobedience." – Curtis Hutson

LORD OUR RIGHTEOUSNESS – March 20

"*'Behold the days come,' saith the LORD, 'that I will raise unto David a righteous Branch, and a King shall reign and prosper, and shall execute judgment and justice in the earth. In His days Judah shall be saved, and Israel shall dwell safely: and this is His name whereby He shall be called, THE LORD OUR RIGHTEOUSNESS*" (Jeremiah 23:5-6).

The capital letters that spell this title were not mine, but are this way in the Bible. I am thinking doing this shows we ought to respect and honor this Person. The "*LORD OUR RIGHTEOUSNESS*" is an incredible blessing to me. The reason this title touches my heart so much is because I know who I am. I know my sinful nature very well. I know if I were to stand before our holy God in my own accomplishments, and my own righteousness I would be in big trouble.

You might be thinking you really aren't too bad … think again. The prophet Isaiah, under the inspiration of the Holy Spirit wrote: "*But we are all as an unclean thing, and all our righteousnesses are as filthy rags; and we all do fade as a leaf; and our iniquities, like the wind, have taken us away*" (Isaiah 64:6). There you have it clearly placed on the pages of your Bible. In our own strength and abilities, no matter how strong they are, are still lacking so much that God views them as "*filthy rags*."

Again, here we all were in the same boat, sinking in our sins without hope. I am reminded of that verse in the old hymn, Love Lifted Me. "*I was sinking deep in sin far from the peaceful shore, very deeply stained within, sinking to rise no more. But the Master of the sea heard my despairing cry. From the water lifted me, now safe am I!*" That Master of the sea is none other than the "*LORD OUR RIGHTEOUSNESS.*"

Have you noticed none of the titles God gave to Jesus would fit anyone on this earth except Him? Oh, there are many who promote themselves on this earth today, but the reality is there is only one "*LORD OUR RIGHTEOUSNESS.*" There are many who teach things contrary to the Word of God and want us to believe they are much smarter than we are, and we should trust their words above the Word of God. I am sorry, but they are not the "*LORD OUR RIGHTEOUSNESS.*" I choose to depend upon His promises in His Word to direct my path today! I will not depend upon my own understanding, but fully lean on the instruction He has given me in the Bible. Praise God we have a "*LORD OUR RIGHTEOUSNESS*" we can depend upon today!

Love is the Motivation – March 21

What motivates your everyday actions? I have noticed guys who fall in love with a girl will change all kinds of personal habits they might have had before. I have even known guys to start using deodorant and brushing their teeth. Some have changed the clothing they wear, or the time they wake up. I have seen some change their friends because of the love they have for that girl! It is amazing what love will do to a person. Real love influences everything in a person's life.

When Jesus was asked what the greatest commandment was, He replied; *"Thou shalt love the Lord thy God with all thy heart, and with all thy soul, and with all thy mind. This is the first and great commandment. And the second is like unto it, Thou shalt love thy neighbor as thyself. On these two commandments hang all the law and the prophets"* (Matthew 22:37-40). Do you think love is an important thing in the plan of God?

I believe the Bible teaches love is the underlying motivation to the things God wants us to do with our lives. When we think about the commandments, we often think of a list of *"do's,"* and *"don'ts."* When God thinks about the commandments, He thinks about a love that motivates us to please the One we love. We all have changed behavior, thinking, clothing, and time schedules for the love of someone else in our lives.

I remember when our first child was born. Our whole world changed at that moment and has never gone back to "normal" again! I'm glad for the change, because love has filled the changes from the beginning until today. Love for that little girl (and all our other children / grandchildren since) has made a drastic and wonderful change in our family. While others might have viewed children as a tax-write off, or a bother, we have seen them as an opportunity to love and to be loved back.

I learned an important lesson from a childhood friend about discipline. Both he and I were disciplined often as kids. One day we were discussing a time when he had been disciplined. He told me he never cried when his father (Step-father) spanked him, explaining he did not love his father. I told him I start crying way before I was spanked. I understood for the first time that day that I was crying because I had disappointed my Mom and Dad, who I loved very much. Do you love God enough to want to obey His commandments? He made you to love God fully each day! Obey today!
"Did I do my all ... when no one knew and no one saw?" – Dr. Ted Camp

Get Your Binoculars! – March 22

When I am in the woods in the fall months, I am looking for something very specific. I want to see the antlers of a nice deer. Many times after seeing the body of a deer in the distance, I have picked up my binoculars to see if I can see those treasured antlers on his head. There have been times when I have strained my eyes looking for that very specific thing on a magnificent deer. I find I have great patience and persistence while looking to see the thing I am hoping to find. I will move to different positions, I will wait, and wait, and wait some more in order to get a better look.

This morning I read a verse that reminded me of this kind of effort, but in pursuit of a different treasure. The psalmist wrote; *"The works of the LORD are great, sought out of all them that have pleasure in them"* (Psalm 111:2). There is no question the works of the Lord are great! There are so many wonderful things God has done and is doing all around us. An old hymn encouraged us to count our blessings ... name them one by one. This is a good practice for us to do. Take some time today to look at the things God has done for you in your life. Take some time to thank God for having an active role in your life. Don't spend so much time looking at the bad things that have happened to you, that you miss all the blessings. This verse simply states God has done wonderful things.

The second part of the verse encourages us to look for those things. We are told to search for those things as if they were treasure to be found. We are living in a time in history when we have almost suffered "information overload." We have so many ways to get more and more information. We can access encyclopedias and all kinds of resource materials, with just a few clicks of a computer mouse. In the same way we ought to spend a great deal of time seeking for the things God has done, not only for us, but for those mentioned in our Bible. We ought to actively pursue everything we can in order to know our God better.

The promise here is, if we will actively search for the things God has done, we will find great pleasure in them. There is nothing like reveling in the goodness of our God! He is so incredible that the review of what He has done for us should cause great joy to come to our hearts every time we think about it. When things start becoming discouraging ... think about all God has done for you and praise Him. It will do you good! Keep your spiritual binoculars ready at all times!

"It is a terrible thing to see and have no vision." – Helen Keller

He Remembers Me – March 23

I remember as a young boy going to our local fair in the town we lived. I was just a boy, but I was always amazed when we would pass people and they would remember my dad. My dad had played football, baseball, and basketball in High School. There were many people who had been in the stands when my dad was playing sports, and they still remembered how he had played many years later. They remembered my dad in days I had never known (it was obviously before my time). They remembered my dad, but I noticed many times my dad had no idea who they were.

For many of us, we have never been famous, and probably will never be famous. However, there is one Person Who will remember who you are. The psalmist wrote, *"Surely he shall not be moved forever: the righteous shall be in everlasting remembrance"* (Psalm 113:6). Everlasting remembrance ... I like the sound of that. I am amazed God remembers me. I am so thankful that no matter how many people here might forget me, I have a God in Heaven Who will keep me in *"everlasting remembrance."*

Each of us ought to thank God for the truth He will always remember us, but there is something He cannot remember ... *"And their sins and iniquities will I remember no more"* (Hebrews 10:17). Did you catch that? God will never forget you, but He has chosen not to remember your sins! It doesn't get better than that for the Christian. You may have trouble forgetting your sins, but God is committed to not keeping them in His memory. The Bible says after you trust Him, He removes your sin as far as the east is from the west! God will not remember your sin, but He certainly remembers your name.

One day, my life on earth will end, but it is a wonderful thing to know my name has been written in the handwriting of Jesus Christ in the Book of Life! When God opens the book to reveal who has been forgiven, He will see my name and yours (if you have trusted Christ). The truth is when I step into Heaven, God Himself, the Holy Spirit and Jesus Christ will all remember my name (like the people remembered my dad years ago)! I am thankful even though I sometimes forget about God and go about my own way, rebelling against Him, He still remembers me and will keep me for all eternity. Think about the security you have in Jesus Christ, and take the time to thank God for keeping you close to His heart.

"Your life would read like a beautiful story, if you would just let God write it." – Unknown

Don't Stay Down – March 24

There was a movie which was made years ago that is still very popular today because of the main character. The name of the movie was also the name of the main character. The movie was simply entitled, "Rocky." One of the reasons the movie became such a hit was because the boxer, named Rocky, was the ultimate underdog, and he never, ever quit. He was fighting the champion, but every time he got knocked to the canvas, he would pull himself back up and get back in the fight.

This really is a picture of our Christian lives. We are sinners by our nature trying to please a perfect, pure, righteous and holy God. We will fall, we will fail, and we will need to stand back up again. The Bible simply says, *"For a just man falleth seven times, and riseth up again: but the wicked shall fall into mischief"* (Proverbs 24:16). Every person reading this devotional today is going to have times in your life when you fall. There is no one who is exempt from falling. There is no such thing as a "super-spiritual" Christian. All of us at best are simply sinners who have been saved by grace! We are very clearly warned if we think we are standing, we should take heed, or pay attention, because we will then fall.

I don't want to waste time debating the fact we all will fall. What I would like to focus on is the "getting back up again" part. It is not hard to fall ... it is sometimes hard to get back up. Sometimes it's hard to get back up because we cannot believe God could forgive us. Please understand that way of thinking is sin. It is sin because it involves doubting the mercy of God. It is sin because we assume our God is not capable of that kind of forgiveness. It is sin because the very character of God is questioned and all of the promises He makes throughout the Bible are in doubt. Don't question God's ability to help you get back up. Don't even wonder if God could ever use you again. God can do things that are impossible with men.

Do not misunderstand ... I am not saying there will be no consequences to our sin. There is always a time of reaping what we have sown. What we plant will definitely grow some fruit we might not like but we will need to deal with. The emphasis of this verse is when we fall, we need to stand up and go on with our lives, trusting God to bring triumph out of tragedy. He can do what we think is impossible, all to create a trophy of His grace. Don't stay down. Get back up and allow God to use you again!

"Don't let failure discourage you." – Curtis Hutson

Let Your Humility Promote You – March 25

My senior year of playing soccer in college was the year I was aiming to be called the "Most Valuable Player." I worked hard that year for that goal. I know it may seem strange, but I have heard if we aim at nothing we will hit it every time. I wanted to be voted as the most valuable player on our team my last year. It all started off good; I was voted as one of the co-captains of the team. I led the warm-up drills, and even when practice was cancelled because of bad weather, helped to organize practices without our coach. I was scoring a good amount of goals, and as the end of the year approached, I was thinking I was going to achieve that goal. On the night of the awards banquet, I was fully expecting to hear my name called ... and then the moment came, and one of my best friends won!

I remember the disappointment I felt internally. I could not feel too badly, I had voted for my friend with many others, and he was very deserving of the award. There have been other times when I have been given recognition and I had no idea it was coming my way. How sweet those times are when you are unsuspecting! The Bible has a truth that is repeated in both the Old and New Testaments. *"For better it is that it be said unto thee, 'Come up hither; than that thou shouldest be put lower in the presence of the prince whom thine eyes have seen'"* (Proverbs 25:7).

As always, the Bible is absolutely correct! It is far better to be unsuspecting of a promotion while living in genuine humility, than to be expecting something like that and it never comes. In the New Testament, Jesus emphasized this same point when He said it is better to be invited to sit in the better seats, than to assume you are sitting there and to be asked to move. Today I want to encourage you to consider yourself with humility rather than pride. We each battle with pride on a daily basis. We all think more highly of ourselves than we really ought to. Humility does not come easy to any of us, but it is a key component to being greatly used of God.

I have noticed in my own spiritual life the people who have most impacted me have been the most humble people. Those who have been presented with the most pomp and circumstance (I don't even know what that means), have made the least impact on my life. I want to be humble so God can use me. May I encourage each one reading this to make it a goal today to remain humble so God can exalt you in His due time! God has a way of moving you upward or downward at just the right time.

"If successful – don't crow! If defeated – don't croak!" – Samuel Chadwick

Mighty God – March 26

"Ah Lord GOD! Behold, Thou hast made the heaven and the earth by Thy great power and stretched out arm, and there is nothing too hard for Thee: Thou shewest lovingkindness unto thousands, and recompensest the iniquity of the fathers into the bosom of their children after them: the Great, the Mighty God, the LORD of hosts, is His name" (Jeremiah 32:17-18).

The title, *"Mighty God"* appears nine different times throughout the Old Testament. Can you believe it is possible for you to have a personal relationship with the *"Mighty God"* Who spoke the worlds into existence? I am thankful this is my Heavenly Father! I'm thankful I am depending on His one and only Son to forgive my sins! I'm thankful His Holy Spirit is the One that lives within me and convicts, and guides, and leads me into all truth!

The next time you are tempted to feel sorry for yourself, remember Who your Father is! Have you ever looked at the child of a wealthy person and thought about how fortunate that child is not to need to worry about finances throughout their whole life? Or have you thought about a child that is born into a royal family. Have you thought they will be set for the rest of their life, simply based on the family they were born into? I have great news for you who are a child of God today ... your Heavenly Father is *"Mighty God."* I would rather live in poverty here on earth and know the *"Mighty God"* is my Father, than to have untold riches here on earth and not know anything about Him.

Sometimes we focus far too much on the things that are right in front of us, and we miss the whole picture of what God wants us to see. A number of years ago, we went on a family vacation to a place in the Smoky Mountains of Tennessee. We were told of a trail we could hike and then have an incredible view. I remember the hike well. There was nothing much to see. We had to continually watch where we were walking so we didn't step into the muddy puddles. Our kids topped the mountain and began to explain what they were looking at. My wife and I finally reached the summit to look out on one of the most impressive sights I can remember seeing.

Our lives are very much like that. We walk through life looking down for the muddy puddles we might step in ... while our *"Mighty God"* knows what is in front of us, and is guiding us along the way. I'm thankful today for my Heavenly Father, Who is also the *"Mighty God."* I'm thankful He has power to guide me today, just like He did to create the world!

A Gift Given to God is Never Wasted – March 27

Just before the crucifixion of Jesus Christ, a woman came with an alabaster box of very precious ointment. While the men were eating, she poured the ointment on the head of Jesus Christ. This ointment was very expensive, and invoked a strong reaction from the disciples.

Consider two different people in this story with me today. First, meet a woman who openly displayed her love for Jesus Christ when she anointed Jesus' head. She gave a gift that may have cost her about one year's pay. She did not hesitate because the gift was representative of how much she obviously felt she owed Jesus. The others were not concerned with offering Jesus anything, but this woman gave something that cost her dearly. Can you imagine the scene as these others (who were so concerned about their own issues that they had forgotten the Son of God had come to redeem them) began to smell the sweet fragrance of that ointment? Their attention was immediately drawn to this woman. You might think that their reaction would be to thank her for doing what they each should have been willing to do … but that was not their reaction at all. Hold that thought for a moment.

Second, we see the very disciples of Jesus. One of these disciples was very close to betraying Jesus Christ for thirty pieces of silver (not nearly as much as the woman had paid for the ointment). He is one of the loud protestors of this gift. These men would also very soon all forsake Jesus and run away at His arrest in the Garden. Some faithful followers they were! They make this statement I want to focus on today: *"But when His disciples saw it, they had indignation, saying, 'To what purpose is this waste'"* (Matthew 26:8)? Notice that this question was asked by these men, not the Pharisees.

The disciples called this precious demonstration a *"waste."* I want to emphasize in this devotional any gift you give for the use of Jesus Christ could never be considered a waste! Believe me, after these disciples realized Jesus was crucified for their sins, and He rose from the dead … each of them wished they had been the giver of such a wonderful gift! What do you have that is of great value to you today? What is your most prized possession? Are you willing to give it up, and give it away for the cause of Christ? Give God your absolute best today. You will never regret it for all of eternity. He is worthy of all that you have.

"He is no fool who gives that which he cannot keep to gain that which he cannot lose." – Missionary Jim Eliot

Who is Your True Friend? – March 28

It was a summer afternoon in the empty lot next to our neighbor's house. My "friends" and I were playing baseball, and I was up to bat. I hit a screaming line drive toward our neighbor's house. While I watched in horror as the ball crashed right through their kitchen window, I turned to see all of my friends running for home ... leaving me standing at home-plate holding the bat in my hand. Every person reading this today has had someone tell them they were their friend, only to see them running away when a tough situation arose. Do you have a friend who will stay with you during the tough times?

When Jesus was here on the earth, He chose twelve men to be His closest followers we call, disciples. When Jesus came to the most crucial time in His life, one of these disciples turned his back on Him in the worst way. There was an interesting thing that took place during the betrayal of Jesus. When Judas approached Jesus, here is what happened ... *"And forthwith he* [Judas Iscariot] *came to Jesus, and said, 'Hail, master;' and kissed Him. And Jesus said unto him, 'Friend, wherefore art thou come?'"* (Matthew 26:49-50).

This makes me think of an old hymn entitled, "What a Friend We Have In Jesus." Could there be a more faithful friend to a sinner than Jesus Christ? Could there be anyone who could love you more faithfully and with more force than Jesus? Even when Jesus knew Judas Iscariot was coming to betray Him ... to send Him to the cross ... to cause Him physical, and emotional anguish; He still called him *"Friend."* The actual reality was Jesus was dying as much for the sin of Judas Iscariot as for anyone else's sin! What an incredible love that drove Him! What an incredible Savior! What an amazing Friend you have if you know Jesus Christ as your personal Savior!

The absolutely clear truth is Jesus Christ is a friend to you ... the real question to be answered is, are you a friend to Him? Will you turn and run to hide when challenges to Him arise? Will we deny we know Him when others are clamoring so loudly He does not exist? Will we tell our family, friends and neighbors there is only ONE Way, Truth and Life? Stand for Jesus Christ today; He is standing for you at the right hand of God in Heaven!

"I have called you friends, who can you call a friend?" – John 15:15 –
Dr. Ted Camp

Only Begotten Son – March 29

*"No man hath seen God at any time; the **Only Begotten Son**, which is in the bosom of the Father, He hath declared Him."* (John 1:18). *"For God so loved the world, that He gave His **Only Begotten Son**, that whosoever believeth in Him should not perish, but have everlasting life"* (John 3:16). *"In this was manifested the love of God toward us, because that God sent His **Only Begotten Son** into the world, that we might live through Him"* (I John 4:9).

I grew up living on John 3:16. I trusted this *"Only Begotten Son"* as my own, personal Savior fifty plus years ago. I have been holding on to God's *"Only Begotten Son"* and trusting Him to both forgive my sins, and give me a home in Heaven when my life here is through. I am madly in love with the *"Only Begotten Son"* of God!

I cannot get out of my mind the love God had for sinners like us. He loved us so much He sent His *"Only Begotten Son!"* He didn't send a message simply through a prophet ... He sent His *"Only Begotten Son!"* He did not simply change His rule on Heaven being able to accept sinful, but well-intentioned men ... He sent His *"Only Begotten Son!"* He didn't allow men/women who had done more good than bad to have an excused entrance into Heaven ... He sent His *"Only Begotten Son!"* He did not say if people would be sincerely religious He would accept their attempts to please Him through that religion ... He sent His *"Only Begotten Son!"*

Will you stop the rush of the day to just park on that thought ... He sent His *"Only Begotten Son"* because that is the only way your sins can be forgiven! It is the only way a holy God could accept an unholy people into His Heaven! He loved you enough He willingly sent *"Only Begotten Son."* His *"Only Begotten Son"* loved you enough to humble Himself to the point of death ... the death of a cross ... to redeem your soul from Hell.

I was thinking recently about the day Abraham took Isaac to Mt. Moriah to sacrifice him. When questioned by Isaac, Abraham told him God would provide Himself a lamb. That day, as Abraham raised his hand to kill his own son, God provided a ram whose horns were caught in the thicket. Let me leave you with this thought ... the day the Lamb of God walked up Golgotha's hill ... there was no "ram" ... there was no other worthy substitute for our sin. The Lamb of God can only be the *"Only Begotten Son"* of God! He is the only One Who can forgive sins ... and He came just for you and for me! Praise God ... Praise God ... Praise God ... He came!

Hold Up the Shield – March 30

When I was a young boy, my cousin and I had a favorite "past-time." His yard was lined with large walnut trees. He would position himself along one side, and I would position myself along the other side, and we would spend hours throwing green walnuts at each other. I learned some very important lessons during the "walnut wars." One thing I learned, it was very important to gather your walnut arsenal at the proper time. If you were stuck with no walnuts within reach, it could be a painful experience to gather more ammunition. For that reason, I tried to move from tree to tree, using the large trees as a shield from my attacker (cousin Earl).

The writer of Proverbs wrote, *"Every word of God is pure: He is a shield unto them that put their trust in Him"* (Proverbs 30:5). I always thought my cousin Earl had incredible accuracy during those times I would venture a little too far from the safety of the shielding of my tree, but I have found my adversary, the Devil has even better aim when I wander too far from the safety of the shield of the Word of God. Somewhere way back in my past, a preacher made the following statement: *"The Word of God will keep you from sin … sin will keep you from the Word of God."* I have found that simple statement to be very true in my life. When I am saturating my mind with the Word of God, I enlarge the hiding place from the fiery darts of the Devil. When I neglect the reading of the Word of God, I realize his darts find their target in my testimony much easier!

I am flattered so many of you read this devotional on a regular basis, but I want to tell you from the bottom of my heart, these few words are not enough to take you through a day. You need to personally get in the Word of God daily, so the Word of God can get into you. The Bible repeats this theme all throughout itself. Just today in my devotions I read about Nehemiah and the completion of the rebuilding of the wall around Jerusalem (Nehemiah 8). The first thing the people did was stand to hear Ezra read from the Word of God. I then flipped the pages of my Bible to begin reading the longest chapter in the Bible; Psalm 119. All but five of the 176 verses spoke about the importance of the Word of God. Then I read this thirtieth chapter of Proverbs and saw this wonderful verse. I think God wants us to realize the importance of the Word of God to our everyday lives. Read your Bible; hide behind its truths; obey what it says; tell others what you have learned. It is a wonderful guide for the life of a Christian.

"The Word of God never loses its effectiveness." – Unknown

The Poor and Needy – March 31

If we are not careful, we will begin to live our lives in such a way we will forget about the needs of those around us and focus solely on our own concerns and needs. Our Bible is filled with instruction to look to help those around us. I believe God places daily opportunities before us to help us serve Him by serving others. You will notice I write often about humility in these devotionals. There is a reason for that repetition. I need to be reminded over and over again I need to remain humble in order for God to bless me. Today I read a verse that touched my heart, and I hope will touch yours too.

"Open thy mouth, judge righteously, and plead the cause of the poor and needy" (Proverbs 31:9). The last phrase really touches my heart. I was raised in a family which practiced looking to the poor and needy. My grandparents raised their families during the Great Depression. I have heard stories of very "poor" times in my family, and it could be those days served as a constant reminder to my family to reach out to those in need. I can remember many times when our family reached out to those who could not help themselves.

Today we see some extreme poverty around us I would like to challenge you to consider today. I believe this verse is talking about having a heart for those who are physically poor and needy. While I think there is a great need for us to help them today, I would also like you to consider another form of poverty we see all around us today. Oh, don't mistake what I am saying … we have more money today than we have ever had, but there are more people who are walking around in spiritual poverty than ever before. Someone needs to have a heart to get the riches of the Word of God to those who need them most, and have so little of it. Will you have a heart for others today? There are great needs represented in every person we see today. Care for the poor and needy you will see today.

I believe this simple verse is encouraging us to lift our eyes off of what we need to see the needs others have around us. There may be someone you work with, go to school with, and live in the same house with who is poor and needy. Be willing to leave your comfort zone today to go to those who are poor and needy today. You will be following the steps of Jesus when you do that. What a great path to walk!

"Others" – William Booth

MONTH OF
April

An Anchor in the Storm – April 1

We spend a good bit of our lives worrying how we will endure the storms of life. The reality is there is no way of knowing until you are in the storm. The further reality is if we have not made proper preparation before the storm, we will sink in disaster when it finally does come. God has placed me many times in places when I was offering comfort to others in distress. There have been many times when I was encouraging people to hold on to Bible truths in the midst of extremely difficult situations. I have told many others to trust God ... while wondering in my own mind if I would be able to do that if the roles were reversed and I was in their place.

The writer of the longest chapter in our Bible made this statement: *"It is good for me that I have been afflicted; that I might learn Thy statutes"* (Psalm 119:71). May I join him in this same testimony? I echo this same truth in my own life. When in the early days of our ministry I would give the advice I mentioned above, as life marched on, I had the opportunity to put into practice what I had advised others to do. I can tell you with a whole heart when the most difficult times of life come upon you, God's Word is a strong anchor! When troubles hit you, one after the other, like huge waves you think will swallow you alive, turn to the Word of God. It will not move, it will not waver, and it will not leave you without a firm foundation!

I can honestly say I thank God for those difficult times in my life. I remember vividly running to the Word of God ... not walking ... not being forced by some feeling of obligation to read it ... not being coerced by some spiritual leader of mine ... running to it with all my hope resting in it! It was during these times in the Word of God when God spoke so tenderly and directly to the challenges I was facing. I will never forget those intimate times between God and me. I would not trade them for the world. *"It is good for me that I have been afflicted; that I might learn Thy statutes!"* Sometimes there is no way to learn with depth, the truths of the Word of God. When you are in a storm in life, you need an anchor that will not shift with your emotions, or even the opinions of others. God's Word is the sweetest book you could ever hold. Love it, read it, obey it. You will never regret the time you have spent in it. It will change your life!

"... everything you need – everything pertaining to wisdom and love and success and happiness and life everlasting – lies between the covers of God's Word." – Ron Mehl

A Gracious and Merciful God – April 2

There are times in each of our lives when we like to judge other people as we see them doing things wrong, or failing the Lord. I can tell you every time we revel in another person's failure, we are giving in to our own sin nature, and we are guilty too. I am so thankful none of us are the ultimate Judge. I am thankful the God Who invented mercy and grace has judged my sin on the cross of Calvary. I am taken with the idea all my sin ... ALL my sin was placed on Jesus Christ, and has been forgiven! We, who are saved, can rejoice over that for all eternity!

When Nehemiah and those helping him finished the building of the wall, they confessed sin, repented and got back on their feet again to serve God. Nehemiah made this statement about God: *"Nevertheless for Thy great mercies' sake Thou didst not utterly consume them, nor forsake them; for Thou art a gracious and merciful God"* (Nehemiah 9:31). Our forgiveness for sin is totally the responsibility of God ... we cannot forgive our own sins. The grace and mercy we desire so much comes directly from God ... we do not deserve either grace or mercy. All the good things we enjoy as Christians are gifts from our Heavenly Father. You and I ought to stop right here and thank God for that grace. God giving us a blessing what we do not deserve. We ought to stop and thank God for His mercy. God withholding the justice and condemnation we do deserve.

The thought I would like to challenge you with today is, how much grace and mercy have you shown others? After all, we have been shown unlimited grace and mercy for what we deserved, from the One Who had the right to bring justice and condemnation. If He has offered us grace and mercy, don't you think we ought to do the same to those around us? We are on this earth today to represent our God the best we can. We were created in His image, and we ought to attempt to live in a way that will reflect His glory on a regular basis. Today, just as God offered you His grace and mercy, offer someone who has wronged you the same grace and mercy. God has been faithful to you; you ought to be faithful to Him.

Praise God Jesus' death, burial and resurrection have opened the door wide for God's grace and mercy to be poured on us! We, who were without hope, have eternal hope and life because of the grace and mercy of God! Much has been given ... much is required. Thank God for grace and mercy! Without it, we all would be in trouble. Give it away today!

"Don't let success go to your heart or success to your head." – Unknown

A Heritage Forever – April 3

I will thank God for eternity for allowing me to be born into a home with a father and mother who were both saved. I am so thankful for them following the directive of God to be equally yoked – a believer marrying a believer. It made for a wonderful environment to grow up in. No, we did not have a perfect home, but it was a place where Christ was exalted, and decisions were made based on the principles of the Word of God. The Word of God had been passed from previous generations as the guiding map for life in general, and for living a life pleasing to God. Our home was built on the truths from the Word of God.

The psalmist wrote, *"Thy testimonies have I taken as a heritage forever: for they are the rejoicing of my heart"* (Psalm 119:111). When I read that verse it made me think about my motivation for this devotional. I want to pass along to our children a godly heritage. I want them to use the Word of God as their guiding map through life. I want to see our grand-children and generations to come following the same Word of God. It has been a blessing to me, and I am hopeful it will remain the guide for the future of our family.

When I think about a heritage being passed along, I do not think of finances. That is probably because our family never had much in the way of money to pass along. I am thinking of the things which have been given to me that are far more valuable than money. I have been given the heritage of fiercely defending the Word of God (after all it is the absolute truth)! I have been given the heritage of hard work. I have heard the phrase, *"If the job's worth doing, it's worth doing right;"* many times. I have been given the heritage of loving others who have been overlooked. I have been given the heritage of sacrificial love for those in our family and friends. I have been given the heritage of keeping your word after you have promised something. I have been given the heritage of standing up for what you believe in. I thank God for the heritage that has been passed along to me.

As you read this devotional today, you are reading part of my attempt to continue passing along the challenges of the Word of God to you on a daily basis. Let me encourage you to keep building a heritage for those following you. This is not a quick race, but a steady, consistent walk with God while those who are following watch how it is done. Be faithful today … others are watching and copying your actions!

"By perseverance the snail reached the ark." – C.H. Spurgeon

Turn to God – April 4

All of us have gotten news that disturbed us. All of us have gotten word that an enemy has a plan to do something to hurt us. All of us have faced problems which were far bigger than the resources we have had to fight the problem. Today I was reading about the king of Judah and a challenge he faced from the countries of Ammon and Moab. What he did first, is what I believe we all ought to do when facing a problem. *"And Jehoshaphat feared, and set himself to seek the LORD, and proclaimed a fast throughout all Judah"* (II Chronicles 20:3). His first reaction was to see the Lord. What good advice that is for any of us facing hard situations. We ought to run first to God and then wait for His solution for our problem.

I believe there is one key to this that is very important. We cannot make this a "9-1-1 call" to God. God desires an ongoing, daily relationship with us. One of the reasons for this devotional is to give you a time each day when you stop looking at all the problems around you, and look directly into the face of God. He is the answer to the problems and worries of our lives. It is His face we ought to seek when things get tough. Jehoshaphat not only sought the face of God, but obeyed exactly what God told him to do. God promised him he would not need to fight on this day and He would take care of the enemy. I wonder how many times God would have fought for us if we would have totally depended on Him for the victory? I wonder how many defeats we have experienced that were totally unnecessary if we had just yielded to His control.

Later in this same chapter there is a description of the army of Judah approaching the place where the enemy was gathered, only to find them all dead and with great riches laying with them! God did it again ... He has a way of conquering the enemies in our lives that we could never imagine every being defeated. He also did it without the help of King Jehoshaphat, or any of his well-trained, but highly outnumbered soldiers. There is a lesson for each of us to remember ... God is enough all by Himself. He does not need us, but we desperately need Him. Lean on Him today. Trust Him fully for the answers to today's questions. Don't try to fight the battles all alone. Walk with Him intimately today. Talk with Him about your challenges. Trust His almighty hand to come through for you, exactly when you need Him! Trust God for the challenges you face today!

"When you can't see the hand of God ... look for the heart of God." – Unknown

He Hears Me – April 5

"In my distress I cried unto the LORD, and He heard me" (Psalm 120:1). What an incredible thought … the God Who created this universe actually takes time to listen to the cares and concerns that are on my heart today. So often we carry the burdens of the day from one day into the next. What a waste of time for the Christian to bear a burden that could easily be taken care of by our God! The psalmist probably had problems that were similar to ours in the times he was living, but he had learned to take his burdens to God and allow Him to take care of them for Him.

I remember a number of times when I had issues at a job I was working on, and voiced those concerns to the manager, or boss. Many times it seemed my suggestions had not been considered correct, or important enough to act upon. In one case, I shared a burden I had for a potential problem I could foresee coming, and I was told my worries were not justified. I felt as if the person I had shared the concerns with had not really listened to what I had told them. Almost one year later, some changes took place within the organization that showed me the person I had shared with had actually been listening. Changes came that addressed my initial concerns. I remember telling my wife, *"They actually did listen!"* It was such a comfort.

I have learned through experience whether I am casting my burdens upon the Lord or sharing a concern with a boss/leader, the timing does not always fit what I want, but it is always just at the right time. There have been times when I have taken concerns to the Lord and thought there was no answer. I have found out the answer was on the way, it was just unseen by me at the time. Because of this realization, I want to learn the lesson God is always in control, and He will always do what is best for me at exactly the best time.

The application for today's verse is, it is always good to leave your burdens with the Lord, but it is also best to trust His timing in providing the answer to the problems you face. He does hear us … and His answer will always come at exactly the right time. Don't despair; God is still on the throne. Don't complain, simply trust Him for whatever is facing you right now and know in your distress you can call upon Him, because He does hear you. There is great comfort in knowing God not only has the answer, but the ability to meet any challenge you are facing today!

"Take your burden to the Lord and leave it there …" – Charles Tindley

Stay in Touch – April 6

One of my favorite stories in the Bible is about a woman who had been struggling with a continual flow of blood for twelve years. She had spent all she had on doctors to try to cure her without success. She had such solid faith in Jesus, she made this statement, *"… If I may touch but His clothes, I shall be whole"* (Mark 15:28). She knew without a doubt if she could simply touch the clothing of Jesus her sickness of twelve years would be healed! What incredible faith!

Do you have that kind of faith today? We all struggle with things that have caused us pain and turmoil in our lives. When we have a problem, we are all too willing to spend our money in an effort to try to "fix" those problems, often without any good results. We get advice from other people and even complete strangers, when all we really need to do is to get in touch with Jesus Christ. For the remainder of this devotional I would like you to consider some ways to touch Jesus Christ.

Obviously we can see Who Jesus really is on the pages of our Bible. It is in this wonderful book where we can see what Jesus did; who He touched; what touched Him; and what He provided for us. When I want to touch Jesus, I run to the Word of God. When I get to it, I ask God to help me get into the Word of God, and for it (the Bible) to get into me. I realize the more I apply my life to the principles of the Bible, the more I will act, think and live like Jesus Christ. Apart from the Bible, I have no hope of ever knowing what Jesus is like … no hope of living a life that is pleasing to Him.

Another way I can touch Jesus Christ today is through prayer. This has always been a very convicting area of my spiritual life. I can get so busy in "doing things" that I have a hard time slowing down to just talk with my Heavenly Father. When I take the time to speak with my God, I must do it through Jesus Christ. When I have sin in my life, I must go through my Advocate, Jesus Christ. When I have a need that is beyond my abilities, I trust Jesus Christ to prop me up and provide all I will need. These times of prayer, are some of the most intimate times I have ever had with God. It is during these times of prayer when I feel I get to know my Savior even more. Don't continue struggling through your problems alone … touch the hem of His garment today through reading the Word of God and in prayer. You will see remarkable results!

"If you don't have enough faith, then borrow some from someone else." – Unknown

I Love Church – April 7

"Do we have to go to church today?" This statement was never spoken in my house growing up that I can remember. Other people might have hated going to church, but not our family. When I was growing up, we lived about thirty minutes from the church we attended. I can remember getting up early on Sunday morning; coming downstairs for breakfast; and hurrying to get back upstairs to get my church clothes on. You might ask, "Why?" My mother always put a stack of records (these are round plastic things that an arm with a needle would sit on and they played music) on the record player and we would have about an hour and a half of music on Sunday morning. I can remember sitting on the couch, singing along with our favorite singers until it was time to leave for church. We would then get into our car, and many days would sing all the way into church. Dad whistled because he wasn't the best singer (although I've heard worse). I don't want to paint an improper picture ... there were times we argued on the way into church, but there were not many of these.

By the time we arrived at church, I was excited to hear what was going to be taught in my Sunday School class, in Junior church, or by my pastor. Today I read this verse from the Psalms: *"I was glad when they said unto me, 'Let us go into the house of the LORD'"* (Psalm 122:1). This verse has been my life's story! I have been and am glad to go to the house of God still today! You see, our family was centered on the Word of God, and it was at the house of God where we learned from it every week! Our best friends were at church. Our fellowship and activities were all based there. When my friends in High School were planning for a beer party on the weekends, I was looking forward to a teen retreat, or activity, or opportunity for ministry.

I don't think my parents had any idea they were creating an enthusiasm for church in us, but they did a great job. I still love to go to the house of the Lord today. Do you have this same passion for your local church? If you don't ... put on some good music; sing in the car on the way there; memorize verses together; and get in a church that teaches clearly the Word of God! I think you will join in with the psalmist and me and say you are glad to go to the house of the Lord!

"The secret of success of everyone who has been successful lies in the fact that he formed the habit of doing things that failures don't like to do." – Albert Gray

Keeping an Eye on Heaven – April 8

When I was in elementary school, one of my favorite things to do was to look up at the ceiling as though I was looking at something very interesting. I did this, not because there was anything interesting to look at, but simply to see how many of my classmates I could get to look at the empty ceiling. I know, I was an ornery little kid when I was young (still am ... just older). Today I read an interesting verse that made me think about where I am making people look now. *"Unto Thee lift I up mine eyes, O thou that dwellest in the heavens"* (Psalm 123:1).

It is my desire to have a very clear look at my Savior on a daily basis. I want to always have one eye toward Heaven to see what my marching orders might be for the situation I am facing. I want to gaze into my Savior's face, looking for instruction for how to live more like Him every day. I want to realize eternity is real, and the things I am facing today are just temporary. I want to keep a perspective that will keep my thinking straight and my steps in line with His perfect will for me.

I want to keep a good balance with my view. I do not want to be guilty of looking so much toward Heaven that I forget the needs of those around me today. I do not want to be so heavenly minded that I am no earthly good. I want to have the vision Jesus had here on this earth. He never forgot the will of His Heavenly Father, but He also never missed an opportunity to meet the needs of those around Him on earth. I want to keep my heart close to God in Heaven, while having a heart that is easily moved to help those around me. I realize in order to do all these things, I must keep an active view of the Word of God, and the heart of God. I want to keep my heart focused on the Word of God daily so God can whisper and I will be able to hear it loud and clear.

I am so thankful I have a Heavenly Father Who is not caught up in the "normal" pressures of life on earth. I am thankful for His omnipotence. I am thankful I can look to Heaven for every answer to every question or challenge life throws at me. Our challenge for today is to keep our eyes focused on Him and not on our situations. Let me encourage you to look up today (like I used to do in elementary school). This time, I promise you, there is a God worth seeing there in Heaven! Look up today and encourage someone else to do the same.

"It's wonderful to climb the liquid mountain of the sky. Behind me and before me is God and I have no fears." – Helen Keller

Resting Time is Needed – April 9

I'm not sure how it is with you, but there are many times when I feel guilty if I take some time off ... a vacation ... even a nap. I don't know why, but I feel driven to always be doing something. I remember having tremendous feelings of guilt when my mother was nearing her home-going to Heaven. She had been diagnosed with liver cancer and was nearing the end of her life here on earth. I struggled mightily with the decision to cancel meetings and stay home to be with my father when that moment came. I did not want to hinder the ministry for the sake of my own personal desires, but I also wanted to be a good son to my parents and a good brother to my sister.

I read a story today in Mark 6 about when John the Baptist was killed by King Herod. When Jesus heard the news of the death of His faithful servant, He said to His disciples, "... *Come ye yourselves apart into a desert place, and rest a while ...*" (Mark 6:31). Jesus realized the need for some time apart from the ministry in order to gather thoughts, heal and re-charge for future ministry. I want to encourage you today to take time to get away from the hustle and bustle of life for some rest time. You are no better than the disciples of Jesus. He needed the time away ... they needed the time away. A time of rest is necessary for all of us. You may feel the ministry/job you have cannot go on without you. I will tell you it can. Actually, your ministry/job will benefit with a "fresher" you, than you when you are worn out and tired.

God was gracious to me when my mom was close to death. He allowed me to have a heart issue that forced me to remain at home for two-months for recuperation. It was during this time when my mother gracefully stepped into Heaven. She did that with my father, my sister and me sitting with her, holding her hand, kissing her forehead and telling her we loved her. What a blessing from Heaven! Yes, meetings were postponed ... appointments were put off a few weeks ... preaching assignments were rearranged ... but the time of rest away from it all enabled me to minister to my dad and sister. It also allowed others to minister to me. Most importantly to me, it allowed me to honor my mother until her last breath. I want to encourage you to step back from your busy schedule once-in-awhile to allow God to minister to your heart. You will never regret it. Sometimes the fast pace of life hides the face of God from us.

"When God bolts a window, don't try to go through a door." –
Curtis Hutson

What's in Your Heart Today? – April 10

We worry so much about what we look like on the outside that we often neglect the things that are on the inside. Or, we think if we dress up the outside well enough, others will not notice what is on the inside. The reality is God does not look on the outward countenance of a man (woman), but on the inward motivations of our heart. So much of what we see being done under the title of "religion," or "church" today is simply an outward display of pseudo Christianity. This display has nothing to do with a deep relationship with God, but simply an outward display to make it appear that we have that relationship.

It is amazing no matter how much things seem to change, they really remain the same. In the days of Jesus, the strongest opponents of His earthly ministry were the religious leaders, not the Romans. He faced pressure all throughout His ministry from those you would have thought would have been waiting in line for His coming! He chastised these religious leaders often throughout His teaching. He encountered a group that challenged the fact his disciples ate with unwashed hands. The Bible says of them: *"For the Pharisees, and all the Jews, except they wash their hands oft, eat not, holding the tradition of the elders"* (Mark 7:3). That last phrase caught my eye this morning ... *holding the tradition of the elders ...*

I wonder how much we do today because it is the tradition of those we want to please. It is not always a long standing tradition that is a tradition. There are many churches today that are doing things in their normal service time that are what is considered the "norm" among religious leaders today. I often wonder how much we are following the Holy Spirit's guidance, and how much we are following other men? Jesus warned these people with these words: *"Well hath Isaiah prophesied of you hypocrites, as it is written, 'This people honoreth Me with their lips, but their heart is far from Me'"* (Mark 7:6).

God is not interested in what you say, sing, or do. He is far more interested in what is in your heart that is motivating your actions. You see, the traditions of men do not come from your heart; only those things directed by the Holy Spirit. Today determine to walk completely led by the Spirit of God, and see what wonderful things He will do in your life today!

"Be calm, cool, and corrected" – Unknown

Laughter is a Good Testimony – April 11

"Then was our mouth filled with laughter, and our tongue with singing: then said they among the heathen, 'The LORD hath done great things for them'" (Psalm 126:2). Sometimes when I am driving down the road, I like to look at the faces of the people driving toward me. I have noticed there are not very many smiles, or even friendly looking faces. There is an abundance of gloom and despair on their faces. We are living in a world that does not have much to smile about. There is constant news of killings, financial ruin, health issues, and troubles beyond our ability to handle. But, for the Christian, we have hope! When was the last time your smiling face made a difference for someone without hope? As a Christian, God expects us to show the joy of the Lord so others outside of Christ will want what we have. I have seen many Christians who look like they are drinking the juice out of the dill pickle jar. When you ask some believers how they are doing, you must give them a half hour to list all their aches, pains and problems. That should not be our testimony.

The psalmist here mentioned that people noticed their laughter and immediately connected that to the blessings of the LORD. If that is true, doesn't it make sense the opposite is true as well? Doesn't it make sense if we are constantly depressed, and dwell always on the negative things that are happening around us, we are a bad testimony to the goodness of the Lord? God has done so many wonderful things for us, we ought to dwell on those things rather than the challenges we are facing on a regular basis. Each of us faces difficulties. Each of us has problems. Each of us struggles in different areas of our lives. However, each one who believes in Jesus Christ for their forgiveness of sin has a joy that is far deeper than the problems we are facing.

It is important we each realize our faces and our countenances are a billboard advertisement for what God is doing in our heart and life. When you give a smile to a person today, you are telling them you have something they ought to desire to have in their life. When you join them with a "gloom and doom" face, you are telling them they are right–there is no hope. You ought to thank God today you are alive with the hope you have in Him. There are unending possibilities of people you can touch today if you will keep the right attitude and laugh a little. You might be the only person who will have a smile on all day long. Use it well!

"Ninety percent of this game is half mental." – Yogi Berra

Who Built Your House? – April 12

We moved from one state to where we live right now. I can remember searching for months with a realtor to find a house that would meet the needs of our family, as well as the budget we had to live within. I was frustrated after searching and searching to find nothing that met the need. I can remember being in some beautiful houses and then finding out they were far out of our reach. I can remember opening the door of a house we could afford, only to be met with an aroma that I could not live with. We looked and looked until finally we found a piece of property we were able to build the house where we now live. My best friend built our house, and he did it with incredible skill and craftsmanship.

As good as he was at building a solid house for us; he could not build our home. Let me explain what I mean. *"Except the LORD build the house, they labor in vain that build it: except the LORD keep the city, the watchman waketh in vain"* (Psalm 127:1). My best friend can put wood and bricks together to build a physical house, but my Heavenly Father is the only One Who can build the hearts of a family together. God has a plan for the husband/father that is unique to our Bible. I would like to encourage the men/ boys who are reading this to look for those places in your Bible that refer to the responsibilities for leading a home. God also has a plan for the wife/ mother that is equally as unique to our Bible. I would like to encourage the women/girls who are reading this to find those passages to learn how to be a godly woman. God has a plan for parents and children that is also unique to the Bible.

If we want to build a successful home, the main ingredient will always be God. If He is the Master-builder, we will have a home that will endure the winds and storms of life. If we depend on the wisdom of people on this earth, we will find our house falling to the ground at the first sign of trouble. Without the help of God, the watchman watches for danger in vain. There is no help when you see trouble coming if you do not have God's help. Today, surrender your life and the life of your family to the hand of God. He will make something beautiful come from ordinary lives if you will trust Him to do it. There are thousands of people who are trying to find the answer for a successful family. Show them your family, led by God Himself, and let them come to know Him through you.

"Your highest compliment as a leader is that other leaders will follow you." – Unknown

Don't Give Up! – April 13

"And many charged him [blind man named Bartimaeus] *that he should hold his peace: but he cried the more a great deal, 'Thou son of David, have mercy on me'"* (Mark 10:48). I love that one line in this verse, "*... but he cried the more a great deal ...*" He was not slowed down by the people who told him not to bother Jesus. He did not hesitate, or lower his voice, or even stop altogether ... he simply cried out more and more and louder and louder! I wish I had that kind of staying power in my prayer life! How many times have we asked the Lord for something once, and when we did not get it, we gave up and forgot about it? How many times have we not even bothered to pray about something, thinking the Lord surely would not answer us?

This man asked for the impossible to be done! This man was blind and was asking for his sight to be restored! Everyone knows that can't happen ... unless Jesus gets involved! Our God is capable of so much more than we believe He can do. After all, the God-head had made the eyes of this blind man. They knew all the intricate things our modern day scientists are just now discovering with all their new and modern technology. Jesus Christ stood directly in front of this man and represented the answer to the longing of his heart for most of his life. When others told him to remain quiet, he just raised the volume level a little higher and started crying out a little more often! What a great example this man is for us today. The reason was the answer to his problem had just arrived on the scene and he was not going to miss his opportunity!

Regardless of how much people around you try to deny the awesome power of your God, don't listen! As much as people tell you prayer is a waste of time ... religion is simply a mental crutch ... the Bible is full of stories that are nothing more than myths written long ago ... or fellowshipping in church with other believers is not necessary to spiritual growth ... etc., keep crying out to the Master of this universe. He will never fail you. As the skeptics around you increase, allow your faith in your never-failing God to increase as well. Remember, the cynics that were near this blind man went home just like they had come ... in unbelief. He went home and saw his family for the first time! He experienced the joy of not giving up and seeing God do miraculous things! He had a story to tell for the rest of his life. What about you and me today?

"Small deeds done are better than great deeds planned." – Peter Marshall

Don't be a Hot-Head – April 14

When I was a young man, I hate to admit it, but I had a very short temper. There are still times when my temper gets the best of me. I can remember a number of times when I was a young man playing in a sport where I let my temper control my actions. I can also remember coming home after finishing the game and being so disappointed in myself. I knew at the time I was losing my temper, my actions were not following those of Christ. I knew when I would return home I had disappointed my Heavenly Father, as well as my earthly parents (many times). I cannot tell you the numbers of times I would pick up the phone to call someone to ask them for forgiveness. I remember many times when I needed to go to someone face-to-face to ask them to forgive me for my horrible attitude.

Of course, the Bible speaks to this very clearly. *"He that is slow to wrath is of great understanding: but he that is hasty of spirit exalteth folly"* (Proverbs 14:29). In my flesh it is very easy to lose sight of what God wants for my life. There were times when I would win an argument, and realize in the end I had really lost because I did not control my temper. What a great personality trait to be slow to wrath! I have a very good friend from Jamaica who is like this. It takes a great deal to get him upset. I remember one day before a softball game when he was sitting on the bench and I was warming up, swinging a bat. I thought it would be cool if I could knock his hat off by hitting the brim with my swing ... I think you know where this is going ... Let's just say it didn't work out exactly like I had envisioned it in my mind. I hit my friend in the head with my swing. He looked at me and simply asked, *"Why did you do that?"* He was slow to wrath (thank God for that!).

Today make it your goal to be slow to wrath. There will be people who disappoint you (hopefully none will hit you in the head with a bat), and there will be situations where you might be justified in being angry. Be careful to not have a hasty spirit. Be careful to act, not react. When we react, many times, we must then go back and repair the damage we have created. I want to be a man under control today. I want to be ready if God wants to use me today. I don't want to be fuming about something I think was unfair, or when I did not get my way. I want to be this wise man described in Proverbs 14.

"God is more interested in making us what we ought to be than in giving us what we think we ought to have." – Unknown

113

Will Your Anchor Hold? – April 15

I can remember fishing on the Connecticut River just below a dam with my dad and some friends who lived in Connecticut. It was something very different than anything I had ever done in my life. I can remember them driving the boat directly toward the dam, getting as close to it as possible to get in the "prime spot," and dropping anchor. We then sat there for hours casting our line toward the dam to catch a fish called a shad. We caught a bunch of this large fish that morning. I remember it because I never have caught so many fish in my life! I also remember it because the fish were big and it was exciting to see them on the end of your line. There was something I did not give much thought to as a boy, but that was very important to our success on that day. If our anchor did not hold us in that "prime spot," we would not have enjoyed the success we had.

As a Christian, there is certainly a strong current from this world that will push against us. These people (representing the current) are interested in moving us off our position of trust in the Word of God and in the God of the Word. It is important we realize we need an anchor firmly set in the strength and power of our God. We cannot withstand the attacks from the enemy without Him! The psalmist wrote, *"Out of the depths have I cried unto Thee, O LORD. Lord, hear my voice; let thine ears be attentive to the voice of my supplications"* (Psalm 130:1-2).

There is a God in Heaven. That God is interested in helping His children endure the tests life brings our way. It is important we surrender to Him each and every day. It is important today to cry to the One Who can help you in the situations you are facing right now. There is a God Who can lift you out of the miry clay you find yourself in. He is waiting for your call today. He can hear your voice ... have you called? His ear is turned toward you ... have you asked for His help? He is not sleeping, but is fully aware of the challenges you are facing. As a matter of fact, God has allowed the very storm you find yourself in. He has a plan to use that storm to draw you to Him. Is your anchor firmly attached to Him? If you are trusting in your finances as your anchor, you are, or will be in trouble. If you are depending on friends/family/church/health/success ... all these will miserably fail you in the middle of the storm. God and His Word will never fail you. Trust Him today. Cry out to Him ... He is listening!

"In order to realize the worth of the anchor, we need to feel the stress of the storm." – Unknown

God Honors Faithfulness – He Hates Pride – April 16

There are many times in life when we feel we are not getting what we deserve. There are times you might be doing the right thing while all others seem to be doing the wrong thing and you wonder if it is worth it. You need to take time to read the book of Esther in the Old Testament to see God is totally aware of what you are doing and He will honor faithfulness to Him. In this book, we are introduced to a Jewish man named Mordecai who is in captivity in Persia. His cousin, Esther had been placed into the position of Queen. There was a man named Haman who hated Mordecai (and all Jews as well) because Mordecai would not bow to him when he came through town. Haman had tricked the king into signing a decree making it legal to kill the Jews. He then went home and built a set of gallows to hang Mordecai on.

Mordecai had done the right thing earlier by warning the king of a threat to kill him, but it seemed his good deed was forgotten. The king had a night when he could not sleep. He asked for the book of the chronicles to be brought in to be read to him so he would fall asleep. During this reading, the story of Mordecai saving his life was read to him. As the king was considering what to do to reward Mordecai, Haman entered to talk about hanging Mordecai. The king asked Haman what he ought to do to honor a person who deserved honor (Mordecai). Haman assumed the king was speaking about him. He laid out an elaborate plan to honor this mystery man. I love God's sense of humor ... here is what happened following this: *"Then the king said to Haman, 'Make haste, and take the apparel and the horse, as thou hast said, and do even so to Mordecai the Jew, that sitteth at the king's gate: let nothing fail of all that thou hast spoken'"* (Esther 6:10).

Oh ... those gallows Haman was preparing for Mordecai were never used by Mordecai, but Haman and his family. Please do not forget today God is not mocked ... whatsoever a man sows that will he also reap. It is always best to do what is right, whether you are noticed for it or not. Men around you might not notice it, but God in Heaven is very much aware of what you are doing, and at exactly the right time will make sure the honor you deserve is given to you. Also realize evil will not triumph, even though it may appear to be winning at the time. God honors faithful obedience and He opposes pride. Haman was filled with pride and lost the battle he was fighting. Mordecai remained humble and was honored.

"You can borrow brains, but you cannot borrow character." –
Bob Jones Sr

Keeping the Main Thing the Main Thing – April 17

When Jesus was asked by one of the scribes what the first or most important commandment was, Jesus answered; *"And thou shalt love the Lord thy God with all thy heart, and with all thy soul, and with all thy mind, and with all thy strength: this is the first commandment. And the second is like, namely this, Thou shalt love thy neighbor as thyself. There is none other commandment greater than these"* (Mark 12:30-31).

Is it possible in all the hustle and bustle of our normal ministry we could forget these simple truths? Is what you are planning to do for God today within these guidelines? Do the efforts you put forth revolve around loving the Lord with every fiber of who you are … your heart, soul, mind and strength? It seems to me we start serving this Lord with this as the goal, but if we are not careful the praise of men flatters us so much we begin to serve God for what "others" will say about us. We become so enamored with hearing how good we are from others we forget we originally were doing it for the love of God. Jesus stated this so clearly we should never forget it, but we seem to do it regularly.

Think about it … the last time you sang a song in church; did you do it for others to hear you, or to glorify God? The last time you gave an offering; did you do it to please your pocketbook? to impress the person next to you? or because you would give all you have to show your love for God? The last time you shared a testimony, or prayed publically in a meeting; were you trying to use vocabulary you knew would impress those in the room with you, or were you pouring your heart out to your God? The last time you shared your faith with an unbeliever; did you do it to fulfill a requirement of a class, or to impress others with how many tracts you handed out, or were you about your Father's business?

Sadly it seems today we all do "spiritual" things for very "unspiritual" reasons. Today is a day for you to love the Lord your God with all you have; and then to demonstrate that by loving those around you like He would. Verse 31 speaks to the proof of loving God with all your being. If we really do love Him that way, we will love those God has placed around us, like He would do it in our shoes. The proof of loving God with all you have is to love those He sent His Son to save!

"People don't care how much you know until they know how much you care." – John Maxwell

Don't Waste Your Time – April 18

Think for a moment about how much time you waste in a normal day. There can be quite a lot of "down time" if we are not careful. We look at our day and think about the things we would like to accomplish. We then begin to attack those challenges, only to be confronted with other options that take our attention away from our original plans. Before we know it, we have wasted away a whole day. I believe it is the same in our Christian lives. We have all had times during a service where God specifically prompted our hearts to accomplish something for Him. Before we know what has happened, we find we have wasted away the opportunity, and we have turned our focus onto a totally unrelated area. This creates a list that seems to grow all the time of "unfinished" tasks.

Jesus made a very strong statement I believe we all ought to take time to consider today. He said about the rapture of the church, *"Take ye heed, watch and pray: for ye know not when the time is"* (Mark 13:33). Jesus was making the point that our time is limited to serve the Lord here on earth. It is important to do the things that are MOST important, and leave those things that serve only as distractions alone. I have heard it said before the enemy of BEST is GOOD. Be careful today to do the things that are most important for the cause of Christ before you waste your time on things that will not last for eternity.

Think about the things you are planning to do today. If you accomplished all of those things, how much of a difference will it make in eternity? If you don't accomplish those goals, how many other people will be affected for eternity? If you do not have plans to make an eternal difference for someone today, consider changing your plans. If you have plans that will affect someone else's eternity, don't let anyone pull you away from the completion of those goals. Have a bull-headedness that will keep you on the mark until you complete whatever it is God has touched your heart with. Others may tell you, you are foolish to pursue that goal ... if you know God touched your heart to do it, don't let anyone pull you away from it. There is a day coming when the trumpet will sound, and all our earthly efforts will be done. Don't waste a minute today. Do all God has touched your heart to do while you have the chance. Share your faith; read your Bible; teach that class; sing for the Lord; go on visitation; volunteer for the nursery; visit a shut-in; learn Sign Language ... Do it now!

"Your lifetime is just a hyphen on a tombstone." – Unknown

Where is Your Heart? – April 19

I was reading about one of the good kings in the history of Judah named Hezekiah. When he took over as the king, he made some radical reforms. He actually cleaned out the temple and encouraged the Jewish people to turn back to God and worship only Him. He also made a way for all the people to sacrifice to God. He did all this because he had his heart in the right place. *"And in every work that he began* [King Hezekiah] *in the service of the house of God, and in the law, and in the commandments, to seek his God, he did it with all his heart, and prospered"* (II Chronicles 31:21). When my eyes crossed these words, it was like the eyes of the Holy Spirit crossed over my heart. I wondered ... if God was writing my life's story, could He write these words about my passion for Him?

Unfortunately, I believe many are serving in churches today "half-heartedly" or without any fervent heart for God. How can we do that when we are serving a God Who demonstrated His heart for us on the cruel cross of Calvary? He gave all He had in order to demonstrate His love toward us. He did this *while we were yet sinners*. Today, I do not want you to think of anyone else but yourself. Are you serving God with a whole heart? Are you living 100% for God today? Are you totally committed to His will for your life? Are you fully surrendered and going forward in that direction with all your might? That is what God deserves ... that is what God demands if you want to have success in your Christian life.

Hezekiah sought God with that whole heart. Hezekiah sought the laws and commandments of God. When he did that, he did it with all His heart! Are you seeking God wholeheartedly today? Have you considered what He wanted you to do with this day before you started on your path? Did you dig into the Word of God this morning to give light to your path? Have you had the Word of God convict you to the point when you decided to change your attitude or direction to match what you read? You cannot have a heart for the things of God without having a heart for the Word of God. I'm not talking about reading this devotional as your spiritual food for the day. I'm hopeful this is your spiritual appetizer, the thing that leads you into the main course you will find between the pages of God's precious Word.

I want to be a man whose heart is fully surrendered to God and His will for me today. I want to be a man who can prosper in the way I am going, because I am going in the way He has chosen for me!

"God is more concerned about your heart than your health." – Unknown

What Change has He Made in You? – April 20

When Jesus was being led up Calvary's hill to be crucified, He fell beneath the weight of the cross. The soldiers compelled a man named Simon to help carry the cross. *"And they compel one Simon a Cyrenian, who passed by, coming out of the country, the father of Alexander and Rufus, to bear His cross"* (Mark 15:21). Simon was a Cyrenian who was probably in Jerusalem for the Passover festivities that were about to take place. An innocent by-stander, minding his own business ... asked to help carry the cross of Jesus. Imagine his horror, as he shouldered the cross and saw the blood of Jesus all over his own clothing, and I am sure, on him as well. He had no idea the very blood would free all mankind (who call upon the name of Jesus) from their sins! He had no idea this was the blood from the Lamb of God Who takes away the sin of the world! Here was a common man, from another country, who was "volunteering" to help carry the cross of the Son of Almighty God!

As far as we know, Simon did not know about Jesus. He was obviously visiting in Jerusalem, as many Jews would do to commemorate the Passover. He was placed in the position of giving help to Jesus Christ in His time of need. What he might not have initially realized was the fact that Jesus was about to give His life up for his sins, and the sins of his sons, and for whosoever will ... The mention of these sons names in particular leads me to believe they were known of the apostles. As a matter of fact, Paul mentioned a man named Rufus in Romans 16:13 with very kind words. I'm not sure if he is the same man that was Simon's son, but it made me think about the impact this contact with Jesus would have, not only on Simon, but also on these two sons of his. When a person meets Jesus Christ, it will make a difference. What difference has it made in your life? Can others tell you have had an intimate encounter with Jesus Christ? Can your friends and family see the difference He makes? Can those co-workers and fellow students see a difference in you? The question for today is simply this; can other people tell you spend time with Jesus Christ? If you do, it will show up in your language, attitude, and heart for lost people, in your habits, and in how you serve Him. If you know Jesus as your Savior, but are not surrendering to Him as the Lord of your life, you are missing out on a tremendous blessing! Why not stop what you are doing right now and give God permission to rule your life? It will be a great decision today!

"Be willing to come up and out of your comfort zone." – Unknown

Mercy That Lasts – April 21

"... *The heart for mercy cries* ..." is a line from an old hymn I love. In reality, all of our hearts cry out for the mercy of God. We really do not want the justice we deserve, but we want God's mercy in its place. Psalm 136 has the phrase, "*His mercy endureth forever,*" twenty-six times. In the margin of my Bible at the end of this great chapter, I wrote; "I think God wants us to know His mercy endures forever!" I am so thankful for a God that gives me what I don't deserve, rather than giving me all I have earned in my sinfulness.

Too much of our lives are spent thinking about how much good we deserve that we are not getting. In other words, there are times when others are promoted, and while we are clapping we are thinking we deserved the recognition more than they did. We constantly view the world through our own opinions and think less of the people who do not share our thoughts and ideas. If we are not careful, we actually begin to think we are the king (queen) of our domain and all others should bow to us. Time for a reality check today ...

Here are the facts ... "*They are all gone out of the way, they are together become unprofitable; there is none that doeth good, no, not one*" (Romans 3:12). You are I are nothing without the mercy and grace of God. Today as you begin this new day, why not pause and thank God for His mercies. Psalm 136 lists some things we have received as a result of the mercy of God. He does great wonders ... in His wisdom He made the heavens ... He stretched out the earth ... He made the great lights ... He made a sun to rule our day ... He made the moon and stars for the spectacle at night ... He conquers enemies for us, and without our help ... He divided the Red Sea for Israel to pass through and then collapsed it just at the right time to destroy the powerful Egyptian army ... He has conquered powerful and famous kings ... He remembers us when we are low and no one else cares about us ... He redeems us from sin ... What can we say except, "*His mercy endureth forever!*" Thank God today He has not given you the things you deserved, again, and again, and again. In the place of what we deserved, God has given us grace. He has pardoned our sin through His Son, by His grace. Don't take these blessings for granted today. Look at your own life; thank God for the times of mercy He has poured out on you.

"*We are all flawed, bruised, and broken people needing the Lord.*" – Unknown

Sing Your Song – April 22

Have you ever felt so "down in the dumps" you did not feel like singing? That is exactly the time when you ought to sing. Have you ever felt God had forgotten you and you had no hope? That is a great time for a song to cross your mind and lips. In Psalm 137, the psalmist writes of a time like that and asked this question: *"How shall we sing the LORD's song in a strange land"* (Psalm 137:4)? The writer was obviously discouraged and thought it was a bad time for a song, but the reality is we ought to always have a song on our hearts we can lift to God.

Do you remember two men in the early church who had been thrown into a jail in Philippi? At midnight they were singing and praising God. Paul and Silas had learned the value of a song while in tough times. Later that night, God not only opened the gates to the prison, but also to the heart of that Philippian jailor! What a great God! A God that is worthy of our praise all the time, not only in the good times.

If we are not careful, we each can focus on the bad things that are happening around us, or to us, and we can totally miss the good things our God has done and is doing. Take a moment today to sing a little for your God. He is absolutely worthy of our praise, and there are many things I am sure you can be thankful for today. A friend of mine is battling cancer as I write this. I constantly hear her say how thankful she is for all the blessings she has. There is only one way she can make this statement ... God is still God! When we focus our attention on our problems, and ourselves we miss the opportunity to have a godly song in our heart.

I realize today as you read this, you may be facing some very difficult times just ahead of you. I want to encourage you to look to your Heavenly Father and break out in a song of praise today. All around the world today we are seeing people who are in despair; thinking there is no hope. If we believers stop praising God in the challenging times, how will they ever know of the hope we have in our relationship with God? We must sing! It is not an option! Be encouraged today to "pick up your harp" (those Israelites in bondage had hung their on the tree limbs) and play a song to your wonderful God today! He is worthy of the praise, and it will lift your spirit as well when you praise Him. There is a world without hope that needs to hear your song of hope today. If you are having trouble coming up with a song, read your Bible ... it's full of them!

"When you don't know what else to do ... try singing." – Numbers 21:17

Confidence in God – April 23

"And when he was in affliction, he besought the LORD his God, and humbled himself greatly before the God of his fathers, and prayed unto Him: and he was entreated of him, and heard his supplication, and brought him again to Jerusalem into his kingdom. Then Manasseh knew that the LORD He was God" (II Chronicles 33:12-13).

The beginning of this chapter says Manasseh did evil in the sight of God; so these verses caught my attention. In these two verses, the Bible speaks of Manasseh turning back to God, and God taking care of him. Have you ever felt you had sinned against God so many times, or so badly He would never be willing to forgive you? Manasseh might have felt that way, but he did something each of us needs to do on a regular basis. Verse twelve says Manasseh *"humbled himself greatly before the God of his fathers."* When was the last time you humbled yourself greatly before God? Most of us don't have time to humble ourselves greatly. Most of us are too proud to humble ourselves greatly.

I believe we will never see the power of God made evident in our lives until we humble ourselves greatly. I do not mean talking about it … I'm talking about actually doing it. I remember in college during a testimony time hearing a girl say she thanked God for her humility. I almost laughed out loud! When someone feels a need to tell you how humble they are, they typically are not very humble! Don't talk about being humble, practice it today. Go to God with a humble heart and admit your sin. You have sinned … He knows all about it … don't try to explain it away; accept responsibility for it, and forsake it! Go to God with a humble heart and admit you don't have all the answers to the problems facing you. Yield your heart to His and ask for His incredible power to stand in your place! Go to God humbly and trust Him for the provision of your needs. We waste too much time worrying and fretting about how we will meet the needs we have, when in reality, we simply need to humble ourselves before Him and let Him show Himself strong.

After Manasseh made a mess of his life doing it "his way," he turned to the God of his fathers and found forgiveness, and help. That same God is alive and well today and is ready to help you … if you will humbly turn to Him. I thank God for his grace and mercy! I am grateful He does not give me what I deserve, but mercy instead!

"Go as far as you can, then wait on God." – Unknown

Someone's Watching You – April 24

Have you ever had the feeling someone is watching you? I have felt that way a number of times when I am walking through a crowded area. I am sure there have been times when someone was watching you that you did not know about. It can be a weird thing if you think about it, but it can also be a wonderful thing in the case of these verses in Psalm 139. The psalmist wrote, *"O LORD, Thou hast searched me, and known me. Thou knowest my downsitting and mine uprising, Thou understandest my thought afar off. Thou compassest my path and my lying down, and art acquainted with all my ways. For there is not a word in my tongue, but, lo, O LORD, Thou knowest it altogether"* (Psalm 139:1-4).

In one way it is a blessing to know we are never outside the care of our God. What a comfort to know whatever stress I am going to face today … my God is with me and offers help. What a blessing to know when I am lacking in strength, I have a God Who is well able to handle whatever supposedly impossible thing I am facing. I am thankful He even helped me when I read my Bible this morning to understand the truths He had for me there. I am grateful when I pray to Him, pouring out my heart to Him, His Holy Spirit is able to take the language of my heart that I cannot put into words, to the very throne of God! What a blessing to know that He is closer than any brother could be.

In another way, it can be very convicting to think that God knows me so intimately. We all have become very proficient in putting on our spiritual masks so others cannot see the "real" us. There are no masks when we go to our Heavenly Father. He knows, not only what we show Him, but He also knows the thoughts and intents of our heart. He sees all the filth we deal with every day in our own sinfulness. Let's consider this question … if God knows us this intimately, why do we even consider trying to hide our sin, or rationalize it? He already knows what is there … why not simply confess and genuinely forsake it?

I am thankful for this relationship with my Heavenly Father. With this knowledge of how well He knows me, I want to live in a way that will please Him more and more every day. I want to make this day one that will honor Him and be pleasing in His sight. I want to walk in a way that will please my Heavenly Father and demonstrate to the unsaved world that He has made a difference in my life!

"I am not satisfied with me – I am satisfied with God." – Unknown

God Turned the Light On – April 25

There is nothing worse than walking into a room you are unfamiliar with and not knowing where the light is. Recently, we stayed in a Prophet's Chamber (like a hotel room in a church) where we had never stayed before. The church did a wonderful job of converting a couple of rooms in a previous wing of their church into this nice area for visiting pastors and missionaries to stay. One night while we were there, I needed to adjust the temperature in the room. The controls for that were in one of the other rooms the church still used for classrooms for Sunday School. The Pastor had shown me where the controls were when he first showed us our room. The problem was, when I went to change the controls, it was dark, and I could not remember where the light was. I was really thankful there were no video cameras to capture my adventure. I'm sure we could have won something for a funny video!

We all were in darkness … stumbling around in our sin trying to find the switch for the light we needed for our souls. We Gentiles were of all men without hope. The Jews had been given the responsibility of carrying the light through the early history of mankind. They were to take that light to the whole world. God stepped in to provide what man could not do. Here's what the Bible says about the time Jesus was born … *"A Light to lighten the Gentiles, and the glory of Thy people Israel"* (Luke 2:32). God turned on the Light for the world! As we groped about in our lives, searching for something with eternal meaning that would satisfy the longing of our soul, God provided exactly what we needed; Jesus Christ!

I am so thankful today for two things: First, I am thankful God provided the only Light that would conquer the darkness of our sin. Let me be absolutely clear. In a day when we are being told the only important thing is to believe in a "higher power" (whichever higher power you want to believe is okay … as long as you believe in one), I want to tell you clearly there is only ONE Light. That Light is Jesus Christ … THE Redeemer … THE Way … Truth … Life – there is no other light! The second thing I am thankful for is, Jesus came here to the earth for me! I know He came for the whole world, but He actually came to rescue me from my sin! MY sins are forgiven by the blood of Jesus Christ! My debt is paid in full! I have a Savior, Who has taken away the sin of the world, including mine!

"Faith is the strength by which a shattered world shall emerge into the light." – Helen Keller

124

No More Important Than a Rock – April 26

We often flatter ourselves by thinking God somehow needs us. The reality is that God is able to do whatever He likes with or without us. The truth is God has accomplished many things in my life in spite of me, not because of me. I can recall many times when I asked God to give me something, or do something that later I realized was exactly the opposite of what I actually needed. God is so good to us to give us what He thinks is best. John the Baptist said it this way: *"Bring forth therefore fruits worthy of repentance, and begin not to say within yourselves, 'We have Abraham to our father:' for I say unto you, 'That God is able of these stones to raise up children unto Abraham'"* (Luke 3:8).

The Jews of John the Baptist's time were so confident in their heritage they considered themselves something special when compared to the rest of the people on the earth. I would love to look down on them, but I am guilty of the same thing most days. I like to think my opinions are the only correct ones. I also think everyone ought to like the same things I like; rout for the same teams I like; enjoy the same kinds of food I enjoy; and generally allow the world to revolve around me. I can't understand why the rest of you won't get with the program!

The bottom line is God was and is completely capable of choosing any people group to carry His message to the lost world. I have found others don't need to agree with me to receive God's blessings. I have also learned if I refuse to serve God, He will use others to serve Him totally without my help, or advice! It amazes me God can use people who think differently than me, but He does. The most important thing I learn from this passage is that I want to be used of God more than anything. I don't want God to give that blessing to a rock. It is not something I like to admit, but I realize God is still not dependent upon me today to do anything.

God can reach the lost world any way He desires, but I praise God, He has chosen to allow me to be a part of the process of reaching this world for Him! What a great honor we have today to be a part of His Divine plan for this world! As you finish reading this today, thank God along with me that even though He does not need us, He has chosen to use us. What a great privilege to serve the God of eternity past and future! There is no greater joy than to stand for God where we go today!

"God can do extraordinary things with ordinary people." – Ted Camp

My Hiding Place – April 27

When troubles come and you don't know where to turn ... there is a God in Heaven. The psalmist said, *"I cried unto Thee, O LORD: I said, 'Thou art my Refuge and my Portion in the land of the living'"* (Psalm 142:5). What a comfort to know we can call upon the Lord. According to this verse, He is a place of refuge. Literally this means God is a hiding place for the believer. He is a shelter in the middle of the storms of life. He is also described as our portion. This has the idea of being our inheritance. God provides not only a place of shelter in troubled times, but He is our inheritance as well. He will take care of us into the future. God is that welcomed place of peace in the otherwise turbulent world we are living in for the Christian.

This description of what God provides for me is a welcome and comforting thought. I seem to spend far too much time in fear of what "might" happen, when I need to learn to simply trust on this God Who promises to be a refuge for me, as well as my portion for the things that are coming. Fear is a result of a lack of trust. When I am fearful about something, or someone, I am looking in the wrong place. When I allow my focus to move off God, and onto my circumstance or situation, I have begun to live a life that is "faith-less." As easy as it is to say this, it is tough in our daily life to practice it. I want to be a person who fully relies on God to take care of me, both in the area's I am facing today, as well as with the control over things that are going to take place in my future.

As a child, I was blessed to have parents who loved me and were a beautiful picture of the meaning of this verse. I had a father who provided comfort for me when fear seized me. He also provided for my daily needs, so I never had to worry about where our next meal was coming from; or where I would get the clothing I would need to wear for school. In the same way, we should not waste a moment in fear and anxiety as a Christian. We have a Heavenly Father Who is far more capable of providing for our needs than my earthly father was. As a child, I never worried about those things because my dad was taking care of it. As a child of God, I should not worry about these things, because my Heavenly Father is taking care of me. Today, rather than spending a moment in fear or worry, turn to your God and thank Him for taking care of all of your needs today.

"There are always better things ahead than any we leave behind." –
C.S. Lewis

Choose Your Friends Wisely – April 28

There was a familiar statement my parents made to me many times when I was growing up. It went something like this; "Birds of a feather flock together." Another saying I heard many times was, "If everyone else jumps off a bridge, will you jump too?" The idea is the same ... the people you spend time with will heavily influence the way you think and eventually act. It is so important we have good relationships with godly people who will be able to influence our way of thinking. Our way of thinking will eventually result in actions that will determine the success or failure of our lives.

"Whoso keepeth the law is a wise son: But he that is a companion of riotous men shameth his father" (Proverbs 28:7). There are two keys in this verse that really set out the plan for living a successful Christian life: The Word of God; and the right friends. I cannot stress enough the importance of making the Word of God the foundation upon which you build your opinions and convictions. It is not a good idea to allow your friends to build your foundation. God alone is the One to give you the truths to build your life upon. God has the wisdom for all the situations you will face in your life, and He has provided the owner's manual for your life ... the Bible. Don't ever minimize the importance of allowing the Word of God to seep into your heart. Those truths are the ones that will hold you when everything and everyone around you is spinning out of control. Without a firm foundation, other people can easily move us from the truth to a lie without us even knowing what is happening.

The second thing is to find friends who also want to stand on the Word of God as their foundation. There is something about the fellowship of people who are standing with you during the tough times. When I was in High School, we did not have a full-time Youth Pastor, so we took it upon ourselves to serve God and to stand strong on the truths we were being taught. I do thank God for lay leaders who influenced our lives as teenagers. We needed that adult influence for sure. I am also thankful I had Christian friends who encouraged me to stand for Christ in a public school, and not to bend to the pressures of teenage years. God allowed us to be involved in precious ministry opportunities as young people that have held strong all these years. Make the Word of God your foundation and stay in the truths of the Word of God. Then choose the right people to stand with today!

"Begin to be now what you will be hereafter." – William James

People Are Depending on You – April 29

Nothing is quite so convicting as knowing other people's eternal destiny is partly your responsibility. We know none of us can "save" another person … we cannot even save ourselves. What we have is a responsibility to tell others, who have not heard, about the way to Heaven. We must understand most of our lives are spent looking out for ourselves, while ignoring the needs of those around us. We have become a very self-centered people. Today I want you to consider the great responsibility you have to those around you, and encourage you to take your eyes off yourself, and consider the needs of others.

"Where there is no vision, the people perish: but he that keepeth the law, happy is he" (Proverbs 29:18). Simply stated … without someone having a vision, there will be people who perish. Immediately my mind runs to the importance of having a vision for the souls of men/women in sharing the Gospel, but the truth of this verse goes far beyond that. We as believers need to get a glimpse of the things which are most important to our God. We need to get a "heavenly outlook" rather than the one we normally have … simply looking at what we want and need.

I was cutting grass a few days ago and was hurrying to finish. I was so focused on the grass in front of me that I was startled to feel a pain on my face and something striking it. I immediately stopped, but not in time to avoid a stick hanging down from a tree. I was so intent on the grass in front of me, I missed the danger of the stick that scratched my face and caused some pain. I now wear two large scratches on my face as a reminder of my lack of vision.

This is a reminder to me of the danger of becoming so focused on what we are facing that we forget those outside of the love and forgiveness of Christ will suffer the pain and anguish of Hell for eternity! I don't want to lose sight of that today. Interestingly, in this verse it clearly states if we are a people of vision we are also keeping the law. I want to be obedient to the Word of God, and I want to have a vision for the things God wants me to do today. Don't fall prey to the traps of the flesh today and focus on yourself and your desires. Give God first place and live sold out to attaining the vision He has given you to accomplish with your life. We have one life, and God has a plan for us. Use your day to His glory today!

"One person with a belief is equal to a force of ninety-nine who have only interests." – Peter Marshall

The Doctor Is In – April 30

Nobody likes to admit they need a doctor … especially a man. There are times when everyone need to go to the doctor. If you are like me, you will wait until the last minute, when all other options have been exhausted. I must tell you I don't like to go to the doctor; except, when I am really hurting, or in trouble … I'm glad there is a good doctor I can go to for help. A few years ago I had a problem with my heart and had to go to the emergency room for help. After an examination, it was determined I had a possible blockage in my heart, and could have even had a heart attack. Heart problems are common in my family, and I knew this day would eventually come. God blessed me with a very good cardiologist at that time. He began to unfold the situation to me and offer me options. After he gave all the options, I informed him I had prayed for him, and I would trust his judgment and experience to make the right choices for me. You see, when you realize you are sick, you also realize you need the help of those how have spent their life-time studying and practicing to help problems like yours.

In the same way, we must all realize we have a sin problem we do not have the ability to remove. Jesus Christ came into this world to offer forgiveness, and "healing" (as it were) from our sin. However, when He arrived and offered the help, there were many who refused to admit they had a need. This is still a major problem today in this world. Look at this interesting verse from Luke. *"And it came to pass on a certain day, as He was teaching, that there were Pharisees and doctors of the law sitting by, which were come out of every town of Galilee, and Judea, and Jerusalem: and the power of the Lord was present to heal them"* (Luke 5:17). Did you read it carefully? The power of the Lord was available to heal the Pharisees and doctors of the law. You see, these men thought they had the "sin thing" all figured out, and they were clean. The reality was they were in much in need of spiritual healing as all the others who were there who came for physical healing.

Don't be so spiritually stuck-up that you do not realize today at your best, you are simply a sinner saved by grace. There is a great deal of spiritual pride in our churches today. We need to be willing to admit we need Jesus every minute of every day, all day long! Trust Him today!

"God does not bless programs or plans, but God blesses people." – Unknown

MONTH OF
May

What's in a Name? – May 1

I have heard this question before … *"What's in a name?"* or stated a little differently, *"What makes you more important because of your name?"* Names in the past were given with some thought to a character trait of the person to whom it was given. Sometimes the meaning of a name was the goal a parent had in mind for a child for their future. In the case of our God (the God-Head), we find these names revealed the character and the very nature of our God. The names given to our God have been a powerful reminder for me. I hope it reveals some things about God that perhaps you have not considered before.

Paul wrote: *"Let this mind be in you, which was also in Christ Jesus: Who, being in the form of God, thought it not robbery to be equal with God: But made himself of no reputation, and took upon him the form of a servant, and was made in the likeness of men: And being found in fashion as a man, he humbled himself, and became obedient unto death, even the death of the cross. Wherefore God also hath highly exalted him, and **given him a name which is above every name:** That **at the name of Jesus** every **knee should bow,** of things in heaven, and things in earth, and things under the earth; And that **every tongue should confess** that Jesus Christ is Lord, to the glory of God the Father"* (Philippians 2:5-11).

If the study of the names of God becomes an academic study for you, you have missed the point entirely. I would like you to consider a few of these names for our great God, in the hopes they will inspire you. I am hopeful they will bring you comfort. I am hoping the word pictures God has used to describe Himself through these descriptive titles in our Bible will help you to see Him more clearly than ever before. I hope you can use these names to look more directly into the face of your God, and allow Him to look deeply into your soul as well.

One day, every knee will bow and every tongue will confess Jesus is Lord! Every name we will see is true, but none of these names can completely explain the splendor and depth of beauty our God deserves. When you bow your knee to Jesus Christ, you are obeying the desire God has for your life. If you have refused to recognize Jesus is the Son of Almighty God; and He came to die in your place; and He rose from the grave to conquer your sin, you have disrespected God. Bow your knee to him today, while you live in the age of God's grace! You will bow in the future if you refuse today. Praise the NAME of the Lord!

Jehovah-Rohi – The LORD my Shepherd – May 2

"The LORD is my Shepherd; I shall not want. He maketh me to lie down in green pastures: He leadeth me beside the still waters. He restoreth my soul: He leadeth me in the paths of righteousness for His name's sake. Yea, though I walk through the valley of the shadow of death, I will fear no evil: for Thou art with me; Thy rod and Thy staff they comfort me. Thou preparest a table before me in the presence of mine enemies: Thou anointest my head with oil; my cup runneth over. Surely goodness and mercy shall follow me all the days of my life: and I will dwell in the house of the LORD for ever" (Psalm 23).

When I was a little boy, I memorized this chapter. I must be honest and tell you I did not memorize it for any spiritual reason … I won a glow-in-the-dark mold of praying hands. I may not have memorized this chapter for the right reasons, but I am thankful I have hidden this part of the Word of God in my heart. I cannot tell you how many times the simple words from this chapter have passed through my mind. Those glowing praying hands also helped me as a young boy growing up to realize my Shepherd was always close.

Like sheep, we often are not paying much attention to the dangers around us. We simply are concerned about satisfying our own appetites. We want safety. We want to know we can live comfortably. We want to know our opinion is thought of as something important. We want to make sure the things we prefer are what others will do for us. We are very selfish people as a general rule. It is a good thing *"The LORD is my Shepherd."*

This is good for multiple reasons. First, it is good *"The LORD is my Shepherd"* because He never leaves me or forsakes me! He never takes vacation. My warranty on salvation never runs out! The company I got my salvation never moves or closes down! *"The LORD my Shepherd"* is also far more powerful than any enemy who might come against me! My Shepherd can defeat any trivial problem I have … He is bigger than any challenge that faces me. Even death does not scare my Shepherd … He conquered that at the empty tomb!

I could go on and on, but I just want to close by telling you *"The LORD is my Shepherd."* You see, it is very personal. I know He could be your Shepherd too, but I know He is mine. There are many troubles outside my door, and I will trust Him to guide and guard me today!

Jehovah-Shammah – The LORD Who is Present – May 3

*"This is the land which ye shall divide by lot unto the tribes of Israel for inheritance, and these are their portions, saith the Lord GOD. And these are the goings out of the city on the north side, four thousand and five hundred measures. And the gates of the city shall be after the names of the tribes of Israel: three gates northward; one gate of Reuben, one gate of Judah, one gate of Levi. And at the east side four thousand and five hundred: and three gates; and one gate of Joseph, one gate of Benjamin, one gate of Dan. And at the south side four thousand and five hundred measures: and three gates; one gate of Simeon, one gate of Issachar, one gate of Zebulun. At the west side four thousand and five hundred, with their three gates; one gate of Gad, one gate of Asher, one gate of Naphtali. It was round about eighteen thousand measures: and the name of the city from that day shall be, **The LORD is there**"* (Ezekiel 48:29-35).

The book of Ezekiel ends with these verses. This chapter describes the division of the land for Israel. These last verses describe the names for each of the gates in the city. The last phrase in the last verse of the book of Ezekiel is *"Jehovah-Shammah"* – *"The LORD is there."* This is a good title for each of us to memorize and repeat throughout our day today and our lives for the future. *"The LORD is there!"*

If you are headed into a challenging area of life you have never been in before; *"The LORD is there."* Remember, He is the One Who left Heaven with the task of living in a sin-cursed earth without sin. He is the One Who walked the hill of Calvary and died in the midst of cursing and mocking and still asked for forgiveness for His accusers. He is the One Who rose from the dead ... need I say more? I know some who are reading this are facing challenges like never before in life ... trust that *"The LORD is there."* He can handle whatever challenge you are facing today.

If you are facing a crisis you have never faced before; *"The LORD is there."* There are points in each of our lives when we are on the edge of disaster. These times are opportunities for each of us to turn to *"The LORD Who is there."* Daniel, Peter, David, Moses and multitudes of others turned to Him in their crises and He was true to this title. *"The LORD is there."* If you are facing temptation you think will overwhelm you; *"The LORD is there."* Remember, Jesus was tempted in all points like we are, but He did not sin. Turn to Him for strength today. Don't try to win on your own! What a joy today to know no matter where we go ... no matter what we face today, *"The LORD is there!"* Praise God!

Jehovah-Rapha – The LORD that Healeth – May 4

"And the people murmured against Moses, saying, What shall we drink? And he cried unto the LORD; and the LORD shewed him a tree, which when he had cast into the waters, the waters were made sweet: there he made for them a statute and an ordinance, and there he proved them, And said, If thou wilt diligently hearken to the voice of the LORD thy God, and wilt do that which is right in his sight, and wilt give ear to his commandments, and keep all his statutes, I will put none of these diseases upon thee, which I have brought upon the Egyptians: for I am the LORD that healeth thee" (Exodus 15:24-26).

Is there a little "bitter creek" running through your heart today? Jehovah-Rapha, *"the LORD that Healeth"* is available for you today! This is a good day to get rid of bitterness and allow the Lord to heal your soul. When the Israelites came to these bitter waters, they did not know what to do. When you have bitterness you might try all kinds of positive thinking and tricks to rid your heart of it, but only *"the LORD that Healeth"* can remove it from your heart.

There are many illnesses which are not physical that need the healing touch of *"the LORD that Healeth."* If you are plagued by doubt and fear, you need to run to *"the LORD that Healeth."* Our Lord that heals is well able to take care of anything you will face today or in the future. Rest in the arms of *"the LORD that Healeth"* today. He is able to take you through every challenging situation you will face in the future. Trust Him for everything you will need today and tomorrow.

If you have a sin that has been showing up wherever you go, don't try to make excuses, take it to *"the LORD that Healeth."* There is no sense in asking friends to help you to heal that sin; they cannot. It is a waste of time to "try harder" to stop that sin; you cannot. The thing to do is to go to *"the LORD that Healeth;"* He can take care of you. He is the same One Who died to pay the ultimate price for your sin! What a great Savior we serve today!

There are many sin-sick souls that are searching for the prescription for sin. They are searching the horoscopes, physicians, psychiatrists, and even preachers. There is no medicine, no antidote, no help apart from *"the LORD that Healeth."* These folks may be depending on you to introduce them to *"the LORD that Healeth."* Don't be selfish and hold the good news to yourself. As the Lord has healed you, He is also waiting to heal them. What a great God you have ... tell others about His healing power today!

Jehovah-Tsidkenu – The LORD our Righteousness – May 5

"'Behold, the days come,' saith the LORD, 'that I will raise unto David a Righteous Branch, and a King shall reign and prosper, and shall execute judgment and justice in the earth. In His days Judah shall be saved, and Israel shall dwell safely: and this is His name whereby He shall be called, **THE LORD OUR RIGHTEOUSNESS**" (Jeremiah 23:5-6).

What sets Christians apart from all other religions in the world? We have *"THE LORD OUR RIGHTEOUSNESS."* Most other religions are focused on many becoming righteous in his or her own works. Our faith is not founded on what we can do, but on what our Savior has done! Thank God the righteousness we have is not what we can build up and display. Our righteousness is not our own, but His! It is Jesus Christ we depend upon to be *"THE LORD OUR RIGHTEOUSNESS."*

The Apostle Paul wrote it this way: *"Not by works of righteousness which we have done, but according to his mercy he saved us, by the washing of regeneration, and renewing of the Holy Ghost"* (Titus 3:5). I am sure of Heaven today because I am not trusting in any "man-made" religion to get me there. I am not depending on my own ability to live a righteous life ... I know that isn't possible! I have tried and failed many times to live on my own righteousness. I try every day to live just one day without sin ... and then I step outside my bedroom, and all is lost!

What a great joy it is to know *"THE LORD OUR RIGHTEOUSNESS!"* The struggle to earn Heaven with my own works is over for me. Now I want to surrender to *"THE LORD OUR RIGHTEOUSNESS"* daily so He can help me to overcome my own flesh with its sinful desires and practices. Now I have freedom to rest in Jesus, but to show my good works to glorify Him in Heaven (Matthew 5:16). Now I have freedom to rest in His saving grace while working to draw as many others to Him as possible.

Do you realize the world around us is struggling to find the peace I just described? They have tried different religions and found none to be perfect (not even your own church). They have tried riches to give that peace, and nothing they can buy satisfies for very long. They have tried fame, but it quickly fades and can turn back on them. They are trying drugs, sex, work, cars, houses, clothing, and on and on the list could go. None of these offers what *"THE LORD OUR RIGHTEOUSNESS"* offers! Let me encourage you to live your life to please Him. The only way the world is going to see Him today is through the change He has made in you.

Jehovah-Jireh – The LORD will provide – May 6

*"And Abraham took the wood of the burnt offering, and laid it upon Isaac his son; and he took the fire in his hand, and a knife; and they went both of them together. And Isaac spake unto Abraham his father, and said, 'My father:' and he said, 'Here am I, my son.' And he said, 'Behold the fire and the wood: but where is the lamb for a burnt offering?' And Abraham said, 'My son, God will provide himself a lamb for a burnt offering:' so they went both of them together. And they came to the place which God had told him of; and Abraham built an altar there, and laid the wood in order, and bound Isaac his son, and laid him on the altar upon the wood. And Abraham stretched forth his hand, and took the knife to slay his son. And the angel of the LORD called unto him out of heaven, and said, 'Abraham, Abraham:' and he said, 'Here am I.' And he said, 'Lay not thine hand upon the lad, neither do thou any thing unto him: for now I know that thou fearest God, seeing thou hast not withheld thy son, thine only son from me.' And Abraham lifted up his eyes, and looked, and behold behind him a ram caught in a thicket by his horns: and Abraham went and took the ram, and offered him up for a burnt offering in the stead of his son. And Abraham called the name of that place **Jehovah-Jireh**: as it is said to this day, In the mount of the LORD it shall be seen"* (Genesis 22:6-14).

Are you close to a place in your life where you think there is no escape? Look around, *"The LORD will provide."* I want you to think about something. If you are walking in the center of the will of God, there are going to be times when there is no way to turn but up! There is no way God can use a servant who is not totally dependent on Him! We love to be self-sufficient people, but that is not the key to successfully walking with God!

We often focus on Abraham and Isaac in this story, but I want you to look at what the angel said to Abraham. He said, *"… now I know that thou fearest God."* To be greatly used of God, a person must surrender everything fully to God. I don't believe God fully uses a person until He has fully broken them. We serve *"The LORD Who will provide."* The problem is we are uneasy with going to places, and doing things we have trouble doing. Have you obeyed God to your Mt. Moriah yet? Some have … and all who have also know *"The LORD will provide."* Those who have not come to a place where they must have God or they will fail will have a limited ministry until that time comes. Praise God! The same God on Mt. Moriah is ahead of you today, waiting to prove Himself all-sufficient for you!

Jehovah-Nissi – The LORD our Banner – May 7

*"And the LORD said unto Moses, Write this for a memorial in a book, and rehearse it in the ears of Joshua: for I will utterly put out the remembrance of Amalek from under heaven. And Moses built an altar, and called the name of it **Jehovah-Nissi**: For he said, Because the LORD hath sworn that the LORD will have war with Amalek from generation to generation"* (Exodus 17:14-16).

This title, *"The LORD our Banner,"* is a picture of the banner that each country carried into war. Here in America we have a very special song entitled, *"The Star Spangled Banner."* It is a song about our *"banner,"* the American flag. It was a symbol to Francis Scott Key when he saw it still flying, that America had not been defeated by the bombardment that had been hailed upon it. When Moses used the term, Jehovah-Nissi (*"The LORD our Banner"*), he was telling Joshua and the rest of Israel the Lord was still in control, and the Lord would bring the victory.

I am sure you have faced, or are facing challenges you may feel are more than you can handle. I am sure there are days, and moments when you feel defeat is inevitable. I am sure as you look around your country you wonder if anyone will stand for Christ again. Please take heart … look up to *"The LORD our Banner."* He has not changed! He has not moved! He is not dead! It is God Who is our Banner, and nothing this world can do or say will change the fact He is God!

One of the main problems I see in myself and other believers today is, we are placing far too much emphasis on what we can do. We are thinking too much about what others can do to us. When do we stop to think about what our God can do? When do we tell Him we are completely trusting in Him for the victories in our lives and nations? When do we stop worrying and fretting and trying to solve all the problems on our own and in our own power?

Make no mistake about it … *"The LORD is our Banner!"* Regardless of how many bombs the world may launch at our God, He is still in the same place of authority He was before they started the attacks. God's power is in no way affected by the assaults of our world against Him! God is God whether the world thinks so or not! God's Word is true regardless of how many "educated people" agree He is or not! He is Jehovah-Nissi–*"The LORD our Banner."* Hold Him high today, and allow Him to be the standard you live by! He will lead to victory!

137

Jehovah-Shalom – The LORD our Peace – May 8

*"And when Gideon perceived that he was an angel of the LORD, Gideon said, Alas, O Lord GOD! for because I have seen an angel of the LORD face to face. And the LORD said unto him, Peace be unto thee; fear not: thou shalt not die. Then Gideon built an altar there unto the LORD, and called it **Jehovah-Shalom**: unto this day it is yet in Ophrah of the Abiezrites"* (Judges 6:22-24).

There is a part of an old song that says, *"Peace, peace, wonderful peace. Coming down from the Father above ... sweep over my spirit forever I pray, in fathomless billows of love."* We are living in a world that is in a desperate search for peace. Men have searched many different places to find peace. There was a time when it was thought there would be peace if we just had enough money. Others thought peace could be found if there was a huge amount of strength gained. It doesn't take long for this kind of peace to show itself as very temporary. A down-turn in the economy ... the word, cancer ... a threat from a bully ... that kind of peace is not a lasting peace.

There is a Savior Who came to us bringing everlasting peace with Him. He is Jesus, Jehovah-Shalom; *"The LORD our Peace!"* While so many search for world peace; peace in their workplace; peace in their school; peace at home ... the reality is without *"The LORD our Peace"* there will be no lasting peace. Others have and will mock true Christianity, but all must admire the peace believers have shown throughout the history of man that Christians have had in difficult situations. Paul and Silas were singing in the bowels of the prison at midnight because they had this peace. Horatio Spafford was able to write the words to the famous hymn, It is Well With My Soul after losing four of his daughters in an accident at sea.

Real peace comes from knowing Jesus Christ – He is *"The LORD our Peace."* When facing trouble; turn to Jesus. When a family member steps out of this life and into Heaven; hold firmly to the hand of Christ. When challenges present themselves to you, and you think there is no way of escape; Jesus holds the key to peace. If you are facing life without lasting peace in your heart, you need to get to know *"The LORD our Peace."* I have met Him ... I have trusted Him ... everything I have written today about Him is absolute truth from the pages of the Bible, but I have found them to be true myself. If you don't know Him today, please take a moment and ask me about Him. I would love to introduce Him to you! He can be your peace in the middle of the storms life brings you.

Jehovah-Sabbaoth – The LORD of Hosts – May 9

*"In the year that king Uzziah died I saw also the Lord sitting upon a throne, high and lifted up, and his train filled the temple. Above it stood the seraphims: each one had six wings; with twain he covered his face, and with twain he covered his feet, and with twain he did fly. And one cried unto another, and said, 'Holy, holy, holy, is **the LORD of hosts**: the whole earth is full of his glory'"* (Isaiah 6:1-3).

Can you imagine the splendor of what Isaiah saw in this vision? He got a peek into the glory of Heaven. With all the incredible things about Heaven we normally talk about, Isaiah was totally consumed with Jehovah-Sabbaoth, *"The LORD of Hosts."* There were angels who sang/sing constantly, *"Holy ... Holy ... Holy"* because they are so taken by the presence of our God! He really is *"The LORD of Hosts!"* The angels cannot help themselves, but must constantly give praise to *"The LORD of Hosts."*

The LORD has revealed His power and authority to us here on the earth, but make no mistake about it; the angels of Heaven (the Host) are well aware of His power and glory as well. It is a shame, but there were one-third of the angels who believed a lie, and like many in our world today, were deceived by Lucifer (the Devil). Martin Luther wrote a powerful hymn in the 1500's that described this battle well. Look carefully at these powerful words. Also, look for the title we are talking about today.

A Mighty Fortress is our God, a bulwark never failing: Our Helper He, amid the flood of mortal ills prevailing. For still our ancient foe doth seek to work us woe; his craft and power are great, and armed with cruel hate, on earth is not his equal.

Did we in our own strength confide, our striving would be losing; were not the right Man on our side, the man of God's own choosing. Dost ask Who that might be? Christ Jesus, it is He; LORD Sabbaoth His name, from age to age the same, and He must win the battle."

God sent the defeating blow to the cause of the Devil when Jesus Christ came to this earth and died as a perfect payment for our sin. The final victory was gained at the empty tomb when Christ rose from the dead. If you had any doubt about whether Jesus is more powerful than the Devil, look to the empty tomb. He truly is *"The LORD of Hosts!"* One day, every knee will bow to Him and every tongue confess He is Lord ... including the Devil himself.

El-Elyon – The Most High God – May 10

*"And the king of Sodom went out to meet him after his return from the slaughter of Chedorlaomer, and of the kings that were with him, at the valley of Shaveh, which is the king's dale. And Melchizedek king of Salem brought forth bread and wine: and he was the priest of **the most high God**. And he blessed him, and said, 'Blessed be Abram of **the most high God**, possessor of heaven and earth: And blessed be **the most high God**, which hath delivered thine enemies into thy hand. And he gave him tithes of all'"* (Genesis 14:17-20).

"The Most High God" is a title only God can rightfully claim as His. What an incredible thought it is for me to know Him personally! He is my God. He is my *"Most High God."* Yes, the God Who spoke this universe and our world into existence is the God I pray to every day. He is the One Who wrote the Bible I have chosen to live by, and He is My Heavenly Father! What a joy to personally know this Source of great power!

When the cares of the world seem to pile up against you, turn to *"The Most High God,"* He has encouraged you to cast your cares on Him. He will be able to handle those burdens for you if you will simply lay them at His feet. So much of life involves really difficult cares and burdens. We try everything we know to lift the burden, but there is only one Who will ultimately offer the peace we need ... laying those cares/burdens at the throne of *"The Most High God."*

When challenges mount which are far beyond your power to solve, turn to *"The Most High God,"* He is well able to handle it. Remember, He is the One Who parted the Red Sea; provided manna for 14,600 days for over 2 million Jews who wandered through the wilderness. He is the same God that rained down fire from Heaven and consumed Elijah's sacrifice; licking up the water in the ditch around it. I could go on and on, but the reality is He can surely take care of the things you and I will need for this and every day.

When you must make a decision that is confusing you, and clarity is not coming; turn to *"The Most High God"* for guidance and instruction. He offers us His wisdom on the pages of our Bible. Take the time to study the Book He has given us for guidance, and then base your actions on the truths you find written in it.

Grab onto the hand of *"The Most High God"* today! He will not fail you!

El-Roi – The Strong One Who sees – May 11

*"And she called the name of the LORD that spake unto her, Thou **God seest me**: for she said, Have I also here looked after him that seeth me"* (Genesis 16:13).

Have you ever had the feeling you were being watched? I have felt that way, and then noticed someone watching me. Well, if you have felt like someone is watching you, it might be because God has His eye on what you are doing and what is happening to you. Have you ever felt no one is watching you? Have you felt like you are all alone in this world, without any help coming from anywhere? Again, let me assure you that the Creator of this world has His eye on you.

This title, *"Strong One Who Sees"* is none other than the Creator of the world, our God! *"For who hath despised the day of small things? for they shall rejoice, and shall see the plummet in the hand of Zerubbabel with those seven; they are **the eyes of the LORD, which run to and fro through the whole earth"*** (Zechariah 4:10). God is concerned about you, and He has His eye on you wherever you might be today, or wherever you might be going tomorrow.

I am happy to know I am never far from my Heavenly Father. Even if I chose to turn my back on Him and wander outside of His will, the *"Strong One Who Sees"* is still watching out for me, and is still watching for me to turn back to Him. Just like the father of the younger son in Luke 15, I believe when a child of God turns and leaves for the far country, God stands on the back porch of Heaven (figuratively speaking) and looks to the place where He last saw us ... waiting for us to return.

Recently friends of ours lost their fourteen year old daughter. As their grief seemed insurmountable, God rejoiced at His daughter's entrance into Heaven. One thing is for sure, God was not surprised by her "unexpected" death. We were shocked, but God has had His eye on her ever since she was conceived in the womb of her mother! He carefully guided her entire life, and He knew when she would step into Heaven. She did not enter one minute too soon, or too late!

Today as you are tempted to worry and fret about the things that are unknown in front of you ... slip your hand into the hand of God and be assured He is watching out for you. He knows what you are facing, even though He might be the only One Who knows. He is going to be with you every step of the way today! Trust the *"Strong One Who Sees."*

El-Shaddai – Almighty God – May 12

*"And when Abram was ninety years old and nine, the LORD appeared to Abram, and said unto him, I am the **Almighty God**; walk before me, and be thou perfect"* (Genesis 17:1).

*"He that dwelleth in the secret place of the most High shall abide under the shadow of the **Almighty**. I will say of the **LORD**, He is my refuge and my fortress: my God; in him will I trust. Surely He shall deliver thee from the snare of the fowler, and from the noisome pestilence. He shall cover thee with His feathers, and under His wings shalt thou trust: His truth shall be thy shield and buckler. Thou shalt not be afraid for the terror by night; nor for the arrow that flieth by day; Nor for the pestilence that walketh in darkness; nor for the destruction that wasteth at noonday"* (Psalm 91:1-6).

Do not focus so much on the things going on around you in this world that you forget you serve El-Shaddai! He is *"Almighty God,"* and there is none other Who can compare or compete with Him! He is the God that gave Abram and Sarah a child when there was no humanly way possible for that to happen. He is the *"Almighty God"* that is our Refuge and Fortress. He is our *"Almighty God"* Who hides us under His wings for safety and protection! Run to Him in your times of fear and doubt. Run to Him when the needs are far greater than the strength to meet those needs.

I sense a growing fear in our hearts as Christians today as we see the things that are happening around us. Don't fear! We serve El-Shaddai! Our Heavenly Father is *"Almighty God!"* Now, if God is not your Heavenly Father, you have reason to fear. If you are reading this and you do not know for sure (100%) you are going to Heaven when you die this *"Almighty God"* has made a way for you to be with Him in Heaven in the future. He offers it to us as a free gift.

If you ever doubted God in Heaven is *"Almighty God,"* simply look at the empty tomb Jesus left behind. Jesus paid what was an impossible debt for us to pay for our sin. He lived a perfect life, and died a sinner's death (not His own, but ours), and He conquered the grave when He rose from the dead! That is an *"Almighty God!"*

This world cannot defeat Him! Those loud critics cannot silence what He can do in a human soul! Those who claim He is not real look more and more foolish the harder they try to prove He does not exist! God is Almighty! He can handle whatever you will face today. Turn your troubles over to Him and let Him prove that He is *"Almighty God"* today!

El-Olam – Everlasting God – May 13

"Hast thou not known? hast thou not heard, that the **Everlasting God**, *the LORD, the Creator of the ends of the earth, fainteth not, neither is weary? there is no searching of His understanding. He giveth power to the faint; and to them that have no might He increaseth strength. Even the youths shall faint and be weary, and the young men shall utterly fall: But they that wait upon the **LORD** shall renew their strength; they shall mount up with wings as eagles; they shall run, and not be weary; and they shall walk, and not faint"* (Isaiah 40:28-31).

What a powerful title for our God. He is not a god like other people worship, one they have made with their own hands. He is the *"Everlasting God!"* He is not a god who had a beginning, and He is not a god who will have an ending. He is the *"Everlasting God!"* He is not a god that will one day be broken and need repairs. He is the *"Everlasting God!"* He is not a god that needs to be woken from a sleep, or has gone on vacation, or needs to hear shouting and crazy behavior until He will come to us. He is the *"Everlasting God!"* Unlike the prophets of Baal, we can call on our God and He is totally aware of everything we need, and He has known it for all eternity past. He is the *"Everlasting God!"*

Isaiah describes us very well in the verses above. When we are in our youth, we have the feeling we can run all day. I mean, we think there is nothing we will need help with ... we are well able to handle life on our own. I love verse 30 when it says *"Even the youths shall faint and be weary, and the young men shall utterly fall."* Praise God, He is an *"Everlasting God"* and He will never need "re-charging." What an incredible thought! When we are young, we think there is nothing we cannot handle ... as we grow older, we begin to see the reality that we have needed Him all along, and we feel we need Him even more in these years.

We all need Him all the time for everything! Don't try to work through your problems today without the help of our *"Everlasting God."* How foolish it would be to try to manipulate situations, and arrange resources without first consulting the *"Everlasting God."* When we were younger we often took the situation in our own hands, and did the best we could and were satisfied with the results. As we grow older, we realize if God does not step in and help, no matter what we do, it will not be enough. What a blessing to know the *"Everlasting God"* personally! He is my Father! He is my Guide ... Guard ... Everything! I love Him so much!

None Else – May 14

*"Tell ye, and bring them near; yea, let them take counsel together: Who hath declared this from ancient time? Who hath told it from that time? have not I the LORD? and there is no God else beside Me; a just God and a Savior; there is none beside Me. Look unto Me, and be ye saved, all the ends of the earth: for I am God, and there is **none else**. I have sworn by Myself, the word is gone out of My mouth in righteousness, and shall not return, That unto Me every knee shall bow, every tongue shall swear. Surely, shall one say, in the LORD have I righteousness and strength: even to Him shall men come; and all that are incensed against Him shall be ashamed"* (Isaiah 45:21-24).

We have studied the different names for our God. What did that study accomplish? Was the purpose of the study simply to increase your knowledge? Was the value of the study simply to educate those who read them? The obvious answer to these questions is these are not the reasons for the study.

Isaiah took two chapters in his book of prophesy to explain the supremacy of God over all other idols/gods. He very clearly describes a man making an idol from a tree. Isaiah pointed out the man cut down the tree, and used part of it to burn to cook his food and then took other parts of the tree to set up in his home as an idol. How foolish can a person be? Let's be sure we don't do this same thing with this study of the names of God. We did not study these different qualities of God for wisdoms sake alone.

I am hopeful our study of the names of God has driven each of us to a deeper conviction of the place God deserves on the throne of our heart. As these verses from Isaiah 45 describe, there is no god … there is no person walking on earth … there is no religion … there is no earthly leader compared to God Himself! In a comparison with God, there is *"none else!"* Just as I wrote previously from Philippians 2, Isaiah confirmed every knee will bow and every tongue confesses one day that God is the only God!

I hope you will bow our knee today to His desires for your life. God has a perfect path for you to follow, but He gives you the freedom to choose whether to walk in it or to follow your own way. Choose God's way today! While on that path, use your words to draw others to the Savior! He is the only hope of the world. There is *"none else!"* I am hopeful I will do exactly this as I go on my way today. What a great God we serve!

Don't Be Afraid – Stay in the Boat – May 15

Life seems to have more stormy days than easy ones. Finances are tighter today than in the past. More people are getting cancer or some other incurable disease than I ever remember in the past. Churches attendance seems to be generally decreasing, or the stand for the Word of God is decreasing (in many). We are hearing of draughts and earthquakes and tsunamis and climate change. Families are breaking down even farther than we expected. I'm not just talking about single parent families (although they seem to be on the rise with no hope of change), but I'm speaking about families that live in the same physical dwelling, but don't interact or connect at all. It seems like we are always in the middle of some kind of storm in life.

The disciples found themselves in the middle of a literal storm on their way across the Sea of Galilee to Capernaum. While fighting for their lives (or feeling like they were fighting for their lives), Jesus walked to them on the water. They were afraid ... they were undoubtedly bailing water out of the ship ... they were sweating, and beginning to feel there was no hope of survival when "*... He saith unto them, 'It is I; be not afraid'*" (John 6:20). What a phrase for us to hold onto today ... '*It is I; be not afraid.*' He is still alive and in control today. He can still calm the storms of your life. He can still speak a word and the ship will calm under you. He is still as much God today as He was when walking on the water to these men in the ship.

As I always try to do with these devotionals ... let's get this story to the place it touches us personally today. Here are a few simple lessons for us from this story. There was no way this storm the disciples found themselves in was going to destroy them. God had plans for these simple men, and dying in a ship on the sea was not in the plan. God has a plan for your life. Understand nothing can touch you or your life that has not passed by His stamp of approval. Understanding that will allow us to stop complaining, and start looking for the good in God's plan ... even in the middle of the storm.

The last thing I will leave you with today is this thought ... with Jesus in the ship there is peace (regardless of where you find yourself) ... without Jesus there is fear and trembling. Rather than try to launch out today into whatever you are planning to do without the stamp of approval of Jesus, why not stop now and ask Him for wisdom for the steps you will take today. In the center of the will of God there is peace and contentment. Outside His will there is nothing but turmoil and discontentment. Stay in His boat!

Mono-mania – May 16

A good friend of mine introduced me to this word about thirty years ago, and I have not gotten it out of my mind ever since. By the way, he mentioned this phrase to me in a very casual conversation, and God has used that simple conversation to concrete this idea into my heart for all these years. The words you will use today could have that kind of impact on someone else today. You might say the words in passing, but ask God to help you carefully choose your words to leave a deep impression on someone. Our words can be used negatively as well and have an equally damaging effect on someone.

The word "*mono-mania*" (mono = one thing / mania = crazy about, or consumed with) is a term that implies being crazy about, or consumed with one thing. When men brought a woman caught in the very act of adultery before Jesus hoping for some condemning words, they got a far different response from Jesus. Twice it says Jesus reacted by stooping and writing on the ground as if He had not heard them (John 8:6, 8). Can you imagine what was running through the heart and mind of Jesus at this point?

These men were bent on trapping Jesus in some intellectual maze that He would not be able to escape from. Jesus had come to this earth (in His own words) "*to seek and to save that which was lost*" (Luke 19:10). While the Pharisees and scribes were rejoicing in the "catch" they had made of this woman taken in the very act of adultery, Jesus had a heart of compassion for her. He had come to the earth for this woman, and people just like her who found themselves in desperate situations without any hope of forgiveness. He knew her name! He knew where she lived. He fashioned the fingerprints on the ends of her fingers. He painted the color in her eyes as He desired.

She had gone astray ... He came to bring her back! She had messed up the perfect plan God had for her when He made her ... He came to give her new hope! She would live with the shame of her sins for the rest of her life ... He came to give her the promise of life everlasting with a clean slate! She came into that room filthy and vile ... He came to lay on a cross ... take all her filth and sin ... and die for her! He came to die for me! They came to trap Jesus with some intellectual exercise (of which He showed His superiority), Jesus came to seek and save the lady they dragged into the room! He came to save them too, but they didn't know they needed saving. Will you love others today like Jesus loves them, or will you allow your inner-Pharisee to rule your heart today? Jesus stayed focused, will you?

Left Alone – May 17

*"And they which heard it, being convicted by their own conscience, went out one by one, beginning at the eldest,, even unto the last: and Jesus was **left alone**, and the woman standing in the midst"* (John 8:9).

When permission was given to cast the stones at the woman in judgment, I'm sure the scribes and Pharisees were delighted ... until they heard the stipulation that they must be without sin themselves. Put yourself in their position. If someone were to say today, *"Everyone without sin can go out to the desk and receive one million dollars ..."* none of us would be able to leave the room! We would all need to sit here in disappointment at the prospect of what could have been ... but what is real. There is no one reading this today who can claim to be perfect ... without sin!

These scribes and Pharisees were no different. There is no religious leader on the face of the planet in the history of the world who could claim sinless perfection. Oh wait ... that's right ... there is One! That One stood before this condemned woman and asked her about her accusers. That One sits on the right hand of the throne of God right now making intercession for everyone who has come to Him by faith for salvation! We have a Redeemer that makes us *"accepted in the Beloved."*

When Jesus stooped the second time to write in the dirt floor of the temple there on the Mt. of Olives, I believe He began to write some specific things. He was not drawing arbitrary things, or simply doodling on the ground. I believe He began to write specific sins of the accusers in the dirt. What other explanation is there for these men to exit the room in order from the eldest to the last? Jesus knew the hearts of these men as well as they knew their own heart.

These men had been guilty of something we do often. We are experts at judging the sins of others, while ignoring our own sins. Jesus talked about a splinter in an eye while having a beam in our own eyes – same idea. The saddest part of this story is not the woman caught in the very act of adultery, she is the best part of the story! The saddest part is those men exited the temple that day **with** their sin ... sin that Jesus could have forgiven. The beauty of the story is the woman the world condemned left the room **forgiven** of her sins! The weight had been lifted. When the man without sin in the room was revealed ... that's right, *"Jesus was **left alone**"* in the room! It is Jesus alone Who stands for you before God today. He is the One and Only Person you and I can depend upon for forgiveness!

Sweet Forgiveness – May 18

"When Jesus had lifted up Himself, and saw none but the woman, He said unto her, 'Woman, where are those thine accusers? Hath no man condemned thee?' She said, 'No man, Lord.' And Jesus said unto her, 'Neither do I condemn thee: go and sin no more'" (John 8:10-11). *"Neither do I condemn thee ..."* were not the words this woman must have expected to hear in her wildest dreams! Can you put yourself in her place for a few moments? She was absolutely guilty. She had been caught by others in the very action of sin. She had no excuse ... no alibi ... no one to stand to defend her. She was absolutely guilty of the charges that had been laid to her account. She had nowhere to turn for help.

All this changed when she met the Lord of all lords and the King of all kings. Of all that could accuse this woman, Jesus held the final gavel in His hand as the ultimate Judge of men/women's sin. Here she was in front of the one Who knew everything about her ... the details of all her sin (not only the most recent). There was no fancy lawyer to get her out of this situation. I can imagine this woman, with disheveled clothing ... hair strewn all over her head ... face to the dirt ... cringing at every little sound ... anticipating the bone-bruising effect of the stones buffeting her body.

Instead, she hears a gentle, yet powerful voice asking two simple questions: *"Woman, where are those thine accusers? Hath no man condemned thee?"* At which, I believe possibly for the first time, she raises her eyes to look at her accusers. She is incredulous, seeing they all have gone! Where did they go? Why had they not stoned her to death? Why had they not carried out the judgment on her they were so committed to on the trip to this temple? She replies simply, *"No man, Lord."* I'm sure she now anticipates judgment from Jesus. He is the only man without sin in the room! It's still what she deserves.

Jesus had come to offer mercy and grace to sinners just like her ... and me. Praise God! Rather than feeling the bruising effect of the stones upon her physical body, she realized the soothing balm of the forgiveness of sin from Jesus! This is incredible! Forgiveness in the place of justice! Can it be true? Can it be true, not only for this woman, but for me too? Yes, it's true! I have been forgiven of much ... I want to be willing to offer this same forgiveness to others who have offended me. Those who have offended me pale in comparison to the sin Jesus had to forgive me. I am thankful for God's forgiveness of my sin, and want to be ready to forgive others as well.

Carry the Light – May 19

"Then spake Jesus again unto them, saying, 'I am the light of the world: he that followeth Me shall not walk in darkness, but shall have the light of life'" (John 8:12). I have been on a few trails in the woods at night. One of the most important questions is, *"Who has the light?"* My cousin and I have made many trips through the woods in the dark of night. I always find it very comforting to be behind him when he has the light as we walk through the woods. He is always very thoughtful. If he crosses over a hole in the ground I might fall into, he always keeps the light on the hole until I have crossed over it. He also knows the importance of the light to me who is following.

In much the same way, if you have trusted Jesus Christ as your personal Savior, God has placed the Light for the world inside you. Did you catch the last phrase in that verse? *"… but shall **have** the light of life."* When you trust Christ as your Savior, God places that *"Light"* for life inside you. That means there will be people following you who are dependent upon you to show them the holes they could fall into without your Light. In order for you to do this, there are some important things at work.

First, you must have the Light yourself before you can show it to others, or for others. Yes, you must first have received Jesus Christ for your own payment for sin. This is more than knowing His name, or some facts about Him that might win a trivia game. This means knowing Him intimately. Before you can lead someone to salvation in Jesus Christ, He must first be your own personal Savior. One of the greatest thrills in my life today is the opportunity to tell someone else what I know of the way to Heaven, and a right relationship with God.

Second, after you have received Jesus (the Light) for yourself, you need to allow Him to rule your decisions and your life. There have been times when my cousin and I set out on one of our trips in the dark woods, and he will turn and say, *"I should have charged my batteries earlier."* The Christian life is a time of continual "battery charging!" This devotional today is meant to encourage you to run to the Bible yourself to allow God to speak to you through His Word every day. If we do not spend time with God alone in prayer, Bible reading, and confession of sins, we will never experience the relationship like God intended us to enjoy.

You are carrying the Light today. Charge up your batteries and get out there and help someone who is in the darkness see the Light today!

One Way – May 20

It has always amazed me how we created beings think we know better than the Creator. There is a natural arrogance in each of us that makes us think we are always right. I know myself when I discover I was wrong about something, my first inclination is to try to find a way to make my wrong opinions seem right. I know in me, within my human nature, is the desire to always be right. Jesus faced this all throughout His ministry, and we are still facing it today.

For thousands of years, men have thought they knew better than God about what it takes to reach Heaven. Men have even introduced terms like "Nirvana," and "the higher power" to describe things that are close to the Bible, but not correct. We have called sin simply a "disease." We have rationalized away many things that are a direct attack on the purity of God, by saying, *"That's just the way I'm made ..."* or, *"I'm that way because society has led me into that habit."* What bothers me most of all about these kinds of things is when we think we have outsmarted God when it comes to reaching Heaven.

I absolutely love Jesus' direct approach. *"Then said Jesus again unto them, 'I go My way, and ye shall see Me, and **shall die in your sins**: whither I go, ye cannot come'"* (John 8:21). Jesus could not lie, and He said exactly what needed and needs to be said. Without Him, we are doomed to an eternity separated from God in Hell. It isn't pretty, but it's true! Jesus knew if He did not die to pay the price for sin, no man on earth was going to step into Heaven.

The people Jesus was talking to were the most religious people on the earth … but every one of them was a sinner! There was not one perfect person in the group. Earlier in this chapter, the woman caught in the act of adultery was brought before Jesus, and He allowed the man without sin to cast a stone at her. They each left with their sin in their heart. The most righteous person reading this today is at best a rotten sinner deserving of Hell! The greatest news of your life-time is Jesus was not satisfied with that, and He left Heaven to come to die in your place.

The reality is you can die for you own sins, or you can accept the gift of God through Jesus Christ, and have your sins forgiven by Him. I am thankful I took the gift more than fifty years ago. I am saved! I don't need to pay the penalty for my sin, it has already been paid. I have trusted THE only way to Heaven! Jesus died for me! I am blessed today.

Rescued – May 21

Many years ago, my family went to a Bible Conference in the mountains of Pennsylvania for vacation. I loved it because it was nice and cool at night and they had two swimming pools. They had an indoor pool if it was raining and an outdoor pool if the weather was good. One of the days we were there it was raining, so I raced to the pool when it was our time to swim. I remember standing in a long line of very excited boys waiting to be allowed into the pool. The lifeguard was not nearly as highly motivated as we were, and he was late showing up to open the door.

When the lifeguard finally arrived, he told us we could begin swimming. He was busy setting things up when we all lined up at the diving board. While the lifeguard was finding his whistle, and the round life preservers, and all the other lifeguarding stuff, we started jumping off the diving board and swimming to the ladder on the side. There was a boy in front of me who jumped off and started toward the side. I followed with an extremely impressive cannon ball.

As I reached the ladder, I saw the boy who had gone in front of me going up and down beside the ladder. I thought at first he was just playing some kind of game. After watching him a couple of times I realized he was drowning. By that time, I was standing on the side of the pool, and I reached my hand out to him. He grabbed it and thanked me over and over again for saving his life! I was on solid ground ... he was sinking. This is a perfect picture of where we are without Jesus.

"And He said unto them, "Ye are from beneath; I am from above: ye are of this world: I am not of this world"" (John 8:23). We ought to thank God Jesus left Heaven to come here to rescue us from our drowning in sin. Just like the pool story, we are stuck in an endless set of calisthenics of trying to please God with our outward demonstrations of religion, while internally we are drowning in our sin! Just like that boy going up and down, struggling and unable to signal to anyone he needed help, no matter how good we look on the outside, we are without hope, and many times don't know how to say anything.

We each ought to praise God He came to us when we were in this condition spiritually. We all were drowning without hope until Jesus left Heaven. We could not go to Him, but He came to us! What a great feeling to reach out and take the hand of the One Who came from Heaven! Praise God for the great rescue Jesus performed for us!

Jesus ... Lifted Up – May 22

"Then said Jesus unto them, 'When ye have lifted up the Son of man, then shall ye know that I am He, and that I do nothing of Myself; but as My Father hath taught Me, I speak these things. And He that sent Me is with Me: the Father hath not left Me alone; for I do always those things that please Him'" (John 8:28-29).

Jesus was confronting His doubters face to face. They were challenging everything He did, every word He spoke, and every miracle He performed. When they challenged Him about Who His Father was, He responded with these verses in John 8. Verse 28 really hit my heart today. Jesus would be lifted up on the cross at Golgotha ... and it would be these very challengers He faced in this chapter who would deliver Him to be crucified. He spoke very true words in these verses (as always), when He said He was doing nothing of Himself, but was simply following every wish of His Father.

You and I are the reason Jesus had to be lifted up from the earth on that cross. It was our sin and God's love that sent Jesus to the cross. Today as I think back to that horrible day when Jesus was crucified, my heart is torn. On one hand I am incredibly ashamed at my sin that demanded such a high price. On the other hand I am incredibly thankful for the love of God that would not allow me to slide into Hell without Him offering me an option of forgiven sins and Heaven! What incredible love this was and is!

Jesus also said when they lifted Him up on that cross, they would realize He was Who He said He was. They would find out He was the very Son of God! The Romans centurion who came to remove Jesus' body from the cross made that very statement ... *"Truly this was the Son of God"* (Matthew 27:54). When the sun went dark in the middle of the day; and the earth shook; and the veil of the temple was ripped in two from the top to the bottom; and graves were opened ... and three days later Jesus was seen walking the streets again ... there would be no doubt!

It is important today to realize the crucifixion and resurrection of Jesus Christ is not simply a good story, but it is the pivotal point in the history of the world. If it is not the pivotal point in your own personal life, it must be before you can touch Heaven. For those of us who are saved, it is imperative we continue to lift our Savior up in our lives. Elevate His love in your life today. Lift high His passion for the lost. Honor the Word of God like Jesus did in His life. Live totally sold out for God like Jesus did and allow Him to draw men to Him. He deserves the place of prominence!

Freedom – May 23

"As He spake these words, many believed on Him. Then said Jesus to those Jews which believed on Him, 'If ye continue in My word, then are ye My disciples indeed; And ye shall know the truth, and the truth shall make you free'" (John 8:30-32). We love to quote that last phrase, but we need to make sure we keep it in the context in which Jesus said it. Of course, the phrase, *"ye shall know the truth, and the truth shall make you free"* is accurate all alone, but there is a depth that comes when you see it with the verses before it. Jesus made a statement to those who were in front of Him, but it is a statement that reaches all the way to where we are today.

Jesus was telling us it is not enough to simply believe what He is saying. *"Many believed on Him,"* but not all would be committed to *"continue"* in His word. The word, *"continue"* here has the idea of remaining in, or living in something. In essence, Jesus was telling those who want to be His disciples that it will involve more than a lunch where 5,000 are fed … or getting your friend healed … or water turning into wine. It will mean you stay, and stay, and stay in His Word.

One of the reasons I began these devotionals was because I wanted to encourage our children to be in the Word of God every day. I don't want them simply visiting their Bible on Sunday morning, and possibly Sunday night, and once-in-awhile on a Wednesday night. I wanted to encourage them to be in the Word every day of their lives. I know what a difference the discipline of reading the Bible has meant to me. I cannot imagine trying to go through a day without some guidance from the words in my Bible. I make a mess of things even when doing this; I would hate to see what would happen if I didn't have its influence in my life daily.

As I said earlier in this study, we often hear verse 32 quoted … but let's not miss the connection with verse 31. I think we are in desperate need of truth in our world today. I think we are in desperate need of clear truth in our churches and individual lives as well. I also think it is not enough to know the truth (to *"believe"* as many did in verse 30). I think we need to take those truths we see and learn from our Bible and put them into our daily lives and in our behavior! Today determine you will put flesh to the truths you read in your Bible. Decide to show your family, your neighbors, your friends the Word of God in your actions. Belief is not enough. We need to continue in the Word that Jesus gave us. Live in those truths and allow them to live in us. That's where true freedom comes from!

Forever Free – May 24

"Jesus answered them, 'Verily, verily, I say unto you, Whosoever committeth sin is the servant of sin. And the servant abideth not in the house forever: but the Son abideth forever'" (John 8:34-35).

When I was a young boy learning about the history of America, I can remember clearly when we discussed the time of slavery. I remember pictures (painted) of the slaves standing on the auction-blocks with people bidding to buy them. I can remember the hopeless looks on the faces of those being sold into slavery. It touched my heart very deeply as I considered what it might have been likes to be thought of as only a piece of property, and not a real person.

There are some beautiful words in our Bible that take me back to the same scene in my own life. The words are *"redeemed"* and *"redemption."* Our Bible only has these English words to choose from, but the original language had three words we translate in English to the words, *redeemed* and *redemption.* The first of those words had the simply idea of buying someone from the market. The second word went a little further and meant not only to purchase from the market, but then to remove the slave from the auction. The third is deeper still. The third meant to pay the full price at the market; to remove from the sale; and then the slave was set free!

Go back to that auction block again in your mind's eye with me. Put yourself in the place of the slave being sold. One bidder is the Devil himself. He has a stronghold on your life. After all, you continue to sin and sin, and there seems to be no hope of you ever escaping that pattern. The look of hopelessness I remember seeing in the paintings of the slave trade here in America, is squarely on your face. There seems to be no way to escape a final destiny of Hell for you.

Then a second Bidder stands. He not only purchases you at the market … He removes you from ever being sold again … but there's more. He then tells you, you now have freedom to live for Him without coercion. You are free to live for Him … or to wander back in sin … but He has redeemed you forever! You see, *"the Son abideth forever!"* Now, I don't know how you can experience this forgiveness and not feel an eternal indebtedness to this Savior! I want to please Him today more than anything else in my life! I want to do the work He wants me to do, and live in a way that will please Him today. I am free to serve Him, and I want to do my best for Him all day today! You see … I was once bound by sin … but He set me free!

What Will Others Remember About You? – May 25

"... be thou an example of the believers, in word, in conversation, in charity, in spirit, in faith, in purity. Till I come, give attendance to reading, to exhortation, to doctrine" (I Timothy 4:12b-13).

Memorial Day ... what does it mean to you? Memorial Day is the day in this month when we set aside time as a nation to look back at those who have sacrificed for the freedom we enjoy here in America. It is a good day because we are encouraged to take our eyes off ourselves, and consider all that has been done for us to enjoy the blessings of this land. I will say there is no other country like America. It is not because of our resources, although we are a rich land in what is available to us here. It is not because of our education ... other countries have many good institutions of instruction as well. It is not because of our people ... I have met many people in other countries who were of the quality of people I have met here. It is not because of the bounty of our finances ... there are many impoverished nations that are quality nations as well. I believe the thing that separates America from many other nations is freedom!

Our forefathers decided freedom, and particularly religious freedom was worth fighting and dying for. Praise God for that freedom today! However, freedom does come with a high price tag. The verses above show the price we ought to be willing to pay still today. Realize as much as we look back on those who have gone before us, there will be a day when others will look back at what we have left for them (in the future). I want to leave some things that are worth fighting and dying for. What are those things? They are listed in the verses above.

I want to be an example in the words I use. I want to speak words that edify and exhort others to live for Christ. I want to be an example in my lifestyle (conversation). I want others to be able to follow me to righteous behavior. I want to be an example in the love I have for others, regardless of what they can give me. I want to be an example in my spirit. I don't want to be a dark cloud coming into the room, but someone who others want to be around. I want to be an example in faith that steps out where reason will not go. I want to be an example in living a clean and pure life in an unclean and impure world.

I want to give time to reading the Word of God. I want to give time to challenging others with the truths I learn from the Book. I want to give time to solid doctrine when other are wavering. I want to leave deep footprints!

The Book with All the Answers – May 26

I am so thankful to God for my Bible. In a world that has far more questions than answers, I am glad to have a Book that has even more answers than I have questions! I was reading Revelation 1 just a few days ago, and saw a verse I have marked as the key verse in the book. *"Write the things which thou hast seen, and the things which are, and the things which shall be hereafter"* (Revelation 1:19).

The Bible God has given us is not limited by our human limitations. It is an eternal book. It is the Word of God, so it does not have the "normal" limitations that we have. The truths held in the Bible are true (that sounds like a stupid statement, but it is true). Truth has no expiration date. Truth is always going to be true, regardless of what generation it appears. The Bible we hold in our hands contains the words of life. It has all we have ever needed, and will ever need.

This verse tells us the Bible is good for understanding three things. It is good for the things that have happened earlier (*"the things which thou hast seen"*); it is good for understanding the things that are happening now (*"the things which are"*); and it is good for helping us to know what is going to happen in the future (*"the things which shall be hereafter"*)! Ask your morning newspaper to do that! Ask your favorite news station on TV, or on the internet to do that! Ask your weatherman to do that! The reality is that man has tried to duplicate that, but all have failed.

We can depend on the historical information that is contained in our Bible. It is 100% accurate ... much to the demise of the skeptics, doubters, and Atheists! We can depend on the Bible to tell us what the events happening around us today mean to us. I have been amazed over and over again as I hear of current events that are falling into place as the Bible predicted just like a puzzle piece falls into the remaining empty place. Because of these two evidences of the authenticity of my Bible, I am equally sure the things that are written on its pages which tell me what will happen in the future will come about just like it says as well.

I don't need to worry or fret about what is coming tomorrow. The reason for that is, my Bible gives me assurance that even though things may look like they are out of control right now, God still is in the "driver's seat." For me, that means all is well. As one Gospel song put it ... *"I've read the back of the BOOK ... and we win!"* What comfort I find in the book with all the answers. Don't neglect your Bible today. It is worth the time to read it!

Adopted – May 27

My wife and I were reflecting just the other day about a young lady who was adopted by a wonderful couple in our church We were blessed to have a small part in the adoption about ten years ago. We knew someone who had become pregnant and did not want to keep her baby. We also knew of this couple in our church who had been pursuing the avenue of adoption. We felt the situation the baby was being born into would not be the greatest if she remained with her birth mother. We also knew this couple from our church to be of very high character. We praised God back then, and we are praising God today to see this young lady become a godly person in a great home!

If you are saved, you have been adopted into God's family. Jesus described us very accurately this way … *"Ye are of your father the devil, and the lusts of your father ye will do. He was a murderer from the beginning, and abode not in the truth, because there is no truth in him. When he speaketh a lie, he speaketh of his own: for he is a liar, and the father of it"* (John 8:44). We were born in sin, and we learned the tricks and trades of sin from the day we began to breath. We had no hope of ever escaping the depths of our sin, until Jesus stepped in to save us.

Just like the girl I described above, we could see very little hope of a good outcome. But, just like the girl above, Jesus stepped in to remove us out of the depths of our situation, and He gave us a completely new home and hope. We were children of the Devil … the father of liars … and we had no hope in and of ourselves to remove ourselves from that condition. Praise God! Jesus came to us when we could not reach Him! Jesus did for us what we could not do for ourselves! Jesus paid the price for sin that we could never pay because it was a sinless life!

When I read this verse in John 8 today, it reminded me of how good I have had it as a believer since Jesus rescued me. I don't deserve to have a mansion built for me … or to walk on streets of gold … or to cross through a gate made of pearl. I deserve an eternal separation from God and an eternity crying out in anguish from the pit of Hell. I have been adopted by the God of the universe! I have been removed from the auction block of sin (like we discussed in an earlier devotional). I have been changed from the son of a liar, to become a son of God! I have literally passed from death unto life! What a great truth! I want to thank God today for coming to rescue me. I cannot help but want to tell everyone about the transformation He has made in my life. I am His child, and He is my Father!

LIFE – May 28

"Verily, verily, I say unto you, 'If a man keep My saying, he shall never see death'" (John 8:51).

Life is such a precious thing. I can clearly remember seeing each of our four children being born. It was always a time of extreme celebration as well as thanksgiving and the thought of a huge responsibility! I can remember seeing those little lives for the first time. We always took time to give our children to the Lord from their first few breaths. What a joy to know the Lord would be helping to raise those four children, and He would be there for them when we could not be. We have also had the joy of welcoming eight grandchildren into the world! Life! It is an incredibly valuable thing!

Jesus made the statement above about more than life itself ... it was made about eternal life, or everlasting life. Ever since I was a little boy, I have loved the word, "everlasting." I memorized John 3:16 as a little boy, and I always loved when it said Jesus offered everlasting life! Even a little boy knows that is better than the life we have here on the earth. I love the thought to this day of never needing to die. Loved ones, who were saved, never experienced the blackness of death, but stepped from this life into everlasting life! What a thought! That is our "blessed hope."

The statement Jesus made is so very definitive! There is no doubt, no debate, and no question as to its truth. We know it is true, because Jesus followed it up by rising from the dead! His statement would not have had any authority and power if the remains of His body were still in a grave somewhere. His resurrection from the dead made this promise become a reality for whosoever calls on His name! It also condemns any idea which suggests another alternative way to Heaven.

This means we who know Him, and understand He is the only way to Heaven, need to get busy telling all the others about it before it is too late! It is always the right time to tell someone about Jesus! There is never a bad time to share your testimony, or hand a tract, or explain the plan of salvation! There is only one way to Heaven! All who accept Jesus Christ and follow His path will arrive in Heaven. All who reject Jesus Christ and do not accept His plan will surely arrive in Hell. Don't wait to tell someone you love about Jesus and His plan for Heaven. Don't wait until everything seems perfectly lined up to share. Tell someone today! Life is precious and eternal life even more so! Don't put it off!

The Pivotal Point in History – May 29

"Your father Abraham rejoiced to see My day: and he saw it, and was glad. Then said the Jews unto Him, 'Thou art not yet fifty years old, and hast thou seen Abraham?' Jesus said unto them, 'Verily, verily, I say unto you, 'Before Abraham was, I am'" (John 8:56-58).

Many people think there are two ways to Heaven. There is the Old Testament way of following the Ten Commandments, and there is the New Testament way of accepting Jesus Christ. That is flawed thinking! There will not be one person in Heaven from Adam to the last person born who did not come to Heaven through Jesus Christ! When Adam and Eve sinned, God sacrificed a lamb to clothe them. He instructed them from that point forward to offer a blood sacrifice for their sins. All of this was a picture of Jesus coming to pay off the sin debt of men.

I have always loved the fact that when Adam and Eve sinned in Genesis 3:6, the promise of redemption followed in Genesis 3:15. God did not waste any time in revealing His plan to mankind. By the way, God did not come up with that plan in Genesis 3:6 after the first man and woman sinned. He had that plan in place since eternity past! Man's sin did not surprise God. He was prepared, and ready to offer His Son as the payment for sin. It is important to understand every person in Heaven will be there by coming through the perfect sacrificially offering of Jesus and His resurrection from the dead.

Jesus made the statement in John 8:56 that Abraham would rejoice when He paid the price for sin. Abraham, even though revered by the Jews, was a sinner in need of a Savior! Every other Old Testament hero was looking forward to the cross. Just as we look back to the cross, the Old Testament believer looked forward to it. Keeping or trying to keep the Ten Commandments never saved anyone! Those commands were to reveal our sin to us, not forgive it! There has never been any person who has followed the Ten Commandments completely ... with the exception of Jesus Himself.

These Jews who were arguing with Jesus, and would want to kill Him for claiming to be God (John 8:58), were looking into the eyes of the only human being to ever live Who obeyed all ten of those Commandments all the time! They were looking at Him, but they didn't see Him. The whole needs to look at the cross ... the pivotal point in the history of man. Some will look there and reject Jesus just like these Jews in John 8, but some will receive Him. Don't be ashamed of the cross today. It is important!

The Touch of God – May 30

I have been thinking back a great deal lately, about what it was that moved me to the decisions I have made in my life for God. There are a number of "mountaintop" experiences I have had that really touched my heart and life. But, I must honestly say most of the life-changing things that have happened to me would not be seen as "lightning bolt" experiences. When I look back, many of the most significant moments in life were just "normal" days when God whispered in my ear. Don't get worried, I have never heard an audible voice from God; but I will tell you I have known the direct and obvious leading of the Holy Spirit. Now, before you think too highly of me … I did not always agree with the Holy Spirit at the time He spoke to me, but I knew I needed to if I wanted to stay in the center of Gods will.

When I was a young teenager, God touched my heart on a hillside in Kentucky on a Thursday night standing next to a campfire. It was there I felt the leading of the Holy Spirit to surrender all of me there was, to serve God for the rest of my life … pimples, goofiness, awkward times, limited intelligence and all. I surrendered it all to Him to use that night. There was no great sermon preached or an altar call. It was just the still small voice of God speaking from His heart to mine.

Later, after a few years in full-time ministry, the Spirit of God whispered in my ear that it was not right that Deaf people in America, or any other country, should die without seeing the Gospel in their language at least one time. I agreed with Him and determined to learn enough Sign Language to tell a Deaf person about the only way to Heaven. Again, there were no trumpets blaring, or bright lights, or earthquakes. It was just the still small voice of God speaking from His heart to mine.

Today I want to encourage you to stay close enough to God that when He whispers to you in that still small voice, you can sense His instructions and obey with all your heart all He touches your heart to do. Once you have heard that voice, then I would tell you "… *whatsoever ye do, do it heartily, as to the Lord, and not unto men*" (Colossians 3:23). We've got far too many people in our churches today from preachers to pew sitters who are doing what they do to please others. Whatever God touches your heart to do, turn the controls over to Him and do it with every fiber of your life! Don't hold back! If God gave you something to do, you have received marching orders from the King of all kings and the Lord of all lords. Do it!

A Savior with No Limits – May 31

"Then Jesus said unto them, 'Verily, verily, I say unto you, Before Abraham was, I am'" (John 8:58).

WOW! What a powerful statement! The Jews that Jesus was talking to, revered Abraham as the father of their race. There were not many who would be spoken of in the history of Israel who could supplant Him in that position. Here Jesus made a simple, but profound statement ... *"Before Abraham was, I am!"* Jesus spoke the world into existence! Colossians 1:16-17 says, *"For by him were all things created, that are in heaven, and that are in earth, visible and invisible, whether they be thrones, or dominions, or principalities, or powers: all things were created by him, and for him: And he is before all things, and by him all things consist."*

Jesus made a simple statement, but an absolutely true statement! He breathed the life into the man formed from the dust! He causes the sun to rule by day and the moon by night. He holds the oceans of the world in the palm of His hand. He brings the rain, snow, and the wind. He is the Creator and Sustainer of life itself! When Jesus made this statement, He identified Himself with God. Only God was given the title, "I AM." When Jesus said this simple verse, the Jews picked up stones to kill Him. The only problem they had was, He was telling the whole truth! He is God! He was exactly Who He said He was!

One thing touched my heart about His statement there in verse 58. If the Jews could have called Abraham from paradise at that moment and taken a word of testimony from him ... Abraham would have agreed! Abraham was in paradise waiting for Jesus to conquer his own sin so he could follow Jesus into Heaven (remember the story of Abraham, Lazarus, and the rich man?). Abraham himself, the father of the Jewish nationality, needed Jesus to be Who He said He was as much as any of us, including the men who were ready to kill Jesus.

Jesus Christ is Who He claimed to be! Jesus is God! Now let that thought sink into your heart for a moment. God truly left Heaven to die for your sins! God's one and only Son paid the price for the redemption of your soul! If God's one and only Son paid the price for your salvation, I think you can rest in His saving power to keep you saved! I will not arrive in Heaven one day and God require something else, other than the blood sacrifice of Jesus to have paid off my sin debt. That was HIS plan, not ours. I am safe forevermore in the arms of Jesus my Savior! Praise God!

MONTH OF JUNE

Precious Promises – June 1

*"According as His divine power hath given unto us all things that pertain unto life and godliness, through the knowledge of Him that hath called us to glory and virtue: Whereby are given unto us **exceeding great and precious promises**: that by these ye might be partakers of the divine nature, having escaped the corruption that is in the world through lust"* (II Peter 1:3-4).

Read those verses again slowly and let their truth sink into your heart today.

God reached out to us and saved us from certain corruption ... certain eternal damnation in Hell for eternity. I am sorry, but I always need to pause and let that one sink in to my heart to get that idea clearly! I was headed to Hell without hope, but now I am guaranteed Heaven for eternity! I cannot get over the grace and mercy of God. The reality is, that great truth is only the beginning! The other blessings which are attached to that truth are overwhelming to me.

Not only have I passed from death unto life, but I have also been given a multitude of promises in the Word of God! One person counted 3,573 promises in the Bible! I'm not sure if that is an accurate number, but I know this ... any promise from God is one I can build my life upon! I am thankful I was taught from the time I was a small boy to trust God! My family grew up reading the Bible, and making it our measuring stick for life. We built our lives upon the truths that are clearly seen in the Bible.

We have all had people who made great promises to us, only to turn back on their word and leave us wanting. I can remember one situation I thought was crucial to us getting started as missionaries. A man made a grand promise to us that I depended on, only to change his mind when the time came to come through on the promise. I remember being very disappointed and wondered how we would ever make it. The great thing was, even though this "man" failed on his promise, my Heavenly Father was absolutely true to His promises, and we survived and went on just fine.

Obviously there is not space enough in this short devotional to review the promises of God. What I would like to challenge you with today is to find one or two promises that touch your heart and thank God for those today. I know this ... God must be true to His Word! He cannot lie, and He is omnipotent (all powerful). I hope you are depending on Him today more than others around you, or an institution. Our God is faithful to do exactly what He has said He would do. He has rescued us from corruption, and provided many precious promises for us to hold on to today.

New Heart ... New Spirit – June 2

Each of us needs a visit to the ultimate "heart Doctor" once-in-awhile. Recently I went to the drugstore to pick up my pills I must take to keep my heart in line. When I arrived at the counter, the person giving me my pills told me they could not refill my medication any more until I visited the heart doctor. It had been awhile since I had been there last, and a visit was required. The same is true with each believer and our God. We need to visit Him often to make sure everything is okay with our heart. Today I read a wonderful verse at the end of Ezekiel 18.

"*Therefore I will judge you, O house of Israel, every one according to his ways,' saith the Lord God. 'Repent, and turn yourselves from all your transgressions; so iniquity shall not be your ruin. Cast away from you all your transgressions, whereby ye have transgressed; and make you a **new heart and a new spirit**: for why will ye die, O house of Israel? For I have no pleasure in the death of him that dieth,' saith the Lord God: 'wherefore turn yourselves, and live ye*" (Ezekiel 18:30-32).

Through the Old Testament prophet Ezekiel, God begged His people to turn back to Him and from the false gods. You and I are in danger of turning our back on God just as easily today. We may get caught up in a hobby, or a habit, or a pleasure, or just plain spiritual laziness. Sometimes we can even become so busy we neglect spending time alone with God for Him to speak to us.

The point is, each of us can easily fall into the trap of allowing our hearts to become cold and indifferent to the things of God. One of the reasons I continue to write this devotional is not for your benefit, but for mine. It is refreshing and challenging for me to listen to the Word of God each day for something that touches my heart, and then to share it with you. Over the years of writing this, there have been times when I thought I would stop. Each time that thought has come to me, I remember the benefit this is to me to have my heart and spirit renewed each morning. Frankly, whether anyone reads this or not, I will continue to write it to keep my own heart tender toward God.

Don't let your walk with God become common and ordinary today. Ask Him for that new heart and new spirit Ezekiel was talking about. Ask God to allow you to be so deeply in love with Him that the thought of Him thrills your soul! Ask God to draw you close enough to His side that you can feel His heart beating against yours and stay right next to Him all day.

My Lawyer – June 3

When someone comes to you with some trouble you have gotten into; wouldn't it be nice to simply say, *"Call my lawyer!"* It would be nice to have a lawyer on call to be able to get us out of the trouble we seem to find ourselves in. As a believer, we have a Lawyer far better than any earthly lawyer Who defends us when we sin. His name is Jesus Christ!

*"My little children, these things write I unto you, that ye sin not. And if any man sin, we have **an advocate** with the Father, **Jesus Christ the righteous**. And He is the propitiation for our sins: and not for ours only, but also for the sins of the whole world"* (I John 2:1-2).

Can you picture the courtroom scene that might happen? There in the front of the room, raised up from the level where the common man stands, sits the righteous Judge, our God. Down below we stand at the desk in front of the judge's seat with nothing more than our own guilt and sin. There is no denying the fact we have been less than perfect. There is no denying we owe a penalty for the things we have done wrong. Next to us stands the Devil with a smile from ear to ear because he knows we are filled with guilt and sin.

About that time, the back doors of the courtroom open and Jesus Christ, our righteous Advocate enters the room. It's interesting how the smile now fades from the face of the Devil, and is transferred to the Judge! After all, Jesus Christ is His only begotten Son! As Jesus comes to the seat next to us, He reveals His nail-scarred hands ... we realize some things that day with Jesus. First, we are absolutely guilty and have a debt to pay for our sin. Second, He took that sin to the cross and suffered our penalty for that sin. Third, our acceptance of His death on the cross means our debt for that sin has already been paid.

Jesus doesn't need a briefcase ... He doesn't need a legal pad with notes scribbled all over it ... He doesn't need witnesses to come ... He doesn't need a fancy speech at the end of the trial. He simply brings with Him one book. He opens the Book of Life to the section that contains your name. He approaches the Judges bench (God) and shows Him the page. God asks all to rise and makes the declaration. This sinner is forgiven! This sinner has their name written in the Lamb's Book of Life and the Lamb of God Who takes away the sins of the world is here to prove it! WOW!

When the Devil tries to convince you today that you are unworthy, or you have no right to do anything for God ... take Him to your Advocate!

Speak Out! – June 4

Imagine you and your family going on a camping weekend in some beautiful mountains. Imagine you rented a cabin and while walking into the room you noticed a rattlesnake in the corner. Of course, you would run from the danger of a rattlesnake … but wouldn't you also warn the rest of your family about the danger of the snake? Surely you would! God painted a picture for us using this same kind of example.

… When I bring the sword upon a land, if the people of the land take a man of their coasts, and set him for their watchman: If when he seeth the sword come upon the land, he blow the trumpet, and warn the people; then whosoever heareth he sound of the trumpet, and taketh not warning; if the sword come, and take him away, his blood shall be upon his own head. He heard the sound of the trumpet, and took not warning; his blood shall be upon him. But he that taketh warning shall deliver his soul. But if the watchman see the sword come, and blow not the trumpet, and the people be not warned; if the sword come, and take any person from among them, he is taken away in his iniquity; but his blood will I require at the watchman's hand. So thou, O son of man, I have set thee a watchman unto the house of Israel; therefore thou shalt hear the word at My mouth, and warn them from Me" (Ezekiel 33:2-7).

This is a simple truth, but it is so powerful at the same time. We have a responsibility to keep our eyes open for dangerous situations for the people we know and love. We then have an added responsibility to warn them of danger that is approaching. When we have seen danger, we have two choices. We can either warn others (helping them miss the danger), or we can remain quiet and let them face the danger on their own.

If we choose not to warn, and damage comes to them; we are responsible for their destruction. God clearly says here their blood will be upon our hands. If we decide to warn them, and they ignore our warnings; the results are on them and is their responsibility.

We have seen the danger that comes when we walk away from God, or when we walk in ways that are opposite of the plan of God for us. It is good for us to warn others of what can happen.

If you know the way to Heaven it is time for you to tell others how they can miss the dangers of Hell, and turn toward Heaven. Don't hold the truths in today you know so well. Tell someone about the things you have learned in the Word of God today!

Bringing Bones to Life – June 5

"Therefore prophesy and say unto them, Thus saith the Lord GOD; Behold, O my people, I will open your graves, and cause you to come up out of your graves, and bring you into the land of Israel. And ye shall know that I am the LORD, when I have opened your graves, O my people, and brought you up out of your graves, And shall put my spirit in you, and ye shall live, and I shall place you in your own land: then shall ye know that I the LORD have spoken it, and performed it, saith the LORD" (Ezekiel 37:12-14).

A few weeks ago, my father came and asked me if I remembered what my first sermon was. I thought for a moment, and told him I thought it was a sermon about dry bones coming together and coming to life. He agreed with me. He had found one of my mother's Bibles, and in Ezekiel 37 he saw her notes on that sermon. At the bottom of the notes she had written, *"Jim's first message."*

These verses were written as prophecy to the nation of Israel. It was a promise of God bringing them back into their land again (which He did). I preached that first sermon about God being able to bring to life things we had thought were dead and buried in our lives. I still think that theme is applicable for us today. There are things in your life you have considered dead and buried, without hope of ever coming to life again. There are relationships that have been damaged that you think can never be restored. There are bridges you have thought were burned and destroyed.

All of us have things that have happened in our lives that we wish we could go back and "fix." However, just as Israel would learn in the days that followed Ezekiel's prophecy, we need to understand that God can do the seemingly impossible things in our lives. God can bring life from things that are dead. God can breathe life into your life and relationships to bring them back to where they were before and even better.

The key is that it is God that provided the breath for these dry bones. You and I can try everything we know, and we cannot restore life to dead things. This is nothing hard for God. He spoke and created the earth and the universe in six, twenty-four hour days! He took the dust and made a man. He breathed life into Adam, and He can breathe life into the things that have died in your life. The most important thing we can do today is to remain close to the Creator. Gather the "dry bones" of your life together today and let God bring them to life. You cannot manufacture this ... it will happen in God's timing, not yours. Be patient and wait for Him to give life!

Keep Christ First – June 6

There is one thing false religions have in common. Each of them denies Jesus is the Son of God and the singular Savior of the world. They each err in some way or another on the doctrines that involve the truth about Jesus Christ. It is very important we realize everyone who claims to love God is not always on the right track. If a person claims to love and follow God, but refuses to accept the fact Jesus is the Christ, is not a follower of God. You cannot have God without His Son. A person cannot approach God without Jesus opening the way for that to happen.

John warned us to watch out for this kind of erroneous teaching in our times. *"For many deceivers are entered into the world, who confess not that Jesus Christ is come in the flesh. This is a deceiver and an antichrist. Look to yourselves, that we lose not those things which we have wrought, but that we receive a full reward. Whosoever transgresseth, and abideth not in the doctrine of Christ, hath not God. He that abideth in the doctrine of Christ, he hath both the Father and the Son. If there come any unto you, and bring not this doctrine, receive him not into your house, neither bid him God speed"* (II John 7-10).

This is a very strong warning given to us. When you know someone denies Jesus is the Son of God ... don't let them cross into your house. Don't invite them in for tea or a cookie. Don't allow them to put in your mind they are just like you except for a few small differences. If they don't believe Jesus is the One and only way into Heaven, they should not be given any opportunity for fellowship with you. You might ask, *"How will I know?"* Ask them if they believe Jesus Christ is the Son of God. Ask them if they believe He is the only way into Heaven? Ask if they believe Jesus lived without sin ... died and was buried ... rose from the dead in His physical body after being dead for three days.

Don't ask if they believe in Jesus ... they will say yes. What they mean is they believe Jesus existed on the earth. They are not saying they believe He is the only way to Heaven. Many exalt their religious leaders to an equal place with Jesus. Some exalt His earthly mother to a place of equality with Jesus. Some say the angels are equal to Him. The reality is, Jesus is THE way, truth and life. The truth is, no man will approach God without Jesus' payment on the cross on their account. Make no mistake ... Jesus is very important. I hope you will take the warning John gave us very seriously, and you will be on the look-out for those who deny the truth about Jesus. Stay close to Jesus today!

Decisions Determine Direction – June 7

During a time of captivity in the history of Israel, a young man immerged who was a shining light in a very dark time. God will always have faithful people who will not bend regardless of the situations they are facing. Can He count on you? Daniel and a few of his friends were taken from their families and homeland and placed in the center of the great nation of Babylon. Babylon was known as a very powerful nation, but it was also known for its idol worship and pagan practices. Daniel, as a young man made some very crucial decisions that determined the direction his life would take.

Daniel would serve as a trusted advisor to three different kings while he lived in Babylon. He would be the mouthpiece of God before these pagan and unbelieving kings. I believe there is a possibility Daniel may have had a part in some of these kings actually turning to God and away from their idols. How did all this happen? It all comes back to a simple statement made in the very beginning of the book that is named for him.

*"But **Daniel purposed in his heart** that he would not defile himself, with the portion of the king's meat, nor with the wine which he drank: therefore he requested of the prince of the eunuchs that he might not defile himself"* (Daniel 1:8). Did you catch that beginning phrase? Too many of us would focus on the fact that Daniel would not eat meat offered to idols ... or that he would not drink wine. I'm afraid if we do that that we are missing the most important thing. The meat and wine were simply by-products of the decision Daniel made in his heart years before.

The word, *"purposed"* carries the idea that Daniel decided beforehand what he would do. You see, Daniel had made deliberate decisions in the times of peace, so when the times of captivity came in his life, he would be ready to do the right thing. Daniel decided long before his feet left Israel what his convictions would be. He decided where he would stand, and when he would flee. He was committed to do what his heart told him was right to do, regardless of what the king commanded. I believe Shadrach, Meshach, and Abednego did something similar to this as well.

In a day of increasing pressure to compromise what God speaks to your heart about, let me ask you to consider this question. Are you willing to decide some things before the pressure is on? Will you simply agree to what the loudest voices are saying in order to keep a peaceful situation? Stand tall for God today. Your decisions will determine your direction!

Committed – June 8

King Nebuchadnezzar threatened three captives in his country … "*"Now if ye be ready that at what time ye hear the sound of the cornet, flute, harp, sackbut, psaltery, and dulcimer, and all kinds of music, ye fall down and worship the image which I have made; well: but if ye worship not, ye shall be cast the same hour into the midst of a burning fiery furnace; and who is that God that shall deliver you out of my hands?' Shadrach, Meshach, and Abed-nego, answered and said to the king, 'O Nebuchadnezzar, we are not careful to answer thee in this matter. If it be so, our God Whom we serve is able to deliver us from the burning fiery furnace, and He will deliver us out of thine hand, O king. But if not, be it known unto thee, O king, that we will not serve thy gods, nor worship the golden image which thou hast set up"* (Daniel 3:15-18).

When your beliefs are threatened, how quickly will you cave in to the pressure? How many of us retreat when opposition to our faith comes? It is time for us to believe in our God so strongly that we are willing to take a stand for what He has taught us, and what we believe the Bible to say. For example; many people tell us the bible has errors all through it. When we hear that, we often stop trying to talk about the Bible. Why not challenge the accuser to find just one of those "errors." Chances are the one who said that to you has not read a verse in the Bible, let alone found an error!

Nebuchadnezzar puffed out his chest and challenged the God of Heaven when he asked, "*Who is that God that shall deliver you out of my hands?*" He got to see first-hand the Son of God walking about in the middle of the fire that killed his strongest soldiers while throwing the three Hebrew guys in the fire! He got a first-hand look at the power of our awesome God, but he got that demonstration because these three young men were willing to stand and be counted when the pressure was on them.

God may be waiting to do some incredible things in your life, but you have not given Him the chance. What I am trying to say is, if you never step out by faith, you will never know how powerful your God actually is. If we never tithe, we will never learn God can help us do more with 90% in obedience than we can do with 100% in selfishness. If we never step out to witness to our neighbor, we will lose the blessing of seeing them come to faith in Jesus Christ! If we never attempt to read our Bible through in a year, we will never learn the incredible satisfaction that comes with obedience to the Word of God! Step out by faith today and enjoy the ride!

I Know THE Man – June 9

Have you ever heard the statement, "*It is not what you know ... but who you know ...?*" That is such a true statement. I have known some people who were considered important by others, and it offered me opportunities that I did not deserve. Well ... I know THE man!

"'*I am Alpha and Omega the Beginning and the Ending,' saith the Lord, which is, and which was, and which is to come, the Almighty*" (Revelation 1:8)

"*And when I saw Him, I fell at His feet as dead. And He laid His right hand upon me, saying unto me, 'Fear not; I am the First and the Last: I am He that liveth, and was dead; and, behold, I am alive forevermore, Amen; and have the keys of hell and of death*'" (Revelation 1:17-18).

It pays to know this man. Of course, there is only one Person these verses could describe. My Savior, Jesus Christ of Nazareth!

He is the Alpha (the Beginning) – there was none before Him because He is eternal. He had no beginning. He has always been and was in control of everything from the beginning of man.

He is the Omega (the Ending) – He will have no end because He is eternal. He will have no ending at all. Just like He has always been ... He will always be in control throughout eternity future.

He is the Almighty – He is God in flesh! He is completely God, but also became completely man. He became man to conquer our sin debt!

He is the One that liveth – He was born in a stable in Bethlehem and laid in a manger. God in human flesh came to the rescue of all of us sinners! He lived here on the earth for all to see! What an impact He made in just thirty-three short years. He made enough of an impact that the people who hated Him then are still making sacrilegious movies about Him today. He made enough of an impact that those of us who love Him are still willing to stand and die for Him today.

He is the one who was dead – notice the "was" there. He went all the way to death for us on the cross, but His death is past-tense. The next phrase says He is "*alive forevermore!*" There He is! That's my Savior! I am following this Man! I choose to live for this Man today! I want to introduce everyone I meet to this Man! I want this Man to be exalted in my life so much, my behavior is affected and others see Him in me today. I want others to know Him as I have known Him!

Open the Door – June 10

Today I want to share a familiar verse we have all probably used out of its context. Jesus, speaking to John on the Isle of Patmos said, *"Behold, I stand at the door and knock: if any man hear My voice, and open the door, I will come in to him, and will sup with him, and he with Me"* (Revelation 3:20). If you are like me, you have used this verse to encourage an unsaved person to open their heart's door to Jesus and allow Him to enter and become their Savior. While I think this is an appropriate picture of what God desires with us, it is not what this verse is talking about. Let's add the verse before it to the verse and see the real meaning. *"As many as I love, I rebuke and chasten: be zealous therefore, and repent. Behold, I stand at the door and knock ..."* (Revelation 3:19-20).

Do you see whose heart Jesus is knocking on? Yes, it is our heart after we have turned away from him to follow our own plan for life. The last part of this chapter in Revelation is Jesus giving a warning to the church in Laodicea. They had been on fire for God at one point, but had sadly drifted into a "lukewarm" condition. Jesus had rebuked them earlier in the chapter telling them He wished they were either hot or cold. Their lukewarm condition sickened Him.

Jesus was knocking on their heart's door to allow Him back onto the throne of their lives. He was asking permission to return to them in the way they had once known Him. He was asking to renew the fellowship that had been broken between them. The King of all kings was asking admission into their lives again. How sad is this picture? He, Who gave all He had to redeem us from our sin ... begging to have an intimate relationship with us again!

How is it with you and Jesus today? Do you know that sweet intimacy with Him, or have you grown a little "lukewarm" in your relationship with Him? He's standing at your heart's door–knocking today. He's looking for you to open that door to allow Him back onto the throne of your heart. It is easy to allow other things to crowd our attention and take His place on that throne. It is usually a "good" thing that replaces Him ... like a family member ... job ... ministry ... a focus on the world rather than Him. It can be any number of things. It is not so important what it is ... the fact that it is there and He is not what is important. Today is a good day to go answer the door ... Someone very important is waiting to come into your life! Don't leave Him standing out there one more day!

Make a Difference – June 11

"We sure do live in a very wicked world." "If ever the world needed some committed Christians, it needs them today." "Things are getting worse and worse all the time ... is there any hope for our world?" Maybe you have heard statements like these before, or maybe you have made statements like these yourselves. The question really is whether or not there is hope for our world today. As always, the Bible has the answer.

God's formula for changing the world is given in the minor prophet Hosea's book. *"Sow to yourselves in righteousness, reap in mercy; break up your fallow ground: for it is time to seek the LORD, till He come and rain righteousness upon you"* (Hosea 10:12).

There are three things I see in this verse that hold the key to us making a difference in the world today. First, we need to sow ourselves in righteousness if we want to reap mercy. You reap what you sow. If we want to see our world affected for the cause of Christ and for good, we need to make sure we are planting righteousness in our own lives. It is always far easier to criticize and see what others need to change than it is to make the changes ourselves. We can point to the wickedness of the world around us, or we can move toward righteousness ourselves. It's your choice ...

Second, we need to break up our fallow ground. I love this picture. In the last two months we have seen the farmers in our area breaking up the fallow ground. The ground that has been untouched for the winter months have now been plowed and broken up. Why? Because it is time to drop seeds into the ground to ensure a harvest in the fall. If we want to make a difference in our world today, we need to allow God's holy plow to make some rows in our hearts and let Him plant the seed of His word. If we want to see mercy produced in our lives, we need to break up the fallow areas of our hearts and let God do His work in us.

Third, we need to seek the LORD! Sounds simple doesn't it? I love the concept of the word, *"seek."* I love the fact Jesus came to this earth to *"seek and to save that which was lost."* I am glad He did not come to stroll through life, but to actively pursue us with the Gospel. I'm thankful for His pursuit of me, but I am convicted at my lack of pursuit of Him. Is it true *"As the hart panteth after the water brooks, so panteth my soul after Thee, O God"* (Psalm 42:1)? If we want to see my world turn back to Christ, we must seek Him with our whole heart. Will you join me in pursuing Him today? Our world needs us today.

The Key to Heaven – June 12

"And when He had taken the book, the four beasts and four and twenty elders fell down before the Lamb, having every one of them harps, and golden vials full of odors, which are the prayers of saints. And they sung a new song, saying, 'Thou art worthy to take the book, and to open the seals thereof: for Thou wast slain, and hast redeemed us to God by Thy blood out of every kindred, and tongue, and people, and nation; and hast made us unto our God kings and priests: and we shall reign on the earth'" (Revelation 5:8-10).

The picture that is painted in Revelation 5 is one of desperation. A book is found no one can open. No political leader had the key required to open it. No religious leader (Buddha, Mohammed, Joseph Smith, my pastor) had the key to open it. I certainly do not have the key to open it on my own, regardless of how good a person I think I am. When all hope was lost, the Lamb of God stepped onto the scene. He had the key … His own precious, sinless blood was the key required.

Today in our world of tolerance, and acceptance, a key is still needed. Think about it. You have keys to your house. You have keys to your car. You have keys for locks you have put on garages, or sheds, or the places you store things. You have a key for your locker. Those keys are meant to give you and those who share that key access into whatever you have thought valuable enough to protect. That key is necessary if you want to enjoy whatever it opens. You can have the most beautiful car in the world, but without the key all you can do is look at it. You can have extremely valuable gems in a locked vault somewhere, but without the key, you cannot get to them.

Heaven is no different. The only key that will open Heaven is the blood of Jesus Christ! You may have thought your blood and Jesus' blood were the same, but you would be mistaken. Jesus' blood is the only perfect blood that has ever been offered for forgiveness of sin. Jesus' blood is the only blood that is the key to opening Heaven. The good news is, it is the key that opens Heaven! It is, however, the key only for those who have received Jesus' sacrifice on the cross for their payment for sin! You need the key to get in. I recently had a lock on a trailer that I put on it for protection. I had about fourteen different little lock keys hanging on our key rack. I tried each of them. Some went into the lock perfectly, but none were the right key to open the lock. Don't make the mistake of thinking your key will work because it looks right. Only Jesus' blood opens Heaven!

Decisions ... Decisions – June 13

"Multitudes, multitudes in the valley of decision: for the day of the LORD is near the valley of decision" (Joel 3:14).

We have no idea when Jesus Christ will return, but it could be at any moment. I believe God planned it that way because He knew it would keep us close to Himself. He knew if we knew the day and the hour we would become spiritual procrastinators ... putting off living for Him until the last minute. As it is today, Jesus could come. He will come as a thief in the night. He will not make an announcement. He will not call us ahead of time and make an appointment. He will come when least expected ... but be sure of this ... He will come!

We are a part of the multitudes the prophet Joel described that are in the valley of decision. We are there every day of our lives. Today you will make decisions that will affect your future. You will make decisions that will affect not only you, but your family as well. You will make decisions that will determine your spiritual success or failure today. It is important for us to make good use of our time. It is important each of us sees the importance of the days we are living in, and we use every opportunity we have to serve our Lord and make a difference where we live while we have the chance.

The fact Jesus could return at any moment, should make each of us realize we should do the important things today. A few years ago, my mother stepped into Heaven as a result of a battle with cancer. We knew her days were numbered, and she would not be with us much longer. We said things to her we wanted to make sure she understood. She did the same with us. We knew the time was approaching and we wanted to make good use of every minute. We didn't spend much time on entertainment during those days. We did spend a great deal of time making sure the other person knew how much we loved them. It's funny how important things came to the surface, while the "normal" things we would have wasted time on disappeared.

Today we are in the valley of decision. Make sure you do the important things first today. Don't put off telling your loved ones you treasure them. Don't miss the opportunity to hand out a tract, or witness to a neighbor. We are in the valley of decision. Today is the day to do everything you have planned on doing for God while you have the opportunity. This is a great day to serve the Lord!

Family of God – June 14

"After this I beheld, and, lo, a great multitude, which no man could number, of all nations, and kindreds, and people, and tongues, stood before the throne, and before the Lamb, clothed with white robes, and palms in their hands; And cried with a loud voice, saying, Salvation to our God which sitteth upon the throne, and unto the Lamb. And all the angels stood round about the throne, and about the elders and the four beasts, and fell before the throne on their faces, and worshipped God, Saying, Amen: Blessing, and glory, and wisdom, and thanksgiving, and honour, and power, and might, be unto our God for ever and ever. Amen" (Revelation 7:9-12).

All different ... but all the same. From every nation ... kindred ... people ... and language we will come to Heaven. We will all come from different places, with different languages, and different cultures. We will all come with the same Savior! We will all come because of the *"Salvation of our God."* We will all come because of the *"Lamb of God which taketh away the sins of the world."* We are all going to have the opportunity to touch Heaven because of one Man ... Jesus Christ!

There was a song I heard a while back that had this phrase ... *"I don't know what a sinner you are, but I know what a Savior He is."* I don't know what path you have come on to arrive where you are today, but I know if you are going to enter Heaven it will be because you have Jesus Christ as your Savior! I don't know what sin has trapped you over and over again, but I know His grace is sufficient for you. I don't know what your background has been ... what horrible things might have happened to you in your past, but I know there is a loving Father Who sent His Son to a sin-cursed earth to pay your penalty and buy you back out of sin!

How can we remain quiet today about our incredible God, and His great love for us? How can we not join with the saints saved during the tribulation that are described in Revelation 7? I have heard people say many times before, we ought not to wait until someone has died to buy them flowers, but should buy them as a gift while they are still alive. The same is true with our praise today. We don't need to wait until we see our Heavenly Father face to face to praise Him. Today is a good day to join the chorus that will be sung in Heaven.

Read the words out loud today ... *"Amen: Blessing, and glory, and wisdom, and thanksgiving, and honor, and power, and might, be unto our God forever and ever. Amen!"*

Ready to Meet God – June 15

"Therefore thus will I do unto thee, O Israel: and because I will do this unto thee, prepare to meet thy God, O Israel. For, lo, He that formeth the mountains, and createth the wind, and declareth unto man what is his thought, that maketh the morning darkness, and treadeth upon the high places of the earth, The LORD, The God of hosts, is His name" (Amos 4:12-13).

We seem to easily puff our chests out thinking we are the most important thing in the world. The reality is God is the most important and we ought to have the goal of glorifying Him in all we do and say. God Who formed the mountains ... and created the wind ... makes the light come in the morning ... deserves our attention. Too many of us go through our days without much thought as to what God wants for us in our lives.

He is the Creator, and Sustainer of our lives. He deserves some thought. He deserves to be considered before we make any decisions in life. Today is a good day to begin asking Him what He wants us to do with this life He has given us. Don't wander aimlessly through the day just letting whatever happens happen without a plan to glorify God. He has given us this day as a treasure. We will never have this day again. Use the hours God will give you today to bring glory to His name, not your own.

The reality is, there is coming a day sooner than we might think when we will meet God face-to-face. The challenge is given in these verses to prepare to meet our God. It seems strange to me we will spend hour upon hour making plans for life insurance, and a casket, and the songs to be sung at our funeral, and many other things. At the same time we don't give much time to thinking about what we will offer our God when we meet Him face-to-face. That day is surely coming. What will you be able to offer Him on that day?

Are you making preparation for the day you will meet God? Are you doing things today He will be pleased with? Are you investing in the lives of those He would like you to reach with the life He has given you? Are you passing along His grace and mercy to the people you will be with today? Or are your plans for the day to give as little time to God as possible, and then to get on with the things you think are important? I hope you will prepare to meet your God today. I hope you will live every moment of today with His goals for your life in mind. I hope you will make an eternal difference in the lives of those God will draw across your path today.

Eat Up! – June 16

There are few things I like more than eating really good food. I have been blessed to have some of the best food I think exists on this earth. I have also had some food I would not feed a dog (if I had one). I have tasted some things, that as soon as they hit my tongue, I realized they were obviously not meant for me to eat. However, there is one banquet table where I sit at that never ever disappoints. Every morning it has been my joy to pull up to the table where the Word of God is available for me. I have enjoyed food here for my entire life. That's right; I was memorizing Scripture long before I knew what it meant. I am still enjoying the feast of the Word of God today!

The prophet, Amos, told us this would not always be the case. "*'Behold, the days come,' saith the Lord God, 'that I will send a famine in the land, not a famine of bread, nor a thirst for water, but of hearing the words of the LORD'*" (Amos 8:11). Many might say we are in that time of famine right now. I totally disagree! We have more availability of Scripture today than we have ever had in the history of mankind. Most of us have multiple copies of the Bible in our homes. We have the Bible available on CD's (or cassette tapes for those old people among us). We have the Bible available for our computers. Most Christians I know have the Bible on their phone.

There is no famine for the Word of God today ... but that day is coming. Rather than spend a moment today complaining about how far down our nation has gone from the Word of God, why not open your Bible and eat up!? Instead of pointing out all the flaws in our churches today, why not beg God to feed you from His Word today and stay in it until you feel He has!? Rather than look for the faults and sins of another person, why not pull up to the table of the Word of God and ask Him to reveal areas of your own life that need some work, and allow the Holy Spirit to clean you up today!?

Today we have an abundance of the Word of God ... but there will be a day when that abundance will turn to famine. What are you doing to make sure you offer the bounty of the Word of God to those who have never heard it before? Rather than wasting another minute on the other things that could consume your time, why not ask God to feed you ... and then ask Him to lead you to someone who needs to feast on the same truths you have discovered? I want to be a man of the Word today. I want to share with others the things God touches my heart with. I want to "feed the world!"

Don't Take a Ride in a Whale! – June 17

Many today think it is impossible for the world to have revival. I disagree! I have seen proof that nations can fall on their knees in repentance. The real issue today is not whether nations need to repent. The real issue is not whether or not God wants nations to repent. The real issue is not if nations will repent. The real issue is not even if God would receive a repentant nation. The real story of the book of Jonah is whether believers who have been given the task of reaching the world will do their part in preaching the true Gospel!

Take a look at the mercy of our gracious God today! "*And Jonah began to enter into the city a day's journey, and he cried and said, 'yet forty days, and Nineveh shall be overthrown.' … For word came unto the king of Nineveh, and he arose from his throne, and he laid his robe from him, and covered him with sackcloth, and sat in ashes. And he caused it to be proclaimed and published through Nineveh by the decree of the king and his nobles, saying, 'let neither man nor beast, herd nor flock, taste anything; let them not feed, nor drink water: But let man and beast be covered with sackcloth, and dry mightily unto God: yea, let them turn every one from his evil way, and from the violence that is in their hands. Who can tell if God will turn and repent, and turn away from His fierce anger, that we perish not*" (Jonah 3:4, 6-9)?

If the pagan king of Nineveh turned to God, there is hope for any nation in our world today. This king had no idea about repentance until Jonah showed up. We focus far too much attention on the belly of the whale in this book, when we ought to be talking about the unlimited mercy of God in Heaven. God is able to do exceedingly, abundantly; above all we can ask or even think! He is able to save to the uttermost, all those who come to Him in repentance! He is able to remove sin as far as the east is from the west! He is the God that sent His Son to hang on a cross! He is the Savior Who cried out from the cross … "*Father, forgive them … for they know not what they do!*"

While you and I (and Jonah) are having thoughts of revenge and justice, God is having thoughts of grace and mercy. Perhaps this is because God knows the terror of Hell. Perhaps it is because He knows the absolute beauty of Heaven. Perhaps it is because God knows the value of the human soul. We realize we are not God … but we are His messengers. There are plenty of whales in the ocean God can use to get our attention today. Don't make God use a whale; go tell someone about Him today!

179

Good Words – June 18

There is a sweet phrase within a verse that really touched my heart today, and gave me time to thank God for the Bible. "*O thou that art named the house of Jacob, is the spirit of the LORD straitened? Are these His doings? Do not My words do good to him that walketh uprightly*" (Micah 2:7)? Did you catch that last question ... "*Do not My words do good to him that walketh uprightly?*" The answer is that the words of God have done good for me, and I want to walk uprightly today.

When my dad was a young boy, they were encouraged to memorize Scripture to win a free week at a local Christian camp. My dad memorized enough to be able to go to camp. His father died in a car accident when he was a year-and-a-half old. He grew up very poor and would have had no other way to go to camp. He went to camp and someone shared the Gospel with him and he trusted Christ as His own Savior! I would say the Word of God was good to my dad ... and to me! Because of the Word of God, I had the opportunity to be born into a Christian home.

When I was a boy growing up in our local church, we had a program that encouraged kids to memorize Scripture. It was called Bible Memory Association. I don't know if it still exists, but it was an incentive-based program that challenged young people to memorize the Bible. I was heavily into the program. Largely because (I hate to admit) there were prizes if you memorized enough verses. Many of those passages of Scripture are still in my memory bank until this day. Sometimes I can't find the withdraw slip to pull them out, but many times those same verses pop into my mind at the exact right time!

The last part of the verse is so true. Walking uprightly ... walking in the right ways, in the ways you know are right ... is a key to the power of the Word of God in a life. Today I have no doubt about the power of the Word of God! I have seen it crush my hardened heart like a hammer. I have felt the heat of it as a fire in my soul at times when I needed the inspiration. It has been a soothing balm, a salve as it were to my heart when it was hurting. It has been a foot launching me into the will of God when I was stuck at the shore of indecision and doubt. It has become my entire source for preaching and teaching material. It is a never-ending spring of wonderful truths that have transformed my life, and the lives of those who have heard the same truths and trusted the same Holy Spirit to do a work in them. I love my Bible! I love my Bible! I love my Bible! Oh, and by the way, if I haven't told you lately ... I love my Bible! Walk uprightly in its truths today!

What God Wants From Us – June 19

"Will the LORD be pleased with thousands of rams, or with ten thousands of rivers of oil? Shall I give my firstborn for my transgression, the fruit of my body for the sin of my soul? He had shewed thee, O man, what is good; and what doth the LORD require of thee, but to do justly, and to love mercy, and to walk humbly with thy God" (Micah 6:7-8)?

God wants me to do justly. God just wants us to do what is right and fair. We are living in a world which has said rules don't matter anymore. If you don't like the rule ... break it! If you don't like the rule ... ignore it! If you don't like the rule ... pretend it isn't there. God wants you and I to walk in righteous paths. He wants us to live in a just way that others may see His influence in our lives. He wants you and I to be fair with others and to treat them right, regardless of how they treat us.

God wants me to love mercy. Again, there is a great deal of anger and vengeance in our world today. God wants us to look for opportunities to demonstrate real mercy. I have found Christians in general are far better at justice than they are at mercy. I want to be merciful ... but it's not easy. It is very easy for me to execute justice when someone does something against me, or against something I believe in. Can you imagine how tough it was for our perfect Savior to put up with imperfect humanity for thirty-three years? At the end of it all, He loved us so much He laid down His life so we could become the righteousness of God. If He was so patient in giving out mercy to us, don't you think we could be a bit more merciful today?

God wants me to walk humbly with Him today. If I am going to walk with God, it must be in humility! If I allow pride to overtake my attitude and actions, God must resist me! If I will become humble and remain that way, I can walk alongside Him. One of the great joys of my heart is to take a walk with our children, or grandchildren. Before, our grandkids needed us to pull them in a wagon, or to hold their hand. Now they are growing up, and their independence is shining through. They can ride the bike themselves (with the help of training wheels). They can walk by themselves. But what a joy now when they choose to walk hand-in-hand with us! God wants to take a walk with you today.

These are the three things God wants from you today ... do justly today ... love mercy ... and walk humbly with Him. He is waiting with an outstretched hand toward you today. These are the gifts God wants from you today.

He Will Turn Again – June 20

"Who is a God like unto Thee, that pardoneth iniquity, and passeth by the transgression of the remnant of his heritage? He retaineth not His anger forever, because He delighteth in mercy. He will turn again, He will have compassion upon us; He will subdue our iniquities; and Thou wilt cast all their sins into the depths of the sea" (Micah 7:18-19).

Check out all the things these two verses say that God will do for us. First, He pardons our iniquity. Recently my mentor, Ted Camp, wrote an article on what a "pardon" really is. The idea we are familiar with is when a governor "pardons," or frees a prisoner from prison. This is what God has done with each guilty sinner who comes to Him by faith! The righteous God offers pardon for every sinner who repents and trusts Jesus Christ for forgiveness of sin!

Second, God *"passeth by the transgression"* of His people. He not only passes by our sin, he does not *"retain His anger"* for our sin. God does something for us in regards to our sin that we cannot do ourselves! He not only forgives our sin … He chooses not to remember it or to dwell on it! He actually, totally forgives our sin! He does this because *"He delighteth in mercy."* He finds joy in forgiving and offering mercy in the place of judgment! He is giddy with joy when He pours His mercy on a sinner who deserved judgment and condemnation!

Third, He turns back to us again! I absolutely love this picture! When Jesus was on the cross bearing our sin and shame, God turned His face from His only begotten Son. Three days later, God received the offering of Jesus' blood as the payment in full for the sins of the world. Jesus is seated at the right hand of God today making intercession for me and for each of you who is saved! God is not turning His back on us today … because of the payment for our sins His Son provided for us. We, like the prodigal son returning home, will find our Heavenly Father on the back porch looking for us to return from our folly. He turns back again! He has compassion for us.

The last thing these two verses show us is, God conquers our sin, and He casts them into the depths of the sea! I am in love with this powerful God Who loves me so much! I am in love with my God Who not only forgives my sin, but also removes them never to be seen again! I love how He loves me so deeply. These verses make me want to live for God today! Run from sin and toward His righteousness today. Turn back to Him in all areas of your life today. Don't run away from Him today … run toward Him!

My Stronghold – June 21

"The mountains quake at Him, and the hills melt, and the earth is burned at His presence, yea, the world, and all that dwell therein. Who can stand before His indignation? And who can abide in the fierceness of His anger? His fury is poured out like fire, and the rocks are thrown down by Him. The LORD is good, a stronghold in the day of trouble; and He knoweth them that trust in Him" (Nahum 1:5-7).

None of us deserve to stand before this holy and righteous God. The questions the prophet Nahum asks provides an obvious answer ... no one is worthy to stand before God. The beauty of these three verses is Nahum takes us from the realization that we are nothing, and for no one to think they should have an audience with God; to the place of calling Him our stronghold in the day of trouble.

What a joy to know God personally! Don't take that for granted today. You and I have the opportunity to know this God! It is this God Who sent His Son to take my place of punishment on the cross of Calvary! It is this God ... the God that causes the hills to melt, and the earth to be burned up ... that loved you enough to pay the price for your sin! That is "my" God!

The power He displays that makes the hills melt and the earth to be burned up is at my disposal for any of the challenges I am facing, or I will face in the future. He is my "stronghold." He is the place of strength where I run to for protection. I'm glad today there is a God Who is well able to handle whatever comes across my path. I'm glad today with all the challenges life presents that I have a God to run to Who makes the hills melt and the earth to burn up! There is no problem, challenge, or difficulty I can face today that He cannot handle.

I will certainly face things which are far beyond my ability to handle. I will not face anything He cannot handle. I am going to make a choice today to trust God. I could spend the day trying to fix my own problems ... without success. I am planning to start this day within the protection of my Stronghold and to remain there all day long. I will need the help of God to do this, because my natural response to trouble will be to try to handle it on my own. I know there are very few things I can handle on my own. I am hopeful I can surrender to my God when these challenges of life come my way. What a joy to know God can be our stronghold in the day when trouble comes! You know troubles will come. Don't try to handle them on your own today. Run to your Heavenly Father for help!

God Alone ... – June 22

"And they sing the song of Moses the servant of God, and the song of the Lamb, saying, 'Great and marvelous are Thy works, Lord God Almighty: just and true are Thy ways, Thou King of saints. Who shall not fear Thee, O Lord, and glorify Thy name? For **Thou only art holy**; *for all nations shall come and worship before Thee; for Thy judgments are made manifest"* (Revelation 15:3-4).

These are the praises that will be sung to our God. There is something that pierces my heart as I read these verses. The simple thought is about the holiness of God ... contrasted with my sinfulness! I am constantly aware of my sinful behavior and thoughts. I would love to live one day without any sin whatsoever ... but, unfortunately by the time lunch rolls around, I have already sinned (really its breakfast, but I don't want you to stop reading). My point is, we serve a holy and righteous God, and He alone is holy!

His holiness causes me to fear Him. I yearn for His approval, but I often wonder how I can please Him when I am such a sinner. I believe I have found the answer. The answer is that He knows me ... He knew me before the foundation of the earth was established. He knows me, and He loves me! He knew all the sin I would ever commit and He loved me in spite of my sin, or as Paul wrote in Romans 5:8, while I was yet sinning!

No wonder these saints in glory will be singing out, *"Great and marvelous are Thy works!"* Today I want to join this chorus! His judgments will be made manifest ... meaning the entire line of humanity, from the first man to the last man will testify God and His works are wonderful and magnificent! All those who scoff at God today and criticize Him and His Bible will one day admit along with everyone else that God is God! All will bow the knee in humility to this wonderful God! I think today is a good day for each of us to bow our knee to Him and open our heart and hands to whatever He has for us to do.

God alone is holy! God alone is worthy of our worship and praise. Man ... regardless of how good he is ... regardless of the wonderful things he has accomplished ... is still man. We have sin at our core. Praise God that He reached to where we were to provide a Lamb Who is worthy to be praised! He sent the Lamb of God Who has the ability to take away the sins of the world! He sent the Lamb that died, but also rose from the dead for us, and is now seated at the right hand of the throne of God. That Lamb, my Heavenly Father, and the Holy Spirit alone are holy!

Seed in the Barn – June 23

It has always amazed me how one simple phrase can touch my heart from the Word of God. Even one word has incredible power when found within the Word of God. When I was in Bible College we made the claim that we believed in the verbal, plenary inspiration of the Word of God. I still believe that! What does it mean? It means I believe God breathed the very words, and even affected the grammatical structure of the verses by His Holy Spirit. It means the Bible is unlike any other book in the history of mankind! It means when all other books have faded away, and their importance with them, the Bible still is the Book of the Ages!

Today I read one short phrase that really touched my heart. "*Is the seed yet in the barn*" (Haggai 2:19)? God has been using the Old Testament prophet Haggai to chastise His people during the days of King Darius. God asked this simple question in the last chapter of Haggai's book. I believe God was saying something like, "*Are you telling me that after all these years of having My commandments … My statutes … My judgments … My instructions for righteousness and godly living that you have left that precious seed in the barn?*" How absolutely foolish could God's people be? We would love to shake our finger at them in condemnation … but … are we not just as guilty as they are?

We have far more than Genesis through Song of Solomon (which may be all the Word of God they had at this time … if they were fortunate). We have all sixty-six books! We have the "*all Scripture*" Paul was talking to Timothy about in II Timothy 3:16-17! We have every word God desired for us to have to give His complete thought and instruction on the things He knew we would need. We certainly have all the seeds for truth that any person in any generation could ever want or need!

Let me ask the same question to each of us reading this today … "*Is the seed* [of the Word of God] *yet in the barn?*" Did you wake up this morning and run to "*the seed*" and sprinkle those seeds of truth all over your fertile heart before getting started? Or is your Bible in the same place you left it from yesterday? Have you prepared your heart before reading those words and asked the Lord of the Harvest to spring up fruit from the seed you are about to read? Have you taken the time to pull out the weeds of sin and doubt that often creep into our hearts? Have you made sure when you are hearing/seeing preaching that your heart is open to receive those words? The question here is … what are we doing with the seed God has given us?

Which Way Will You Turn? – June 24

"Therefore say thou unto them, Thus saith the LORD of Hosts; 'Turn ye unto Me,' saith the LORD of Hosts, 'and I will turn unto you,' saith the LORD of Hosts. 'Be ye not as your fathers, unto whom the former prophets have cried, saying, "Thus saith the LORD of Hosts; 'Turn ye now from your evil ways, and from your evil doings:" but they did not hear, nor hearken unto Me,' saith the LORD" (Zechariah 1:3-4).

"Draw nigh to God, and He will draw nigh to you. Cleanse your hands, ye sinners; and purify your hearts, ye double minded" (James 4:8).

In both the Old and New Testaments God has put out a plea for men to turn toward Him. There are two thoughts that come to my heart today while reading these verses. The first thought is, it is awesome to me to think the God Who created everything on the earth and in the universe wants to spend time with me. I am very humbled by that thought. I don't feel very important most of the days I live (and when I do feel important, it doesn't take much to make me realize who I really am). The thought that God desires to spend time with me … that He really does want me to get closer to Him … is such a blessed and rich thought to me. I am very humbled by this thought.

The second thought that occurred to me was, it is a shame this much deserving God should need to challenge us to spend time with Him! He should never need to encourage us to turn to Him. He should never need to invite us to draw nigh (near) to Him. He should not need to challenge us on a daily basis to come to Him for help. He ought to be the first person we turn to on a daily basis. After all, He is the One with the Words of life! He is the One Who invented love. He is the One that reached out to us when we could not reach out to Him. He created the universe and has all the answers to how it works!

It is not about what others are doing with God; it is about what you are doing with God. These devotionals are meant to be personal. The goal of these are to help each of us to draw into a more intimate relationship with our God on a regular basis. So, the chastisement for not going to God for help should be a personal thing for each of us. The encouragement for the blessings that come when we draw near to God is personal as well.

I don't know about you today, but I am going to need Him all day long. I have things I need His help with. Run to Him today for all you will ever want or need. Our loving Heavenly Father is waiting for His child.

The Main Character – June 25

Yesterday my wife and I had the opportunity to go see a drama about the life of Moses. There seemed to be no doubt the main character in the story would be Moses. However, as the drama unfolded, it became very obvious the main character was not Moses at all, but the God of Moses. Today I read one of my favorite verses again. The prophet Zechariah wrote this: *"Then he answered and spake unto me, saying, 'This is the word of the LORD unto Zerubbabel,' saying, 'Not by might, nor by power, but by My Spirit saith the LORD of Hosts'"* (Zechariah 4:6).

There is a very important message in this verse I believe many of us are missing in the world today; and unfortunately, in our fundamental churches as well. The main character in our story should not be us ... but our God! Just as Moses' life was filled with his inabilities; his insufficiencies; his sinful pride; and even his sinful actions ... we are nothing to brag about. We like to portray ourselves as being good people, but the real truth is at our best we are wretched sinners who have been saved by the grace of God!

Again, He is the Main Character! He did the saving! He does the cleaning up! He does the training to help us to know the right way to go! He does the convicting of sin! He draws us closer to Himself, when our natural inclination is to walk away from Him! He is the One Who breathes life into the work we do for Him! It is all about the Main Character ... God!

If you would be honest with yourself, you will see sin dominates our lives. We think sinful thoughts. We do sinful actions. We have sinful attitudes. We waste time. We waste money. We are selfish and greedy and seek revenge whenever possible. We generally think of us first and others a distant second. We want everything done our way, in our time, in ways that will please us. We are sinful people. There is no way we can take the place of main character, even in our own life's story.

Without the Spirit of God working and moving in our hearts ... nothing good will come of us. With the Spirit of God in control of our life, there is nothing God cannot do. You see, He is looking for a yielded vessel to work in and through. When Moses started his life in his own energy, it ended in disaster. When Moses came to God with nothing but a stuttering tongue and a rod he had found in the desert, God made possibly the greatest leader the world has ever known of him. What do you have to offer God today? Are you willing to turn that over to the Holy Spirit?

Are You Listening? – June 26

When I was a little boy ... a teenager ... a young married man ... a middle aged man ... I guess I can say my whole life has been a challenge to really pay attention! I can remember hearing my mom ask if I was really listening to her when she was talking to me. There are times my wife is talking to me and she will pause to ask simply, *"Did you hear what I was saying?"* Just last week our daughter called and asked me to do her a favor. Later that day she showed up at our house, and I remembered I had totally forgotten the favor!

Zechariah the prophet wrote these words from the Lord to the people of his day: *"Thus speaketh the LORD of hosts, saying, 'Execute true judgment, and show mercy and compassions every man to his brother: And oppress not the widow, nor the fatherless, the stranger, nor the poor; and let none of you imagine evil against his brother in your heart. But they refused to hearken, and pulled away the shoulder, and stopped their ears, that they should not hear'"* (Zechariah 7:9-11).

God gave His commands very clearly through His prophet Zechariah to the children of Israel, but they were not listening. What good is instruction if those who need it are not paying attention? What good is a Bible if all we do is read its words without obeying its principles? What good is preaching or teaching if all we do is look for a place to say, "Amen" but we never change our behavior after hearing it?

Zechariah continued ... *"Yea, they made their hearts as an adamant stone, lest they should hear the law, and the words which the LORD of hosts hath sent in His spirit by the former prophets; therefore came a great wrath from the LORD of hosts"* (Zechariah 7:12). Be sure if you refuse to allow your heart to be changed, judgment is coming!

Today you have read some good instruction for living. God wants us to live in a way that we demonstrate justice ... meaning we are going to live by the laws we know to be true. God also wants us to live showing mercy and compassion to those around us. When we walk according to the laws we have seen in the Bible and couple that with mercy and compassion on others, it will make a huge difference!

Now the question for the day is this: will we live the way we have been taught by the verses to live, or will we also close our ears to the instruction and harden our heart? It is totally your choice. No one can make this decision for you today. Walk with God show His compassion to others!

In the Book – June 27

"And the sea gave up the dead which were in it; and death and hell delivered up the dead which were in them: and they were judged every man according to their works. And death and hell were cast into the lake of fire. This is the second death. And whosoever was not found written in the book of the life was cast into the lake of fire" (Revelation 20:13-15).

After a funeral service for a dear Christian friend of mine, a Deaf man approached me. He worked his way through many people and when he reached me, he simply signed, *"Is my name in the book?"* I was confused, thinking he was talking about the guest registration book that is often in the lobby of a funeral service to record who attended. I signed back to him I was sure the book was still in the lobby and he could go back to sign in whenever he could get back there. He adamantly shook his head, and signed again, *"Is my name in the book?"* He then told me he was sure the man who had died was in Heaven, but he was not sure he would be there when he died.

I took that Deaf man into a back room where no one could see us, and explained as clearly as I could the Gospel message of Jesus' death, burial and resurrection. I asked him if he believed all that. His response was a definite 'yes.' I then asked Him if he wanted to ask Jesus to become His Savior. Again, he replied, 'yes.' He followed me in simple, but clear prayer following the guidelines of Romans (3:23; 6:23; 5:8; 10:9 – by the way, it is the Gospel of Jesus Christ that is the power of God unto salvation, not some fancy worded prayer) and asked Jesus to become His Savior.

When he finished praying, he looked at me with the most sincere eyes and asked again, *"Is my name in the book?"* I then acted out for him the scene I pictured in Heaven. I showed Him God looking down and seeing him preparing to ask Jesus to forgive him – God calling for the book of life to be brought to Him. Then I explained as God watched him signing he knew he was a sinner – God asked for the pen. As God saw him say that he believed Jesus died, was buried and rose from the grave for his sin – God leafed through the pages to the place where his name would go. As he signed 'Amen' – God wrote his name in the book of life and slammed it shut and signed, 'FINISHED!'

Has there been a time when God could do that for you? I would not want to risk missing Heaven! If you're not sure, please take the time to be sure! Praise God if you know your name is there!

Scars – June 28

Ever since I was an eight year old boy, I have carried three different scars on my right bicep. My family and I lived in a duplex house (a house where the right side of the building was ours and the left side of the building was a separate house for another family). I can still clearly remember one summer afternoon when I went over to my neighbor's house (in the other side of my house) to prepare to go fishing. We got our fishing poles together and the bait and I started out the back door to go fishing. When I stepped out of the door, I saw his collie dog snarling and looking at me funny. The dog attacked me and I turned to toward the house. He bit my right arm, and clawed at my back. Quickly my neighbor came out of the house and got his dog to release me. I jumped the fence between our houses and ran inside my house. After what seemed like an alcohol bath (not really), we made a trip to the hospital and I got seven stitches in my arm to repair the places his dog had bitten me. Almost fifty years later, I still have the scars to remind me of that incident.

There is a verse in Zechariah that touched my heart today. It simply says, *"And one shall say unto Him, 'What are these wounds in Thine hands?' Then He shall answer, 'Those with which I was wounded in the house of My friends'"* (Zechariah 13:6). I believe this is a peek into Heaven and into the future time we will spend with Jesus there. I believe we will be able to view the scars in the hands, feet and side of Jesus Christ for all eternity. They will be a constant reminder to all of us who are redeemed through the blood of the Lamb, of the tremendous cost He paid for our sin. Make no mistake about it; our sin cost Jesus something! The cost of our sin was not cheap. The gift of forgiveness is free, but there are scars that will serve to remind us of the incredible price Jesus paid for us.

Jesus said He got those scars *"in the house of My friends."* Stop and think on that for a moment. He got these scars *"in the house of His friends."* There is an old hymn that says, *"Jesus, what a friend for sinners ... Jesus lover of my soul."* When Judas Iscariot made his way into the Garden of Gethsemane to betray Jesus with the kiss, Jesus called him *"friend."* When Jesus hung on the cross, the first words He spoke were, *"Father, forgive them for they know not what they do."* Jesus is the friend of sinners. Praise God for that because I am a sinner! You should praise God as well, because you are a sinner too! One day we will see the scars on the hands of Jesus there in Heaven. Start thanking Him today for those scars. His scars have deep significance to us both today, and throughout eternity!

Let the Whole World Know – June 29

"'*For from the rising of the sun even unto the going down of the same My name shall be great among the Gentiles; and in every place incense shall be offered unto My name, and a pure offering: for My name shall be great among the heathen,' saith the LORD of hosts*" (Malachi 1:11).

Think about the significance of this verse! From where the sun rises to where the sun sets ... every place on the face of this globe ... God's name will be great! A college professor of mine told many stories of being a missionary in a very primitive, tribal country. He told about being the first white man the people had ever seen. He then told about how they had to learn the language of the people and develop that language to a written form. Their goal was to present the Gospel to the people in their own language. I believe it took them three years to get to the place where they knew enough of the language to tell the people about Jesus Christ.

When they finally told them about Jesus, most of the people they told, including the tribal chief, trusted Christ. As they learned more of the language and were able to communicate with the people they discovered that within the traditions that had been handed down from generation to generation, these people had been told a great bird would drop a white man into their tribe to tell them about God. When this missionary got off the plane (the great bird), and eventually told them His message of God and His Son, this tribe was ready to respond!

I can remember sitting spell-bound to this story. This missionary (later my professor) was used by God to establish 100 churches in a little over ten years in that field! All because God promised from the rising of the sun to the going down of the same people would know about Him. They not only would know about Him, but they would offer their hearts to Him! What an incredible journey we have to be on as Christians in this world today.

Rather than cursing the darkness we see around us, let's do as Peter Beneson encouraged us, and light a candle! I know our world is turning darker and darker with each day, but we have the light of the Word of God! We know the Light of the world, Jesus Christ! With all the technology God has blessed us with today, let's do our part to get the word out to the uttermost parts of the world. Jesus came to save sinners! Jesus is the Light of the world, and men do not need to live in darkness anymore! It is a great day to live for God! Tell someone about Him!

Don't Waste Your Worship – June 30

We worship athletes today … only to find out they do not have the character they should have and we are disappointed. We worship political leaders today … only to find out they do not fulfill the promises they made. We worship spiritual leaders today … only to find out they too are just flesh and blood like us and they fail as well.

In the last chapter of the last book in our Bible, we read a very clear and important message that was given by an angel to John as he neared the completion of this great book of Revelation. He could not help himself, as he heard these great promises for the future. *"And I John saw these things and heard them. And I fell down to worship before the feet of the angel which showed me these things. Then saith he unto me, 'See thou do it not: for I am thy fellow servant, and of them which keep the sayings of this book: Worship God"* (Revelation 22:8-9).

We are living in a world where we are seeing people worship the strangest things. Some worship their cars. Others worship their houses, or gardens. Some worship their work. Others worship their boat or camper. Some worship an author. Some worship a preacher or teacher, politician or world leader. Others worship a stone … bone … shroud … stain on a paper … a cloud in the shape of something … you can fill in the blank. We are living among a generation of confused worshippers.

Let's not be too critical … the Apostle John himself was confused. There have been times when I have seen a majestic sunset, or sunrise and have been tempted to worship the beauty of it. The angel gave us all good advice. Be careful not to worship the creation … go to the Source and worship the Creator! Don't worship the messenger, the Pastor, the teacher, the author; worship God! Don't worship the church building or the things in the building; worship God! Don't worship the choir, or the music, or the instruments; worship God! Don't worship your children, or your parents, or your family; worship God!

When all is said and done and we finish this race we call "life," we will appear before God face to face. We will not be tempted to worship anything else in Heaven. There will be streets of gold … we won't care. There will be gates of pearl … we won't care. There will be walls made of precious stones … we won't care. Why? Because God will be there and He will far surpass all these other "things" we think are so important here on earth! Don't sing for the praise of men! Worship God today!

MONTH OF
July

Others – July 1

I have committed to reading my Bible through every year that I can. These devotionals are written out of what God touches my heart with in those daily readings. As a result, you are traveling on the journey through the pages of the Word of God with me each day. I have been praying about what God would have me do now that the reading schedule is complete for reading my Bible through this year. I was advised by a trusted counsellor to do a study that is in an area of need I have right now. Recently I have started a whole new phase of our ministry that both scares and excites me! Because of this new adventure, I have felt led to study the book of Nehemiah. The devotionals for this time will be lessons I am learning from Nehemiah and passing along to you.

This morning I read of Nehemiah's heart for his people. *"That Hanani, one of my brethren came, he and certain men of Judah; and I asked them concerning the Jews that had escaped, which were left of the captivity, and concerning Jerusalem"* (Nehemiah 1:2).

God touched my heart with a couple of thoughts from this verse. First I was impressed Nehemiah had such a heart for others. Too many times I feel like I wander through an entire day only thinking of myself and the things I want to accomplish. On those days, I am like a steam-roller, just going through my day flattening all who are in my path. Nehemiah was genuinely touched by those who were still in Jerusalem that were his countrymen who were in need of help. When was the last time you thought about others who have needs you might be able to help? Don't miss the opportunities to serve someone else today.

The second thing that struck me is the blessing of having a burden. I love to look at faces. I know it's strange, but when I am driving, or working in my yard, or in the mall (at Christmas time) … I look at the faces of people who are passing. I have noticed in general people today are living very bored lives. There are many times when I see blank expressions, or depressed looks. I am thankful God has given me a burden for the Deaf! What a privilege it is to me to wake up every morning with a purpose for the day. I want to make a difference just like Nehemiah wanted to make a difference for the people in Jerusalem.

If you do not have someone, or some people that you have a heart for today, ask God to give you this same passion for someone other than your-self! Life is too short. Make a difference for someone else today!

Open Eyes and Ears – July 2

"Let Thine ear now be attentive, and Thine eyes open, that Thou mayest hear the prayer of Thy servant, which I pray before Thee now, day and night, for the children of Israel Thy servants, and confess the sins of the children of Israel, which we have sinned against Thee: both I am my father's house have sinned" (Nehemiah 1:6).

Nehemiah heard about the walls of Jerusalem being in ruin and it drove Him to His knees in prayer. In the process of that prayer, Nehemiah asked God to keep His eyes and ears open to his prayer, and eventually to the prayer of His people, Israel. When was the last time you went to God in prayer for something that seemed to have a greater sense of importance than normal? When you knelt in prayer, did you consider asking God to turn His full attention to what that situation?

One of our grandsons was born with some physical challenges. There have been a few times in his first year of life when he needed to make a return trip to the hospital. During his last "run" back to the hospital, we happened to be in Canada in meetings for two weeks. Of course, our hearts were burdened because we wanted to be there for our family, but realized there was nothing we could do. By the way ... God's timing is always perfect.

When we got the call that our grandson was being taken to the hospital, we realized things were potentially more serious than they had been before. Immediately we began to pray. Not like you might pray before a meal, but like Nehemiah might have prayed in the verse above. We were asking God to focus His attention on that hospital room, and specifically our grandson and his family. We quickly went into action and began to tell many of you about the need for prayer. What a blessing to know believers all around the world were praying for a little guy not even a year old at the time.

God worked in a very powerful way, but it was a vivid reminder of how important prayer really is in the life of a believer. All throughout this book of Nehemiah we will read of the prayer life of this dear Christian man. It strikes me that even though he had a very good relationship with the King of Shushan that he did not go to him first. We ought to take note Nehemiah had even better connections than that! He knew the King of all kings, and the Lord of all lords! He went straight to the top! Let's do the same thing today as we face challenges that are beyond our scope of power and ability. Thank God He does not need a wake-up call. He is always on duty and always ready to help in time of need! What a God we serve!

Turn Back to God – July 3

*"Remember, I beseech thee, the word that Thou commandest Thy servant Moses, saying, 'If ye transgress, I will scatter you abroad among the nations: But if ye **turn unto Me**, and keep My commandments, and do them; though there were of you cast out unto the uttermost part of the heaven, yet will I gather them from thence, and will bring them unto the place that I have chosen to set My name there'"* (Nehemiah 1:8-9).

I think God gets far too much blame today for the condition our world is in. I often hear things like, *"If God is a loving God, why does he allow rape …famine …earthquakes …"* and any other disaster that comes. Why don't we place the blame where it belongs? We are the ones who have sinned, not God. God has never changed, nor will He ever change! I'm thankful His plan has not changed either.

God created an incredible earth and universe, and made it to bring glory to Him and pleasure to His children. The problems we see today are not a result of God's unfair treatment of those of us on the earth. The problems we see today are a direct result of a people turning their backs on God and doing things that seem right in their own eyes. These things are detestable in the eyes of a holy and righteous God. It is so typical of we who are humans though … when we are caught in our sin; we often strike out at the One Who is without sin.

Nehemiah realized if there was ever going to be a restoration of the wall around Jerusalem, that there would first need to be a turning back to God by His people. If we are going to see revival in our world today, there must first be a whole-hearted turning back to God by His own people. If we would simply turn back to Him … if we would simply return to His commandments, the principles in the Word of God … if we would just *"do"* the things we know to do from the Word of God … I believe God has the same mercy and help available today that was available for Nehemiah.

How many times I have stood with my hands extended toward our children/grand-children with the offer of help … I am more than willing to help, but am waiting for them to turn to me. God is the same. He has all the answers for our lives today. Don't waste one more minute trying to solve the problems that will face you today on your own. God is waiting for us to turn back to Him and to do the things He has told us to do in His Word! Just like Nehemiah and those people in captivity needed to return to God in their day, we need to turn back today. God is waiting with opened arms!

Smile – July 4

Have you ever noticed how many people you pass on a daily basis that look like they drank dill pickle juice for breakfast instead of orange juice? They look like someone has stolen their joy. You are afraid to ask them how they are doing for fear you will be trapped for an hour as they explain everything that has gone wrong in their life for the past ten years! Unfortunately, it seems even our churches have been infected with this mentality.

I was reading about Nehemiah's burden for rebuilding the wall and noticed an interesting phrase. *"And it came to pass in the month Nisan, in the twentieth year of Artaxerxes the king, that wine was before him: and I took up the wine, and gave it unto the king. Now I had not been beforetime sad in his presence"* (Nehemiah 2:1). *"Now I had not been beforetime sad in his presence ..."* Can you say that about your relationships here on the earth?

Nehemiah had a very strong testimony before this heathen king. The king surely saw people on a daily basis who had great riches, but no joy. He, himself might have experienced the lack of genuine joy in a life filled with all the benefits of the position of a king. There was something different about this Hebrew man named Nehemiah. Every morning, every meal, every time he saw Nehemiah, he was impressed with the joy he displayed. Now, for the first time in the time he had known him, Nehemiah is sad.

What is your testimony today? Oh, listen ... Nehemiah surely had difficulties. His life was not an easy one at all, and yet he was displaying something King Artaxerxes could not buy with all his riches. Nehemiah knew the *"joy of the LORD"* (Nehemiah 8:10). I know each one reading this today could make a long list of things that are burdens, or challenges, or problems today. Nehemiah could have surely matched your list, and might have added a few more. I'm guessing none of us reading this today are slaves. I'm sure very few of us have been separated from our home land and family.

With all that in mind, when the king noticed Nehemiah's sad face, it was so unusual that he asked him about it. Nehemiah might normally have been the one bright spot in the kings day, and on this day, his smile was gone. May it be that you and I are the bright spot in someone's day? I hope you will make this your goal, not only today, but for every day God gives you life on this earth!

Got Junk? – July 5

I have heard an advertisement on the radio that asks this question. Do you have junk you want to get rid of? We will come and take away all your junk for you ... you don't need to do a thing! I think that sounds pretty good! Unfortunately, I think we all have some "junk" we would like to get rid of. Much of the junk we are faced with on a daily basis is junk of our own making ... meaning, we have done things which have created junk.

One of the main enemies of Nehemiah and those rebuilding the wall was a man named Sanballat. When he heard the Jews were rebuilding the wall "... *he spake before his brethren and the army of Samaria, and said, 'What do these feeble Jews? Will they fortify themselves? Will they sacrifice? Will they make an end in a day? Will they revive the stones of the heaps of the rubbish which are burned*" (Nehemiah 4:2)? He was worried the Jews would be able to make something out of the "junk" they had left them when they had conquered Israel years before.

Sanballat was talking about physical rubbish, but I would like to draw a spiritual truth from what he said. If you knew the rest of the story of the book of Nehemiah, you would know these Jews did rebuild this wall in only fifty-two days! An amazing architectural challenge given the tools and personnel they had working! Sanballat worried these people of God, under the direction of God, and with a vision from God might do something that would be so amazing it would result in the defeat of Samaria.

God is able to take ordinary people, like us, and do extraordinary things with us if we will simply follow His plan for "rubbish removal!" There are things in your life you might have the same viewpoint of that Sanballat had of the wall around Jerusalem. *"This is just "rubbish," whatever good thing could come from this?"* I want to tell you the same God that empowered this remnant of Israelites, is still alive and well, and is still in the "junk removal" business.

Later in this book, the book of the law was read in the presence of these people, and revival spread throughout their lives. Revival may seem impossible today, considering all the "rubbish" that surrounds our lives. Revival may seem impossible to you in your own personal life because of the "junk" you have accumulated in the last few weeks and days. I want to leave you with this incredible thought ... God is able to take your "rubbish" and do exceedingly ... abundantly ... above all you could ask or think with it if you yield it to Him. He is the Master Builder! Let Him work in you!

The Good Hand of God – July 6

"And the king said unto me, (the queen also sitting by him), 'For how long shall thy journey be? And when will thou return?' So it pleased the king to send me; and I set him a time. Moreover I said unto the king, 'If it please the king, let letters be given me to the governors beyond the river, that they may convey me over till I come to Judah;' And a letter unto Asaph the keeper of the king's forest, that he may give me timber to make beams for the gates of the palace which appertaineth to the house, and for the wall of the city, an fro the house that I shall enter into. And the king granted me, according to the good hand of my God upon me" (Nehemiah 2:6-8).

There will be times when you feel you are living in a world where everything seems to be going against you. There are times it will seem as though every opinion you hear is against the truths of the Word of God. There will be times when even Christians refuse to stand where it is right to stand, and you will feel as though you are all alone in the world. Don't believe that at all! When you stand where it is right to stand, you have a powerful Heavenly Father standing beside you!

Nehemiah was a captive in a foreign land. The people who surrounded him did not believe in God, and may have even mocked Nehemiah and the other Jewish slaves by reminding them their God was unable to protect them or their land. But, as is the case today, Nehemiah knew His God was still on the throne and still firmly in control. Nehemiah and the other Jews who were in captivity knew very well it was they who had turned their backs on God and not God Who had turned from them. In spite of the bad conditions ... and in spite of the fact that Nehemiah was in a pagan land that worshipped multiple gods, when Nehemiah made a request the king, the king gave him all he asked for. The key is that small phrase at the end of verse 8. *"According to the good hand of my God upon me."*

Have you experienced that "good hand" upon you and your life? God is still alive and well today. He can function regardless of the political or economic situation we face. He will choose to show His good hand regardless of what else is happening in the world ... but He will only reveal it through faithful believers. Nehemiah had remained faithful to God in spite of the captivity of him and his people. I am convinced God is ready to show His power still today. He can still stretch out His hand and bless the efforts of His people today. Are we living in a way that allows Him to show His power in our lives?

Mono-mania – July 7

One day a friend of mine told a story about three boys who were playing together after a fresh snow had fallen. I thought would be appropriate for this summer morning! The three boys loved to compete with each other about everything. They were standing together on one side of a field where no one had walked across yet. They were competing to see who could make the straightest line across the field with their footprints. The first boy started out with a plan he thought would bring him victory. He put the toe of his right foot up against the heel of his left and alternated all the way across the field, really concentrating on his feet. When he arrived on the other side and looked back, he had made an arc all the way across … not straight at all. The second boy learned from the first boy and did his plan with the toe to heel method, but he picked a tree on the other side and would periodically look up to get his bearings from the tree. He looked back at a zig-zag line all the way across. The third boy learned from the first two. He also did the toe to heel method, and using a tree on the other side of the field, fixed his eyes on the tree and walked straight across the field.

The term, "*mono-mania*" was invented by my friend to mean being "crazy about one thing." Nehemiah found the value of this singular focus on the thing that God gave him to do as well. He tells of his first trip to view the fallen walls around Jerusalem, and gives this description at one point. "*And I arose in the night, I and some few men with me; neither told I any man what my God had put in my heart to do at Jerusalem …*" (Nehemiah 2:12).

There will be times when God will place something on your heart to do that no one else sees as a burden to do. It is at that time when you need to follow the example of the third boy in the story above. You need to fix your eyes on the goal God has given you. You need to keep your feet in line with the Word of God. You need to move across that field whether or not anyone else comes with you. There was going to be a time for Nehemiah to share his vision with the others, but you will notice he did not reveal it all to them before he started.

I believe there are too many people who have shared their vision too soon with others, and were discouraged by those others when they asked questions and challenged the vision. Whatever God has placed upon your heart to do today, my advice is to begin to walk toward that goal and don't let anyone stop you! I am thankful for the burdens God has placed on my heart. I am thankful for His strength and guidance for pursuing and accomplishing those goals when others doubted! Step out w/mono-mania!

Strengthen Your Hands – July 8

"Then I told them of the hand of my God which was good upon me; as also the king's words that he had spoken unto me. And they said, 'Let us rise up and build.' So they strengthened their hands for this good work" (Nehemiah 2:18).

Nehemiah finally began to reveal the plan God touched his heart with to those who would help him. He told of the burden God gave him originally. He then told about how the king gave him permission and letters to get the materials they would need to build. Their response was, *"Let us rise up and build."*

Notice the vision God gives to a person begins in the heart of one person. It then takes a time of preparation and counting the cost. It then moves to passing that vision on to others who will be able to help. I am thankful God placed this book of Nehemiah in the Bible for us to see His plan for making a vision become reality. Many times I have had a plan, or a burden, but I never saw it actually come to pass. There have been other things God has touched my heart with, and now those things are happening and have become reality.

Look at how a vision becomes reality using this devotional as an example. This daily devotional began when our youngest daughter asked me to write something for her while in college. I began with the goal of finishing devotions for her freshman year in college. The vision for this began with a need. The need was seen and passed along to me from our daughter. The cost of doing this was evaluated. I realized it would take some time every day to do. I would need an internet connection to be able to email it to her. She would need to accept the responsibility to read it every day.

In order to make a vision become a reality, we need God's good hand to be upon us. If a vision is 'man-made' it will crumble and fail eventually. If a vision is going to become a reality, we will need to then strengthen our hands and do our part of the work. The men/women who built the wall in Jerusalem, could not 'pray' the wall up ... they had to get their hands involved! If we want to see God's work done in our lives, we must accept responsibility and do our part. In order for a vision to become reality, we need to continually strengthen our hands for the work. It is not a once-and-done thing, but an on-going process that needs effort to be finished.

Strengthen your hands today for the things God has placed in your hands to do. You will never regret following through. You will regret not doing it!

Faith and Works – July 9

In the New Testament book of James, the Holy Spirit reminds us there is a spiritual/physical combination God views as essential in order to live by faith. We hear a great deal about living by faith today, and much of it has nothing to do with Biblical principles. Today I was reading about Nehemiah and the remnant building the wall. As always, when we attempt anything for God, there will be those who are against us. If you have no opposition … you're probably not making that much of a difference.

Nehemiah faced this same thing. Look at his reaction (and the reaction of those building) … *"Nevertheless we made our prayer unto our God, and set a watch against them day and night, because of them"* (Nehemiah 4:9). Did you catch the mixture of faith and works there? First, they prayed to their God. A good habit to develop is to pray first, and act second. I must admit I usually find myself reversing that order. Unfortunately, I have tried too many times to take things into my own hands and try to fix whatever problem was facing me before asking God for help or guidance.

Nehemiah and this remnant first went to God for His help. But, they also did an interesting thing following that prayer to God. They set a watch, day and night on the wall. They added some effort to their prayers. They were asking God for His help, but they were not foolish enough to just sit still and complain when God didn't come through for them. They followed up their faith with their own efforts.

I still believe the first thing I ought to do is to pray and ask God for His help and guidance; but I also believe I then need to do the things He touches my heart to do. Common sense is largely missing in our society today. We need to exercise some Spiritual common sense when we pray as well. If I am challenged in a specific area, and I know something is a problem for me, I ought to do everything I can to get as far away from that thing as possible.

There are some things I am thinking of right now that are areas of challenge for me in my own personal life. I am going to ask God for help in those areas, but I am also going to set a watch on the wall day and night for them. I'm not going to go near the things that would cause me to fall. I'm going to set up all the protection for my heart that I can to guard myself. I think we all need to exercise some work to follow our faith in God. Let's determine today that we will trust God to do His part; but then let's also do all we can to be faithful in doing our part! Teamwork with God!

Fight For Your Family – July 10

"Therefore set I in the lower places behind the wall, and on the higher places, I even set the people after their families with their swords, their spears, and their bows. And I looked, and rose up, and said unto the nobles, and to the rulers, and to the rest of the people, 'Be not afraid of them: remember the Lord, which is great and terrible, and fight for your brethren, your sons, and your daughters, your wives, and your houses" (Nehemiah 4:13-14).

When the opposition came to Nehemiah and the Israelites who were building the wall, Nehemiah did something very interesting. He set the people in building the wall according to their families. I think it means he put families related to each other together ... side-by-side. He put them next to each other so if they needed to fight, they would have a deeper purpose and reason to fight. They would fight to protect and guard those they love.

I believe in fighting for your family. I have seen many families who have decided the best thing to do is to fight with their family. I don't believe that is the most productive thing we can do. I know there will be times within a family when we do not see things with the same perspective, but we ought to fight for our families nonetheless. I know there will be times when we disagree within our families, but we still need to stand beside each other and do our absolute best to stand tall for God. I know there are times when we will need to resolve conflict within our families, but I also believe it is worth the effort.

When we are in the battles of life, and we are working through the issues that face every family, the most important thing to do is to *"remember the Lord."* As I wrote recently, it is more about Him than it is about us. It is more about what He wants for our families than it is about my personal goals or desires. If we will keep the Lord first in our families, then we can fight for our sons and daughters; for our brethren and wives. The danger comes when we remove God from His rightful throne in our lives and we place ourselves, or our desires above His.

We are certainly in a battle today. There is a battle for our time, money, energies, and for our purpose in life. I want to encourage you today to keep your focus on the Lord. Remember Him in all the battles you are facing in life, and then fight hard to keep your family close to Him. Don't allow this world to be the major influence in the lives of you or your wife/husband, or your children. Remember the Lord today and fight for Him!

Hear O God – July 11

There are times in life when it is important to be so singularly focused on God that the clamoring of the world around you becomes dull and unimportant to you. I feel that way many times in the days we are living. It seems the opposition to God and His Word is increasing daily. Those who are willing to stand for the Bible and its truths seem to becoming less and less each day. There are times when I get to feeling like Elijah when he was hiding in the cave, complaining he was the only faithful prophet in all of the land. Just as it was with Elijah, I am reminded by God that I am not the only one standing for Him. Just as it was with Elijah, I am not the only one … but I am one! I need to take my stand where I believe the Bible says I ought to stand regardless of what others are doing, or not doing around me.

While in the building process of the wall, the Israelites heard some opposition and some mocking statements. The statements were not as important as the response of Nehemiah and those building the wall. *"Now Tobiah the Ammonite was by him, and he said, 'Even that which they build, if a fox go up, he shall even break down their stone wall.' 'Hear, O our God; for we are despised: and turn their reproach upon their own head, and give them for a prey in the land of captivity'"* (Nehemiah 4:3-4).

I want to follow Nehemiah's example and immediately turn to my God to defend me. Oh, how hard it must have been for Nehemiah not to fire back a sharp answer to defend himself! He probably wanted to stop what he was doing and go down and pound on Tobiah for a bit. I'm glad he turned to His God for his defense. What a great example his response is to me today. There are many who mock what we do when we are serving God. There are many (including some Christians) who will offer far more discouraging words than encouraging.

When others complain and make fun of what you are doing for God, just keep building the wall and pray to God. Just stop for a moment to pray and ask God to take care of them and their accusations. We need some folks who will have such a spiritual resolve that a little mocking will not stop them or slow them down. I want to be one of those people! I want to put aside my own feelings and opinions and stay singularly focused on what God has for me to do.

Whatever your "wall" may be, follow Nehemiah's example. Ignore those who are against you, and focus on the One that is for you! God has a listening ear pointed in your direction! Trust Him and obey Him today!

Holy Heartburn – July 12

Have you ever had a case of "holy heartburn?" If you haven't, you are not walking close enough to God. God has a heart that burns for many things. He has a heart that burns for the lost to be saved! He has a heart that burns for each of us to desire the truths found in His Word. He has a heart that burns for our families to walk in righteousness with Him daily. He has a heart that yearns for every last person as far as the uttermost parts of the earth to have seen/heard a clear presentation of the Gospel before they pass into eternity.

Without "holy heartburn" we may drop the ball on the things God has hoped and dreamed we would accomplish with the life He has given us. When Nehemiah heard of the broken down walls in Jerusalem, this was his response: "*And it came to pass, when I heard these words, that I sat down and wept, and mourned certain days, and fasted, and prayed before the God of heaven*" (Nehemiah 1:4).

The verses that follow are Nehemiah's prayer to God. It strikes me that before he prayed; he had an incurable case of "holy heartburn." His heart was so deeply burdened for the needs he saw, it affected everything about him. He did not just become discouraged, but if you notice there were some actions involved right from the beginning. He sat down ... he wept ... he mourned certain days ... he fasted ... and then he prayed.

Would you consider honestly today this question: When was the last time you were so burdened with "holy heartburn" that it sat you down? When was the last time that burden drove you to tears? When was the last time you mourned for days for a burden God gave you? When was the last time you missed a meal to pray for a burden? When was the last time you poured out your heart to God in sincere, deep prayer for that burden?

I am afraid with our busy life-styles today, we have very little time for a God ordained case of "holy heartburn." I am sitting here writing this and thinking about how I can carve out time for the things that "must" get done in the next week. Most of the time when I am doing something important I am texting someone, or I am checking email, or answering a phone call, etc. Where is the time for "holy heartburn?"

If we are going to have a healthy case of "holy heartburn" we are going to need to give God time. Yes, T-I-M-E, time. Are you willing to put aside your phone, computer, TV, book, and play time to spend time with God so He can burden your heart with the things He thinks are important?

Our Direct Line – July 13

Do you remember the old suspense movies when someone would walk over to the "red phone?" That phone was the one you never used, except for when you were in an emergency and you needed to get through to the "top" person for help. Today I was reminded of our "Direct Line" to Someone Who can help us in any situation we face at any time. What a joy to know God as our Heavenly Father! What a joy to know He loves us and is vitally interested in what is happening in our lives. When faced with the huge vision of rebuilding the wall in Jerusalem, Nehemiah spent most of the first chapter of the book named for him, pouring his heart out to God!

"And it came to pass, when I heard these words, that I sat down and wept, and mourned certain days, and fasted, and prayed before the God of Heaven, and said, 'I beseech Thee, O Lord God of Heaven, the great and terrible God, that keepeth covenant and mercy for them that love Him and observe His commandments: Let Thine ear now be attentive and Thine eyes open, that Thou mayest hear the prayer of Thy servant ..." (Nehemiah 1:4-6a).

Think about Nehemiah for a moment, and then consider yourself. Nehemiah was in a foreign country. He was nothing more than a servant, but God had allowed him to be the cupbearer for the king. He had no way to return to Jerusalem. He did not have the resources needed to rebuild the wall. He did not have anyone else he knew of, who committed to helping him with this job. He had no idea of the actual condition of the wall, or the opposition he would face once he arrived there to work. Nehemiah had far more questions than answers ... but he knew the God that could make the difference!

You may feel like the world has changed and you are living in a foreign country. You may not have a position that anyone recognizes as having much authority. You may feel there is something God wants you to do, but you are not qualified, or capable of doing what He has asked you to do. You may not fully understand all the ramifications of what you will need until you actually get fully committed and involved. You may feel very much like Nehemiah must have felt in chapter one. Do what Nehemiah did.

Today is a good day to take all your burdens and cares to God and trust Him to provide the wisdom and all the things you will need to accomplish what He has touched your heart to do. Nehemiah was able to watch God do some incredible things, because he trusted Him! Step out and trust God yourself!

Get Ready– July 14

There are many people with many questions today in the world we are living. We as believers ought to be ready to give an answer to them whenever the question might come. You never know when someone you work with is going to ask you why you spend your Sundays in church. You never know when a neighbor will have a health issue and will ask you to pray. You never know when a complete stranger will offer you the opportunity to talk with them about the troubles they are facing. When these times come, we need to be ready.

Nehemiah heard of the crumbled walls of Jerusalem. He had prayed and fasted and asked for healing for his people and land. When he stood before the king with a sad face (for the first time), the king asked what was troubling him. Nehemiah was ready with an answer. "*And said unto the king, 'Let the king live for ever: why should not my countenance be sad, when the city, the place of my fathers' sepulchres, lieth waste, and the gates thereof are consumed with fire*" (Nehemiah 2:3)? He did not stumble or stammer, but clearly explained his burden. Can you do this with the burden God has given you?

I remember the reaction of a pastoral candidate when I asked him what his vision was for ministry. It struck me when he had to think for quite some time before answering the question. I believe if God has given you a burden today for a portion of His ministry you ought to be ready to give an answer for why you are doing what you are doing. If you questioned me today about why I am doing what I am doing, I ought to have a plan in place and be working that plan. If I don't have a plan, chances are I am not going to be very successful today.

You might be thinking, "*I don't have a burden or vision for anything like that.*" If that is where you are right now, I would get on my knees and ask God for a burden … a vision … a ministry He wants you to do. I am sure God has not saved any one of us to sit and complain about what others are doing. I believe God saved us to serve Him. I also believe God has a job for everyone who is in His family to do to His glory!

Nehemiah was ready to tell the king what God had placed on his heart in a very clear and concise way. Can you do that? If you are a bit blurry on how to communicate your heart, spend some time today thinking about it and ask God to help you be able and ready when the time comes. Then you better get ready! God wants to use you to accomplish His work today!

When a Plan Comes Together – July 15

There was a TV show a while ago where the leader of a team would say, "*I love it when a plan comes together.*" Do you have a plan for your life? Do you have goals you are aiming for, and things you want to accomplish with the time you have here on earth? Do you have something that drives and motivates you? Your goal(s) will determine your plan. Each of us ought to have a plan for where we are going and what we are doing with our lives. God did not give us life so we could aimlessly wander through and eventually reach Heaven. He made us to accomplish His will and His plan!

Nehemiah, when asked by King Artaxerxes what he wanted to do about the crumbling walls of Jerusalem, had a plan. He immediately responded, "*Moreover I said unto the king, 'If it please the king, let letters be given me to the governors beyond the river, that they may convey me over till I come into Judah; and a letter unto Asaph the keeper of the king's forest, that he may give me timber to make beams for the gates of the palace which appertained to the house, and for the wall of the city, and for the house that I shall enter into.' And the king granted me, according to the good hand of my God upon me*" (Nehemiah 2:7-8).

People who are in the world, and are not a part of the "ministry," have a plan. They expect we believers should have a plan too. I know some Christians who live very haphazard lives ... waiting for the wind to blow them in a direction and trusting God sent the wind. This should not be the case with your life! This is not the way God designed you. King Artaxerxes was not taken aback by Nehemiah's request. He expected if Nehemiah had a burden, then he also would have a plan.

Nehemiah had a plan at this point of his journey, but he did not have all the details he would have after seeing the condition of the wall. That fact did not slow or stop him. He gave the plan he had to the king with the information he had. Having a plan that is developing is better than having no plan at all. This is a good place to remind us all we should not wait to have all the details on God's will for us before stepping out and taking action. I believe it is easier for God to direct a moving believer than one who is sitting in the pew, just waiting for something to happen!

Get a burden ... develop a plan to make that burden become a reality ... and then step out by faith. Have the spiritual sensitivity to God that He can adjust your plan as you go along the way toward the goal. Don't waste a moment. Get up and get going with the plan today!

Hear From God ... Do it! – July 16

"And I arose in the night, I and some few men with me; neither told I any man what my God had put in my heart to do at Jerusalem: neither was there any beast with me, save the beast that I rode" (Nehemiah 2:12). Nehemiah gives us a good order for doing the will of God in our lives. I know when God touches my heart about something, it is best to solidify the call in my own heart first. Normally when you tell someone else what God has touched your heart to do, they will ask too many questions, and bring up too many objections and you may decide it was not God's plan.

It has been my experience that the things God has called me to do, if thought about logically, did not make too much sense "humanly speaking." I saw a quote just the other day that said something like, *"God does not call the qualified ... He qualifies the called."*

That has been my experience too. I have rarely felt qualified to do the things God has touched my heart to do. I have entered most of the things God has touched my heart to do with the thought there must be someone more qualified and capable than me to do the work. I have begun many things that God touched my heart with, by looking around to find that qualified and capable person ... generally speaking, they have not showed up ... so I just keep doing my best at the work God has given me to do.

Too many of us feel the call of God and then ask our family, friends and even strangers what they think we should do. Nehemiah did not tell anyone what God had lain on his heart to do. He understood what God touched his heart to do. He then went to look things over in Jerusalem (2:11-16). He did not tell others what God had touched his heart for until he had fully surveyed the situation and had developed a plan in his heart and mind.

There is a key phrase in Nehemiah 2:12 – *"... what my God had put in my heart to do ..."* Today I want to encourage you to do the thing God puts in your heart to do! Don't take a popularity poll! Don't discuss and allow anyone to 'talk you out of it.' Don't look at the thing God has asked you to do through your eyes only; remember God touched your heart and He will prop you up where you sag the most! When you experience the touch of God for something ... do it! Don't waiver ... step out by faith and do all God has touched your heart to do! What a thrilling thought! God has something for me to do for Him in His service! I don't know about you, but I am overwhelmed with joy that I have the opportunity to serve the King of all the kings who have ever been on this earth! Go build your wall today!

Check it Out – July 17

"And I arose in the night, I and some few men with me; neither told I any man what my God had put in my heart to do at Jerusalem: neither was there any beast with me, save the beast that I rode upon" (Nehemiah 2:12). Nehemiah showed us a key to making a vision become a reality. When God touches your heart to do something, it is always good to "Check it out." Nehemiah had the burden for re-building the wall. He had verbalized it to King Artaxerxes when asked about it, but from that point until this in chapter two, he had not told anyone else.

Now that he had the vision for re-building the wall; had gotten approval from the king; had gotten the papers to help him get the materials he needed; then he actually went to see the wall. At this point, he still had not revealed to the men who were with him, the burden God had given him. Nehemiah had enough leadership skills that men were willing to go with him without even knowing where they were going, or what they were doing. It is possible he took these men along for protection, but also so they could catch a glimpse of what had touched his heart already.

My father always taught me ... *"Anything that is worth doing will cost you something."* Nehemiah knew this lesson too. He wanted to get a look at the condition of the wall so he knew the proper steps to take. There have been many times in my life when I had a burden and just blasted ahead ... only to realize I didn't have the things I needed to accomplish the goal. Nehemiah had received the burden, but now he was going about the task of determining the problem ... discovering what would be needed to solve the problem ... solidifying the vision in his own heart so he could pass it along to those who would help to re-build the wall.

Pursuing the vision God has given you requires work on your part. It requires you to take the same steps Nehemiah was taking. Having a burden, or vision for something is just the first step. Determining what is needed to bring that vision to reality is the second step. Going through the steps of what it will take to pass that vision along to others who can help you reach the goal is the next step. Actually picking up a hammer (figuratively speaking) and doing the work will be the easy part!

"Anything that is worth doing will cost you something." The question for the day is, are you willing to pay the cost for the thing(s) God has burdened your heart to do? Are you willing to give the time and energy to making the vision become reality? Pursue the dream God has given you!

You Are Not Alone – July 18

Have you ever had the feeling there is no one alongside you as you are doing the things God has touched your heart to do? Have you ever felt like Elijah when he ran to the cave and complained to God that he was the lone remaining faithful prophet in Israel? I'm sure you have felt this way ... just like me. There are times in all our lives when we feel we are carrying the burden God has given us, all alone! I'm sure Nehemiah might have felt this way. God touched his heart for the re-building of the wall in Jerusalem. He went and checked out the damage. He developed a plan for what it would take, and how to get it done.

Chapter 3 of this book named for him, lists forty-five different people, or groups of people who were lined up to do the work with Nehemiah. Many of us, when facing a chapter like this in the Bible, think about how boring it is to read name after name. I want to tell you, each of the names listed in this chapter meant something very special to Nehemiah. Each represented a family. Each represented a part of the wall he would not need to build himself. Each in their own way was telling him this was the work of God, and not only him.

There is an interesting group which touches my heart every time I read this chapter. "*And next unto them the Tekoites repaired: but their nobles put not their necks to the work of their Lord*" (Nehemiah 3:5). This group of Tekoites are mentioned a second time in verse 27 of this chapter. No other group is mentioned twice. But that's not what grips my heart! The phrase "*... but their nobles put not their necks to the work ...*" arrests my attention.

There are three lessons I get from this chapter, and verse. First, be sure when you are doing the work of God, you will not be doing it alone. It may seem like you're alone, but God has people helping you that you might not even know about.

Second, even though it may not seem like anyone knows what you are doing, God knows. It is better to hear a "*Well done, thou good and faithful servant*" from Him than to hear the praise of men here. It is also important to note He knows both who is working and who is not working! The Tekoite nobles were pointed out to have done nothing!

Third, when you are pursuing the vision God gave you for your life, you are involved in the work of the Lord ... not your work ... not your pastor's work ... not your family's work. Make sure you are doing what you are doing for the right person. Do what God has called you to do today!

211

Share Your Vision/Burden – July 19

"Then said I [Nehemiah] *unto them, 'Ye see the distress that we are in, how Jerusalem lieth waste, and the gates thereof are burned with fire: come, and let us build up the wall of Jerusalem, that we be no more a reproach.' Then I told them of the hand of my God which was good upon me; as also the king's words that he had spoken unto me. And they said, 'Let us rise up and build.' So they strengthened their hands for this good work"* (Nehemiah 2:17-18).

God touched one man's heart about the need for re-building the walls of Jerusalem. He surveyed the situation and saw the needs that were there. He did not tell anyone at first; but the time came when he needed to share his vision ... his burden with those who could help him make it happen. I have learned God does not give us all the same burden. Some look at a situation and see one thing; while others look at the same situation and see other things, or don't see anything at all. I have a burden for reaching and teaching Deaf people. Not everyone sees that need – but that is the vision ... the burden God has placed on my heart. A few years ago, my wife and I were at a mission conference where a young lady was sharing her burden to help in translation of the New Testament into the language of a tribal people. As she talked, all I could think was, *"I wonder how many Deaf people live in that tribe?"* That's my burden ... my vision.

I want you to see the things Nehemiah did, and the order in which he did them to get this wall rebuilt. First, he shared his burden in a way that it could touch their hearts like it had touched his heart. Look at the opening phrase he gives to these men: *"Ye see the distress that we are in ..."* Before we can get others to come with us to help us accomplish our vision, our burden, we need to be able, in a persuasive way, to share the things we have seen and why there is a need. Nehemiah was able to do this by allowing them to see the broken down walls, and then telling them he was here to do something about it. They said, *"Let us rise up and build."* I think they got the vision/burden.

Nehemiah did not just share his vision/burden; he also shared his preparation, and his plan. It is not enough to inspire people for the work; we also need to show them how it is going to get done. Evangelist David Wood once said, *"Inspiration without education leads to frustration."* I agree. Do you have a burden today? Do you need help to get it done? Follow these simple steps Nehemiah showed us and get the work done for God. It is important for us to accomplish something for God in our life!

Main Character – July 20

Years ago I was a referee for soccer in the county we were living. One of my goals was not to become the main focus of the game. I had seen far too many referees/umpires who thought they were the main attraction and tried to make sure the attention was focused on them rather than the game itself. I realized if that happened while I was the referee I had not done my job very well. It was great if the coaches, players, and fans never knew my name. If that happened, I had done my job well.

The same is true in our lives today. The goal in each of our lives as Christians ought to be to make sure people know the name of our God … not us. You see, the Main Character in your life story should be God! Nehemiah understood this truth and made sure others around him knew it too. *"Then answered I them, and said unto them, 'The God of heaven, He will prosper us; therefore we His servants will arise and build: but ye have no portion, nor right, nor memorial in Jerusalem"* (Nehemiah 2:20). Take the time to read that verse one more time! Did you catch that short phrase in the verse "… *ye have no portion, nor right, nor memorial* …?"

We have one life to live. The sad thing for many people is they live and die and no one remembers anything they did with their life. I have preached funerals for many families who did not have a church home. I always tried to meet with the living family members to learn what I could about the person who died. It always saddened me when these living family members could not remember anything important or unique about the person who had just died.

On the other hand, I have a grandfather who died long before I was born. I have heard so many stories about individuals he touched for Jesus in his short, fifty-two years of life! He understood what Nehemiah was telling the builders of the wall. Nehemiah told them long after they were gone, people would remember God allowed them to build the wall in Jerusalem. He told them regardless of the opposition coming against them during the building, God would triumph and the wall would be built. He was telling them this before they had lifted one hammer!

Whatever you put your hand to do today, make sure you are doing it for the glory of God! He should be the Main Character in your life today. If you go through this day trying to get people to remember your name, it will be an unsuccessful day. If you go through this day trying to get people to remember His name … that is success!

God Knows Your Name – July 21

Have you ever had the feeling no one knows what you are doing for God? Have you ever been left off the list of names when the Pastor is giving praise to those who helped out with some special activity? Have you ever been asked to be ready to share something at a meeting, and everyone else had the opportunity to share, and you were forgotten? Did your name ever get left off a list of names in the bulletin, or program? Have you ever worked yourself to the point of exhaustion, only to hear someone complain about the one minor thing you did wrong?

All of us have had feelings at one point or another when we have had some of these feelings. We have all felt slighted at some point or another in our lives and in our ministries. I must be honest and tell you even though we say we are working to please our Heavenly Father, a little encouragement from those around us now and then is really nice. It would be good to remember that the next time someone helps you with something.

Today I came upon a listing of names in Nehemiah 3. Normally, I struggle through trying to figure out how to pronounce the names listed, or I simply rush through them to get to something more "important" to me. The thought came to my mind today while reading these; that chapters filled with names is a reminder that God remembers every person's name!

While working as an Associate Pastor in a large church, I went to visit the home of a new couple who had begun coming to our services. When I asked them about whether or not they knew they were going to Heaven, their answers stopped me in my tracks. The wife told of being saved when she was a young teenager. The husband said he had just trusted Christ a few weeks before. He had come to the church with skepticism because of past bad experiences. When this couple was leaving his first morning service, they met our Pastor. He decided he would return one last Sunday. When they walked in the door, our Pastor greeted him by name! He told me he decided then, that any Pastor who could remember his name out of the 1100 people in that church deserved his attention. He got saved at the end of that service!

This list of names here in chapter 3 (45 people or groups named) tells me God knows my name. He knows both what I am doing … and what I am not doing. He knows the minutest detail about my life and takes an interest in what I am going to do with this day today. Make your life count today! Do something to build the things God gave you the tools to build!

Don't Focus on the Opposition – July 22

There will always be plenty of people who are willing to stand against you! There will always be plenty of thoughts in your own mind about your weakness, or your inabilities. While there will always be those people and thoughts that easily slow you down, or stop you from doing what God called you to do … there is a solution!

"But it came to pass, that when Sanballat heard that we builded the wall, he was wroth, and took great indignation, and mocked the Jews. And he spake before his brethren and the army of Samaria, and said, 'What do these feeble Jews? Will they fortify themselves? Will they sacrifice? Will they make an end in a day? Will they revive the stones out of the heaps of the rubbish which are burned?' Now Tobiah the Ammonite was by him, and he said, 'Even that which they build, if a fox go up, he shall even break down their stone wall.' Hear, O our God' …" (Nehemiah 4:1-4a).

I love the response of Nehemiah to the opposition. He immediately went to God and asked in essence … *"God, did you hear that?"* I remember when I was coaching basketball one year. We had made the playoffs in our state for Christian schools. Don't be too impressed … we had a team of only six guys, all under six-feet tall. We were the lowest seed in the playoffs, and we were going to play a school that was almost ten times the size of our school. It was truly a "David against Goliath" story. We had to travel to their gym for the game. Our guys were warming up on the court when their locker room doors opened. They ran out on the court in a single-file line and ran toward the basket. The first six players who ran onto the floor dunked the ball to start their warm-ups. At that time in high school basketball, it was a technical foul to dunk in warm-up. I noticed the referees following them out of the locker room. I simply walked to center court and pointed at the rim and caught the referee's eye. He nodded he had seen it. I wanted to make sure the right person saw what had happened.

There are times in your life when unfair things are going to happen. There are times when the enemy seems to be triumphing unfairly. There are times when the good guy seems to get the bad end of the deal. Don't lose heart! We have a God in Heaven Who is keeping the score! He has not missed a thing that is happening in our world, or in your life. He is still in control! I want to encourage you today, God is still on the throne, and He has not, and will not ever move! Stand where God called you to stand! Do what God called you to do! Be faithful to what God called you to be faithful to, and He will take care of the rest! He is not sleeping today. Trust Him today!

Don't Turn Right ... or Left ... Stay on Course – July 23

"Hear oh God; for we are despised: and turn their reproach upon their own head, and give them for a prey in the land of captivity" (Nehemiah 4:4). One of the greatest tools of the Devil throughout the history of mankind ever since Adam and Eve has been distraction and deception. Just as the serpent approached Eve and enticed her just slightly off the plan of God, the Devil still tries to get us just slightly off the "main thing" today. I have noticed in my life the most dangerous traps are the ones that are "good" but not "best." Things that are okay and would not be considered sin, but things nonetheless that moves my steps from the "main thing" onto something that is secondary.

Nehemiah and the others were really committed to the rebuilding of the wall. There would have been a great temptation to stop building for just a bit to defend what they were doing. It would have been easy for Nehemiah to come down from the building of the wall to explain how he had originally gotten the burden for building this wall. He could tell how he went before the king and how King Artaxerxes not only gave him permission, but also letters for cedar and the other materials they would need. He could easily have done this ... but all the while he was doing that "good thing," the wall would remain in a shambles.

I noticed Nehemiah depended on God to fight these "other" battles, while he remained on that wall to continue building. I don't know what God has touched your heart to do today, but I am sure the Devil has offered some very "good" alternatives for you to do in the place of that "best" thing that God has given you. Let God take care of those "other" things while you stay on the wall and do the thing God so deeply touched your heart to do.

Don't waste one minute today coming down to defend what you are doing for God. Let Him fight those battles for you. Stay at it! God is depending on you to be faithful to Him just like Nehemiah was faithful at this wall. After the fifty-two days it took to build the wall, Nehemiah would have plenty of time to talk to these people. It's very interesting to notice in Nehemiah 6:15 we read of the completion of the wall in fifty-two days. The last time Sanballat's name appears in the book is in Nehemiah 6:14. Stay on course! Don't worry about what others are saying! Be true to what God called you to do. Let Him take care of closing the mouths of those who are against you. He can do it better than you can. Keep at the work God has given you and finish your wall!

Someone is Depending on You – July 24

"So built we the wall; and all the wall was joined together unto the half thereof: for the people had a mind to work" (Nehemiah 4:6).

The burden to re-build the wall was obvious in Nehemiah's life. The opposition that always follows God's calling was also obvious. The resolve of these builders kept them on the wall and building. Progress was made and the wall began to take shape because these folks just stayed at the work. What a blessing to be around a group of people who have a mind to work!

I am sure when they first started the work, and they looked to their left and right and saw nothing but destruction and waste, their hearts were a little overwhelmed with the job in front of them. However, they noticed there was someone else to their right, and someone else to their left who was feeling the same way. They might have also noticed the person to their right and the person to their left had picked up a hammer or a saw and had started to work. They also picked up their hammer and saw and began to do the little they thought they could accomplish. Before they all knew it ... half the wall was built ... because each person there had a mind to work!

There are a number of lessons I learned from this verse. First, there are many times when God has called me to do something new that has initially given me a feeling of being far beyond my ability to perform. I have learned when I simply pick up my "hammer and saw" and start to do the smallest part of what God gave me, the work begins to progress! It's exciting to look back after having accomplished a part of the work God has given me to see that progress has been made.

Second, it always stirs my heart to know others have come alongside me to help in the work. These are usually people who have very different gifts and abilities from mine. As we work side-by-side, I am totally dependent on them to do their part because I could not do what they do in one million years! I need them, but they also need me. This is the way God has made us as the Body of Christ! We are to be "fitly joined together."

The third thing I see in this verse is that little word, "we"–the third word in. I love that the work of God is not something any one man/woman can claim they have done. If we are going to accomplish anything for God, we will need to work together with others from the Body of Christ! If you have gotten, or already have the "Lone Ranger" mentality ... it's time to get over yourself! We each need the help of God and others. So, grab your hammer and saw today and do your part on the "wall!" We need you!

Watch and Pray – July 25

"Nevertheless we made our prayer unto our God, and set a watch against them day and night, because of them" (Nehemiah 4:9).

It is very important for us to pray about the things we are facing today. There are many things that are beyond my abilities, or my strength. I need to spend time praying; asking God to step in and do the things I cannot do. I need to be a man who quickly prays when facing decisions about the future or decisions that need to be made which will affect my family and those who are following me. Prayer should not be our "last resort," but it ought to be our first step in any process.

All throughout the book of Nehemiah, we have seen him practice what I have written above. There are multiple times recorded in this book when challenges arose where Nehemiah's first response was to stop all he was doing and to pray about it. I am always very convicted when I write about prayer. Prayer is something I recognize as vital to the success of what I am doing, and yet it is something I struggle daily to make time to do. I want to become more of a man of prayer.

I want to emphasize that as important as prayer is, I believe it is equally important to keep the watch for what God wants us to do. If all we do is pray about God's leading, and we fail to keep our eyes open for His answer, we are missing the boat. I believe prayer is not simply me giving God my "shopping list" of needs, but it is also a time for me to listen for that "still small voice of God" as well. Don't be so consumed with the asking part of prayer that you neglect the watching part of prayer.

When we pray we ought to be expecting an answer from God. I want to be a man of prayer. I also want to be a man of action. I don't want to simply ask God for things and then sit back as though God needs to answer everything I have asked for. I want to ask and then watch to see how God leads. In the case of Nehemiah and the others building the wall; I believe they were asking God for protection as they built. I believe they were probably asking for strength and wisdom to build the wall as quickly and as well as they could. I am sure while they were praying, they were building ... but they were also watching for what God wanted them to do, as well as for the opposition they knew was there.

We are living in a time when much work needs to get done. We too need to be watching and praying. Ask God to do some big things for you today. Follow the leading of God in your life, but keep your eyes opened too!

Greater Is He That is in You – July 26

It seems there are enemies on every side today. I believe most days my greatest enemy is my own sinful nature! What do we do when it seems everyone is against us, and even our own nature betrays us? Turn to the Holy Spirit within you. John wrote the Holy Spirit within us is greater than the enemy that is outside us (I John 4:4). That includes those opposed to us ... our own sin nature ... and the physical enemies of our faith that we can see.

Nehemiah wrote, *"Therefore set I in the lower places behind the wall, and on the higher places, I even set the people after their families with their swords, their spears, and their bows. And I looked, and rose up, and said unto the nobles, and to the rulers, and to the rest of the people, 'Be not ye afraid of them: remember the Lord, which is great and terrible, and fight for your brethren, your sons, and you daughters, your wives, and your houses"* (Nehemiah 4:13-14).

Remember the Lord ... and fight! Fight for your brethren ... sons ... daughters ... wives ... and houses. These are things worth fighting for. What exactly are we fighting for today? I know these people were fighting to complete the task they felt God had given them at this time ... the re-building of the collapsed wall around Jerusalem. What should I be fighting for today? There are a number of things I believe we ought to fight hard for when it comes to our families and ourselves.

I want to fight hard to maintain a spiritual walk with my God today. This is a real battle for me. I am so easily drawn into my sinful thoughts and behavior. I wish that my flesh did not pull so hard against the things of God, but it does! I want to stay in the Word of God today so I walk closer to God today than I did yesterday. I have regrets from yesterday, but God has given me renewed mercies this morning for today, and by His grace I want to walk more faithfully with Him today than I did yesterday.

I want to fight today to lead my family in service to the King. I am prone to laziness spiritually, and today I want to hotly pursue my God! I want to read His Word with an aggressive heart to find all He has for me in it. I want to pray before I act today. I want to stop and reach out to that person who normally I would walk past today. I want to demonstrate a godly love for my world that does not allow me to criticize first, but to pray and attempt to love them. All this takes work! All this goes against my natural tendencies. I want to stay on the wall for my family today.

God is in Control – July 27

"And it came to pass, when our enemies heard that it was known unto us, and God had brought their counsel to nought, that we returned all of us to the wall, every one unto his work" (Nehemiah 4:15).

There is no doubt about the fact there are enemies to our faith. There is no doubt those enemies love to threaten, and try to intimidate us to stop what we feel God has called us to do. There is also a very real truth that our God is in control and He is well able to not only defend us, but allow us to move forward for Him in the work He has called us to do. That work? To tell everyone in the world Jesus died in their place as a perfect sacrifice. To tell them He was buried in a grave that was protected by a group of Roman soldiers. To tell them in spite of these trained soldiers watching that tomb, night and day, after the third day, Jesus rose from the grave! To tell the world Jesus loves them and did all this to restore a right relationship between them and our holy God!

It is important for us to remember what our goal in life is today. Don't let the threats and cares of this world slow you down in pursuit of this goal. It is our responsibility to do what God has called us to do, not to worry about the other "things." I was reminded of Elisha and his servant when the enemy surrounded their town. The servant saw only the enemy. Elisha knew God's protective hand was upon them. He asked God to open the eyes of the servant so he could see the protection He had provided. When God did this, it revealed the angels of Heaven were surrounding them!

God is not dead today! God is much alive today as He was when Elisha was a prophet in Israel. There may be people who speak against you. There may be people who don't like your church. There may be people who say the Bible is outdated and it has no relevance for us today. There may be people who tell you the old-fashioned way of serving and worshipping God doesn't work anymore. I will tell you there will always be opposition to the things of God.

I want to close today by telling you God is still in control! He has not taken vacation from you (even though you may take a vacation from Him). He has not forgotten you or the work He wants you to do. It is safer for you in the center of His will today than any other place where someone or something else offers you. Stay close to your Heavenly Father today. Lean into Him and trust Him to take care of you wherever you go. I am so thankful He is alive and well today!

Do Your Part – July 28

"For the builders, every one had his sword girded by his side, and so builded. And he that sounded the trumpet was by me. And I said unto the nobles, and to the rulers, and to the rest of the people, 'The work is great and large, and we are separated upon the wall, one far from another. In what place therefore ye hear the sound of the trumpet, resort ye thither unto us: our God shall fight for us'" (Nehemiah 4:20).

Nehemiah realized the workers were scattered from one end of the wall to the other. They were not grouped closely together in the case of an attack. He devised a plan that he would keep the trumpet player with him (in case of an attack), and the trumpet player would sound a warning if danger came. The people were all carrying their swords. They were not building the walls with their swords, but were ready for battle even in the middle of the building project. If they heard the trumpet sound, they were to stop the building, and run to help wherever the need was.

How does this apply to us today? Too many times I have been guilty of asking God to do something for me without doing my part. I have treated God like a "genie in a bottle" that I go to and give my requests, and then sit back waiting for Him to give me what I have asked Him to give me. I am not saying we should not ask God for the things we need. I am saying if I ask God to help me, I should be ready to work as hard as I can to accomplish the thing I have asked Him to help with. I should keep my sword close by while working toward the goal.

If you want to learn more about the Bible (praise the Lord), you need to spend time in the Word. You cannot simply ask God to help you understand it and then only visit it on Sundays and Wednesdays. If you want to become a soul-winner, you cannot just pray in your house for souls to be saved. You need to go out where the unsaved are, and tell them about Jesus! If you want be a better father/mother/child, it will take more than prayer, and you will need to work on improving specific areas of your life!

You can be sure of this one truth … God will do His part! Nehemiah had no doubt God would fight for them. What he emphasized was, they did their part! God cannot be anything but faithful, it is His character. Let's determine today that we will do all we can to accomplish the work God has given us to do, and we will trust Him to do His part in that work! Don't sit around today waiting for something to happen. Do your part and watch as God amazes all by doing His part.

Good Ole Fashioned Work! – July 29

"Yea, also I continued in the work of this wall, neither bought we any land: and all my servants were gathered thither unto the work" (Nehemiah 5:16). I have noticed we are living in a world that has decided if it isn't easy to do, we just aren't going to get involved with the work. I find myself falling into that trap as well sometimes. If something requires strenuous work, I begin thinking, *"There is probably a machine that would do this a good bit easier."*

I still remember one of my early jobs. One of my uncles asked if I wanted to make some money. At the time I was saving up to buy my first car, and I quickly agreed before asking what we were going to be doing. I showed up at his house very early in the morning and followed him down the hill behind his house to a place where he was trying to make a pond. It was then I spotted the bull-dozer buried in mud above the tracks that made it move! My uncle handed me a shovel and a pair of boots. We shoveled mud that stuck to the shovel all day long. Finally, at about four in the afternoon, he suggested we hook the tractor to the bull-dozer and try to pull it out. I must tell you it was at this point I became a man of prayer! I drove the tractor while he tried to drive the bull-dozer. I praised the Lord out loud when I felt that thing moving out of the "never built" pond! I have never been so tired in all my life! I also have never been so pleased with what a good days work can produce! I'm also thankful my uncle gave up on the idea of having a pond in his backyard!

Today there is a great deal of work that needs to be done for the Lord. I want to encourage you to grab your spiritual shovel and start digging in for the Lord! I spend many days very tired from the work God has called me to do. I often fall into bed with a very weary mind and body. What a joy it is to look back and see something accomplished … something much better than a bull-dozer on high ground! If you have not attempted much for God lately, then I want to ask you a question. What are you waiting for?

Jesus told us not to look four months ahead at what we think might be a harvest. He told His disciples they needed to lift up their eyes and look on the fields directly in front of them, because they were white, already to harvest! I believe as Nehemiah and his servants worked tirelessly, we need to be involved in doing what God has touched our heart to do as well. They may not have felt wall was too important at the time, but it was what God had given them to do. What God has touched your heart to do today may not seem that important, but stay at the work until completion!

The Enemy of "Best" is "Good" – July 30

Our enemy is very good at deception. He offers alternate plans that seem very good. The problem is the time we spend on doing that "good" thing robs us of the time we should be spending on what is "best." That was the case when Nehemiah was building the wall, and it will be the way it is today in your life too. Nothing has changed. The enemy of "best" is still "good."

"Now it came to pass when Sanballat, and Tobiah, and Geshem the Arabian, and the rest of our enemies, heard that I had builded the wall, and that there was no breach left therein; (though at that time I had not set up the doors upon the gates); That Sanballat and Geshem sent unto me, saying, 'Come, let us meet together in some one of the villages in the plain of Ono.' But they thought to do me mischief" (Nehemiah 6:1-2).

The request to come and meet may have seemed like a "good" thing to do … but it would have taken Nehemiah away from the "best" thing God had called him to do. I find this battle going on every day with my schedule, and the things I have planned to do. It is so easy for me to start on the path of doing the "best" things, only to get side-tracked into doing things that are "good" but not in the original plan. I believe distractions have caused many unfinished walls in my life, and perhaps yours too.

Just like Nehemiah, we need to recognize the danger of the "good" things taking the place of the "best." He made a very strong statement at the end of verse 2 when he said, *"they thought to do me harm."* We need to understand doing something that is "good" at the expense of the things we know are "best" ultimately do us harm. Those "good" things, although they have some positive results, may actually kill the opportunity to accomplish the "best" things.

With all the technology available today, I find sometimes I can spend a day "tweaking" a program, or setting up something on my computer or phone, only to look back and realize I have spent far too much time on something that did not give an end result that really mattered! What a waste of my time! I want to make sure I guard my time just as much as Nehemiah guarded his time in the building of the wall. I doubt very highly Nehemiah and the others would have finished building this wall in fifty-two days if they had stopped for too many coffee breaks!

Keep the "best" thing at the top of your list today. Don't allow the "good" distractions to pull you away from what God intended this day to produce.

Great Work Deserves Full Attention – July 31, 2014

How important is the work you are doing for God today? Do you see it as vital to the cause of Christ, or is it just something you are doing until something better comes along? One of the greatest joys of the Christian life is life has meaning for us! There is something ahead of us that is far bigger and far more important than us. We have a reason to live and do the things we are doing. Unlike the world we are living, we are not pursuing riches that can vanish, and will certainly never satisfy.

Temptation came to Nehemiah as he was working on the wall in the form of an invitation to "take a break." There are many times when we are warned against "burn-out." We are encouraged to "take our foot off the gas pedal" in life and slow down. While I understand the importance of taking a break now and then, I think there is also a case for keeping the pedal to the floor for as long as possible. Balance is essential, but be careful of the trap of leaving the work God has given you.

"... *Sanballat and Geshem sent unto me, saying, 'Come, let us meet together in some one of the villages in the plain of Ono.' But they thought to do me mischief. And I sent messengers unto them, saying, 'I am doing a great work, so that I cannot come down: why should the work cease, whilst I leave it, and come down to you*" (Nehemiah 6:2-3)?

Once the job is seen clearly, and the materials are in place, and the blueprints have been clearly understood, it is time to work, not talk. Nehemiah had the goal clearly in focus. He had the people to do the work. He had a passion pushing him toward the goal. The last thing Nehemiah needed was to "discuss" things with those who were opposed to him. Even people who are well-meaning may pull you from your "wall." Stay there and keep on building.

I have often said (and believe with all my heart) when we finally stand before God in Heaven, we will not say, "*I wish I had taken more time off from spiritual things while on the earth*." On the contrary, I think we will all be saying, "*I wish I had done far more for the Lord while I was on the earth*." We need to keep our focus on what is important ... on what our "wall" is that God has called us to build. Be careful to plan well, but also be careful not to waste time in idle conversation about what you know very well God has called us to do. Remember, the house is on fire! There is no time to lose! Do all God has put in your heart to do and do it with a passion that will not allow you to come down from the wall! Stay at it!

MONTH OF
August

O God, Strengthen My Hands – August 1

"And thou hast also appointed prophets to preach of thee at Jerusalem, saying, 'There is a king in Judah:' and now shall it be reported to the king according to these words. 'Come now therefore, and let us take counsel together.' Then I sent unto him, saying, 'There are no such things done as thou sayest, but thou feignest them out of thine own heart.' For they made us afraid, saying, 'Their hands shall be weakened from the work, that it be not done.' Now therefore, O God, strengthen my hands" (Nehemiah 6:7-9).

The enemies of God are stubborn and will not give up easily. When Nehemiah refused to come down from the building of the wall, his enemies used a different tactic. They decided, since they could not trick them into stopping, they would threaten them. They told Nehemiah and the others they would report false things about them to the king in charge of Israel. These accusations would be false and unfounded, but they would be made to the king regardless. This could have stopped the building for sure.

I don't want to focus on these accusations very much. I just want you to be aware the Devil does not try to stop us once and then leave us alone. He is stubborn, and will try multiple times to defeat and stop the work you are doing for God. Your own sin nature will join in this effort. There will be many times when you will feel inadequate, or insufficient for the work you are doing. Don't you dare come down from the wall! Don't think for a moment what you are doing is dependent upon you or your strength, or your wisdom to get accomplished! This is the Lord's work, and He will provide the power and protection if it is to be completed.

Again, I am impressed with what Nehemiah did. Look at the last phrase in the verse. Rather than rallying the workers together and giving a "pep talk," Nehemiah turned to his Rock. *"Now therefore, O God, strengthen my hands."* This ought to be our battle cry today! There will be enemies who are bigger than we are. There will be obstacles in our paths today that will seem insurmountable. There will be far more people who tell us we cannot do what we feel God has called us to do than those who are behind us to help. Don't turn to your own strength today. Turn to the God in Heaven Who called you and enables you!

Whether you are preaching ... teaching ... plumbing ... raising children ... cleaning a house ... or whatever, do it with all your might today. When God puts something in front of you do, do it with all your might! Let Him strengthen your hands for the work! Trust Him today and move forward!

Where's the Beef? – August 2

A number of years ago, one of the fast-food chains had a TV commercial in which an "age-challenged" woman looked directly into the camera and asked the question, *"Where's the beef?"* It was a direct attack on the competitors who used less beef in their hamburgers than this particular restaurant used. Well, today I would like to let you look into my own walk with God. I write this devotional every day. I prepare and preach/teach at least three messages every week of the year. I preach/teach all day rallies for the Deaf in which I will share up to eight short messages in one day. I tell you this to say these things do not guarantee I am walking with God.

I can read my Bible every day, and write a devotional, and prepare and even preach a message and be doing it all in my own strength. If I am not careful, I can learn how to go through the motions of what makes a person spiritual, without allowing God to get involved! I can have a form of godliness, but deny the power thereof. I don't want that for my life! I don't want to play a game of Christian charades! I want to live what I preach! I want to practice what I preach to others! I want to walk so closely with God that when He whispers, I hear it loud and clear and I do something about what He is telling me. I want to live an authentic Christian life! I want to have the "beef" of the Christian life!

At the completion of the wall, Nehemiah recognized publically where the power had come from (where the "beef" was). He said, *"And it came to pass, that when all our enemies heard thereof, and all the heathen that were about us saw these things, they were much cast down in their own eyes: for they perceived that this work was wrought of our God"* (Nehemiah 6:16).

That's the way I want to live today. I want the world to know if they see any good thing coming out of me today, it is my God Who made it happen! I want to walk so closely with God today my feet are landing in the footprints of my Savior! I don't want to read my Bible to watch the words pass by my eyes. I don't want to prepare a lesson for someone else ... I want to study it for me, and for it to change my life. I don't want to preach at you that you should live right, and then coast myself. I want to see the work only God can do in my life.

Join me in this dedication today. I believe we could change our world if we would each follow Jesus in the way He encouraged His disciples to do.

Qualifications for the Leader – August 3

When Nehemiah was planning the leadership roles following the building of the wall, he noted an interesting qualification which I think is good for us to look for in our leaders today as well. *"That I gave my brother Hanani, and Hananiah the ruler of the palace, charge over Jerusalem; for he was a faithful man, and feared God above many"* (Nehemiah 7:2). These two simple things were mentioned for leadership: a faithful man, and feared God above many. I think that sums it up fairly well.

Think about the importance of these two qualities. Faithfulness has been defined as *1. strict or thorough in the performance of duty: a faithful worker. 2. true to one's word, promises, vows, etc. 3. steady in allegiance or affection; loyal.* The meaning of the word in the Hebrew language carries the idea of: *stability; figuratively certainty, truth, trustworthiness:– assured, establishment, faithful, right, sure, true.* Regardless of which one of these you want to choose, I would like to follow a person who demonstrates this characteristic. I want to follow someone who has stayed true to the cause for their lifetime. I want to follow a person who demonstrates that regardless of past failures, they are walking faithfully today in what they are doing for God.

I not only want to follow a person who demonstrates this quality, I want to be that kind of a person. I want to be true to my promises. I want to be steady in my allegiances. I want to be a man who is considered trustworthy. You see, I would like people to be able to follow me to the feet of Jesus Christ! I would like to be a leader of men/women that does not point people to me, but points them to Jesus Christ. This is my goal for today.

The second qualification Nehemiah had for a leader was he be a man who feared the Lord. I don't think we think enough about the day we will stand before our holy God. I don't think we plan our day out enough with the idea that God is watching us and is depending on us to represent Him well wherever we are going, and in whatever we are doing. I think we just "coast" through our lives far too much. I want to live my life with this healthy "fear of the Lord" today.

People tend to work harder if they know the boss is looking over their shoulder. I want to work for my Heavenly Father today with the realization He IS looking over my shoulder; into my heart; and into my dreams! I want to be a qualified leader today! I want God to be the focal point of my thoughts and actions today. I want Him to say, *'Well done!'*

Pay Attention to the Book – August 4

"And all the people gathered themselves together as one man into the street that was before the water gate; and they spake unto Ezra the scribe to bring the book of the law of Moses, which the LORD had commanded to Israel. And Ezra the priest brought the law before the congregation both of men and women, and all that could hear with understanding, upon the first day of the seventh month. And he read therein before the street that was before the water gate from the morning until midday, before the men and the women, and those that could understand; and the ears of all the people were attentive unto the book of the law" (Nehemiah 8:1-3).

After all the effort of the building of the wall was finished; and after all the persecution the people had endured; they did something very important. They opened the laws of God and gave their full attention to the Word. I stress on a regular basis the importance of reading your Bible. I want to use these verses today to emphasize the point that getting in the Word of God, and allowing the Word of God to get into you is one of the keys to walking with God.

This wall had fallen down because of the captivity of the Jews. There was not anyone in Jerusalem who cared about the wall, or saw the importance of it. The Jews were in captivity because they had neglected God Himself, and had turned to the worship of idols. They corporately had decided to ignore the laws of the Word of God in order to fit in to the societies around them. Their compromise on the principles clearly stated in the laws of God, had allowed their hearts to be turned. As a result of their hearts being turned, the law of God had largely been ignored and forgotten.

It impresses my heart, after the victory of the completed wall was accomplished, one of the first things they did was to open the books of the law and give their attention to it! They did what they should have done years before. Perhaps they would not have needed to have made such a monumental effort to rebuild the wall if they had stayed in the laws of God earlier.

Determine to stay in the Word of God today and also to allow the Word of God to stay in you as well. It is not enough to simply read the words of the Bible, we must allow those words to govern our actions and attitudes and thoughts. I want to give heed to the Word of God today, and let it do its work in my life!

Holy Standing Ovation – August 5

"And Ezra opened the book in the sight of all the people; (for he was above all the people); and when he opened it, all the people stood up: And Ezra blessed the LORD, the great God. And all the people answered, 'Amen, Amen, with lifting up of their hands: and they bowed their heads, and worshiped the LORD with their faces to the ground" (Nehemiah 8:5-6).

Think about it with me today for just a few moments ... we rise to our feet when we sing our National Anthem. We rise to our feet at the ball game when someone hits a ball, or scores a basket, or makes a goal. We rise to our feet when someone plays a beautiful song, or we simply want to honor what we consider something outstanding which they have done.

Did you see the reaction of these folks after the wall has been built? Were they looking for others to give them a standing ovation? Were they interested in getting some praise for the effort they had made? Were they waiting for their names to be read, and the part they played recognized in front of all the others? No!

God's Word was read and it (the Word of God) got the standing ovation! These people who had worked twenty-four hours a day; guarding each other when they were not building; fighting against opposition there in Jerusalem, as well as back home with their families. These people, stood to honor the Word of God. They did something we might frown upon today if it happened in our church. They even went so crazy as to lift up their hands ... they bowed their heads ... they worshiped with their faces to the ground!

These people needed to get themselves under control! They were actually showing emotion in church ... and they did it without any music! How is that possible? We need some high quality, emotionally charged music if we expect anyone to worship today! Did you catch why they were reacting this way? It was simply because the Word of God was present and was on center-stage. Man was not recognized. God and His Word had taken the focal point of the attention of all in attendance.

Look at their reaction, and consider following their behavior. Before they knew what they were doing, their hands were lifting in the air. They could no longer look straight ahead, or upward. Their heads bowed in absolute recognition of humility! They could not even look at anyone else! What followed was pure worship. No guitar, drum, trumpet, piano, PowerPoint ... just pure worship of our awesome God. Follow their example today!

Clear Teaching – August 6

"So they read in the book in the law of God distinctly, and gave the sense, and caused them to understand the reading. And Nehemiah, which is the Tirshatha, and Ezra the priest the scribe, and the Levites that taught the people, said unto all the people, 'This day is holy unto the LORD your God; mourn not, nor weep.' For all the people wept, when they heard the words of the law. Then he said unto them, 'Go your way, eat the fat, and drink the sweet, and send portions unto them for whom nothing is prepared: for this day is holy unto our Lord: neither be ye sorry; for the joy of the LORD is your strength'" (Nehemiah 8:8-10).

What a powerful set of verses these are for us to consider today! After the law of God was read in the presence of the people, it was explained so all who were there understood its meaning. We are still doing this today. The thought struck me today that the Word of God is so deep and meaningful simply reading the words does not tell the whole story. If you read a mystery novel, or some person's biography, or some book on history; if you have paid attention, when you finish reading you know all the information and you don't really need to read it again (unless you have a short memory and you enjoyed the book).

It constantly amazes me no matter how many times I read the Bible there are greater depths of the riches to be found on its pages. That is because this book we have is the living Word of God! When these people heard the words they touched their hearts. However, Ezra and the other leaders mentioned took the time to explain the words even deeper. The result was an emotional response that caused the folks as a whole to weep. Nehemiah stopped them and reminded them all these things were for their good, and for their joy!

When was the last time you read your Bible and wept? When was the last time the verses were so sweet to you, they stirred your emotions? When was the last time you read you Bible and laughed out loud? When was the last time you read your Bible?

Make sure you put yourself in a place where the Word of God is being accurately taught, and you will find your heart being moved. I'm not talking about finding an exciting story-teller, or loud voice. Get under the teaching of someone who rightly divides the Word of truth. The messenger does not make the message powerful. The Word of God brings all the power we need for our lives today! Run to the Word today!

Victory in the Trial – August 7

"Nevertheless for Thy great mercies' sake Thou didst not utterly consume them, nor forsake them; for Thou art a gracious and merciful God. Now therefore, our God, the great, the mighty, and the terrible God, Who keepest covenant and mercy, let not all the trouble seem little before Thee, that hath come upon us, on our kings, on our princes, and on our priests, and on our prophets, and on our fathers, and on all Thy people, since the time of the kings of Assyria unto this day. Howbeit Thou art just in all that is brought upon us; for Thou hast done right, but we have done wickedly" (Nehemiah 9:31-33).

Trials in our lives are coming … whether we like it or not. Throughout the Word of God, we have witnessed trials on the people of God ever since time began. We must face the facts these Israelites had to face with Nehemiah. We are sinners that make bad choices, and those choices result in some difficult times in our lives. It is good for us to look back and review these times of difficulty for a number of reasons. Some of those reasons are seen in these verses.

It is good for us to realize when bad things come in our lives, we have had something to do with those things. We are not perfect. When we have gone through a difficult time it is a perfect time for us to reflect on what we have done wrong, and determine to make some adjustments. This is not to say every time something bad happens to us it is the result of some sin in our lives. Remember, we are not living in a perfect world, and there are times when other people's sin will affect us. Trials afford us the opportunity to honestly evaluate where we stand with God.

The best part of a trial is it allows us an opportunity to remember God's grace and mercy! Even during this time of captivity for these Jews, they were able to see the hand of God on their lives at work. They witnessed the favor of King Artaxerxes in the beginning, and the ongoing protective hand when the opposition came on them. They could stand this day and rejoice in the goodness of God in spite of all that had happened to them. Take some time today to reflect on the good things God has done for you in the midst of the storm.

Our trials get our focus on our God, and off of ourselves. Often in the middle of our trial we realize we need Him to come and help us or we are going to be in trouble. We need God every day, all day long … but when things are going good we don't stop to realize that. In a trial we will.

Safe And Secure – August 8

What an incredible book the Bible is for us today! It is like the oasis in the middle of the desert of life. It is like the refreshing cold glass of water on a hot summer day like we are facing right now. It is like the ultimate food that satisfies the longing of our soul, but makes us want more every time we read it! What a great book. Let me share a number of verses with you today and end with one that really touched my heart.

"He that dwelleth in the secret place of the most High shall abide under the shadow of the Almighty" (Psalm 91:1). There is a secret place with God no one in this world can block. Regardless of the situation you are going to face today, or somewhere down the road of life, remember there is a place you have with God that nothing can take away.

"I will say of the LORD, He is my Refuge and my Fortress; my God; in Him will I trust" (91:2). In a day when the economy fluctuates like the waves of an ocean in a bad storm, you have a place to anchor your hope … In your God! Don't waiver when the storms come; run to the refuge … the fortress … your God!

"Surely He shall deliver thee from the snare of the fowler, and from the noisome pestilence. He shall cover thee with His feathers, and under His wings shalt thou trust: His truth shall be thy shield and buckler" (91:3-4). There is nothing more powerful than your God! There is nothing that can penetrate His protection of you! What a beautiful picture of being under His wings … close to His heart … totally at ease from the noise of the world around us. That is our God!

These things are all contingent upon one thing in your life. *"Because thou hast made the LORD, which is my Refuge, even the most High, thy habitation; there shall no evil befall thee, neither shall any plague come night thy dwelling"* (91:9-10). Make the Lord your place of refuge. Make Him the place you live and abide. Make Him the center of your entire life. Every minute of this day and all that follow, allow Him to be the Master! If you and I will do this, we are promised all the blessings of Psalm 91. This chapter has lifted my spirits, but it also sets a great challenge before each of us. We need to get out of the driver's seat of our lives, and let Him have complete control. That is easier said than done. Move on over and let Him have complete control. You will not be sorry!

"When God is in the midst, everyone is affected." – Ted Camp

Talk Is Cheap – August 9

It's easy to make big promises; it's another thing to actually do what you promised. I can remember being so frustrated with myself when I was a teenager, I can remember being so moved by a message I would go forward at the end of a service to surrender my whole heart and life to God. At the time, I was very serious, but there were more times than not when the promise I made died at the altar and never made it into my life. I hated that I made these promises and then did not have the back-bone, or courage to actually make the changes necessary.

There is a great example of this in our Old Testament. Moses was getting ready to go to the mountaintop to receive instructions on living from God Himself. Just before he went up the mountain, this was the scene before the children of Israel. *"And he took the book of the covenant, and read in the audience of the people: and they said, 'All that the LORD hath said will we do, and be obedient'"* (Exodus 24:7). *"We will do, and be obedient ..."* They said these words, I am sure, with the full intention of doing them.

However, we have read the "rest of the story." While Moses was on this mountain receiving the laws God had for them to follow, these same people were building a golden calf (knowing full well the first commandment was, *"Thou shalt have no other gods before Me"* (Exodus 20:3). Am I here to slam these people for their lack of faith and commitment? Not at all ... I'm here to warn each of us about doing the exact same thing.

If these folks were guilty of this, we are even guiltier! They had such a limited library of what God had said, compared to me. In front of me as I write this devotional, is a copy of all sixty-six books of the Bible in my own language. I don't need a translator ... I don't need a guide ... I surely can't complain I did not have all the facts. All I need to live godly today is available to me right now.

I'm not even pointing a finger at you! I'm clearly pointing my finger at myself, and I would advise you to do the same. Any of us can make big promises to God about what we will do for Him. It is quite another thing to actually get out of our spiritual Lazy-Boy chair and actively serve God! Don't put off finishing what you have promised God. Start where you are and do all you can today to obey all you have told God you would do. There is much that needs to be done, and God is depending on us do it.

"Just do it." – Nike advertisement

Don't Forget To ... – August 10

When I was a boy growing up, I can remember hearing a thousand times a day (exaggeration, I know, but you get the point), *"Did you wash your hands ... and face?" "Did you brush your teeth ... all of them?" "Did you put on clean underwear?" "Did you ...?"* It seemed like there were thousands of things a boy had to remember to do each day that had little or no significance to the plans he had in mind. After all, I was thinking about the frogs in the local creek, and the bike that was leaning on the side of my house calling my name, and the bugs that needed to be caught, and ... many other things my Mom did not understand the significance of.

The Bible has some things we ought to be doing everyday too. *"Sing unto the LORD, bless His name; show forth His salvation from day to day. Declare His glory among the heathen, His wonders among the people"* (Psalm 96:2-3). According to the Word of God, I have some everyday things (chores) God wants me to do as a mature believer. I don't want to fail Him today and forget to do these things.

Show His salvation every day. There will be people who I will meet today that will need to know about the salvation that is found in God alone. Am I going to be willing to those who need to hear today? Will I be too worried about my own potential embarrassment to testify for my God? I must remember today God's salvation needs to be proclaimed every day!

Declare His glory to someone who does not know Him every day. Am I going to be willing to tell someone about the blessings of knowing God today? God has done so many wonderful things in my life I want to tell everyone about Him. I don't want to be guilty of receiving so much from Him, and then keeping it all to myself. I want to be a person who declares, and proclaims to the world how great my God is! I have noticed the world is good at declaring the "glory" of their gods. I don't want to be unfaithful to my God.

Show His wonders in my testimony to those who have not seen them. We live in a society which glamorizes movie stars and athletes. If you follow their lives you find they are flawed and sinful, just like us. I want to be sure to speak of the wonders God has done and continues to do on a daily basis. God changes lives every day. Tell someone about it today!

"For the LORD is great, and greatly to be praised: He is to be feared above all gods" – Psalm 96:4

Stay in the Light – August 11

When you see a couple who have been married for an extended time, you will notice they begin to think alike, and most times they will act the same. I have even noticed couples who have been married for a long time will begin to look like each other. There is something about becoming so familiar with someone you begin to think the same way. The same should be true of God and me as we walk through this life. The longer I am with God, following Him and depending upon Him, the more I should resemble Him and act like He wants me to act. I noticed this transformation with my father and mother. My Dad did not enjoy going to the area yard sales each Saturday when my Mom first got interested in that. However, I noticed after a while (some years), he actually started to get the hang of it, and I think he enjoyed it some.

I want to be so close to my Heavenly Father, I begin to act like Him and think like Him. The Bible says, *"Ye that love the LORD, hate evil: He preserveth the souls of His saints; He delivereth them out of the land of the wicked"* (Psalm 97:10). When we become Christians, we bring with us a natural love for this world. The longer we are saved, the less pull the world should have on us. The less we should love the things we knew there. Actually, this verse says we ought to hate the things we see going wrong in this world. The problem I see in many individual Christians as well as many churches today is, we are trying to snuggle up as close as we can with the world, without stepping over the line of actual sin.

If you and I are going to resemble our Heavenly Father, we must learn to love the things He loves, and to hate the things He hates. Be careful today to keep your distance from evil. Don't snuggle up to evil, but snuggle up to what is good. Stay close to the things you know are right to do, and run away from those things that look evil! I know you might think you will be able to "rehabilitate" some of those things that are so horribly wrong, but you need to heed the warning of the Word of God! Run from those things you see that are evil. If you will do your part, God will do His part. If you will run away from sin, He will preserve and deliver you.

I want to walk in the light today so I stay away from the pitfalls the Devil has waiting for me. Please walk closely to your Heavenly Father and hate the evil that is in this world. It may seem all the world is against you now, you will be glad you walked with God when you meet Him!

"The worst sin is not being aware of sin." – Ted Camp

Let the Whole World Know – August 12

"The LORD hath made known His salvation: His righteousness hath He openly showed in the sight of the heathen" (Psalm 98:2).

When you hear someone say God is not right to send people to Hell, remember this verse. God has not sent one person to Hell in the entire history of the world. Every man/woman who has gone to Hell has done so by their own choice, not by God's. His heart is for the whole world to be in Heaven. The Bible says over and over again God is not interested in seeing people go to Hell.

If you don't believe me, ask Jonah. Jonah had no desire to see anyone from the nation of Nineveh go to Heaven. He thought they all deserved to burn in Hell for their response to God and His people. You may have similar feelings to a person, or a group of people today. If you do … you are not in agreement with God! From this verse in the book of Psalms, you can see God wants everyone to know about the salvation He offers. He openly showed His plan for forgiveness, even to the heathen. If you have not been thinking this same way, today would be a good day for repentance.

Let's move to the second step we all need to take after we agree the whole world needs to hear this message … will we do our part to make that happen? You might never board a plane or ship to go to a foreign country to reach the "heathen," but you can help others get there! We always hear there are more missionaries returning from the mission-field than there are going as new missionaries. We often look down on people for not surrendering to go to the mission-field; but I have seen this from a little different perspective. I see many young families who are surrendered, but struggle to raise the needed support to go! Do your part, and get involved!

Before I go much further, remember there are heathen who live in your own town, and you don't need to fly, or ride somewhere to meet them. The question then becomes, are you doing all you can to reach those who are without Christ who live in your own area? You can hand a tract to that stranger you will pass. You can be friendly and help your neighbor, after building a relationship you will be able to share the Gospel. You can visit a lonely person in a hospital with the message of hope. You can join in a soup-kitchen ministry, or prison ministry, or bus ministry, or _____. Don't sit by and let this generation go to Hell! Do your part!

"Missions is not geography, it is people." – Ted Camp

237

Just Around the Bend – August 13

When God asks us to follow Him, He does not always show us the final destination. When we get ready to travel to a different area than we have been in before, I always pause at the end of our driveway and ask the question, "*Which way am I headed?*" I don't know the final place ... we have never been there before ... but I need to know where the first turn in the road is. The Christian life is very much the same. We know where we are headed, but we don't know all the turns in the road along the way.

God told Abraham He wanted him to take Isaac, his only son, the son he loved, and to offer him as a sacrifice in the place He would show him. Abraham and Isaac, by faith, made that journey. Along the way, it dawned on Isaac they had all the things required for sacrifice, but there was no lamb. When he asked his father about it, Abraham replied: "*My son, God will provide Himself a lamb for a burnt offering ...*" (Genesis 22:8). The last part of that verse says, "*... so they went both of them together.*"

Abraham and Isaac were going to totally depend on God to reveal His plan to them. They did not need to know all the details, but simply needed to know God had a plan and they were a part of it. You see, God will not always reveal all the steps to you for the plan He has for your life. He will let you know the final destination, but the turn-by-turn directions will be shown to you as you take the steps by faith.

We do not typically like to operate this way. We all like to have the steps clearly laid out far ahead of time. My cousin is preparing for a trip across the country with his family in their camper. He has explained to me how far they plan to go each day, and where they will stop. It is good he has a plan. The reality is, his actual trip will be affected by things along the way that he cannot plan for, but will enjoy nonetheless.

In the story of Abraham and Isaac, God provided far more than a ram in the thicket. God provided a lesson for all of us to see about complete trust and faith in Him. Today is a good day to demonstrate your trust in God. That "lamb" you are looking for will come at just the right time, in just the right place. The key to this walking by faith is, faith is the unseen reality God will show you. He can see clearly what is in front of you. You are sitting at the end of your "driveway of life" and should just ask, "*Which way am I headed?*" Don't be so concerned about the final destination you miss the blessings of the sights along the way! There is some beautiful scenery you will not want to miss ... just around the bend.

Fully Persuaded – August 14

"And being fully persuaded that, what He had promised, He was able also to perform" (Romans 4:21). What a great confidence we can have in our God to do exactly what He promised He would do! Abraham and Sarah were promised a son. Old age had seemingly overtaken the natural ability to have a child. Sarah was ninety, and Abraham was older than her. Praise God, He is not limited to nature. Our God made nature. Abraham had two choices at this point in his life. He could either doubt God's ability to do the impossible, or he could demonstrate simple faith and trust Him.

You have these same two choices today. Will you doubt God's promises, or stand firmly on them (regardless of how foolish it may seem). The world we are living in (and even most Christians) will try to talk you out of standing by faith. Your choice today is just as clear as Abraham's was. There is no middle ground in this area of your Christian life. I know it seems crazy to think it ... but God really is able to do all He promised He will do.

The real question is not whether or not God can do what He promised, but whether or not we will trust Him today. The words, *"fully persuaded"* mean to carry through to the end, to accomplish it. Make no mistake; God is going to do exactly what He said He would do! There will be no loose ends with God's plan. He will do exactly what He said He would do. Let's make it personal for you. If God touched your heart for a certain ministry, He will provide all the things necessary for you to accomplish that ministry! He will give you all the tools; He will provide all the supplies necessary; He will give you all the education you need; and He will bring about the end result.

The key to all this is for us to remain fully persuaded that He can and will do it. The key is for us to completely (100%) trust Him to do what He promised He will do. Don't waste time debating something you know God wants you to do. Don't hesitate for even a split second when God makes His will known to you. Don't ask for the opinions of others; don't seek outside counsel; don't make a list of "pro's" and "cons." Step out by faith and do what God has touched your heart to do! Hesitation at that point becomes disobedience! Follow Him ... He will never fail you! Know His will ... He wants to reveal it to you, if you will seek Him. Sell out 100% to Him, and follow the path He has for your life!

"Faith is stronger than fear." – Unknown

Walking Through the Front Door – August 15

There was an old saying about a person who was trying to get away with something they were not supposed to be doing. We used to say that they were trying to "*Sneak in the back door.*" This implied that the action they were doing was either illegal, or unethical, or something they knew was not going to be accepted. The opposite of that saying was also true. When it was said of a person, "*He/She walked through the front door ...*" it implied that they were not ashamed and were very bold to stand for what they believed. These folks were not afraid of rejection.

Did you know that God made a wonderful way for you to do that very thing as it regards Heaven? "*Therefore being justified by faith, we have peace with God through our Lord Jesus Christ: By Whom also we have access by faith into this grace wherein we stand, and rejoice in hope of the glory of God*" (Romans 5:1-2). When you have received Jesus Christ as your payment for sin, you don't need to invent some sneaky way to slip into the gates of Heaven ... you can walk through the front door! We will not walk through that front door with our chests puffed out in pride, but with a lowliness of mind and heart, realizing we did nothing to deserve that opportunity. We will know it was completely by faith in Christ that we have come there.

The Bible says we are "*justified by faith.*" This word, "*justify,*" does not mean that it is "just as if I never sinned." Many have said this because it is easy to remember, but does not give the depth of what that term means to the believer. The word means that God knew all of our sin (every one); it means that as a righteous Judge, He accepted the death of Jesus, and placed His blood on our account. Thereby declaring an ungodly, undeserving sinner like us completely forgiven (made just), in the death, burial and resurrection power of His Son! Now I'm sorry, but that's good stuff!

I thank God today that I am completely justified in the sight of God, even though I still battle sin in my life on a daily basis! I am complete in Jesus Christ! I have no need to cross my fingers, hoping I will someday "earn" a way into Heaven. I will not trust my good works; my church membership; taking communion; my baptism! No! I will trust Jesus Christ (His death ... His burial ... and His resurrection) alone to save me and give me a home in Heaven. When I come to the gates of Heaven, Jesus will be walking with me. We will go in the front door!

"Jesus alone ..." – Unknown

Yield the Right of Way to Him – August 16

Is it possible to live a holy life in our world today? How can I remain pure in an impure world? Is there a special plan that will result in holiness? Is there a roadmap for a holy life? The answer to these questions is God has given His plan for holiness in our Bible.

"I speak after the manner of men because of the infirmity of your flesh: for as ye have yielded your members servants to uncleanness and to iniquity unto iniquity; even so now yield your members servants to righteousness unto holiness" (Romans 6:19).

You see, holiness, or the lack of holiness is really a choice each of us makes multiple times every day. We either choose to yield the members (hands, feet, mind, tongue, arms, eyes, etc.) to the world and unholiness; or we yield those members to righteous behavior. Which will you do today? When I was working on getting my driver's license (many, many years ago), I remember studying the difference between what it meant to YIELD and to MERGE. The simple difference (that I still remember after all those years) is the person YIELDING will stop and wait for an opening in the traffic on the road they wish to enter. A person MERGING does not slow down, but maintains their speed, blending into the traffic they are joining.

The Word of God urges us to YIELD our members to righteousness. That means we need to come to a stop and wait for God's leadership in our decisions today. There will be multiple decisions you and I will make today that will affect not only our own lives, but the lives of those associated with us as well. If we MERGE without slowing down and thinking about it, we will naturally be making decisions that will lead to uncleanness and sin. I want to urge you today to take the time to stop at the Word of God and ask God to show you the "opening" in the paths you are entering today for His righteousness.

There is a possibility for you and me to live holy lives today. If we are going to do that, it will be because we have allowed God to direct our steps (decisions). If we do that, we will see righteous and holy results. If we do not do this, we will see unrighteous and sinful results. It is not easy to live a holy life in an unholy world. Trust God and yield to Him today. He is the only hope you have of living a holy life! Sell out to Him today!

"God will bring out the best in you. The Devil will bring out the worst in you." – Ted Camp

I Want That Title – August 17

There are many athletes today who are clawing their way through the daily practices, and games in hot pursuit of a championship. They want the title of world champion. There are people in offices, working and planning and striving every day to become the CEO of their companies. There are doctors, lawyers, and teachers who want to be known as being the top in their field. It seems like people are caught up in goals that will give them a title today. I too am in pursuit of a title.

Here is what I would like to be said about me: "*There was a man in the land of Uz, whose name was Job; and that man was perfect and upright, and one that feared God, and eschewed evil*" (Job 1:1). No, I am not changing my name to Job ... I'm talking about the description the Bible gives us of Job. I would like God to be able to describe me as, "perfect and upright," and "*one that feared God,*" and as a person who "*eschewed evil.*"

Most of the titles I mentioned that we see people chasing today are ones men are impressed with. I think as believers we ought to make the things that are spoken about Job, the goals for our lives today. Knowing what we know about the rest of this book of Job, it is comforting to know where Job started. God described him as a man of integrity and upright in his heart. I want to live in a way that God could say these things about me.

It is important to realize if we want these qualities in our lives, they will not come easily. Just like the championship, or the CEO's chair, or the "top in your field" title does not come easy. Job had to pay the price for these qualities before all the challenges we are so familiar with, came to him.

Regardless of the cost, I would like to be a man who is called "*perfect and upright.*" I want to live my life in such a way God sees me attempting to live a life of holiness and purity. I have not always been holy or pure, but that is what I am striving for today. I would like to be described as a man that "*feared God.*" I want to live in a way that it is obvious to the world I am concerned with what God thinks of me. I want to avoid anything that would tell others I don't care about what God wants; I want to follow the world. I want to make a clear distinction as to Who I am following. I would like to be described as and man that "*eschewed* [hates, or runs from] *evil.*" I don't trust myself, so I want to put as much distance between me and evil as possible.

I want to be like Job. I want God to look at me and give this kind of title!

Brighten Your Day – August 18

Each of us have days when we are discouraged, or depressed as we look at the situation around us, or the things we think are coming toward us. If we are not careful, we will become so focused on the troubles around us, we forget how great our God is. It is good for us to remember all God has done, and is doing in our lives when these times of discouragement come.

"I will sing unto the LORD as long as I live: I will sing praise to my God while I have my being. My meditation of Him shall be sweet; I will be glad in the LORD" (Psalm 104:33-34).

Reflection on all God has done … is encouraging. He has created the world and the universe and holds them together. He placed the sun at the exact distance that is perfect for our good here on the earth. He causes plants to grow to feed us and to sustain us. He continues to cause it to rain to replenish our earth. He does not need my help, and He is bigger than any man/woman on this earth.

Reflection on all God is … is encouraging. God is love, and because of that, we know the blessings of love in our relationships. God is pure. We don't need to worry He will fail to be perfect. It is His character. God is truth. What a great thing to know that whatever He has promised must come to pass. Everything He says He will do will happen exactly as He said it would. God is a Righteous Judge of the world. He will never be fooled on the day of judgment. He is God.

Reflection on all God will do … is encouraging. God has promised to care for His children. He has promised to care for His sheep. There will never be a day in our lives when God is not paying attention to what we are facing. Be comforted to know your Heavenly Father is in control of what is going to happen in your life, not some politician, or banker, or doctor, or lawyer. God is the final authority in this world … don't lose sight of that fact. There are times when the voices that are against God are so loud, if you are not careful you will think they are right. Read these two verses again and remind yourself your God is still in control.

Today there are many things that might discourage you, or cause you to become depressed. When that happens, don't go to the psychiatrist, read these verses again. When looking around you discourages you … look up, you will not be discouraged any more. God is still in control!

Biblical Example – Loving Family – August 19

We all say we love our families, but do we take the time we ought to in prayer for them, and in sacrificing for them? As someone once said, *"Talk is cheap."* The Word of God says *"faith, if it hath not works, is dead"* (James 2:17). Look at the description of Job's demonstration of love for his seven sons and three daughters: *"And it was so, when the days of their feasting were gone about, that Job sent and sanctified them, and rose up early in the morning, and offered burnt offerings according to the number of them all; for Job said, 'It may be that my sons have sinned, and cursed God in their hearts.' Thus did Job continually"* (Job 1:5).

Job loved his children with such depth (while loving His God with his whole heart) he felt compelled to do all he could to make sure they were living right with God. He sanctified them, and offered burnt offering for them before God. He did this just in case they were not living as they ought to live before God. Remember, one of the things God said about Job was he was a man who feared the Lord. This understanding of the holiness of God and the unholiness of himself and his children drove Job to do this for his children.

How often do we show this kind of love for our own children today? When was the last time you went to your Heavenly Father and begged Him to put a hedge of protection around your children? The word *sanctified* in this verse has the idea of making them clean. We know in the New Testament it means to set apart, or to make holy. I think the meaning is basically the same. I believe Job went daily before God asking Him to keep his children away from sin. I believe Job not only feared God, but he also feared his own sinfulness, and the potential sinfulness of his children. Knowing my own natural tendency to sin, I ought to pray more fervently for our children to stay away from sin.

Job not only sanctified his children, but he made sacrifices on their behalf, just in case they had forgotten to do it. He was asking God to forgive them if they had sinned without going through the proper channels for forgiveness. This is love! The end of the verse says Job did this *"continually."* Can't you see Job making this trip every day on behalf of his children? What about me and my children? Am I running to the throne of grace regularly for our children? Are you realizing the pit-falls that could trap your family and asking God for deliverance and protection for them today? I hope you and I will love our families like Job loved his family.

What Can I Say? – August 20

"Likewise the Spirit also helpeth our infirmities: For we know not what we should pray for as we ought; but the Spirit itself maketh intercession for us with groanings which cannot be uttered" (Romans 8:26).

Has there ever been a time in your life when you were so overwhelmed with the situation facing you that you bowed your head to pray ... but words to describe your hearts burden could not be found? Have you ever had joy that was unspeakable and you bowed your head to offer thanksgiving to God ... but the words to describe your heart of joy could not be found? These times come to all of us. You might be in one of these two right now. If you are, I am hoping it is the heart of joy you have.

The moment you asked Jesus to forgive your sins, and you claimed Him as your Savior, Jesus sent the Comforter (the Holy Spirit) to live within you. The book of I Corinthians speaks about your body becoming the temple of the Holy Spirit. You have living in you, God Himself! He ministers to us in many ways throughout our lives. We sometimes do not even notice. One of the things He does is described in Romans 8. During these times when words fail us, He has a way of communicating to God exactly what we want to express but cannot.

I remember a time when I was standing with a father who just lost his three-year-old son in a house fire. The father fell on me and screamed the question, *"What do I do now?"* I did not have the answers he was asking for. My training for ministry did not equip me for this kind of situation (none could). My experience in ministry past did not help me. I could not think of one Bible verse I felt would meet the need this father had at that moment. I whispered a prayer to my Heavenly Father, but even in whispering the prayer, I could not find the appropriate words to speak.

The blessing to my heart was the reality of this verse. I did not need to put my desires into words; I had and have a Holy Spirit living within me Who knows exactly how to convey my heart to my Heavenly Father. What an incredible comfort to me! What an incredible comfort to you today. No matter what you are facing, God is able to fully understand your situation and leans toward you with a compassionate ear to listen. What a great God we serve! What a blessing to have the Holy Spirit living within us!

"Sometimes you only see the present – God sees the future." – Unknown

Not the Main Character in the Story – August 21

I remember taking a Literature course while in college. At the beginning of the class, our teacher explained there would be differing points of view in the class, and if we could prove our point of view then she would not consider our viewpoint as wrong. This got my creative juices flowing. The last half of our semester, we all read a story about a doctor and a situation he faced. The final exam was a two question exam … who was the main character, and why. I decided to take the least likely person in the story and try to build a case for them being the main character. The obvious main character was the doctor. The entire story revolved around him … but I chose his father-in-law (mentioned only briefly in the story). I then explained this father-in-law had a great influence on his daughter, and she had the greatest influence on the doctor. I got an A+ (I think it was the first and last of my life).

Today I read a verse which reminded me I am not the main character in my life's story. Paul wrote, *"So then it is not of him that willeth, nor of him that runneth, but of God that showeth mercy"* (Romans 9:16). So many times in our everyday lives, we elevate ourselves to the position of the main character. There are many times when we think the entire world revolves around us and our opinions, or it should! We get the idea our problems are the biggest problems on the face of the earth. We imagine the things we see as right and wrong are the same as what others see as right and wrong. We cannot understand why others don't see our situation and have mercy on us!

The Bible clearly states here all the mercy we will need for this day is in the hand and control of our Heavenly Father! He really does know you and what you need. He is totally aware of what you will face today and He has all the mercy you are going to need for the challenge. You see, He is the main character of any story. We are simply the "character actors" who surround His story. We have value because He loves us! We have value because He cares for us! Take heart today … you are worthy of the love of God! Let's do our very best to make Him clearly known to the world we live in. They need to know the Main Character of the story of life too. Don't become so self-centered today that you miss exalting the One Who deserves all the praise of every person in this world! He is worthy!

"Do all you can – to all the people you can – in all the ways you can – for as long as you can." – D.L. Moody

Who Is Standing Beside You – August 22

"Give us help from trouble: for vain is the help of man" (Psalm 108:12). Give us help ... we have trouble ... we have asked for the help of other men ... they have given it ... we are still in trouble. When will we wake up to the fact there is only one place we are going to find the help we need? We know God is the source of the help we need ... so why is it we continue to trust others more than we trust God? Why is it the advice given to us in the Bible many times is our last resort, rather than our first choice? Why do we depend more on unsaved people and what they think than we do about what our God has to say?

The answer to these questions and others is that it seems easier for us to depend on those we can see as opposed to depending on the God we cannot see physically. There is one other thing I have not mentioned, that is a reality we all need to deal with; we have a sin nature that is absolutely opposed to the holiness of our God. Knowing these things are true, let's determine today to live dependent upon God. Let' live today asking for His advice and help before we ask for others. Let's honestly and repeatedly ask for the help of God. He has the answers and the influence we need for whatever we are going to be facing today.

There have been many times when I was in a leadership position and doubted I had the wisdom needed for whatever decision was in front of me. I can recall during those times having a sense of what should be done, but doubting my own judgment so much I was skeptical about saying what my "heart" was telling me. After following what the Holy Spirit was telling me to do, I saw the incredible blessing of walking in the center of the will of God. I want to encourage you to stubbornly fight to stay in the middle of the will of God. I want to encourage you to listen to that "still small voice" that comes from within you (that is the Holy Spirit).

In the life of every Christian there comes a time when you must trust God fully and ignore the clamoring of the world and other believers. Take time today to ask God for wisdom in knowing what He thinks about what you are facing. Rather than running from friend to friend, or even family member to family member, turn to Him first and last. Give God the opportunity to touch your heart in this busy world today. Read His Word with a heart that is yearning for His wisdom and instruction. Don't turn away from what He reveals to you in His Word. Decide that you will trust the leading of the Holy Spirit today and remember man is vain when compared to God.

Face to Face – August 23

Today I want you to consider an incredible verse describing an amazing meeting between God and man. *"And the LORD spake unto Moses face to face, as a man speaketh unto his friend. And he turned again into the camp: but his servant Joshua, the son of Nun, a young man, departed not out of the tabernacle"* (Exodus 33:11). First of all it amazes me God repeated the Ten Commandments for Moses and the children of Israel. Remember, God had already given these once before and etched them on tablets of stone. While God's finger was writing out these commandments, the children of Israel under the leadership of Aaron were busy breaking them! Moses saw their sin and threw the original tablets to the ground in his disgust with the sins of Israel. God wrote a new set for Moses and these sinful people. Thank God today for His mercy.

What really touched my heart in reading this verse is the response of Joshua to all that was happening around him. Notice the description of him ... he was *a servant ... a young man ...* (but the last phrase is what really touched my heart) he *departed not ...* This young servant knew there was something special in the presence of God! He knew there was more there to be gleaned from time alone with God. We don't know all that happened as Joshua lingered after Moses left because the story in our Bible follows Moses' actions.

Allow me to draw two applications for each of us today from this part of Exodus 33:11. First, I don't care what your position might be in this world today; God is interested in meeting face to face with you on a daily basis. I have noticed God is not nearly impressed with the titles we earn here on this earth as we are. He loves the lowest person just as much as He loves the person we think is important. He brought Joseph out of Pharaoh's prison and placed him second in command. He did a similar thing with Mordecai with King Ahasuerus. Remember today God loves you as much as He can love you, and He has invested all He can invest in you. You can be used by God today if you will surrender to His will.

The second application for us is the obvious one ... Joshua lingered in the presence of God. When was the last time you hated to put your Bible down? When was the last time you needed to leave your prayer time and regretted you had so little time? When was the last time you just took the time to meditate on a truth from the Bible and let it sink deeply into your soul? Linger awhile with your God today. You will not regret it!

I Feel So Weak – August 24

I can remember when I was in high school, lying on my back on a weight-lifting bench. My arms looked more like toothpicks than muscular structures. My body resembled more of a distance runner than a weight-lifter. There I was lying on the bench with about 150 pounds on the bar. While my friends lowered the bar to my chest, I began to try to push it upward. I grunted ... I groaned ... I even squealed (much to my disappoint-ment), but that bar remained on my chest. I couldn't even budge that bar! I realized at that time I was exactly as weak as I looked!

Just as I realize I have physical limitations, I am equally aware I have spiritual limitations that are just as real. The prophet Isaiah wrote, *"Trust ye in the LORD forever; for in the law of the LORD JEHOVAH is everlasting strength"* (Isaiah 26:4). Did you catch that title? The LORD JEHOVAH is our God, not simply the "higher power," or the "big guy in the sky," or some other name that does not carry the respect that is due His name. We hear many people say today it does not matter what you call your god, as long as you have faith in something, or someone who is greater than you.

The reality is the author of the religions of our world today is no other person than the Devil. As non-threatening as other religions may seem, they are definitely a part of the plan of the Devil to deceive men into a false hope for eternity that does not exist. The verse I am writing about today says very clearly the strength you and I need for the day is not going to be found in some religion, but only in a meaningful relationship with the LORD JEHOVAH. Isaiah was living in a time when his own people, the Jews, had become captives because of their worship of idols. Isaiah warned them to return to their own God.

I began this devotional by speaking of my own weaknesses, but the reality is anything or anyone compared to our God IS weak. Today you are going to face challenges and situations which are far beyond what a "reli-gion" can handle. Will you trust your own strength, or will you trust this powerful God Isaiah spoke about. Your natural tendency will be to trust yourself, but I want to encourage you to fully depend upon God and Him alone. Don't substitute anything in the place of God, including your family, friends, or your own wisdom. God alone is able to care for you today and every day. I am so glad I can write this devotional about Him and what I know He can do for you. Trust Him fully today.

I Need More Knowledge – August 25

We are living in a world of information over-load. If you have a question about anything (regardless of how trivial it might seem), you can simply enter it in "Google" and find out more information than you knew existed! We have people who have been attending college for most of their adult life, and if you ask them what their plans are to do when they finish the work for their degree, they will probably tell you they are going to pursue another degree. But you know, for all our learning, we are a very foolish people. I think it's because we are starting in the wrong place. *"The fear of the LORD is the beginning of wisdom: a good understanding have all they that do His commandments; His praise endureth forever"* (Psalm 111:10).

I don't know about you, but I need all the wisdom I can get. The Bible clearly states God has made a way for us to attain wisdom from Him ... it is simply by having a healthy fear of the Lord. We like to talk about God in terms that make us feel better, but we need to realize the God we serve is not only love, but His is perfectly just and pure. That means the sin we normally have in our lives is an offense to Him.

We ought to fear failing our God. The reality of life is, we are not perfect. The best of us is at best a sinner saved by the grace of God. Not one of us has earned the right to stand before a holy God. There ought to be a fear we live with every day. I notice in my own life I often treat sin with a very casual attitude. This is a trap of my own sinful flesh, and one I need to guard against at all cost! When I sin, I am failing my righteous and holy God. This ought to strike fear into my heart! This fear of failing God should drive me to my knees. Fearing God, living in fear of failing God, is simply the beginning of wisdom. It is not the end, but it is the important beginning.

If you ever wonder how exactly you fail God, He gave us a set of commandments that are designed to help us walk in a right way before Him. We fear Him because as we seen His commandments clearly, we realize we have not obeyed those commandments. Today is a good day to begin to see your sins as God sees them. This is the launching point to you beginning to understand the fear of God. Because you are beginning to fear God, you now are also beginning to gain wisdom. The people I have known who walk the closest with God, have all had one common characteristic. They all knew their sinfulness and were overwhelmed with the grace of God in their lives. Join them today and begin to know the wisdom of God!

Light in Darkness – August 26

I will be honest with you ... I don't like complete darkness at all. Light is a wonderful thing! Check out this verse: *"Unto the upright there ariseth light in the darkness: He is gracious, and full of compassion, and righteous"* (Psalm 112:4). I know the reality of this Old Testament verse! I thank God I was raised in a home where the light of the Gospel was shining every day through my father and mother. I am grateful I had two godly grandmothers praying for me on a daily basis for me to know the truth of the Word of God.

When I was just a boy, THE Light rose up and conquered the darkness of my sin. I remember well the day I asked Jesus Christ to forgive my sin and give me a home in Heaven. It was on that day I trusted Jesus' death, burial and resurrection to be payment from my sin that eternal darkness left me! I am so thankful I will never know the horror of the eternal darkness of Hell. The reason is not my own goodness, or my own righteousness, but because the Righteous One came for me! That day I trusted Christ, grace, compassion and righteousness came along with Him! I had no idea the great bargain I was getting when I trusted Christ. I was just thinking of the blessing of having my sin forgiven! Little did I know how great it would be to experience the grace He would give me along my way. I had no idea how wonderful it would be to receive blessings I had not earned. I know very well I deserve the judgment of God, and instead He declared me righteous in His Son! That is what I call "Amazing Grace!"

I had no way of understanding how important the compassion God shows to me on a daily basis would be in my life. While the world beats down on me on a regular basis, I run to my Heavenly Father and find His arms open wide to me, every time. What a blessing to come to myself, realizing my failures in sin; deciding to return to God and ask for forgiveness; and there to see my Heavenly Father waiting for me on the back porch! What compassion! Not only do I receive grace and compassion, but He has declared me righteous too! I do not deserve any of that. LIGHT has come to my life! Knowing all these things about what Jesus has given me, how can I remain quiet about the LIGHT? I don't want to be quiet ... I want to tell His story for the remainder of my days!

"In the vast plain of the North, I have sometimes seen, in the morning sun, the smoke of a thousand villages where no missionary has ever been." – Robert Moffat

251

He Reached Down For Me – August 27

"Who humbleth Himself to behold the things that are in heaven, and in the earth! He raiseth up the poor out of the dust, and lifteth the needy out of the dunghill" (Psalm 113:6-7).

When someone with an important position notices someone who has no position, it has always impressed me. I remember a time when I was fifteen years old and was asked to play my trumpet in an orchestra for a Christian musical. It was an Easter musical that was very powerful. The singers and all of the orchestra, except me, were professionals. There was a 1,000 voice choir that had assembled from different churches in the Philadelphia area. The music was written and arranged by a man named John W. Peterson. This was a new experience for this tenth grader. We only had one practice; the night before the actual performance. I remember showing up for practice and being very nervous. My mother had to drive me into the city to the large Civic Center. We walked into the 10,000 seat auditorium and I was totally overwhelmed. As we approached the orchestra pit, I noticed everyone talking excitedly to the director. It was John W. Peterson himself! I was in shock! At one of the breaks in the practice, John W. Peterson made it a point to come down and talk to me. I was extremely humbled this great song-writer would take time to talk to the least important person in the room.

These verses from Psalm 113 show an even more amazing scene. God, Who must humble Himself to view the things in heaven, reaches even further down than that to reach out to we who are poor and needy and in the dunghill! Can you believe that? The same God Who threw the stars into the heavens and named each one ... the God Who held the oceans of the world in the palm of His hand ... the God Who formed Adam out of the dust of the earth and breathed the breath of life into him, reaches down to you and me.

At our best we are poor and needy. It still amazes me the God of all eternity cares about me ... I really can't believe it! I am amazed not only that He cares about me, but He orchestrates events in my life for my good. I don't always understand everything He does with me, but I am thankful He is in charge. I thank God for this care He shows me. I am going to do all I can today to show my gratitude by serving Him the best I can.

"It's not what happens to, but in you that makes the difference." – Unknown

The Firm Foundation – August 28

The most important part of a house is its foundation. Jesus used this foundation as an illustration about a wise and foolish man. Jesus told us if a man builds his house on sand then the storms of life will cause a great crash. He used the opposite picture to teach us a house built on a rock will stand during the storms of life. The prophet Isaiah knew the same thing. He wrote, *"Therefore thus saith the LORD GOD, 'Behold, I lay in Zion for a foundation a stone, a tried stone, a precious corner stone, a sure foundation; he that believeth shall not make haste"* (Isaiah 28:16).

What an incredible verse! Notice the phrase, *"a sure foundation"* ... that is exactly what Jesus Christ is for we who have placed our faith in Him. We are living in a world where it seems many of the things we thought would never change have shown signs of drastic change. What a blessing to know the Rock that is "sure." Consider Jesus Christ and the descriptions the Old Testament prophet Isaiah gave Him.

Isaiah called Him the *"foundation, a stone."* There is no other name given among men where you ought to build your life. Jesus Christ is a foundation you can trust to remain the same in a changing world.

Isaiah called Him the *"tried stone."* Jesus Christ was tested often by other men when He was on the earth. Each time it was obvious He was far above any of them. He is the One you can trust to be sure for you in this unsure world.

Isaiah called Him the *"precious corner stone."* The stone the rest of the building is built upon is called the corner stone. Jesus Christ is the only stone that would have been totally accepted by our holy God. There is no other religious leader who has walked on the earth who could be accepted by God other than Jesus Christ. He is the only One that could claim the title of the Corner stone.

Isaiah called Him the *"sure foundation."* Almost in repetition, but with the addition of the word, *"sure,"* we are told Jesus Christ will be a foundation despite the storms that might beat upon our lives. Don't try to endure the tests life sends your way with your own wisdom. Trust this sure Rock Isaiah told us would be coming for us. Praise God for the Savior we serve today!

"It is not the position that makes the leader; it's the leader that makes the position." – Stanley Huffty

Hope, Hope, Hope – August 29

"Now the God of hope fill you with all joy and peace in believing, that ye may abound in hope, through the power of the Holy Ghost" (Romans 15:13). Can you imagine what a difference you can make today if you will simply live with hope in this hopeless world? Allow your God to build up His hope within you so others can see it today. We are living in a world that is desperately searching for hope. Finances have left people without hope. Health challenges have left people without hope. Leadership has left people without hope in many cases. As with everything else, the only One Who can provide lasting hope is our God! The world is desperately looking for hope today ... there is no question about that. The hope God gives a person does not end with hope alone. God's hope will also bring joy and peace. Think about it ... as smart as those in the world think they are, they cannot produce hope, joy, or peace. Genuine joy and peace are only possible when the Holy Spirit produces them within a person. Everyone in the world yearns for hope, joy and peace.

As the world searches all the "normal" places for hope and finds none, this verse admonishes us to be people that overflow in hope. Don't look at this world through the glasses of someone who does not know Jesus Christ! You do have hope! You do have a future in Heaven that will be far better than anything you have experienced here on the earth! You do have a Comforter in this world of turmoil. Let the world see the hope the Holy Spirit brought when He indwelled you! There should be an out-pouring of hope from you wherever you go today! This is the hope the world so desperately needs ... and you know the Source!

I am not telling you that you will not have discouragement and bad things happen to you. We are living in a world where bad things do happen to good people, but never forget this world is not your final home. There is a bright future for those who have trusted Jesus Christ to save them! Don't live like this world is the final destiny for you, but live like you know where you're going! Make today a day when you display the hope God gave you when you came to know Him personally. Let the world see a hope that circumstances cannot diminish. Show them a hope that is strong and bright in a weakening and darkening world.

"I can see, and that is why I can be happy, in what you call the dark, but which to me is golden. I can see a God-made world, not a man-made world." – Helen Keller

The Arm of Flesh Will Fail – August 30

I remember a night in December (over twenty-five years ago) when I entered a hospital Emergency Room and saw my father lying in a bed with wires connected to his chest. For the first time in my life I realized my Dad was actually human and had weaknesses. Oh, I knew he was human before that, but that night all my dreams of his power came crashing down on me. I remember looking at my dad and seeing the concern on his face. I remember thinking soon he would just stand up and walk out of that hospital and be as good as new. After all, Dad had always been able to conquer the problems that faced our family. That time in life opened a new chapter for me.

Today I read a verse that brought to light the truth I want to share with you today. *"Woe to them that go down to Egypt for help; and stay on horses, and trust in chariots, because they are many; and in horsemen, because they are very strong; but they look not unto the Holy One in Israel, neither seek the LORD"* (Isaiah 31:1)! You see, it really is not about us, but about Him taking care of us. In the life of every believer today there should be a continual yielding of our will/heart/mind/actions to God on a daily basis. What we normally do though, seems to be quite different.

We often depend on the people around us to supply us with the things we think we need. We ask them for advice ... we depend on them for assistance ... we give them a place of honor because we obey what they say, even if we don't fully understand it. We seem to depend on technology more today as well. If we read something on the computer we assume it is correct without even questioning its validity. If a so-called expert says something about a topic we have interest in, we blindly accept what they say and take it as the truth.

There is no question each of us will need help today. Where we go for help during these times will really determine our success or failure. When tough times come in your life today, and they will, run to your Heavenly Father first. If we will do that, I believe some of those difficulties we seem to think we cannot get past, will fade from view very quickly. Trust in your Heavenly Father today; He is well able to help in your time of need, no matter what the obstacle is you will face. The world will always offer an alternative, but it will always be true that God will be able to help you far more than any horse, or chariot, or man can. Will you trust Him today, or will you continue to struggle? Surrender to Him.

Who Can You Depend On? – August 31

"Trust me ..." Have you ever heard those words and had an imme-diate question mark rise up in your brain? I have heard some people say that to me and I had my doubts. I remember going to buy a car one time. Let me say early in this story, not all car salespeople are bad. I went with a friend of mine named Nate. Nate had found a newspaper advertisement for a brand new mini-van. I was looking for a used van because I did not think I could afford a new one. As we arrived at the lot, we asked to see their "used" vans. The prices were higher on the used vans than on the one in the advertisement Nate found. When he asked the salesman about the van, the salesman read the fine print. There was a very small number at the bottom of the advertisement. The salesmen told us that van was there and we could buy it. There was a slight trick to the advertisement. The car lot sold only that one specific van for the reduced price, but it made it look like they had 100 of those vans for sale at that price. That tiny number spoke of that one van.

I have found over the years trusting a man can lead to those kinds of troubles. Catch this verse today: *"God is faithful, by Who ye were called unto the fellowship of His Son Jesus Christ our Lord"* (I Corinthians 1:9). Those first three words are enough! You could read those, close the book and have a great day believing that alone! I will tell you mankind has been trying to fool God and you ever since Cain offered that sacrifice of vegeta-bles instead of a lamb. There is one thing you can be sure of ... as unfaithful as men can be, God is absolutely faithful! What great news! What does that mean to us today? Every promise that is in your Bible, will come true! God's faithfulness demands He will do what He has promised to do!

As you go through your day today and see the unfaithfulness of men/women around you, take heart ... God is not like them. God will be faithful today and in the future as He has been faithful in the past. Remember His feeding all the nation of Israel every day for forty years while they wan-dered in the wilderness? He can provide for you today. Remember the fire that came down when Elijah trusted Him? That same power is ready for you today. Remember when Jesus healed the blind/deaf/crippled and raised the dead? He is still the same God today He was then. I am trying to tell you God is still faithful today and will be the God you need Him to be all day!

"Be aware of your human limits and His holy 'unlimitations.'"
– Ted Camp

MONTH OF
September

The Stone – September 1

I remember being in Jerusalem and seeing the famous "Wailing Wall," or the western wall of the temple in Jerusalem. We were able to go through a tunnel that follows the western wall, underground. Of course, it would have been ground level during the days of Jesus, but there have been many streets and buildings built on top of it now. It was amazing to see this large stone still in the same place after so many years had passed. There were two things which really impressed me while looking at this huge stone.

First, I was impressed by the massive size of one of the foundational stones that could be seen in the tunnel. The guide told us this one stone weighed over three tons. What was amazing was it was placed in the correct place without the help of any machinery. It was moved into that spot by the strength of many men working together. That amazed me. The other thing that really grabbed my attention was the stone was still there, doing what it was designed to do. Even though the city had changed much above that stone ... the stone remained in its place.

I thought about that stone when reading in Psalm 118 today. *"The Stone which the builders refused is become the head stone of the corner"* (Psalm 118:22). To us today looking at that large stone in its place along the western wall of Jerusalem, we would think it was impossible for it to be cut out of the mountain it was in, and then for it to be moved into its place in that foundation. To the Jews who were alive when Jesus walked on this earth, they looked at Jesus and decided in their hearts there was no way this man could be the Messiah. It did not fit the mold they had invented in their minds for what the Messiah would look like.

There are still many skeptical people around today who reject the fact Jesus Christ is the Son of God. If we want to live successfully in this world, we must realize Jesus Christ should be the centerpiece of whatever we are doing. When you prepare to make a decision today about anything in your life, ask yourself how Jesus would view the situation you are facing. Ask yourself how Jesus would react if He were in your place. Seek to give counsel He would have given. In order to do this, you need to spend time getting to know Him better! The Bible is full of truths about Jesus Christ that I believe are there for our good and our knowledge of Him. It is not enough to know about Him; we must live like Him as well. Let Jesus Christ be the foundational Rock you build your life upon!

"Everyone is facing an inescapable Lord Jesus Christ." – Unknown

Since I Have Been Redeemed – September 2

I have learned this world offers absolutely no lasting peace. I have found the world offers no lasting hope. I have learned no religious leader can offer forgiveness of my sins; after all, that person is just as much a sinner as I am! I have learned there is peace and hope only in one place ... with our God! The good news is, there is real hope with Him!

"And now, Lord, what wait I for? My hope is in Thee. Deliver me from all my transgressions: make me not the reproach of the foolish" (Psalm 39:7-8). This is where the hope really is! I have chosen to hope outside of the realm of my understanding and outside the realm of my own righteousness. I choose to hope in God! Yes, some will call me foolish. Some will scoff at me and mock me for trusting in God. Those are the same people who use drugs, alcohol, sex, sports, work, and many other things to find satisfaction for the longing of their soul. I have found in Jesus Christ the answer to the longing of my soul. I am at rest in Him today.

My heart goes out to people who are using these other things to search for peace, hope, and forgiveness. I have found all those things in an on-going relationship with God Himself. What a great gift God offers us today! He has loved us. His Son died in our place and offers forgiveness for sin. The Holy Spirit takes that offering and puts it on our account, and then stays in us for eternity to help lead and guide us! What a great God!

Edwin O. Excell wrote: **Verse 1:** *I have a song I love to sing, since I have been redeemed, of my Redeemer, Savior, King – since I have been redeemed.* **Verse 2:** *I have a Christ that satisfies, since I have been redeemed; to do His will my highest prize – since I have been redeemed.* **Verse 3:** *I have a witness bright and clear, since I have been redeemed, dispelling ev'ry doubt and fear – since I have been redeemed.* **Verse 4:** *I have a home prepared for me, since I have been redeemed, where I shall dwell eternally – since I have been redeemed.* **Chorus:** *Since I have been redeemed, since I have been redeemed, I will glory in His name; since I have been redeemed, I will glory in my Savior's name.*

We are living in a world that is without peace; we are living in a world that is without hope; and we are living in a world that is without forgiveness. Don't be selfish today. Tell someone about the God you know Who has given you lasting, eternal peace. Tell them of the hope you have for all your needs to be met. Tell them they can be forgiven! Tell them about Jesus!

Showing the Power – September 3

How much of our time is spent trying to impress other people with our intelligence, our skill, our wisdom, our experience, or how much money we have? The answer is, too much time! As a believer, we should do all we can to lift our God up, and to put ourselves out of the picture. Today I read Paul's words to the church in Corinth. This statement Paul made always brings me back to reality. He wrote … *"And my speech and my preaching was not with enticing words of man's wisdom, but in demonstration of the Spirit and of power: that your faith should not stand in the wisdom of men, but in the power of God"* (I Corinthians 2:4-5).

Be very careful of what Paul spoke about here. If we are not careful we can fall into this very trap of trying to impress others. Think about it for a moment; what motivates this kind of thinking? The answer is, it is our pride that drives this desire within us. Our pride is the enemy of God's grace. Our pride will always promote us (and eventually our sinfulness) and will demote God from the place of prominence in our life. Pride will destroy any hope of living in a godly fashion in an ungodly society.

Paul makes it clear his desire was not to depend upon his own wisdom, or even the wisdom of those he would meet who appeared to be wise. His desire was simply to show the power of the Holy Spirit in his own life to those who were watching the way he behaved in this world. His heart's desire was to show this power so other people could build up their faith. He was not trying to prop them up with some fancy way of talking that would "tickle" their ears. He wanted his life to be so controlled by the Holy Spirit that when he would testify, it would be evident God was in control. I hear so many folks today arguing about a specific usage of a word, rather than thinking about the substance of what they are saying. One of the most powerful men in my life was a man who spoke so simply, any child would have been able to understand what he was saying. That is the goal I have for the times I am preaching/teaching. I want the power of the message not to be in the words I choose to use, but in the obvious leading of the Holy Spirit. I want to be hidden behind the Holy Spirit when I have the chance to counsel, teach, or preach to others. Today God will place opportunities in your path for you to make a difference in the life of someone else. Will you try to impress … or will you hide your life in Him and let Him minister?

"To make a message simple is hard." – Ted Camp

What Should I Do – September 4

Just before I was born, a so-called expert came on the scene to tell parents how to raise their children. Dr. Benjamin Spock wrote a book called "Baby and Child Care." It became the standard many parents lived by in raising their children. I'm very thankful my parents did not buy a copy. The counsel given in that book was later found to be absolutely wrong. I am thankful my parents had a copy of the Book of books, the Bible. They practiced what the psalmist wrote in Psalm 119 ... *"Thy testimonies also are my delight and my counselors"* (Psalm 119:24).

Where are you going to get your advice from today? Whose counsel will be most important to you in making life's decisions? Where will you turn when trouble is just ahead? These are choices you are going to make today that will affect where you end up in the future. Ted Camp has said many times *"Decisions determine directions. Directions determine destinations."* The simple decisions you will make today are going to influence where you will go and the direction your life will take.

Bad decisions based on the advice of this world will lead to problems and heartache. Good decisions will lead you to stability and success. Making good decisions (decisions based on the truths of the Word of God) will not always be easy, but they will always be best for your life. There are people in this world today who love to mock the Word of God and the principles that are in it, telling you they are outdated and unreliable. These people do this while fumbling through their lives making a mess at every turn because of ignoring those principles and truths. Don't fall into their trap. A person once said, *"Misery loves company;"* and it is true, these kinds of people want you to agree with them and join their misery. Don't follow them!

The last thing I will say to you today is, there is no value in having a Bible that remains closed. If you want your Bible to become your counselor, you will need to open it and search for the answers to your challenges on a daily basis. You are going to have daily challenges ... you will need daily counseling sessions with the Word of God. I promise you ... the answers you need for the challenges you are facing and will face, are all found in the Word of God. Don't allow this foolish world to decide for you who has the advice you need. Just check out the lives of some of those who are called counselors in our day. They are searching without success for answers themselves. Trust God's counsel, you will not be sorry.

"Make decisions that are best for the ministry." – Ted Camp

Bare Necessities – September 5

When preparing to leave on a trip, I always consider what the most important things I will need are. I hate carrying around baggage that has non-essential things in it. I remember a trip our youngest daughter and I took to Ukraine. Our flight to Ukraine had an unexpected delay after take-off. I remember getting off the ground in Philadelphia and hearing the captain tell us one of the lights in the cockpit was malfunctioning. He announced we were going to land in New York to get it repaired. I was happy in one sense he would not attempt to cross the Atlantic Ocean with something not working correctly, but I was not excited about the delay in the beginning of our long flight.

When we finally arrived in Ukraine, we found our bags had not followed us. For a man this is not the worst news you can receive. For a teenage girl … it's pretty close to the top of the "worst news" list. We were in Ukraine for about ten days. We got our luggage on day seven. Needless to say we had to do a little shopping for the teenager! However, the thing that really hit my mind after we got our luggage was this … why did I bring so much stuff? I had made it fine with one change of clothing!

The Christian life is no different. Check out this wise man's perspective: *"Neither have I gone back from the commandment of His lips; I have esteemed the words of His mouth more than my necessary food"* (Job 23:12). In all the trouble Job faced, he realized the one thing he needed was the Word of God. He could face the challenges that had come to him, as long as he had the Word of God to lean on. He could endure the suffering his body was experiencing if he had the Word of God. He could find the peace for his soul at the death of all his children as long as he had the Word of God. Job's key to life was the Word of God. It was the "Bare Essential" for the life of Job.

How about you today? Is God's Word that important to you? Have you given much thought to what God wants for you in your life today? Have you opened your Bible this morning to get the day started right? Have you checked out your newspaper, local news cast on TV, your Facebook page, or anything other than the Bible to start your day today? This is a struggle for me daily. I want the Word of God to be "… *more than my necessary food*" today and every day. Don't wallow in the past. Begin today to ask God to make His Word as valuable to you as it was to Job. Run to it today for your guidance and help. Lean on the Word of God. It will not fail you.

Run for Your Life … Don't Look Back – September 6

When I was a young boy, I was always the smallest kid in the class. I remember playing in my neighborhood when I was growing up. We met every day in the empty lot next to my house. We played football, baseball, and all kinds of running, active games there. There was one boy in our neighborhood who was sometimes my friend … sometimes my neighborhood bully. There were times when he would become mad at me and begin to threaten to "beat me up." When that happened, I would do what came natural to me … I would run, and run, and run until eventually either the bully "ran out of gas" or I arrived at home! When I was running, I learned a very important lesson … Don't look back!

All of us have times when we need to turn and run from things that would harm us. There are past sins that nag at our hearts … turn, and run for your life and don't look back! There are failures we would love to undo and erase … turn, and run for your life and don't look back! There are people who would drag us down into a pit with them … turn, and run for your life and don't look back! There are habits that can ruin your spiritual life … turn, and run from them and don't look back!

God spared the lives of Lot, his wife and his two daughters by His mercy. The one instruction they were given was not to look back. *"But his [Lot's] wife looked back from behind him, and she became a pillar of salt"* (Genesis 19:26). You and I might read this story and wonder to ourselves, 'How could she be so stupid? She had heard the voice of the angels (in the form of the men that visited their home)! How could she not listen to their clear instructions?' Before we go too far in giving blame to Mrs. Lot, consider the book you have in your house called the Bible. How many of God's clear instructions have you ignored this week? The reality is the best of us will struggle with this daily.

Each of us has a different "Sodom and Gomorrah" in our lives. For Mrs. Lot, it had been her home; her place of comfort; her life-style. We might argue she should not have felt at home there with all the wickedness they showed, but it had been her home nonetheless. She turned back to all she had ever known. Let's learn from her today as we live out this day. There are some things, some people, and some places you and I need to turn our backs on today. There are some things, people and places we ought to run from and never look back. Today is a good day to sing that song, *"I have decided to follow Jesus … no turning back … no turning back."* I hope this story will help you to keep your eyes fixed on Jesus today!

263

God Hears the Voices – September 7

In college, God led me to pursue Missions as my minor. I attended a Bible College where we all majored in Bible. I remember sitting in an early Missions class that was taught by a man of God named Austin Lockhart. He had been a missionary for many years in Papua New Guinea. He told us a story I have never forgotten and would like to share with you today. He told of landing in a very remote part of the world with his family, with the goal of starting a church. He and his family were the first white people the tribe had ever seen. He was amazed at how quickly they were accepted. He and his family began the task of learning a language from nothing. As soon as they felt it was possible, they began to present the Gospel of Jesus Christ to these people. Very quickly the chief of the tribe, as well as many of the villagers responded and trusted Christ. Mr. Lockhart found out this tribe had been handing down a story from generation to generation that God would reveal Himself to them through a white man who would come from a great bird in the sky. Little did my professor know, but they had been waiting for him and his family to arrive long before he had planned to go to them! God had heard their cry for help!

Today I read about Hagar and Ishmael being cast out by Sarah after the birth of Isaac. Just when Hagar thought all hope was gone for her son to survive, this verse says, *"And God heard the voice of the lad; and the angel of God called to Hagar out of Heaven, and said unto her, 'What aileth thee, Hagar? Fear not; for God hath heard the voice of the lad where he is'"* (Genesis 21:17). God heard the voice of the lad … God still has an ear for those who cannot cry out, or don't even know to cry out today! God sent my professor and his family to a very remote part of the world because there had been generations of people there crying out for the Gospel!

Have you ever felt you were crying out, but no one was listening? Have you ever felt you were talking to the wall when you were praying and there was no hope of an answer coming? Have you ever been ready to give up on the whole "Christian thing" and just go back to your old way of living? Take heart today from this story from the first book in our Bible. God hears your voice! God knows your pain, frustration, anxiety, and fear. God hears the voice of those around you who are waiting for someone to arrive with the news of the Gospel for them today.

God hears the voices of those in need. Those around you are calling out to Him today. As Mr. Lockhart was faithful to in his life, be faithful to God's plan for you today. Someone is counting on you!

Comfort Food – September 8

There are certain foods you eat that cause you comfort. For each of us, these foods might differ. You can give me butter covered noodles and a good piece of roast beef and I will be ready to take a nap! You might like jalapeno peppers and pepperoni pizza for your comfort food. The psalmist wrote about the food that comforted him. He wrote, "*I remembered Thy judgments of old, O LORD; and have comforted myself*" (Psalm 119:52).

I was thinking about the things in the Word of God that bring comfort to me. Here are a few I hope will be an encouragement to you too. I am comforted by knowing the Holy Spirit within me is greater, and more powerful than the Devil who is in this world. No matter how bad things look around us in this world, remember our God is still in control.

I am comforted to know God's promise to His children is that He will never leave or forsake them. What a joy to know that regardless of how difficult the things are around me, I have a relationship with God that is strengthened rather than weakened. I have had people who have told me they were friends to me, but when the difficulties came, those "friends" were long gone!

I am comforted by the fact I cannot lose the salvation God has given me. As a matter of fact, Jesus explained He holds me in His hand and no one can pluck me from it. He then added His hand is within the hand of God the Father and no one will be able to take me from His hand! I am told He gives me "everlasting life" and "eternal life" and I will live "forever" with my Savior!

I am comforted to know the Bible I have read my whole life contains the words for life. I am thankful I don't need to trust the opinions of anyone else, or look for another substitute Bible. I am glad the verses I memorized when I was a boy are still real and profitable today. I am glad we have a Bible that is good for what is right (doctrine), for what is wrong that I need to avoid (reproof) for how to make what is wrong, right (correction) and for staying right (instruction in righteousness).

I am comforted to know when I am weak and loaded down with burdens, I have a Savior Who is willing to lift me up and carry me along! What a great God I serve! I cannot tell you how I appreciate the comfort of these things. What is there to fear with this God as my Father?

"*God acts for His glory and for my good.*" – Ted Camp

The Old Book and the Old Faith – September 9

"Princes have persecuted me without a cause: But my heart standeth in awe of Thy Word" (Psalm 119:161). Of all that King David had seen in his lifetime, he made the statement here at the end of his life that he stood in awe of the Word of God. How about us today? Do we stand in awe of the Bible? Do we hold the truths that are on its pages with high respect? When we hear it preached in our churches, do we determine we will let God have His way with us, or do we fight against its conviction?

I never had the privilege to meet my grandfather, Earl Franklin Gable. My grandmother told me so many stories about him, I have always felt like I have known him. One of the stories she told me was how he so simply and completely loved the Word of God. My grandfather was raised in a time in our history when the thinking was that a boy who had reached the eighth grade was educated enough. He never learned to read well. When he was saved at the age of twenty-five, he told my grandmother; *"I've lived for the devil for twenty-five years, now I want to live for God for the rest of my life."* He taught himself to read, basically by giving himself to reading his Bible every day. When visitors came to the Gable home to eat, they were required to take part in family devotions, and to read from the precious book, the Bible. I have my grandfather's Bible on my bookshelf, right in front of me. On the back cover, written by his hand are these words … "P.S. Read." May I encourage you to do the same? Don't just own this precious book … read and obey it! George A. Carr wrote …

Verse 1: *'Mid the storms of doubt and unbelief we fear, stands a Book eternal that the world holds dear; thru the restless ages it remains the same – 'Tis the Book of God, and the Bible is its name!* **Verse 2:** *'Tis the Book that tells us of the Father's love, when He sent His Son to us from heav'n above, Who by richest promise creates hope within, for 'tis thru His blood we are save from ev'ry sin!* **Verse 3:** *'Tis the Book that tells us of the will of God and the Savior's teachings while the earth He trod – How He soothed earth's sorrows and relieved its woe, thru Whom strength is given to conquer ev'ry foe!* **Verse 4:** *'Tis the Book that tells us of eternal life, after faithful service in a world of strife; and this glorious triumph over death's dark fears is the world's best gift in an age of countless fears!* **Chorus:** *The old Book and the old Faith are the rock on which I stand! The old Book and the old Faith are the bulwark of the land! Thru storm and stress they stand the test, in ev'ry clime and nation blest; the old Book and the old Faith are the hope of ev'ry land!*

Is There a Burr Under Your Saddle? – September 10

Why is it we think we can hide things from God? We teach and believe He knows everything, and yet it seems we think we can hide some of our sinful behavior from Him. How foolish we are! God designed us to live godly in Christ Jesus. He made us to want a clean conscience. His will for every believer is to be a light to this darkened world so they will see Him in us and be drawn to our Savior. His will for every believer is to be salt in this world. To offer some flavor, some preservative ... for us to make a difference.

Why is it we then try to snuggle up to the world, and to live as close to the line as possible at times? We should know better, but we are just like those before us who struggle in the battle between our human nature and the Holy Spirit within us. Today is a good day to turn your back on your sin nature and fully yield to the Holy Spirit. Walk in the Spirit today and don't fulfill the lusts of your flesh.

When Jacob finally left Laban to head out on his own, with his own family, there was a situation where Laban claimed Jacob had stolen one of his idols. After searching all, he came to Rachel. *"Now Rachel had taken the images, and put them in the camel's furniture, and sat upon them. And Laban searched all the tent, but found them not"* (Genesis 31:34). Rachel thought she had successfully hidden these idols Laban cherished ... but she had not hidden them from God. This record in Genesis is proof that God knew, but also that the writer of this book knew as well.

There are things in each of our lives we struggle with in that battle between our sin nature and the Holy Spirit of God. There are times when all of us do what Rachel did in this chapter. We think we can hide some of these things from God. The reality is, it is far better to *"... confess our sins"* because *"... He is faithful and just to forgive us our sins, and to cleanse us from all unrighteousness"* (I John 1:9). Why is it we think we can hide things from God? An even more important question is this: Why would we hide things He can forgive and remove?!

I don't want to allow anything to block my relationship with Him today. I am so thankful for the mercies of God that are new every morning! I'm thankful this morning when I woke up that God had a whole new bundle of mercy waiting for me. I'm sure I will use up my allotment today, but He will have a new batch ready for me tomorrow! What a great God! Love Him and serve Him today!

Remember ... – September 11

Today is a day Americans should remember for the rest of our lives. Not necessarily because of the attack of terrorists on American soil, but because of the reality of how short life really is for each of us. On this day, many years ago, we realized life can be taken very unexpectedly. Some of the folks who went to work so many years ago had no idea they would be meeting God face to face before their morning was finished. My first thought was, 'how many of the people losing their lives were saved?' Eternity is not something we often think about on a regular day.

It is important we do consider our eternity on a daily basis. We ought to live our lives as though this is the last day we will live. Today I want you to consider living life as though it could be your last. Don't waste time today on trivial things that will have no eternal value! We waste so much time on insignificant things on a regular basis. I want to look back today and remember how valuable life came into focus on that day so many years ago. I want to make sure I use every minute of this day to make memories that will last into eternity!

As always, I turn to the Bible when thinking about the things that affect my life every day. Today I thought about these verses: *"Remember ye not the former things, neither consider the things of old. Behold, I will do a new thing; now it shall spring forth; shall ye not know it? I will even make a way in the wilderness, and rivers in the desert"* (Isaiah 43:18-19). What a great God we serve! He is ready to do a new work in me for today. I need that new work! He is ready to make a way in the desert where it seems (humanly speaking) there is no way. Not only will he make a way in my desert, but He will provide rivers there. He will provide all I need in that desert.

There is value in remembering events like "9/11." There is value in us remembering the things God has done for us in our everyday walk with Him. We Americans have a responsibility to remember the events of that unforgettable day. We Christians have a responsibility to remember the things that happened to us before our salvation, as well as the things God has done for us since our salvation! We ought to take time today to reflect on the "rivers" God has provided in our "deserts." I am thankful for the "desert" times of my own life. It was there in the "desert" that I grew into a much more intimate relationship with the One I was totally dependent upon. I'm thankful for these times, and want to tell others there is hope, even in seemingly hopeless situations. Remember your God today!

Run to Win – September 12

It was a cold March afternoon with a heavy drizzle falling when we walked onto our High School track for the races that day. I remember well walking through the gates that led to the football stadium where our track was located. I remember how cold I was, but more than that, I remember how excited I was to run in my first official race. I reflected back to a race I ran in second grade of elementary school. There it was, all the kids from first to sixth grade running from the starting point, around the flagpole and back. My cousin and I were the shortest runners, but we finished first and second. This day, some nine years later, I was going to run in my first official race. I remember stepping to the starting blocks and looking up the track to the finish line. I wanted to cross that line first. Nothing else was on my mind, but that goal that was set out in front of me.

The Bible speaks about a finish line that is in front of every Christian today. *"Know ye not that they which run in a race run all, but one receiveth the prize? So run, that ye may obtain"* (I Corinthians 9:24). We are living in a time when people are against competition. This is another proof the world has no concept of how God designed us, or the purpose He designed us to be. God made you and I to try our best to reach the goals that are set in front of us! God made you to try your hardest to be the best you can possibly be! He made us to want to succeed!

We seem to have less trouble with this concept when it comes to business, or our favorite sport, or even in a classroom setting. I wonder how many goals we have set for ourselves that involve spiritual things? Do you have a finish line in front of you when it comes to things that will help you develop your spiritual life? Do you have a goal for reading your Bible through every year? Have you set a goal to be faithful to your local church, regardless of what is on TV? Have you asked God to help you pray more often and with more intensity? Have you asked God to help you to be a witness to a neighbor, family member, or stranger? Have you asked God to help you make changes to match biblical principles in your walk with Him?

It is time for every Christian to focus on the finish line, and to press toward that mark without looking to the right or to the left to see what others are doing. The one thing I loved about running on the track team was that I had no one to blame but me if I lost. Set YOUR sights on the goals God has for you and don't look back or to the side to compare yourself with anyone else. Reach for that crown that awaits the faithful in Heaven!

Run to God for Strength – September 13

"Hast thou not known? Hast thou not heard, that the everlasting God, the LORD, the Creator of the ends of the earth, fainteth not, neither is weary? There is no searching of His understanding. He giveth power to the faint; and to them that have no might He increaseth strength. Even the youths shall faint and be weary, and the young men shall utterly fall: But they that wait upon the LORD shall renew their strength; they shall mount up with wings as eagles; they shall run, and not be weary; and they shall walk, and not faint" (Isaiah 40:28-31).

There are times when each of us feels we are at the "end of our rope." There are times when the gumption to get up and get going has gotten up and gone! There are times, if we are honest with ourselves, when we can become spiritually drained. There are a few things which came to my mind today as I read these very familiar verses. The space here will not be adequate to exhaust those things, but let me mention a few for you to ponder today.

I noticed Isaiah began this great section of Scripture by reminding us of the greatness of our God. Notice the phrases, *"everlasting God,"* and *"Creator of the ends of the earth."* I think Isaiah wanted us to remember when we become weary, we have the ultimate source for strength. Earlier in the chapter (40:12) he had spoken about the immensity of our God. This is good for us to remember when we are so weary we feel like we cannot go forward. Look to the Creator of the ends of the earth ... He can handle it!

You will also notice from these verses this weariness of life does not only come to those who are old, but to all. I like that 30th verse where it makes it clear *"Even the youths shall faint."* We often associate weariness only with older folks. There is a great lesson here for those who are younger reading this today. Young people should be so actively involved in serving God, you can become weary! Sitting around on the couch playing a video game does not wear you out (except for your thumbs and posterior). Get up and get involved today. If you have been feeling weary in doing something for God, be comforted to know He is well aware of that, and He is on call. He is ready and able to help you in your time of need! Run, and He will prop you up!

"There is no thrill quite like doing something you didn't know you could."
           – Marjorie Holmes

Behind the Scenes – September 14

There are times in life when we might feel God is sleeping, or certainly not paying attention to the things that are happening "to" us. We might feel we don't deserve the poor treatment we are receiving, or we deserve better than we are getting. I have gone to God at times and complained I was doing my best to serve Him, and I didn't understand why I had to face the challenges in the center of His will which I was facing. Imagine that! Me questioning God!

When Joseph was in the pit, hearing his brothers discuss killing him; he must have felt that way. When he was sold as a slave and turned to watch his brothers and their sheep fade into the distance on his way to a foreign country; he must have felt that way. When he was falsely accused and thrown into an Egyptian prison to rot for the remainder of his days; he must have felt that way. When the Pharaoh's butler forgot about him for two years; he must have felt that way.

But on that first day when he saw his brothers coming to Egypt for food … it must have all come together in his mind. When he finally told them who he was, he said, *"And God sent me before you to preserve you a posterity in the earth, and to save your lives by a great deliverance. So now it was not you that sent me hither, but God: and He hath made me a father to Pharaoh, and lord of all his house, and a ruler throughout all the land of Egypt"* (Genesis 45:7-8).

Joseph realized something you and I need to get hold of today. It does not matter what things look like through our human eyesight, God has a plan He is working out that will result in our ultimate good! He sees the bigger picture! He knows the end of the story! He has a plan that is working behind the scenes in our lives, that we don't even see or recognize until He is done working and we look back and see His guiding hand all the way through!

Rather than struggle against the plan of God for you today, trust the loving, guiding hand of God! Rest in the fact He never makes a mistake! I would rather have been Joseph … through the pit … the slavery … the prison time … and through the feelings of being forgotten … than to be any of his brothers, or Potiphar's wife (that's a devotional for another time). I would rather be in the center of God's will (testings and all), than to be in the lap of luxury with all my bills paid! We have a great God … trust Him today! He is absolutely trust-worthy!

Hope for Today – September 15

"I have set the LORD always before me: because He is at my right hand, I shall not be moved. Therefore my heart is glad, and my glory rejoiceth: my flesh also shall rest in hope" (Psalm 16:8-9). What a joy to have God so near in such troubling times! All around us we hear of disasters happening. I'm not necessarily talking about tornados, or floods, or earthquakes. I'm talking about people who are committing suicide. I'm talking about marriages that are breaking down after many years together. I'm talking about leaders who are crumbling under the pressures of leadership. I'm talking about men and women who are not serious about their commitment to their families, children and spouses.

We are living in a time of great hopelessness. This hopelessness is not only in the world, but also in our churches. This should never be the case with a believer, and yet we see it happening all around us. Why is this so today? When I was a teenager, someone made a statement I have never forgotten, and have written about many times before. The statement is simply and true. *"If you feel far from God … guess who moved?"* The reality is, God is not to blame for the hopelessness we are seeing all around us today.

As the writer of this chapter said, God is always at the right hand of a believer. If we are going to wander from recognizing the value of the life God has given us and consider suicide, we must let go of the hand of God to do it. If we are going to give up on being faithful to a husband/wife we have been married to for some time, we must push away from an intimate walk with God. If we are going to turn our backs on our responsibilities as leaders in our church or community, we must refuse the commission God has given us. If we are willing to run from our responsibilities as father/mother/children in a family, we must ignore the clear Bible principles that have been given to us.

I don't want this to be a negative thought today, so let's shift our minds from the failures we see around us, and are so easy to fall into. Let's look into the face of our loving Heavenly Father. The reality is, His is at our right hand today! He is there to help you to not move off the mark He has planned for you today. He is the Person we ought to run to for our joy and gladness. This world will fail us, but our God will never fail. He is the place for our hope today, not any government, or money! Draw near to your God today, and you will find Him drawing near to you. What a great God we serve! What an incredible hope we have in Him!

G.P.S. – God's Plan Seen – September 16

I have become very dependent on a GPS to help me find my way to places I have never been before. It's scary how much I trust the little box that sits on the dash of my car. If it says "turn right," I turn right. If it says "recalculating," I tend to panic. I trust a computer and satellites far up in the sky to lead me to places almost every day. When we arrive in an area unknown to me, I simply plug in the destination I want to go to and then I follow the instructions. Why is it so difficult for me to do that with my Heavenly Father?

The psalmist wrote ... *"Show me Thy ways, O LORD; teach me Thy paths. Lead me in Thy truth, and teach me: for Thou art the God of my salvation; on Thee do I wait all the day"* (Psalm 25:4-5). Did you notice the absolute dependence the writer had on God? *Show me ... teach me ... lead me ... for Thou art the God ... I wait all the day.* I like this chapter. Today when I read it, it seemed to be calling my name! Just as I depend on the GPS in my car, I want to follow completely the plan God has for me!

Just as I follow the instructions of the GPS, I want to do these things mentioned in this verse above. I want God to show me where to go. I want to know His ways, rather than stumbling along on my ways. I have run into far too many roads that lead in the absolute wrong direction in my life when trusting myself. I have hit detours and had no idea where to go. I have turned onto roads I thought would bring me happiness, only to find out there is NO OUTLET! I want to follow the guiding hand of God.

I want God to teach me along the way. I have found if I am riding with someone else, I have no recollection of how I arrive at places. However, if I am driving, I can remember for a long time how to get to different places. I want the same to be true of me as I "drive" through my Bible each day and learn its truths. I want to be taught the Words of God for myself, so I can use them for years in the future. I want God to lead me very clearly to the places He wants me to arrive. I want to be willing to trust Him, even when it seems the path I am on could be a mistake. I want to so lean on my Heavenly Father that when He nudges me, I turn without thought!

Why should I turn over the controls of my life to Him like that? Because *He is the God of my salvation; on Him do I wait all the day*! That's why! No other explanation is necessary. You can choose to wander without direction all day if you want, but I'm tired of stubbing my toes on my own plans. I want to trust God's plan for my life today! Recalculate today!

It's Time – September 17

"'Explosives' cut power at Iran nuke plant ..." "War Drums – Syrian jet hits Lebanese territory ..." "Pakistanis try to storm U.S. outpost – 1 killed ..." "D.C. police seek 6-year-old boy in robbery ..." "Dollar hovers near 7-year low ..." "Panetta warns of war ..."

These are the headlines on a popular news website today. *"It is time for Thee, LORD, to work; for they have made void Thy law"* (Psalm 119:126). We all could echo the reality of this verse. May I tell you I believe God is ready to work; He is just looking for some believers who are sold out to work with Him. A.W. Tozer wrote in his book, <u>The Crucified Life</u> (pg. 23), *"Many Christians talk about living the crucified life but nothing in their lives indicates they have even begun the journey."* The reality of the situation we find ourselves living in is that God does need to work. The added reality is God is willing to work, but He has chosen to work through believers. That brings us to the question, "Am I available for God to use me today?"

Are you fully committed to living a righteous life for God today? Can others see a difference in you from those without Christ? Do you dress differently? Do you love differently? Do you speak differently? Do you think differently? Do you view the importance of your money, possessions and time differently? I am not trying to be legalistic at all, but our actions will prove what is in our heart far more than our words will. It has been said before your walk talks louder than your talk. There is a great deal of truth in that statement.

Are you willing to live a separated life today for the sake of the Gospel of Jesus Christ reaching the lost? It seems we love to emphasize our liberty in Christ, but not much about becoming a bond-slave of Christ. Remember the Old Testament slave who loved their master so much they wanted to remain a slave for the remainder of their lives? They would go to the doorpost and allow a hole to be drilled through their earlobe with an awl. Instead of wearing a large hollow button in the ear (popular today), this person showed by an outward display, an inward commitment to their master. Can others tell by how you live that you are totally committed to Him?

I think we all would agree this would be a good time for God to work in our world. Just remember He has chosen to work through you! Today put yourself in a position where God can use you. Release your hold on the things of this world and grasp the responsibility of serving Him fully.

A New Day … A New Opportunity – September 18

"Remember ye not the former things, neither consider the things of old. Behold, I will do a new thing; now it shall spring forth; shall ye not know it? I will even make a way in the wilderness, and rivers in the desert" (Isaiah 43:18-19).

I really needed these verses today. It feels like I have been messing up, more than doing what's right lately. Has that ever happened to you? After all, I am always telling someone else how to live for God, and how to do what's right … then I look at my own walk, and I realize I have a long way to go to become a godly man. That is my number one goal in life … to walk with God in a way that will bless and challenge others. However, preaching about it and living it are two different things.

I remember the frustration I felt as a teenager when I would go forward at the end of a church service to fully commit a part of my life to God, and then struggle in the days following to actually do what I had committed. Nothing much has changed to this point. I still am frustrated with how little effort I seem to give to living out the principles of the Word of God in my daily life. God always brings verses along like these today that bring me back to reality. The reality is that none of us is good enough to walk with God on our own. We desperately need His help! We need His daily guidance and help to get us back on track again and again.

I am so thankful to God that when I wander into the "wilderness" and "desert" areas of my Christian walk, He is there to pull me back to Himself. He actually *"makes a way"* … I picture the father/mother clearing a path for that child who is just learning to walk. I can just see God moving things He knows would hinder my walk with Him so I can find the paths He has for me for each day. How good is that?!

I've got to do my part in this process of finding new paths in the wilderness and deserts of my life. I need to close off the failures of the past. That means I need to seek forgiveness for sins of the past. I then need to repent and turn my back on those sins. It also means I need to remove the power of influence those sins of the past want to continue to have on my future. I want to forget the things that are behind me so I can clearly see the paths in the deserts in front of me. Don't give up today! God is still able to clear a path for your steps. Look for His guiding hand!

"God almost never calls His people to a fair fight." – George Otis

Trust and Obey – September 19

"And the word of the LORD came to Solomon, saying, 'Concerning this house which thou art in building, if thou wilt walk in My statutes, and execute My judgments, and keep all My commandments to walk in them; then will I perform My word with thee, which I spake unto David thy father: And I will dwell among the children of Israel, and will not forsake my people Israel'" (I Kings 6:11-13). That sounds simple … but as we read the pages of our Bible, we realize it wasn't that simple for Solomon, and it continues to be a challenge today. I hope every person reading this has the goal in their heart to serve the Lord and to completely obey His Word. If that is not your goal, today is a good day to make it your goal. The problem Solomon had is the same as the problem we have. We are not perfect, and we live in sinful flesh that wars against the Spirit of God within us. There are no guarantees we will walk with God today. That does not change the fact it should be our goal today and every day we live.

Solomon has been considered the wisest man who has lived (except for Jesus, of course), and yet even after hearing this clear warning and promise, he still turned his back on the truths of Scripture. I want to encourage you today to learn from Solomon's mistake. It is always better to trust God than to suffer the consequences that come from straying away from Him. God has a plan for your life today. Ask Him to help you stay on track. If you get off the track, God loves you enough to do everything He can to guide you back onto the right track. This might include some very tough situations until you yield to Him. Trust Him today, and obey His Word!

John H. Sammis wrote: **Verse 1:** *When we walk with the Lord in the light of His Word, what a glory He sheds on our way! While we do His good will He abides with us still, and with all who will trust and obey.* **Verse 2:** *Not a shadow can rise, not a cloud in the skies, but His smile quickly drives it away; not a doubt nor a fear, not a sigh nor a tear, can abide while we trust and obey.* **Verse 3:** *Not a burden we bear, not a sorrow we share, but our toil He doth richly repay; not a grief nor a loss, not a frown nor a cross, but is blest if we trust and obey.* **Verse 4:** *But we never can prove the delights of His love until all on the altar we lay, for the favor He shows and the joy He bestows are for them who will trust and obey.* **Verse 5:** *Then in fellowship sweet we will sit at His feet, or we'll walk by His side in the way; what He says we will do, where He sends we will go – Never fear, only trust and obey.* **Chorus:** *Trust and obey – for there's no other way to be happy in Jesus but to trust and obey.*

God Enables the Called – September 20

I am sure there have been times when you wished you were different than you are. I know women with curly hair who wish they had straight hair and use some kind of iron thing to flatten those curls. All the while a woman with straight hair spends time with a curling iron to make curls where they did not exist. Men with hair shave their heads so they don't have to work so hard to keep it looking nice, while men who are balding put a patch of fake hair on their head to hide their baldness. We never seem to be satisfied with who we are, or what we are.

When God called Moses to lead Israel out of bondage in Egypt, Moses complained he did not have the ability God was looking for in a leader. He made many excuses, but at one point he told God he was slow of speech. Look at God's answer to Moses, and listen for what God might be saying to each of us this morning. *"And the LORD said unto him, 'Who hath made man's mouth? Or who maketh the dumb, or deaf, or the seeing or the blind? Have not I the LORD'"* (Exodus 4:11)?

God did not make a mistake in making Moses like He made him, and He has not made a mistake in the way He has made you. Regardless of what you may see as a deficiency in your life, God has uniquely made you to serve Him today in some very special place and way. I heard a statement one time that said something like, *"God does not call the gifted … God gifts the called."* The idea behind this, as well as what God was saying to Moses was that He knows us and He will enable us to do what He wants us to do.

Rather than complaining today about the way God made you; why not simply embrace the uniqueness God has given you, and go out and follow His will for your life? Rather than look at others with envious eyes; why not revel in the way God made you and use it for His glory? Rather than consider a weakness you have as a reason for not serving God; why not look for the unique advantages that weakness gives you and jump in and do what you can for the glory of God!

The former record-holder for the longest field goal kicked in the NFL was a man named Tom Dempsey. He was born with only half a right foot. He had a deformed arm as well. Rather than complaining about what he could not do, he decided to kick a football. He had his name in the record books for many years for kicking a 63-yard field goal! He did not consider the limitations he had … he looked at the possibilities that were in front of him and was successful. What are you doing with what God has given you?

Take the World, but Give Me Jesus – September 21

"He delighteth not in the strength of the horse: He taketh not pleasure in the legs of a man. The LORD taketh pleasure in them that fear Him, in those that hope in His mercy" (Psalm 147:10-11).

There it is … God is not impressed with how much horsepower you have in your car's engine. He is not moved by the amount of gigabytes you have in your computer. He is not even impressed with the amount of money you have in your bank account. He does not care how quickly you can run the 100 meter dash; or if you can complete a full marathon. What impresses God? God is looking for people who will fear Him … people who place their hope in Him. If you honestly look at our society in general, and in our churches in particular, you might find these are the two qualities that are lacking most today.

In days gone by, we wore our best clothing to church in order to show our respect and fear for God. We did not worry nearly as much about how comfortable we were in church as we did about how much we exalted our Heavenly Father. We were concerned about our own personal habits not fitting into God's eternal plan; and we wanted to set up standards in our home to ensure we stayed within the boundaries of His will.

In days gone by, we did not have much money, but we gave our tithe and depended on God to provide for the things we would need. We didn't miss a meal, because we hoped in God. Today it seems we hope more in our job than in our God. We seem to depend more on our 401K than we do Romans 8:28 and Philippians 4:13 and 19. These verses clearly state God finds delight in us fearing Him, and then hoping in Him. Follow Him today, and put the world in your rear-view mirror.

Fanny Crosby wrote, **Verse 1:** *Take the world, but give me Jesus – All its joys are but a name; but His love abideth ever, thru eternal years the same.* **Verse 2:** *Take the world, but give me Jesus – Sweetest comfort of my soul; with my Savior watching o'er me, I can sing tho billows roll.* **Verse 3:** *Take the world, but give me Jesus – Let me view His constant smile; then thou-out my pilgrim journey light will cheer me all the while.* **Verse 4:** *Take the world, but give me Jesus – In His cross my trust shall be; till, with clearer, brighter vision, face to face my Lord I see.* **Chorus:** *O the height and depth of mercy! O the length and breadth of love! O the fullness of redemption – pledge of endless life above!*

Trust Jesus for your joy today.

Who's in Control? – September 22

"Remember the former things of old: For I am God, and there is none else; I am God, and there is none like Me. Declaring the end from the beginning, and from ancient times the things that are not yet done, saying, 'My counsel shall stand, and I will do all My pleasure'" (Isaiah 46:9-10).

When there was just darkness and no earth at all ... God was there and in control. When Adam had the breath of life breathed into his body formed from the dust ... God was there and in control. When Adam and Eve ate the fruit from the tree of the knowledge of good and evil ... God was there and in control. When earth was covered with the waters of the great flood and only Noah and his family were spared ... God was there and in control. When Jesus hung between Heaven and earth on the cross paying your sin debt ... God was there and in control. When Jesus burst from the shackles of sin and death in the victorious resurrection ... God was there and in control. The day you repented of your sin and trusted Jesus Christ to forgive you, and you were saved ... God was there and in complete control.

Isaiah stated very clearly from eternity past through eternity future, God will be in charge of what's happening. It is good for us to take a break from the hustle and bustle of life to remember what God has done in the past. God has proven Himself to be God in the past, and it is certain He will prove Himself to be God in the future. I think one of the lessons Isaiah was trying to impress on our hearts was there should never come a time when we trust anyone or anything more than we trust God. This is the place where most religions gets off course. The religious leaders begin to place more emphasis on their rule/standards than they do on a proper relationship with God Himself.

I don't write this devotional to criticize others, I write it to draw our attention to where we are in our relationship with God. How is your time with God? Does He seem like a distant figure you call on when you are in trouble? Is He the first One you run to when you have a burden? Is He the One you live your life for every day, or has someone else taken that place? Make no mistake about it; God is still in control, and He alone deserves all our praise and attention. Don't leave Him out of your day today; rather center your day on Him and what He wants for you.

"My life, my love I give to Thee, Thou Lamb of God Who died for me; O may I ever faithful be, my Savior and My God." – Ralph E. Hudson

The Throne of Your Heart – September 23

"The LORD is my strength and song, and He is become my salvation: He is my God, and I will prepare Him a habitation; my father's God, and I will exalt Him" (Exodus 15:2). These words follow one of the most amazing displays of power mankind has ever seen. Again, God proved His awesome power when He caused such a strong east wind to come, it not only parted the Red Seas, but it kept the water as walls while Israel passed through. The wind caused the normally muddy bottom of the sea to become dry enough for 2 million Israelites to pass through! That's amazing!

It's easy after God has given us some great victory, to place Him on the throne of our heart with the idea He will never move off of that spot! It's quite another thing when things are tough and we become discouraged ... wondering if God is paying attention to us. It is easy to stand in church and give a testimony when you just got a raise at work ... it is another thing to be able to testify when everything that could go wrong has gone wrong. Let me ask you to examine your heart today. Is God there on the throne of your heart?

Moses said he was preparing God a place to inhabit. Today, God is not looking for some cathedral with stained glass as a place to live. God is not looking for some gold-plated throne to sit on. God is looking to the hearts of believers as a place to rule and reign. However, it seems far too many of us have filled that spot with many other things, and God has no place to reside in our heart. It reminds me of some churches. I have seen baptisteries that should be filled with water to baptize new converts ... filled with Christmas decorations ... or VBS supplies ... or choir music. Obviously that is not what that was designed to do, and it is a misuse of the space.

Your life was designed to have God on its throne. Have you replaced Him with something else? Or have you replaced Him with someone else? On the day we read about in Exodus 15, these Israelites were committed to keeping God on the throne of their heart. However, it would not be very far into the future that we will find them complaining about God bringing them into the wilderness to die. In a few years we find these same people making a golden calf while Moses is getting the Ten Commandments. How quickly they turned! How quickly we turn as well! Guard that throne room of your heart today. Don't' allow any "Christmas decorations" to take over the place God alone deserves. Crown Him King of your heart today!

Empty, or Full? – September 24

In most cases, "full" is better than "empty." I would rather have a "full" tank of gas than an "empty" tank any time. I would rather my cup be "full" and not "empty." I would rather have my belly "full" than to have an "empty" stomach that talks to me and everyone around me. I would rather have a house that is "full" than one that is "empty." I would rather have a candy dish that is "full" than "empty." I would rather attend a church that is "full" than one that is "empty." I would rather go to eat at a restaurant with a "full" parking lot than one that has no one parked there. I think you get the idea.

I am teaching my way through the New Testament book of Acts. I just reached the half-way point, and I have noticed a reoccurring theme throughout the book. It is that these early believers were *"full of the Holy Ghost."* In the first thirteen chapters of the book of Acts, it says these early leaders were *"full of,"* or *"filled with"* the Holy Ghost ten times! The last one says, *"And the disciples were filled with joy, and with the Holy Ghost"* (Acts 13:52). This verse describes one of the first towns Paul and Barnabas stopped at on their first missionary journey.

My question for each of us today is simply this ... ***Are you ... Am I filled with the Holy Spirit today?*** It was imperative these early leaders and their followers in the New Testament church be filled with the Holy Spirit. They had a big job to do, and it would be impossible to do it without the help of God and the filling of the Holy Spirit of God! Wait ... we have a huge responsibility today as well! We have been given the impossible task of reaching the uttermost part of the earth! How does God expect us to do that??? Through the power of the Holy Spirit is the answer!

How can I be filled with the Holy Spirit today? I'm glad you asked! Just as a glass can be filled/empty/half full with liquid, our lives can be filled/emptied/or half filled with the Holy Spirit. The filling or lack of the filling of the Holy Spirit in the life of a believer is determined simply by the amount of unconfessed sin in our lives. God's Spirit gives us conviction that He expects will be followed by our confession. That confession must be followed by repentance (a turning from that sin and change of direction). That confession and repentance bring the forgiveness of sins and filling of the Holy Spirit. We need to be filled with the Holy Spirit as much as these early believers in Jesus Christ needed it to launch the New Testament church! To further the New Testament church we need the filling of the Holy Spirit today!

Help is Nearby – September 25

A few years ago, I spent six weeks in Ukraine while my wife and family remained in the states. I had never been away from my wife for more than a weekend at a time (or a few days at the most) before that time. I was not looking forward to the separation. During those six weeks, I learned some life-long lessons. First, I discovered in the times when I felt the loneliest, I sensed the presence of God the most. I also discovered God had people I had known only causally before, who became like a family to me (and have remained that way). I also learned I was not really alone at all. God had not removed His presence from me.

The prophet Isaiah said it this way: *"For the Lord GOD will help me; therefore shall I not be confounded: Therefore have I set my face like a flint, and I know that I shall not be ashamed. He is near that justifieth ..."* (Isaiah 50:7-8a).

As a believer you should never believe that nasty voice inside you that tells you you are all alone. If you have received the forgiveness God offers you through accepting the death of Christ as your payment for sin; and your belief in His bodily resurrection from the dead; God has saved you. But beyond that wonderful blessing is the fact God now indwells you. That sounds complicated, but it simply means the moment you trusted Christ for your salvation, the Holy Spirit of God began to live within you. From the instant you prayed in earnest to receive Jesus Christ's payment for your sin, you have had a new owner of your body/soul/spirit.

It is good news to know you are not alone. When it seems no one understands you ... or you are all by yourself either physically, or in taking a stand for what's right, or simply because you feel strongly on an issue, remember the Holy Spirit of God is within you, and you are as close to God as you could possibly be. Be careful to understand the enemy wants you to believe you are the only one who believes what you believe. He wants you to think you are all alone, and there is no hope unless you join all the others. Don't buy into that thinking. God has placed His Holy Spirit within you ... you will never be alone again. Trust His still small voice of comfort and direction today.

"Nearer, still nearer close to Thy heart, draw me, my Savior, so precious Thou art; fold me, O fold me close to Thy breast, shelter me safe in that Haven of rest." – Lelia N. Morris

Changed – September 26

We hear a great deal about "change" today. I have found "change" is a tough thing, even if it is a good thing. There is an adjustment that is demanded because we must move from what we have always known, and become accustom to that which is unknown (even if it is a good change). When we change vehicles, I have noticed even though the new vehicle may be newer, and nicer, I find myself reaching to the places where the old nobs on our previous vehicle were. I moved the place we put our tea-pot the other day, and I have found myself still going back to the old place. Change is good, but it also demands a price.

A huge part of the Christian life involves change. We often hold on tightly to the old way of thinking, the old language, the old habits, and the old sins. God has a different plan for our lives, and that plan involves changing some things. The change God is talking about does not happen as most change does in our lives. You see, most change we bring on ourselves is from the outside of us that eventually moves to the inside of us. God's changes many times will begin on the inside and eventually show up on the outside of us.

Look at God's idea of how change should come in the life of a Christian. *"But we all, with open face beholding as in a glass the glory of the Lord, are changed into the same image from glory to glory, even as by the Spirit of the Lord"* (II Corinthians 3:18). The change God wants to bring in our lives begins with us fully viewing the glory of the Lord. You see, the change that will result in godliness, does not begin with you and me reading some Christian book, or from listening to messages on a DVD, or from some inspirational input from others. Godly change always begins with us looking to the glory of our God.

Changing to godliness does not end by looking at God, it also involves us copying the characteristics we see in God, into our own lives. It carries the idea of us seeing things in God we do not see in ourselves, and then conforming to the leadership of the Holy Spirit to those characteristics in our own behavior. I want this change in my life. Even though I know it comes with challenges and some uncomfortable days. I want to be changed into the image of my Savior more and more each day. Today I want to yield myself to His plan for me. I want to be changed into His image today, and I want to continue to change to reflect His glory every day.

"Take my love – my God, I pour at Thy feet its treasure store; take myself and I will be ever, only, all for Thee." – Frances R. Havergal

Wood, Hay, Stubble, Converse Sneakers – September 27

I remember buying a pair of Converse high-top sneakers when I was a freshman in college. They were the coolest sneakers in the world. Not only were they canvas Converse high-tops, but they were red! Yeah … when I walked out on the floor with my chicken-legs and those red Converse high-tops on, all the action stopped! Of course that was only in my dreams! Actually, I wore those sneakers to play street hockey. One day I planted my left foot to go around an opponent and the sole of that shoe stayed exactly where I had planted it. The problem was, the canvas was not as sturdy, and my foot blew right through the side of those incredibly handsome sneakers! I had only gotten three years out of those things! I have visions of wearing them well into my 30's (can you imagine that visual picture?).

I realized quickly in life that some of those things we thought would last a life-time might not even make the end of a year, or a month! Things on this earth are at best only temporary. The Bible says it this way … *"While we look not at the things which are seen, but at the things which are not seen: for the things which are seen are temporal; but the things which are not seen are eternal"* (II Corinthians 4:18). What a vivid reminder of the reality of things today. We strive for so many things that are here today and gone tomorrow. Many of the things we place our greatest efforts into, are not even going to matter in the future. Many of the things we spend hours arguing about, or defending, or putting great effort into will not even make the end of the month!

This brings me to a very sobering question for today … what am I doing with my life today that will have eternal value? What project am I working on that will meet me in Heaven? What am I investing my time in today that will outlast my own brief life? Am I wasting time by worrying about things that will last no longer than my Converse sneakers? Am I placing value on things that will be looked at in Heaven as ridiculous? Am I ultimately working towards goals God had in mind for my life when He formed me in my mother's womb? Am I attempting, and achieving things that are worthy of eternity? The things I have wasted time on in the past can never be recouped, but the things I am planning to do today can be turned over to the control of my Heavenly Father. Don't build with wood, hay and stubble today. Let God direct your steps and make a difference for Him today.

"Only one life, 'twill soon be past, only what's done for Christ will last."
– C.T. Studd

A Sweet Reunion – September 28

I have a vivid memory of the end of the summer after I became engaged to my wife. She spent the entire summer on a mission trip to Alaska. You cannot understand the implications of this unless you know my wife. Any temperature under 75 degrees is cold to her. She spent the entire summer working with children and camps in Alaska. I remember a letter where she described swimming in a glacier fed lake. The way she described it, there was not much swimming involved on her part. She told me she felt like a Popsicle when she came out. The August day we met her at the Philadelphia Airport; it was about 98 degrees outside. We all were waiting to see her come off the plane (this was thirty-plus years ago when you could still do this). I will never forget seeing her for the first time since May. She was wearing a turtle-neck sweater under a brown vest suit.

I didn't care she was dressed for the winter in the middle of the summer; this was a sweet reunion for us! There was a sweeter reunion that took place in my life about fourteen years earlier. It was the reunion between my righteous Heavenly Father and me. Paul described it this way: *"And all things are of God, Who hath reconciled us to Himself by Jesus Christ, and hath given to us the ministry of reconciliation. To wit, that God was in Christ, reconciling the world unto Himself, not imputing their trespasses unto them; and hath committed unto us the word of reconciliation. Now then we are ambassadors for Christ ..."* (II Corinthians 5:18-20a).

The word, "reconciliation" literally speaks about a reunion between individuals who had been separated before. My separation with God was a permanent situation until Jesus Christ left Heaven to die in my place. At the moment I placed my faith in Jesus' payment on the cross, and His resurrection from the dead, my sin debt became His, and His righteousness became mine! It doesn't get any better than that! There is nothing on this earth which compares to that!

The thing I want to stress to you today is in the last verse ... we who have been reconciled (re-united with God through Jesus), now become *"Ambassadors"* of reconciliation to others. Don't keep the wonderful message of reconciliation to yourself! Tell all those who are apart from Christ He is waiting for them on the back porch of Heaven right now! God is not willing that any should perish. He wants to save the world, and His love is big enough for the worst sinner! Tell someone about it today!

To God Be the Glory – September 29

"And when all the people saw it, they fell on their faces: and they said, 'The LORD, He is the God; the LORD, He is the God" (I Kings 18:39). This was the response after God consumed the sacrifice of Elijah on the altar. The 850 priests/prophets of Baal had worked all day calling on their god ... but to no avail. The simple reason was because their god did not exist. Elijah did an improbable thing when he poured twelve barrels of water over his sacrifice first. This was a great display of the power of God no one could deny. The thing that really strikes me from this story is Elijah was trying to prove to the people of God that God was real.

There are times still today when we who believe in God need a reminder He is real. There are certainly plenty of false priests/prophets around today, but where are the Elijah's who are willing to stand for what they believe and cry out to the world that God is LORD? There are people with tattoos all over their bodies who "preach" their message to the world. They are not ashamed to put a caricature of something satanic on their body for the rest of their lives. Just yesterday I saw a young man (maybe nineteen years old) with a tattoo on the back of his leg that said, "Rebel." He was not ashamed of rebellion; he was very happy for the world to see his message.

Elijah's message in I Kings 18 was to those who should have been the believers of his day. His message is just as real for us today. *"... How long halt ye between two opinions? If the LORD be God, follow Him ..."* (I Kings 18:21). It is time for us to acknowledge before our neighbors, co-workers, friends and neighbors that we believe in God. We need to be obvious in our love for our Savior! There are plenty who unashamedly advertise their loyalty to athletes, musicians, actors, etc. When will be stand for our God? Fanny Crosby wrote: **Verse 1:** *To God be the glory 0 great things He hath done! So loved He the world that He gave us His Son, Who yielded His life an atonement for sin and opened the Life-gate that all may go in.* **Verse 2:** *O perfect redemption, the purchase of blood! To ev'ry believer the promise of God; the vilest offender who truly believes, that moment from Jesus a pardon receives.* **Verse 3:** *Great things He hath taught us, great things He hath done, and great our rejoicing thru Jesus the Son; but purer and higher and greater will be our wonder, our transport, when Jesus we see.* **Chorus:** *Praise the Lord, praise the Lord, let the earth hear His voice! Praise the Lord, praise the Lord, let the people rejoice! O come to the Father thru Jesus the Son, and give Him the glory – great things He hath done.*

Praise the Lord – September 30

"The LORD hath done great things for us: Whereof we are glad" (Psalm 126:3). Is this verse true in your life? If you are saved and following the principles of the Word of God, then it will be true for you. If you are not saved, it is what God wants to do for you, but cannot until you trust Him. If you are saved, but not living by following the principles of the Word of God that you know, don't expect to see the fullness of the goodness of God toward you. The reality is God has done great things for us, and we ought to be a "glad" people!

I want to encourage you today to put down your cell phone; your tablets; your computer; your radio; your television … and take some time to reflect on how good God has been to you. All of us have challenges and difficulties in our lives, but if you are saved there is a joy in knowing you cannot take a step today without the Holy Spirit going with you! There is joy in that alone! God has chosen to live within me! Wow! What a blessing that is. However, this is also the reason a person who is truly saved cannot just continue in sin without a feeling of conviction or guilt.

The Holy Spirit within you cannot sit back and watch you take your life in a direction He knows will harm you. Call us crazy, but we did not let our children play in the middle of a busy intersection when they were younger, no matter how loudly they protested. We knew the dangers of that intersection, and we warned, and set boundaries for our children to avoid that danger. The Holy Spirit of God will do the same for a child of God who is reading the Word of God and walking in the path the Bible lays out. What a great reason for gladness!

Okay, so take some time to look back at all God has done for you instead of coming up with the current list of complaints about what He has not given you. After you have reviewed all God has done for you, let your face know about it! A Christian who has experienced the blessing of God should be glad! A Christian who has passed from the Hell he/she deserved to the Heaven they did not, should be glad! A Christian who has a Bible in their language should be glad! A Christian who had a local church to attend on the Lord's Day should be glad!

Let's not be guilty of whining about every little thing we see and don't like. Stop that! Take time today to praise your Heavenly Father for all He has blessed you with. If you will do that, you might not have enough time left to complain! That is a blessing in itself! Smile … God loves you.

MONTH OF
October

Why Stand Separated? – October 1

The pattern I have used to read my Bible for the past 30+ years is by reading a single chapter in five different sections of the Bible each day. I am typically reading a chapter from the laws; a chapter from the prophets; a chapter from Psalms; a chapter from Proverbs; and then a chapter from the New Testament. I have loved reading my Bible this way, and it has not grown old to me in all these years. Reading my Bible this way has helped me to see this Book is "supernatural." There is no way man had anything to do with the concepts and principles in this Book with the exception of being the pen-man, and God using their personality to convey His thoughts. Today something happened (this happens often) I feel compelled to write about.

While reading in the Old Testament books of the law I read this clear statement: *"And ye shall be holy unto Me: For I the LORD am holy, and have severed you from other people, that ye should be mine"* (Leviticus 20:26). I was reminded once again God had a purpose for Israel and for His children today. That purpose is for us to be holy as He is holy so the world can see the reality of our God and be drawn to Him. I then read a few other chapters and went to the New Testament chapter and read this: *"'Wherefore come out from among them, and be ye separate,' saith the Lord, 'and touch not the unclean thing; and I will receive you, And will be a Father unto you, and ye shall be my sons and daughters, saith the Lord Almighty'"* (II Corinthians 6:17-18).

Here's when that "supernatural" vision of the Bible becomes clear. Moses wrote the book of Leviticus at least 1,000 years before Paul wrote this second letter to the church in Corinth, but the same Holy Spirit inspired each man! What Moses wrote to the nation of Israel, Paul wrote to the church in Corinth. Ultimately, both men wrote these words for you and me to read today. It seems to me our churches are in deep trouble today (in general). It seems instead of paying attention to these words and separating ourselves unto holiness, we are drawing ourselves closer to the world, and becoming far too loose in our biblical standards. I know, call me an old-fashioned, outdated man ... but, the Bible is still the authority! Our ultimate goal is to reach as many in this world as possible before we die. That will be impossible if we become like this world! There is a reason God desired us to be separated from the world. Not to look down in judgment on them, but to represent Him as clearly as possible. Try to live a holy life today. The world that is watching you is depending on you!

Incredible Love! – October 2

I know this is unusual … I cannot get past the power of Isaiah 53. I am hopeful you will not skim this, but read it with an intimate personal application to your own life. Read these words and think about what Jesus did for YOU. Look at this description of Jesus and His love for you …

"He is despised and rejected of men; a man of sorrows, and acquainted with grief: and we hid as it were our faces from Him; He was despised, and we esteemed Him not" (53:3). In a time when we yearn for the approval of others, Jesus purposely became hated of all … in our place. *"Surely He hath borne our griefs, and carried our sorrows: yet we did esteem Him stricken, smitten of God, and afflicted"* (53:4). While we look for the easy way out of tough situations, Jesus plowed into the depths of sin for us.

"But He was wounded for our transgressions, He was bruised for our iniquities: the chastisement of our peace was upon Him; and with His stripes we are healed" (53:5). Notice the pronoun, *"our,"* and understand the price described here was for your sin, not His. *"All we like sheep have gone astray; we have turned everyone to his own way; and the LORD hath laid on Him the iniquity of us all"* (53:6). Men continue to reject Him even today, yet He continues to offer forgiveness!

"He was oppressed, and He was afflicted, yet He opened not His mouth: He was brought as a lamb to the slaughter, and as a sheep before her shearers is dumb, so He openeth not His mouth" (53:7). Like an innocent sheep paying the price for a guilty human, Jesus paid for you … without saying a word in protest … it's what WE earned.

"He was taken from prison and from judgment: And who shall declare His generation? For He was cut off of the land of the living: For the transgression of my people was He stricken" (53:8). He did not stop short … He was obedient to the death (don't forget the price-tag for our sin is death).

"Yet it pleased the LORD to bruise Him; He hath put Him to grief: When thou shalt make His soul an offering for sin, He shall see His seed, He shall prolong his days, and the pleasure of the LORD shall prosper in His hand" (53:10). To me, the most amazing phrase in this chapter is, "… *the pleasure of the LORD* …" Jesus Christ endured all this so we could be reunited with our perfect, sinless Heavenly Father. He endured the cross for the *"joy"* that was set before Him. The "joy," the *"pleasure"* was the fact that you and me, wretched sinners, could come home through Jesus Christ! WOW!

THE Book – October 3

Why is it we think we need some fancy "trick" to convince people to trust God for their salvation? When a person is saved, I don't believe it has anything to do with us. If we used some slick presentation to win someone to Christ, they probably were not saved. You see, the Bible states over and over again it is not man's abilities, or some "cunning" presentation, but the simple Gospel found in the Word of God. The Old Testament prophet Isaiah was inspired by the Holy Spirit to say it this way ... *"So shall My word be that goeth forth out of My mouth; it shall not return unto Me void, but it shall accomplish that which I please, and it shall prosper in the thing whereto I sent it"* (Isaiah 55:11).

What is the lesson we learn from this verse for the situations we are facing today? We don't need more man-made counseling; or psychiatrists; or prescription drugs; or _____; we need more focus on the Word of God! We don't need more books to be written to tell us how to raise our children, or how to study our Bible, or how to witness to others. What we need is more time in THE Book; the Bible. This Book is the Book of the ages! This is THE Book for everything important in life!

What has happened to us today is we have fallen into the trap of thinking because we have technology ... we have experts who dedicate their lives to the study of one subject ... that somehow these things or people can replace the wisdom of the Word of God. What happened to us that made us think these "substitutes" could replace this Book in our lives? What is it that makes it easier to read the most popular Christian book, than to read the Bible itself? Why does it seem more glamorous to learn the latest witnessing technique than it is to memorize Romans 2:23; 6:23; 5:8; and 10:9-10, 13?

God's plan has never changed! He gave us this Bible with all the things anyone needs to live godly in Christ Jesus! Let me take a moment to explain this clearly. There is nothing wrong with Christians giving their lives to studying topics that will help others. There is nothing wrong with Christian books. There is nothing wrong with Christian counselors. What is wrong is when any one of these becomes a higher priority in helping others than the Word of God. I believe with all my heart THE Book believers need to focus on is the B-I-B-L-E! It is the tool needed to transform a person's life. God will use His Word in the exact way He had it planned all along. Don't give up on knowing your Bible better each day!

As it is Written … – October 4

How well do you know your Bible? Do you think it is important for a believer to know his/her way around the Bible? If someone challenges what you believe, do you know where to go in your Bible for your defense? Jesus was tempted by the Devil in the wilderness. When Jesus was faced with challenging situations from His adversary, He used the Word of God so effectively, the Devil was forced to run away in defeat. The same will be true with us if we are prepared.

Look at the first answer Jesus gave the Devil in the first temptation: *"But He answered and said, 'It is written, Man shall not live by bread alone, but by every word that proceedeth out of the mouth of God'"* (Matthew 4:4). Did you catch this first response? Jesus Himself knew the greatest defense a person has against the Prince of the Power of the Air is the infallible, inerrant, inspired Word of God! Do you know that? Or, do you treat your Bible reading time as an option if you have time in your day?

Job said the words of God were more necessary to him than His physical food. This book we call the Bible is an amazing book! I have never seen another book like it. No matter how many times you read the Bible, it still remains alive and active! How is that possible? Well, it is possible because *"All Scripture is given by inspiration of God …"* (II Timothy 3:16). Every word … every thought … every letter in our Bible has been thought over, edited and put onto paper, directly from the heart of God!

I would imagine if you had received a letter from President Ronald Reagan, you would have it framed and placed in a place of importance in your home. I would imagine if you met Michael Jordan, and had gotten an autograph from him, you might have it framed and in a place of prominence in your "man cave." I would think if you met a celebrity in the airport and snapped a picture of them with you on your phone, you would make sure all your friends saw it!

We have the absolute, infallible, Word of God! What place does it have in your home? What place does it have in your heart? What place does it have in your behavior every day? Jesus knew the importance and power of this book … do we? Today is a good day to begin to allow the Word of God to become a priority in your life. Go to church and hear the preaching with a hungry heart for receiving the Word of God. When you pray; ask the Lord to help you get all you can from the Bible, and "can" all you get!

Salt and Light – October 5

Two of my favorite things … salt and light! I love the taste salt gives to the food I eat. When I enter a room, I like to turn the lights on to be able to see clearly. Jesus is so wise to use these two things as illustrations about what we are to do, and who we are to be as Christians. I have noticed Jesus used common, everyday things to teach Biblical principles. I have also noticed Jesus uses common, everyday people to carry out His will on the earth. The things Jesus taught were meant to touch the heart of the "average" person. He spent a good deal of time fighting with the "religious" people. I'm glad God chooses to use regular folks like us.

In Jesus teaching, He pointed out *"Ye are the salt of the earth: but if the salt have lost his savor, wherewith shall it be salted? It is thenceforth good for nothing, but to be cast out, and to be trodden under foot of men"* (Matthew 5:13). I want to make sure today I touch people in a way which makes them glad I showed up. I don't want them to say (after I leave), 'What was wrong with him today?'

God created you and me to make a positive difference in our world. He did not create us so we would think the world revolved around us and everyone else needed to make sure we were having a good day. God made us to serve and use our lives to draw others to Himself. Think about it for a moment. Salt on a plate all alone is not that appealing. However, a big juicy steak with salt sprinkled over top is … making my mouth water as I write! You, without Jesus Christ, are not that appealing. But, your actions mixed with the message of Jesus Christ can make a powerful difference in the lives of those you will touch today.

Jesus also described what He wanted from us when He said, *"Ye are the light of the world. A city that is set on an hill cannot be hid"* (Matthew 5:14). There is one thing I have notice about light. It cannot co-exist with darkness. Light will drive out darkness every time. God did not make you and me to mimic the world. God did not make you and me to "blend in to the world." God did not make us to be spiritual chameleons. God made us to be different! God made us to stand out in a crowd! God made us to be a light in an ever darkening world! The world we are living in today needs more light. The world we are living in needs more believers who will live authentically different lives that draw attention to God!

How is your salt and light doing in the world today? Are you making a difference? If not, ask God for a new beginning today. If so, keep it up!

Grace for Troubled Times – October 6

Many Christians today are wringing their hands in fear of what is happening around us. These seem to be days when righteousness is attacked and unrighteousness is exalted. Guess what? This is not the first time the world has been in this spot. Don't be surprised when ungodly people act in ungodly ways. This same thing happened years ago, and it was recorded in the first book of the Bible for us. The writer of Genesis described the world in much the same way we would describe our world today, and in the midst of all the negative he described, he wrote, *"But Noah found grace in the eyes of the LORD"* (Genesis 6:8).

I was struck with the idea that no matter how corrupt our world may seem; no matter how corrupt it may actually be; God's grace is still available for His children today. Noah was in a time very much like ours. God poured out His grace upon Noah even though things looked desperate to him. God has grace that is still available for us today, and His grace is sufficient to meet all the needs we have! Today, I want to make a conscious effort to look for the grace of God in the midst of the turmoil of this world. I want to find ways to show the grace of God to others I will meet today, rather than give them the things they have earned.

The verse that follows Genesis 6:8 is a very convicting verse for me. *"These are the generations of Noah: Noah was a just man and perfect in his generations, and Noah walked with God"* (Genesis 6:9). I want the explanation that was given to Noah to be true of me today too. It is convicting to me, because I love to complain about how bad things are around me. I love to point my finger at others when looking for who I can blame. The reality is, it is my responsibility to walk in a just way; in a perfect (complete) way with God today. My walk with God is not determined by those around me, but by my own decision(s).

Okay … the world is filled with sin and sinful people doing their own thing. Okay … the church may not be a strong as it ought to be in standing for what's right. Okay … others may not feel the compulsion to walk with God and stand for God around me. None of this should affect my walk with God today! I am responsible to be a man who is walking with God! I need the grace of God that was showered upon Noah in his day! I need God's hand to lead and guide me today. In and of myself, I will never be the kind of man I want to be, or ought to be. I need to run to God multiple times throughout this day for His grace! I want to be a man of God today!

My Greatest Enemy – October 7

Our natural tendency is to focus our attention on other people's problems rather than our own. The athlete who blames everyone else but himself for not fulfilling his responsibilities ... the politician who constantly focuses the attention on the downfall of his opponent ... the coach who blames his players, and players who blame their coach ... the pastor who complains about his deacons ... the parents who complain about their children ... I think you see what I am talking about. We love to look at the problems of others, while totally ignoring our responsibility.

Jesus spoke to this very directly in His sermon on the mountain. He said it this way: "*And why beholdest thou the mote that is in thy brother's eye, but considerest not the beam that is in thine own eye? Or how wilt thou say to thy brother, 'Let me pull out the mote out of thine eye;' and, behold, a beam is in thine own eye*" (Matthew 7:3-4)?

I would love to write about my greatest enemy being someone outside myself, but the reality is that my greatest enemy is me and my own sin nature! Your greatest enemy is your own sin nature. I have written often we love to blame the Devil for the bad things we do, but the reality is, it is our heart that is deceitful above all things and desperately wicked. It is my tongue that is like a fire that can destroy many good things I want to do. These are my own hands and feet that take me to, and get me involved in sin. It is my own mind that devises evil things about others; and these are the things that come out of my mouth. It is my mouth that can gossip so easily and then sing in church to praise God.

The reality is, I am my own worst enemy. My own sinfulness is what works to my defeat far more than any outside influence does. Just as Jesus taught ... I need to stop focusing on the sin of others, and concentrate on my relationship with Him today. I want to live a pure and holy life today. I don't want to wallow in my sin. I don't want my life to be characterized by a "mote" of sin that is in my eye that everyone else can see, but I ignore.

I want to walk in such a way today that the world sees a person who is in the process of turning over complete control of their life to Jesus Christ. I don't want to promote myself as having arrived, but as someone who in on the journey of Christ-likeness. I want to be a man of character today and take care of surrendering my life to Jesus minute-by-minute. Will you join me? I believe Jesus can do a work in our world if we will surrender to Him.

His Name is Wonderful – October 8

"O LORD our Lord, how excellent is Thy name in all the earth! Who hast set Thy glory above the heavens" (Psalm 8:1).

There are 625 names in our King James Bible that try to describe God. Some of my favorites are: Almighty God; Blessed and only Potentate; Captain; Desire of all nations; Everlasting Father; Faithful and True; God and Father of all; Hope of His people; I AM; JEHOVAH; KING OF KINGS; Lord God Almighty; Master; Our Father; Possessor of heaven and earth; Refuge; Savior; The Rock; Wonderful.

The thought that touched my heart today is this ... of all these 625 names, and numerous descriptions of our God, my favorite name for Him is in Psalm 8:1. The title that means the most to me is simply ... *"our Lord."* You see, God is everything these different titles throughout our Bible describe Him to be. He inhabits all these titles and far more than we cannot put in to words, but the greatest thing to me is He is MY God! He is MY Savior! He is MY High-priest! He is MY Lord! He is mine, and I am His, and we will never be separated by anything that might come along the path of life!

We will live together for all eternity because He loved me at my worst point! I will see Him face to face because it was His Son Who took my place on Calvary's old rugged cross. It is the precious blood of His Son, Jesus Christ that cleansed me from all my unrighteousness, and has written my name in the Lambs Book of Life! It is His own payment for my sin that bought my liberty! You see, for all the fancy titles He deserves, my favorite is *"our Lord"* because He is my personal Heavenly Father!

Is He your Heavenly Father? If you have never come to Him recognizing your own sin, you need to today. None of us is perfect. He is perfect! Anyone who is going to touch Heaven must do it without sin. That is why God sent His only begotten Son to this earth. Jesus lived without sin and offered Himself willingly on the cross of Calvary to pay off your sin debt. Well now, the price has been paid ... and God offers you forgiveness through the blood of Jesus Christ. The only question remaining is; why wouldn't you receive the gift God offers of His Son as payment for your sin? I would not want to face another minute on my own, when God has made a way for me to be in Heaven with Him! Please receive the gift God offers you today of His Son! Jesus is the only way. Receiving Him will allow you to call God ... *"our Lord."*

It's All in Who You Know – October 9

I have noticed from the very young years of my life there is a great deal to be said for knowing the right people. When I played Little League baseball, the boy who was the coach's son got to play all the innings ... I was happy to play the minimum that was required. When I got into High School, my best friend was on the football team, and was a very good player, but did not get to play too much. There was another guy who was the coaches' favorite who played instead. I have had the opportunity a couple of times to be on the other side of that picture. I had the privilege to play my trumpet in front of 11,000 people one time because I knew a guy who deserved to be there and he got me an invitation to the orchestra.

David wrote, *"And they that know Thy name will put their trust in Thee: for Thou, LORD, hast not forsaken them that seek Thee"* (Psalm 9:10). Today is a very important day for you to know Jesus, and for Him to know you. God has a book He called the Book of Life. That book contains the names of all who have been redeemed by the blood of Jesus Christ. It is very important for your name to be there. If, on the day of the Great White Throne Judgment when that book is opened, your name is not found there, you will be cast into the lake of fire forever.

If your name is written in the Lamb's Book of Life, then this verse from Psalm 9 is yours to claim. Every person who is in that book is one of God's chosen people. We are blessed because He knows our name! He knows what we are facing! He is our Refuge (as verse 9 describes). He is our hiding place when things get tough. He is our God and we are His people!

Today when you feel like the whole world is against you, remember this verse. You who know His name have the promise He will not forsake you when you seek Him. That is the key for this day for each of us who knows Him. We must seek Him. Don't take a step on your own today. Ask Him for guidance and direction for each step you take. After you begin to walk in the way which He has planned for you, realize there will not be one place in the center of God's will where you will be on your own! He is there beside you and in you. He will never leave you or forsake you.

If things get tough today (and they might), remember this promise from Him and walk on in confidence that He is able to take you through whatever you are facing! Remember the title for this devotional? It is all about Who you know today. You can walk with the King of kings today if you will seek Him with your whole heart. Do it! He will not forsake you!

Staying Humble – October 10

I believe the verses in the New Testament that tell us God resists the proud, but gives grace to those who are humble. I understand why God hates pride, because I am not fond of people who are arrogant and proud. I prefer a humble and meek person over a proud and arrogant one. Today I read, *"LORD, Thou hast heard the desire of the humble: Thou wilt prepare their heart, Thou wilt cause Thine ear to hear"* (Psalm 10:17). It reminded me once again I ought to desire genuine humility if I expect God's ear to be listening to me.

I want you to know I am no different than any of you reading this today. I love to hear people praise the things I have done. I will even try to "help" people praise me. I love to hear people tell me how much I mean to them, and how much I have helped them, and how great I am ... I think you get the picture. But, before you condemn me for admitting all that, realize it is in the heart of each of us to desire those things. How do I know that?

If you look at the original fall ... not of Adam and Eve ... the fall of Lucifer from the position of one of the three archangels. His fall came when he voiced his desire to be equal with God. He even went so far as to say his desire was to be above God! When Adam and Eve followed and placed their desires above the desires of God for them, they too demonstrated a pride that led to the sinful nature we all possess today. Pride has been, and continues to be one of the major enemies of living godly today.

God's Word clearly says God hears the cries of the humble. God gives grace to those who are humble, and resists those who are not. We have witnessed countless examples of God removing the proud as leaders throughout the Bible, and exalting humble ones to replace them. If you look at the people Jesus chose to be His disciples, I think you will recognize a general quality of humility (with a few exceptions) in these men. Of course, we do see moments when even those men had of allowing pride to get the best of them.

Today I want to be a man who is characterized by real humility. I have asked God to keep me humble in the past and then complained when people did not recognize my accomplishments! Regardless of that, it is my goal today to live a humble life that draws attention to our Savior, and not to me. Let me encourage you to do the same today. If we would humble ourselves, I believe it will exalt our Savior.

Out of Your Comfort Zone – October 11

Why does God force us to leave our comfort zone? Why is it the mother eagle pushes her eaglets out of the nest when everything was going so good for them? Why does your pastor always seems to ask you to do the "one thing" you determined you will never do? Why do you think God asks people who are living in comfort to leave and go to a foreign land with the Gospel? Why is God going to touch my heart today to do things I don't feel comfortable doing? Public speaking ... witnessing to a stranger ... helping in a nursing home ... making a hospital visit?

I am sorry to tell you ... you will find your answer in the Bible. Paul complained about a thorn in the flesh. Something he was bothered with and wished would be removed. As a matter of fact, Paul had asked God three times to remove it from his life! Have you ever asked God to remove the thing that is outside of your comfort zone? Here is the answer God gave Paul, and the answer He is giving us about His reason for pushing us out of our comfort zone nest! *"And He said unto me, 'My grace is sufficient for thee: for My strength is made perfect in weakness...'"* (II Corinthians 12:9a).

You might complain when God requires you to leave your comfort zone; but God replies ... *'My strength is made perfect in your weakness.'* You might argue with God that there must be someone else who would be better qualified to do what He has asked you to do. God replies, *'My strength is made perfect in your weakness.'* You might remind God of past failures in your attempts to do the thing He has asked you to do; but He replies, *'My strength is made perfect in your weakness.'* You begin ... oh ... what's the use? *"His strength is made perfect in your weakness!"*

Paul's response to understanding this is classic, and it needs to be repeated by each of us who has had to venture with fear and trembling outside of our comfort zone ... *"Most gladly therefore will I rather glory in my infirmities, that the power of Christ may rest upon me"* (II Corinthians 12:9b). Here is the question for each of us today ... would we rather stay nestled in the warmth of our supposed comfort zone; or would we rather have the *"power of Christ"* resting on us? One last thought to go along with this idea today: if God calls us to leave our comfort zone, we can be assured He has already stepped through the door of that opportunity, and He is waiting on the other side with everything we will need to accomplish His will. If we don't step out, we are on our own in the comfort zone; not so comfortable!

Living Godly Lives in an Ungodly World – October 12

"The words of the LORD are pure words: silver tried in a furnace of earth, purified seven times. Thou shalt keep them, O LORD, Thou shalt preserve them from this generation forever" (Psalm 12:6-7).

Is it possible to live a godly life in such an ungodly time? Let's ask Daniel there in Babylon. He was separated from his family. He was separated from any spiritual leader who believed in the Bible. He was surrounded by idol-worshipping people who would become his teachers and would try to become his leader. He would be presented with meat to eat that had already been offered to an idol. He would be offered wine that was fermented to drink. Yet, Daniel, just a teenage boy, determined he would not defile himself. The words that describe his stand in Daniel 1:8 are Daniel *"purposed in his heart."* This phrase literally means Daniel made a decision before time. He had rehearsed, he had practiced what answer he would give before the question was ever asked!

According to the two verses from Psalm 12, we too have the opportunity to stand pure in a day of impurity! We too can make some decisions before the test comes that will help us to pass the test with a passing grade. We too have a place to run in time of trouble that will not move, and that will not fail us. *"The words of the LORD are pure words ..."* Is there any doubt in your mind about the truth of this statement? I have no doubts whatsoever about the Word of God being pure. I also believe verse 7 that follows. I believe if a person will make the Word of God his/her compass, God will keep and preserve their lives.

I cannot help but think about jelly when I see the word preserve! But isn't that an accurate picture of what this verse is saying for us. I have watched my grandmother make jelly. I have seen her cook the fruit she had chosen; I then saw her pour it into jars. I then watched her put on these special lids that would seal shut as the pressure built up; and then I remember hearing a "pop" as the seal took and the lid bowed up (please forgive my naïve view of canning ... I was just a kid). I remember how excited I would get to be able to spread that sweet jelly on my bread. My grandmother explained to me that we did not need to put that jelly into the refrigerator because it was preserved, or kept until we opened it. God's words have the ability to keep those who read and obey them too. If you will stay in the Word of God, and allow the Word of God to stay in you, when difficult times come, you will stay true. You can live godly in an ungodly world, following the Bible.

Clean House – October 13

"You know, you really should clean this office..." is a statement I hear often from my wife. I always tell her I know where everything is and if I clean it up, I will lose my fancy filing system. It never fails; shortly after this conversation, I find myself looking for something without success. It is then when I realize it is time to clean my office. Spiritually speaking, every night before we go to sleep, or every day when we wake up, it is time to do some spiritual house-cleaning. David said it this way: *"Search me, O God, and know my heart: Try me, and know my thoughts: And see if there be any wicked way in me, and lead me in the way everlasting"* (Psalm 139:23-24).

I want to recommend a little booklet to each of you reading this. It is entitled, "My Heart, Christ's Home." This little booklet was written by Robert Boyd Munger. When I first went to Bible College, this was required reading. Because it was such a small booklet, I decided to read it first. When I began reading, I was simply fulfilling a reading requirement ... but as I understood the principle behind the book, it changed my life. Whenever I read this chapter in Psalms, I am reminded of the truth of that booklet.

Munger's booklet describes our lives as a house. He mentions the Library as the place we store all the information that comes to our attention. The Kitchen is the place our appetites are fed. The Study is the place we either pass by, or sit down to consider important thoughts ... and so on. In this booklet, Munger goes through each room, surrendering each part of our life to the lordship of Christ. He describes giving over the control of each room to Christ. As the book comes to an end, there is one remaining closet that has not been surrendered. He describes the battle of releasing that room to the authority of Christ. Victory comes with the signing over of the title of the "house" to Jesus Christ.

The key to living a successful Christian life lies in the depth of our commitment to allowing our God to "search" every part of our life; revealing the area's that need to be changed; and giving in to the convicting and cleaning work of the Holy Spirit. Take the time today to pray through these two verses, asking God to reveal any weakness or sin that needs to be forgiven and forsaken. Allow God to do the clean-up work you need today. We are incapable of changing ourselves from the inside out, but He is certainly able and willing to do that with each of us today!

Hope in the Right Place – October 14

Don't place your hope in me to help you ... I will fail you. Don't hope in your money to provide what you will need ... it will fail you. Don't hope in your health to hold you ... it will deteriorate. Don't hope in your religion to hold you (if it is based on traditions and not the Bible) ... it will erode away in times of struggle. Don't hope in world peace in this ever-changing world ... it is not going to happen apart from a Divine act of God.

You might think I have gone off the deep end and need some psychiatric help after reading this! Don't stop reading ... today I read, *"I said unto the LORD, 'Thou art my God; hear the voice of my supplications, O LORD. O GOD the Lord, the strength of my salvation, Thou hast covered my head in the day of battle'"* (Psalm 140:6-7). This is THE ONLY place you and I can find real HOPE! Why is it we spend so much of our time on the other things I listed in the opening paragraph of this devotional? We all have seen these things collapse at different times in our lives, and yet we seem to run to them first.

What a great thing to know God personally! There is nothing that compares to this relationship. I have watched people step into eternity who have been tightly holding onto the hand of God. There is no thrashing, or despair. There is peace and contentment. I have watched people face incredible pressure without fear of what was coming, simply because they were trusting in God and not their situation. I have also witnessed people who had great storehouses of money crumble under the pressure of normal life situations. I have seen people who depended on someone else (who eventually failed them), fall apart themselves when disappointment came.

The real point of the verses I shared with you this morning is that you and I will be an advertisement for one of these two positions in the way we live our lives. Are you going to build a strong relationship with God today so when you are facing the difficulties of life you can have this same kind of confidence? Or, will you trust these other "things/people" and find them totally lacking when you need help in difficult times? The choice is yours, and you will display which choice you have made by who you spend the most time with today. Don't build you spiritual house on the sands of this world. Build you house upon the Rock of Jesus Christ. If you do, you will find there is nothing that can defeat you. When you place your trust in Him, you will find He is trust-worthy.

"... ever-lasting life and light He freely gives." – Norman J. Clayton

The Greatest Co-Worker – October 15

These verses are some of my favorite in all the Bible. *"Come unto Me all ye that labor and are heavy laden, and I will give you rest. Take My yoke upon you, and learn of me; for I am meek and lowly in heart: and ye shall find rest unto your souls. For My yoke is easy, and My burden is light"* (Matthew 11:28-30). These are the words of Jesus to each of us today.

I think we all realize there is a great work to be done today. We realize if we don't get involved, the work God has for us will be left undone. Just as in a factory or on a sports team every individual is important, the same is true in a church body. God has left us with a tremendous work to do. He is entrusting us to be busy about the things that are important to Him. Today I would like you to think about what you will do with the next sixteen hours that will please your Heavenly Father.

As I type these words they are very convicting to me. I can find ways to waste chunks of time in a day if I am not careful. I'm sure you can do the same. God has a job for us to do that requires a lifetime. It is a serious work, and it is beyond our abilities to perform, and yet He hopes we will put our hands to the plow and dig in (forgive the pun). The good news is when we serve Jesus Christ, we will be serving alongside the King of kings and the Lord of lords. The good news is when we come alongside Him, He shoulders the load, and we simply must stay there beside Him and watch what He will do.

I believe many Christians are overwhelmed with the idea of trying to reach the world for Christ. The reality is He is the One Who will reach the world … He just chooses to use our voices, hands, feet, and testimonies to get the message out. Jesus said in these verses, the work would be easy if we would come alongside Him. Look at your plans for today. Do you have time planned that would include you being in the yoke with Jesus today? Have you considered what He would do if He were in your shoes today?

I'm not necessarily suggesting you change your schedule (although that might be a good idea in some cases), but I am suggesting each of us should consider we are going alongside Jesus today wherever we are going. That means He will lead us to opportunities that will glorify His Father in Heaven. We ought to be keeping our eyes open for these people, and opportunities that God will put in our path today. Don't be so focused on yourself today that you miss the fields which are ripe in front of you.

No Excuses – October 16

I think there are far too many people in our world today who want to blame the rest of the world for their personal problems. I'm sorry, but I was raised in a way that taught me to take responsibility for my own actions and accept the consequences of them too. Today I read a verse that has always touched my heart. It is from the report of Nehemiah and those helping him, re-building the wall around Jerusalem. The report of those building the wall includes … "*And next unto them the Tekoites repaired; but their nobles put not their necks to the work of their Lord*" (Nehemiah 3:5).

The last part of the verse is what touched my heart: "*their nobles put not their necks to the work of their Lord.*" Their own leaders did not have the vision to help on the wall. You and I might complain about a lack of leadership in some cases, but this is no excuse for not doing the work God has given us. There may be times when you feel others ought to step up and get involved, but they don't. This is not a reason for you to sit on the spiritual sidelines and not get involved in the game of life!

These Tekoites did not use leadership, or a lack of leadership, as an excuse not to get involved and do the work. They jumped in and did what they could. As a matter of fact, later on in the same chapter we read, "*After them the Tekoites repaired another piece, over against the great tower that lieth out, even unto the wall of Ophel*" (Nehemiah 3:27). Think of the blessings these men received as they had opportunity to work for the Lord! Their nobles missed out on the blessing, but God recognized these faithful workers nonetheless.

Are you busy trying to find someone to blame for your lack of involvement in the work of the Lord today? Are you upset with something that happened years ago in a ministry? Are you blaming your parents, or your government, or your church, or the local Walmart (just threw that in there to see if anyone actually reads these)? We are famous for looking at others and finding a reason not to do what God touched our heart to do. Stop looking for someone to blame and pick up a hammer and get working!

If you are in a position of leading anyone … it could be in your home, in a classroom, or in a ministry … please don't follow the example of the nobles of the Tekoites. Don't allow those who are following you to do all the work, and receive all the blessing. How would you like God's description of you to be that you were absent when the work was getting done? I want to be on the wall doing my part!

Somebody's Listening – October 17

"And it shall come to pass, that before they call, I will answer; and while they are yet speaking, I will hear" (Isaiah 65:24).

What an incredible verse for us to remember! This morning when I sat down to read my Bible, I found this verse written on a small piece of paper by my wife. She gave me something that encourages my heart more than many promises from men could give. This verse has always been very encouraging to me. Do this favor for yourself today. Take some time to really think about what this verse promises each of us who are His children.

"... before they call, I will answer ..." Before you call, God already knows what you need. He knows what is best, and what you might ask for, and He determines to give you what is best, not necessarily what you have asked Him to do. How many times have you asked God for something, only to discover later that if He had actually given it to you, you would have been in trouble? God's answer is always exactly what we need, and it is always exactly on time! He is never late, and He is never early ... after all, He is perfect!

"... while they are yes speaking, I will hear ..." Have you ever been talking with someone and had the distinct feeling all the time you were talking, they were thinking about something else? I remember a time I went in to speak to someone about a decision I was planning to make. This person was someone I trusted, and someone I thought could really help me to make a good decision. From the time I asked if I could see him throughout the time I sat in his office, he kept looking at his watch. I realized even though my voice was making noise, he was totally unaware of what I was saying to him, and the time with him was going to be fruitless.

What a great verse for us to take with us throughout this day! God hears us when we talk to Him, and even before we ask, He already knows about what we are facing. Listen folks ... God is for us! He wants the best for us, and He is actively involved in your life. I am not saying God is some genie that you can make wishes to and He will grant our desires! I am saying He knows what we need, and He will give us what we need, not what will make us happy! If we are walking with God, we will ultimately be happy only when we walk in agreement with His will for our lives. Be encouraged today. The thing that is heaviest upon your heart is already before His throne, and He is working all things together for your good today!

Strong Plants ... Polished Stones – October 18

"That our sons may be as plants grown up in their youth; that our daughters may be as corner stones, polished after the similitude of a palace" (Psalm 144:12). In the verse just above this one, David speaks of his fear of the *"strange children"* of his enemies. There is a definite distinction made between the *"strange children,"* and the *"sons"* that grow *"as plants"* and *"daughters"* that are *"corner stones"*, and *"polished"* stones. We all know David had issues with his children ... but his heart (that was called a heart after God's own heart), was for his sons to grow up like strong plants and his daughters to be like polished stones and cornerstones.

It is important for us to understand if we do not take the care necessary to raise our children in a godly fashion ... the *"strangers"* of this world will be happy to do it for us. I want you to consider the role parents are to take in the *"planting"* and *"polishing"* of their children. We have a responsibility to them, to raise them to be solid and strong in the days ahead.

It is interesting the word pictures God uses in this verse. A plant takes a great effort to get it to grow strong. It takes a good deal of attention to make sure that the plant produces fruit. There is breaking up of the ground required. Sometimes in order to get the principles into our sons that we want, we need to break up a stubborn spirit. After we break up the ground, we need to plant a seed. Of course, the greatest seed we can plant in our son's hearts is the Word of God. We then must make sure weeds do not choke out the good nutrients the plant needs, and we need to water and allow sun to get to it to help it grow. We need to help our sons choose good friends and provide good advice that will help them to have the greatest opportunity for success possible.

We are to polish our daughters so they can be good cornerstones. The process of polishing stones is really interesting. It involves placing the stones you want to polish inside a barrel with other rougher stones and water and allowing them to roll around and around while the rougher stones knock off the rough edges of the stone being polished. This means we need to spend time with our daughters, helping them to recognize the rough areas of their lives and guide them to removing them. It also strikes me that the abrasive process produces the smoothest stone!

Both of these things take a great deal of time, but both are well worth the effort when the finished product is seen. Don't take the easy path in life; give the effort needed to produce what God wants us to be!

A Very Good Thing – October 19

"Whoso findeth a wife findeth a good thing, and obtaineth favor of the LORD" (Proverbs 18:22). We often pass over this verse very quickly, but it deserves our attention. A man who has found a wife has found someone who is good for him. We often use the term, "better-half." There is a good deal of truth in that title. I want to use this time today to thank God for the good wife He has given me.

Before I go any further, I do not believe my wife is perfect and it's a good thing she is not. I am far from perfect, and there is no way we could have remained happily married if she were perfect. I want to tell you how much my wife has enhanced me as a person, and has had tremendous influence on our ministry. The first thing I want to mention is I am so thankful she is nothing like me. I have been in numerous counseling settings where a husband and wife are complaining about how different they are ... I think that's how God intended us to be. I'm thankful my wife is sweet and kind. I am thankful that tears come easily to her eyes (okay, we are alike in that way). I am grateful for her always looking for the good in people. I am thankful for her ability to control her temper. She and I are different in many ways. I'm glad!

Second, I am thankful for a wife who completes me. She fills in the cracks in my personality, in our home, and even in our ministry. I depend on her perspective in our personal lives as well as our ministry together. She is a great benefit to me when I am making preparation for messages I am planning to deliver. Sometimes I rehearse with her what I am planning to share with others, and she helps with adjustments that bring the point home much better. She willingly shares things God has touched her heart with in her devotions, and I preach some of those things to others. We are a team!

Third, I am thankful for a wife who is honest with me about my short-comings. My wife is the ONLY person I trust to honestly answer the question; *"How was that message?"* She does not flatter me, or try to butter me up. She knows I am asking so I can make improvements and better the ministry as a whole. I trust her to help me make wise ministry and family decisions. She is the one person who I know has the ministries best interests at heart. I know she has no ulterior motives in answering honest questions.

I am so thankful for the very good thing God gave me over thirty years ago! I love my wife, and I need my wife! I praise God for her!

The Right Call – October 20

If you have a leaky faucet ... don't call me ... I don't know what to do to fix it. If you have a light that is flickering on and off ... don't call me ... I don't know how to fix it. If your car is making a strange noise ... don't call me ... I only know how to change the oil. If you need money ... don't call me! I think you get the idea of where I am heading this morning. There are certain people to call in times of need. I don't want to call my financial consultant to help me put a roof on my house. I don't want to call my barber to pull a bad tooth. We must learn where to go in times of need.

David said, *"The sorrows of death compassed me, and the floods of ungodly men made me afraid"* (Psalm 18:4). He had a need. Because of the need, he had become afraid. He must have looked everywhere for someone to help him, and he came up lacking the help he needed. He might have asked friends for help ... they could not help. He might have thought about classmates he had in the past ... they could not help. He might have turned to family for help, but they were unable.

Finally, David went to the right person, and he made the right call. *"In my distress I called up on the LORD, and cried unto my God: He heard my voice out of His temple, and my cry came before Him, even into His ears"* (Psalm 18:6). He called the One Who could come to his rescue and He stepped in! The rest of this chapter describes how powerful God is. It would be a good exercise for you to read this chapter today, and put yourself in David's shoes. Maybe you are already in David's shoes, but you have been calling all the wrong people.

Just as David reflected on His God rather than on the things in front of him and behind him, we need to take a long look at our God today. He is well able to care for the challenges you will face. The challenge is not on God's side of things, it is on your side. God will step in if we will yield our will to His will. If you will surrender your dreams and your plans to His will for your life, you will find His powerful hand there to carry it out.

Don't be guilty of trying to fight your way through this day without the help of God! Don't take a step without first asking if this will please God today. Our lives ought to be a series of times of surrender to the will of God. It is not something that can be done once and never needs to be done again. It must be done repeatedly throughout every day we are alive. In your troubles and challenges today, make the right call. Don't lean on your own understanding; turn the controls over to Him today! He is able and ready!

Finish What God Started in You – October 21

It is amazing what God can accomplish with people who will follow His will and who refuse to allow anyone but God to influence them. *"So the wall was finished in the twenty and fifth day of the month Elul, in fifty and two days"* (Nehemiah 6:15). Fifty-two days to completely rebuild the wall around Jerusalem! We can't even get a pothole patched in fifty-two days now! How did it happen? How was it possible for his rag-tag group of people would gather together and accomplish such a great task in such a short amount of time?

*"And it came to pass, that when all our enemies heard thereof, and all the heathen that were about us saw these things, they were much cast down in their own eyes: for **they perceived that this work was wrought of our God**"* (Nehemiah 6:16).

The key is this group of "rag-tag" people had come together at the prompting of God. If you remember correctly, it was God Who originally broke the heart of Nehemiah for this work. It was God Who he turned to again and again throughout this book for help and protection. When a "rag-tag" person or group of people gets together behind the leadership of God ... there is nothing that is impossible for them to accomplish. However, when a person tries to do something in their own strength and wisdom ... very little will get done that pleases God or lasts for very long.

The question in my mind today is simply, what are you building for God? When God touched the heart of Nehemiah, he moved. When opposition came to him, he continued moving forward because he had a mandate from God. God has touched your heart for some kind of service for Him today; are you continuing to move toward completion of that goal, or have you come down from your "wall?"

I have often used this statement, but I believe it fits here and has value for us today: *You can tell the measure of a man by what it takes to make him quit.* Many start something for God, but very few seem to be finishing today. The Apostle Paul said he was confident that what God starts in us, He will perfect, or finish if we remain faithful. I believe God wants to do a work in this world today, and I believe with all my heart He wants to use us to do the work. The question is not whether God can or will work today. The question is will He be able to depend on us to continue to do our part and be faithful. Fifty-two days ... despite opposition and difficult challenges. It can still be done today! Stay on your wall!

Why God Turned His Back on Jesus – October 22

"My God, My God, why hast Thou forsaken Me? Why art Thou so far from helping Me, and from the words of My roaring" (Psalm 22:1)? These words were written by David about 1,000 years before Jesus Christ was born in Bethlehem. These questions were placed in our Bible by the Holy Spirit for a very important reason that we ought to reflect on more often. These two simple questions reveal the depth of **our sin**! These two questions reveal the depth of **the love of God** in spite of our sin!

If we were to "fast-forward" history 1,000 years into the future from the time these words were penned, we would catch a glimpse of a man Who had been beaten beyond human recognition on a cross. We would notice He had been whipped ... His beard plucked from His face ... His mother standing a short distance from the cross observing ... that He was being crucified between two thieves ... that He had been a willing participant rather than thrashing and fighting ... we would notice He was in great physical and spiritual pain.

Finally, we would see Him raise His head with a crown of thorns perched on it and cry out His first words ... *"My God, My God, why hast Thou forsaken Me?"* We might wonder why God would forsake His own Son in the time of His greatest need. The answer is simple and extremely powerful. For the first time in the history (not only of mankind, but history of eternity past), God had turned His face from His only begotten Son.

What could make Him do that? I hate to tell you the answer ... I am a liar ... I am a thief ... I gossip ... I have evil thoughts ... I am jealous ... I am selfish ... it was for my sin. It was because of my sin that my righteous God hates! My sin that is appalling to God! My sin that disgusts God! My sin that had condemned me to Hell! God's face turned because my sin was resting on Jesus' shoulders. Your sins were there bundled up and placed upon the sacrificial Lamb of God Who takes away the sins of the world. Later that afternoon, the sun would become completely dark ... how could it not? God had turned His face from His Son because of our sin!

Closing question ... If God was willing to send His Son to die for you knowing this scene was coming (remember, David wrote Psalm 22 over 1,000 years before Jesus' birth) ... If Jesus was willing to come and suffer this for you ... are you willing to live for Him full out today? What could He ask of us that we would not be willing to offer back to Him after this kind of sacrifice was made for us? What an incredible Savior we serve!

Your Bible ... Impacting You? – October 23

*"And Ezra the priest brought the law before the congre3gation both of men and women, and all that could hear with understanding, upon the first day of the seventh month. And he read therein before the street that was before the water gate from the morning until midday, before the men and the women, and those that could understand; and the ears of all the people were attentive unto the book of the law. And Ezra the scribe stood upon a pulpit of wood, which they made for the purpose ... And Ezra opened the book in the sight of all the people; (for he was above all the people); and when he opened it all **the people stood up**: And Ezra blessed the LORD, the great God. And all the people answered, 'Amen, Amen,' with **lifting up their hands**: and they **bowed their heads**, and **worshipped the LORD with their faces to the ground'** (Nehemiah 8:2-5). "So they read in the book in the law of God distinctly, and gave the sense, and caused them to understand the reading. And Nehemiah ... and Ezra the priest the scribe, and the Levites that taught the people, said unto all the people, 'This day is holy unto the LORD your God; mourn not, nor weep.' For all **the people wept**, when they heard the words of the law"* (Nehemiah 8:8-9).

When was the last time you felt this way about the Word of God? When was the last time you felt honored to read words that came directly from the heart of God designed for your life personally? When was the last time you fell on your face after reading the Word of God? When was the last time you rose to your feet in honor of the Word of God? When was the last time you bowed your head after reading something that convicted you? When was the last time bowing your head wasn't enough to show your humility, and you actually fell flat on your face on the ground before God?

Perhaps we are too spoiled today. We don't understand the value of the Word of God because we have access to it on every side. We have our own personal copy of it ... we have it on our computers ... we have a copy that has notes especially designed for us as men / women / teenagers / singles / married ... etc. We have the Bible on our phones, or tablets. We are saturated with the Word of God, and yet I'm not so sure it is saturating our hearts! We tend to be Bible Trivia experts, but lack the character to actually apply the truths to our hearts. It is not enough to own a copy of the Bible. It is not enough to know the answers to the Bible questions when asked. It is not enough to even read the Bible! There needs to be a contrite heart in us that we saw in these folks. Thank God for your Bible and obey it today!

Who Will Follow You? – October 24

I promise you, there are people following you. You might not think you are influencing anyone, but there are surely people following the direction you are going because of your influence. I read a very sad story this morning in my time in the Bible. It is the story of the angels going into Sodom and Gomorrah to remove Lot and his family before the destruction would come on these cities. If you remember, Abraham had begged the angels not to destroy the city if there were even ten righteous people still there. This is sad in itself. Lot had gone to Sodom as a single man; had married; and had children who were old enough to be married at that time. When the angels went to the city, they were not able to find ten righteous people. Lot had not left much of an impression on his town.

The verse that crushed my heart was this commentary that explained what happened when Lot went to his sons-in-laws and daughters to encourage them to leave with them. It says, *"And Lot went out, and spake unto his sons-in-law, which married his daughters, and said, 'Up, get you out of this place: for the LORD will destroy this city.' **But he seemed as one that mocked unto his sons-in-law**"* (Genesis 19:14). What a sad commentary, not on the sons-in-laws, but on Lot! He had had his daughter's lifetime to display to them trust-worthiness, but he had failed. When the most crucial time in their lives came, they saw him as a foolish old man who did not know what he was talking about.

There is an important lesson here for us to learn. If we talk one way, and we walk a different way, people will believe our walk before they believe our talk! Lot said all the right things in encouraging his sons-in-laws and daughters to leave with them, but his prior behavior did not give any power to his words. He seemed to them as some foolish man spouting out warnings about things that could not possibly happen! What a shame! No wonder Lot's wife looked back! Some of what was happening in that city was her family burning to death!

Rather than pointing an accusatory finger at Lot, and getting on our "high-horse" to look down upon him, I think it would be good for each of us to examine our own hearts first. If we are honest we must admit it is far easier for us to find fault in others than it is to admit our own. We all spend far too much time talking the talk. But do we give as much attention to walking the walk? I want to live today in such a way that I can influence my family to live godly lives. I want to be a pattern they can follow.

Doubly Prepared – October 25

"*Let the high praises of God be in their mouth, and a two-edged sword in their hand*" (Psalm 149:6). Be ready with praise to God and the Word of God close by in your hands! Sounds like a Christian soldier ready for the enemies that are sure to come in this world today. Two things that seem to be lacking in our lives (in a very general sense) are praise to God, and a good handle on the Word of God. Recently a young man who is searching for answers from his Bible told me he has been going from church to church looking for Bible answers to some deep questions in his soul, but he has found the churches he has attended to be more like concerts than church.

In my humble opinion, there is a tremendous amount of emphasis on spiritual entertainment in many churches today, and not so much on solid Bible teaching/preaching. It seems sermons have become sermonettes, and the beginnings of our services have become productions. I was in a church not too long ago to be the speaker for the morning services. An assistant pastor met with me to review the schedule prior to the first service. The first thing I noticed was the schedule was extremely detailed. The second thing I noticed was the music section of the program was a little longer than the time I was given to preach. I do not mean to over-emphasize the teaching/ preaching time in the service, but it seems there is generally an imbalance in many services.

I also do not want to de-emphasize the importance of the "praise" part of this verse. Again, my concern is, often our praise is what pleases us, without too much regard for what might please our God. God made us to praise Him! He has given us plenty of things to praise Him for ... beginning with our salvation and going through all of the beauty we see in nature around us. There is no way we could ever exhaust our praise of all He has done for us. We need to spend more time in simply praising Him for what He means to us.

We also need to be able to handle the Word of God correctly. There are many today who are promoting false doctrine and philosophies. It is important for each believer to know what the Bible has to say about these issues, and be well equipped to defend the truths of the Bible. We have been given a Bible that can pierce to the dividing of the soul and spirit. It is able to discern what our motivations are and to guide us in the right paths. We need to open it more. We need to actually handle it more. We need to memorize and obey it. It should be in our hands daily!

Get Up and Do Something! – October 26

"The slothful man saith, 'There is a lion in the way; a lion is in the streets'" (Proverbs 26:13).

Every time I read this verse, it strikes me as though it is an incomplete thought. However, it is complete. The slothful man, the lazy man, the sluggard sees the danger in the path he is on, but he does nothing about it! He can see the lion clearly. He even repeats his observation twice. He just does nothing about it. How foolish this act would be! But, we do the same thing over and over again when reading the Word of God. We see the truths clearly defined in the Bible, but we do very little to make corrections or adjustments in our lives.

If we are not careful, we can easily become the "slothful man." We recognize Bible truths, but they don't fit into our plan. Or, they don't make us "feel" good. Or they bring conviction to one of our favorite habits, or actions. Each of us must come to the realization that we are not perfect, and God gave us His Word to help us walk more closely with Him. The Bible is meant to be our guideline to living a Christ-centered, Holy Spirit filled life. Our problem is not with having a Bible (seeing the lion in the way) … our problem comes when we are forced to action, or not to act after seeing what is in the Bible.

It has always bothered me when people complain about the government of their country. When you ask them if they voted, they reply they do not because it makes no difference in the outcome. I would like to tell them their complaining isn't making any difference either, but the one single vote they had could accomplish great things if all the people who felt that way (and did not vote) had voted. My point is this … we love to point out things that "should be" getting done, but if we do nothing to affect change we are no different than the slothful man pointing out there is a lion in the way.

In conclusion this morning; I would like to encourage each of us reading this to determine that we will do more than complain about things we see that are wrong today. Let's get up off our spiritual couches, and get involved in the game of life! Yes … getting involved in the game of life will involve some dirty pants, and scuffed up shoes, and bruises, and maybe even a broken bone or two. Regardless of all these problems, you will be able to say you had gotten in the game! I would rather have a dirty uniform than a clean when the game is over! Get in the game of life today!

What Are You Asking For? – October 27

"Ask of Me, and I shall give thee the heathen for thine inheritance, and the uttermost parts of the earth for thy possession" (Psalm 2:8). When was the last time you begged God to save someone? When was the last time you woke up in the middle of the night with someone you know who is unsaved on your heart? When was the last time you saw a missionary presentation and either asked God to save those people, or even offered to go yourself? When was the last time you actually presented the Gospel to a person? When was the last time you went forward and knelt at the altar begging God to give you some spiritual fruit in your life?

Life is far too short for each of us to let even one opportunity pass. Time is one thing that can never be regained! It would be great (as a few movies have suggested), if we could reverse time and go back to change some things we have done, or to take opportunities we have missed. The reality is we cannot do that; we must make good use of the opportunities we have in front of us today. If we do not look for the opportunities God will place in front of us, there is a chance we could walk away from them without noticing. It is important for us to ASK God to give us the opportunities and then to keep an eye open for them.

Some of the best opportunities to lead a person to Christ for me have come from the most unlikely situations. I recall one time going to visit an elderly lady from our church in our local hospital. When I entered the room looking for "Mrs. Jones," I saw a man in the bed. I jokingly said to him, *"I'm sorry, I was coming to visit Mrs. Jones, but you are obviously not Mrs. Jones."* He smiled and assured me he was not Mrs. Jones. As I turned to leave the room, I stopped and turned back to the man. I told him there was a real possibility God had led me to his room to meet him. After a few minutes of explaining the Gospel to him, the man trusted Jesus Christ as Savior. There are opportunities waiting ... we ought to be asking.

There is one thing that is most precious to God today ... it is not the value of the dollar, or the Euro, or the condition of the stock market, or the latest deadly disease. The thing most valuable to God is that person you will pass today who is without Christ. God sent His only begotten Son to this sin-cursed earth to save sinners. You and I will pass plenty of sinners today. God has a heart for each of them ... do you? Ask God to give you that heart today and then begin to look for the opportunities He will place before you. I know He will ... He is not willing that any should perish!

315

A Pig with a Bow – October 28

We seem to love to "dress up" the outside of us, while totally ignoring the "heart" of the matter. Recently I read, *"Burning lips and a wicked heart are like a potsherd covered with silver dross"* (Proverbs 26:23). As always, God says things way better than I ever could. He paints an incredible word picture here I want to apply to my life today, and I hope you will want to apply to your heart as well. The idea of covering an earthen vessel that is made of the mud of the earth with silver seems foolish. However, this is exactly what happens when we try to appear to be something or someone we are not.

This picture reminds me of what Jesus called the Pharisees in the New Testament. These were people who tried to pass themselves off as religious, or pious, or better than the common sinner that might come into the synagogue. Jesus at one time called them *"whited sepulchers."* In my list of jobs I have done in my life, I helped a funeral home for a few years. In that time working with them, I have seen some beautiful caskets. I have seen beautiful and expensive wooden caskets all the way to the shiniest gold and silver looking caskets. The reality is it doesn't matter if it is a pine box, or the most expensive casket in the world, it is still going to house dead bones!

We are very aware of what we can do to appear as though we are spiritual and a good person. The reality is, within each of us is nothing more than an old clay pot! We are just made of the dust of the earth and we are no better than that! Rather than try to fool others, I think it would be better for us to realize our weakness, and allow God to do His work in us. The truth is we are not the ones who generate anything that is good in our lives. If anything is going to come out of our life and testimony, it will be because God does a work through an old clay pot!

I am hopeful God can take something from this old clay pot and make something beautiful today. I know who I am, and you know who you are. I'm not talking about what others think of me or you; I am talking about what I know and God knows about me. I want to yield whatever I have to Him today, and allow Him the freedom to do whatever He wants with me all day long. I don't see much potential in me. He sees what can be done if I will turn over the controls. I want to take my hands off my life, and allow Him to take over. I thank God the Holy Spirit of God now lives in this clay pot, and He can do amazing things if I will get out of His way!

Joy in the Morning – October 29

"For His anger endureth but a moment; in His favor is life: weeping may endure for a night, but joy cometh in the morning" (Psalm 30:5).

This may seem like a strange verse for me to talk about for today's devotional. The reality is God does have anger! We love to talk about the grace and mercy of God. We love to spend hours talking and singing about the love of God. We love to think about the gentleness and kindness of God today. As a matter of fact, if the only information you got about God was from the television preachers, you would feel pretty safe no matter what kind of life you were living.

I would not be fair with you if all I talked about were these things. The reality is our sin makes God angry! If you have not trusted Christ, I want you to know the mercy, grace, and love of God are equal qualities to the righteous anger God has for sin. He cannot look on sin! He cannot stand to allow sin (even the "small" ones we tend to excuse as acceptable) into Heaven. So, yes, there is a part of God which becomes angry! However, as the verse states, God's anger can be overtaken by God's joy. How is that possible?

Just as we witnessed God turning His face from His only-begotten Son there on the cross (when your sin and mine was placed upon Him), He turns His face from us without Christ as our Savior. After Jesus paid the price for our sin and rose from the grave, God accepted His offering of His blood as payment for our sins. He then opened Heaven to whosoever will come by that sacrifice. You and I who earned the anger of God, now have the opportunity to see the joy on the face of God as we accept His forgiveness for sin. That is grace!

I want to caution you not to be too quick to dismiss how angry sin makes God. I also want you to remember God has provided a way for any person who will trust Jesus Christ as Savior, to avoid that anger. I want to encourage you with this thought: as much as you may struggle with sin in your life, keep battling. God has the answer if you will yield to Him. As dark as it may seem today, there is joy coming in the morning if you will run to Him for forgiveness and restitution. I can tell you every time I have felt alienated from God because of my sin, He has been waiting for me in my prayer closet with all the grace and mercy I have needed. Don't run from God. Don't stay away too long. He is eager to give you back the joy you have lost while away in your sin. Trust Him for the joy you need today.

Good News – October 30

I have stopped watching the nightly news on television because it is so depressing! Every story seems to be about some horrible thing that has happened, or is happening all around us. I'm sure the news in your part of the world is no different than mine. However, the one thing I do try to do every day is to reach into my Bible to find some hope for the day. Today I read, "*Be of good courage, and He shall strengthen your heart, all ye that hope in the LORD*" (Psalm 31:24). Now, that's good news!

Think with me for a moment ... God made man for fellowship and for companionship. I love to think of God walking in the Garden of Eden with Adam and Eve before their fall into sin. I love the thought of God speaking verbally with them, and with them all having a good laugh together. I love the idea of fellowship with God unhindered by sin. Those must have been great days!

We have never experienced that kind of freedom today because we are encumbered by our sin. However, God still offers fellowship and companionship today. He gave us His Son to restore our relationship with Him. He has reconciled us to Himself through the blood of His Son and His resurrection from the dead. The reality of this truth is the focus should not be on us, or our sinful behavior, but on the wonderful God we serve! Too much of my time each day is spent on what I want, and what I think, and my plans, and my goals for the day. I hate to admit it, but I have found myself to be extremely self-centered.

That last phrase in the verse is the key to the entire verse. The promise of a strengthened heart is for those "*that hope in the LORD*." If you are hoping in the Lord today, you can have courage for the days you are living. If you are hoping in the Lord today, you will be strengthened in your heart regardless of all that is happening around you. There is hope! There is a reason for courage! There is strength that is offered! It is there for those who place their hope in the Lord.

One of our problems today is, we have become far too dependent on our computers ... on our jobs ... on our governments ... on our pastors ... on our own wisdom and skill ... on our families. The hope we have is not found in any of these things, but is found only in the Lord! Today is a good day to run to Him for your help. Today is a good day to make a conscious decision to stop trusting in man, or in you, and to begin to trust in the Lord! He is the place that hope was invented! He has all the hope you will need!

The Forgotten – October 31

How many people will you pass today who are desperate for someone to notice them? They are everywhere you will go today. It could be the person who works next to you who drives a nice car and lives in a beautiful house. It could be the child who is acting badly in your Sunday School class that you wish would stay home and miss this week. It could be the friend of yours who always seems to have it together, but is struggling internally with things he/she tells no one. It could be your neighbor. I think you get the idea.

King Lemuel's mother challenged him to notice these forgotten people. *"Open thy mouth for the dumb in the cause of all such as are appointed to destruction. Open thy mouth, judge righteously, and plead the cause of the poor and needy"* (Proverbs 31:8-9). Think about this for just a few moments today. This was the king who was being encouraged to speak up for those who could not speak for themselves. If the king needs to pay attention to these people, I think we ought to be able to find it in our hearts to look for them too.

I know sometimes I get so caught up in what "my" plans are or "my" schedule for the day, I don't give God much space to use me in the lives of others. I am convicted when I read these verses. When I awake in the morning, I begin to think of what "I" need to do for the day. I don't always consider some time for God to do what "He" wants to do in my day. I want to be the kind of person that God can depend on to look for those who cannot speak for themselves. I want to have a heart that looks to the poor and the needy who are all around me.

The "homeless" are not the only people who are *"poor and needy"* today. Are you willing to pick up your phone and call a friend you sense might be struggling? Are you willing to go to someone who has been shut-in to stop and brighten their day? Are you willing to stop whatever it is you have planned, to do the things God has planned for you? Will you allow for a "heavenly interruption?"

King Lemuel's mother realized life is too short to simply plow through working our own agenda. We must stop to make a difference where we can, with whoever we can. I believe God has people who will cross your path today who He is hoping you will *"Open your mouth"* to tell about Him. He is the hope for our world today. He is the Person all the hurting people are searching for. Don't keep Him a secret!

MONTH OF
November

Sins Forgiven – November 1

"Blessed is he whose transgression is forgiven, whose sin is covered. Blessed is the man unto whom the LORD imputeth not iniquity, and in whose spirit there is no guile" (Psalm 32:1-2). I hope I never forget the thrill of these verses! I hope I never look at my sins being forgiven as something I deserve, or something that is normal. God literally moved Heaven and earth to pay off my sin debt! He sent His only begotten Son to die in my place when I had no chance to be right with Him. He imputed, or placed my sin totally onto His Son there at Calvary so I could know a relationship with forgiveness from Him! These are monumental thoughts today. Don't ever get to the place where these things become common place to you. Don't allow these events to come to your mind as easily as what you had for breakfast, or where you are planning to do today.

The thought of God taking care of a sin debt I could not pay ought to sit on my heart and mind every day I live! Imagine yourself in an illustration Jesus gave while he was here on the earth. Imagine you owe a huge debt you could never repay to another person. Imagine if that person called you to see him. You would surely be shaking with the bad news that was coming. Your mind would be running to thoughts of slavery, or prison, or even the man bringing bodily harm to you. Imagine how you would feel if, when you walked into his office, you saw the man take the bill you owed, and rip it in pieces. Imagine if you watched him take a match and light it on fire, and you both stood and watched it disintegrate before your eyes. Imagine if the man hugged you and told you he loved you and he, himself, had paid your debt and you were now free from the debt.

This is what God has done for us! He was the One Who paid our sin debt off, the only way it was possible for it to be done! The righteous demand of God was satisfied with the righteous sacrifice of His own Son's blood being shed on the cross of Calvary! There was no other way for this to happen! There is no religious cloak you can lay over your sin that would remove your sin debt! There is not enough money in all the banks of the world that could pay for even one sin, let alone all your sin! Even if you could stop sinning today (which you cannot), who would pay for the sins of your past? Jesus stepped out of Heaven ... lived perfectly on earth ... and voluntarily took your place on the cross ... He rose from the dead removing the debt of whosoever comes to Him by faith! That is great news for today, and every day in which you live all the way to eternity! Thank Him and live for Him!

Longest Word in the Bible – November 2

A very good friend of mine once taught a Bible study on this topic. He went on to explain in his opinion, the longest word in the Bible was the word, "wait." It has been my experience he might be right. I hate the "waiting room" at the doctor or dentist's office. My least favorite part of flying is sitting in the airport for an hour or two waiting for our flight (or for our flight to be delayed). When I played and coached sports, I hated the day of the game, just waiting for the time to click off the clock until game time. I guess you could say "waiting" is a real challenge for me.

Today I read some very simple words that greatly convict me. *"Our soul waiteth for the LORD: He is our help and our shield"* (Psalm 33:20). As much as I hate waiting, I need the help of the Lord, and I certainly want Him to be my shield. When trouble comes to me, I have noticed I find myself rushing about trying to find a quick solution to the problem. According to this verse, and many others, the real solution is to sit still and give God a chance to prove Himself powerful for us. How foolish we are to try to handle our own troubles when we have a God Who is willing and ready, if we will simply wait for Him to work!

I read a little further today and saw this powerful verse: *"He keepeth the paths of judgment, and preserveth the way of His saints"* (Proverbs 2:8). The idea behind the word, **keepeth** is that of a guard being set around us. God guards our paths, and **preserveth** our ways. He can do this when we stop trying to do everything in our own strength and power. He can do this when we yield ourselves to Him. I know you have heard this before, just like me; but are we living this?

I know this is an area of my life where I struggle. I tend to try to control the situations I am in and will face. I realize how foolish this is as I see the words on this page, but it is the reality of my life. I will commit today to trying to wait on the Lord. I will commit today to stay behind His shield of protection with the things I will face today. I will commit to staying within the parameters God sets around me today and to stay within the guarded places He has for me. I will commit to allowing God to direct my steps and choices today.

I will need to make these commitments again tomorrow, and the day after, and the day after. This is a part of the process of God's refining us. He can take us from the filth we bring Him, and make us a vessel fit for the Master's use … but we need to wait on Him! Join me today!

He's Near – November 3

When I was nineteen years old I was lying in a hospital bed preparing for some surgery. I was feeling some nervousness and asked the Lord to help calm my spirit. I closed my eyes, opened my Bible, and pointed my finger blindly at the page the Bible opened to (I do not recommend this, but our Bible is so powerful that even this kind of searching can prove to be very profitable – be warned however, I did hear of one man who was feeling depressed and did this and he pointed to "*Judas went out and hung himself*" ... he was sure he had pointed to the wrong place so he tried again and pointed to "... *go thou and do likewise*" – so it doesn't always work.

That day my Bible had opened to Philippians 4 and I read the phrase, "... *The Lord is at hand*" (Philippians 4:5b). I know it may sound insignificant to you, but it has been more than thirty years since that day in the hospital, and every time I read that phrase I remember God IS in control! What a great God we serve today! I honestly could fill 5,000 pages with praises for all God has done for me through my lifetime, but I will not take the time right now. I do want to praise Him for being "*at hand*" on that day of my surgery, and every day since.

I know some of you reading this today are facing far more pressing issues than I was facing that day. I know some of you are thinking, "*Well, that's good for him, but he doesn't know what troubles are in front of me!*" You are right! I don't know what's facing you, but I want to remind you of a few things ... Our God parted the Red Sea so over one-million Israelites could cross on dry ground. Our God fed those million + Israelites for forty years. Our God defeated 135,000 Midianites with 300 men carrying pitchers of clay, trumpets, and a lamp. Our God used a teenage boy named David to kill a nine-and-a-half foot tall giant named Goliath with a smooth stone. Our God sent His only begotten Son to carry all of your sin to the cross, and He died there to pay the price demanded for your sins to be forgiven. Our God raised His Son from the dead and He is alive right now making intercession for you and me for the problems we are facing today. What am I trying to tell you? "*The Lord is at hand!*"

All morning I've been singing the chorus to myself of the old hymn, "No one ever cared for me like Jesus!" It's so true! I don't know what challenge you are facing today, but I know the Lord is at hand. I don't know what burden you are carrying today, but I know the Lord is at hand.

He's Still in His Place – November 4

When I was a young boy playing in the back yard, there was always something comforting when I saw my Mom or my Grandmom looking out the kitchen window. If I fell and hurt myself, or if the neighborhood bully was about to pummel me ... it was good to know I had "back-up." There was a specific time when I remember my neighborhood bully trying to end my life. He had me pinned to the ground, and I was heavily involved in intercessory prayer ... for myself ... when I heard the sweet, melodious tones of my Grandmother's voice threatening to "shake the liver loose" of the bully if he did not get off me. To my surprise, he responded as my Grandmother had said. I looked over at her and she happened to be waving a cast iron frying pan while issuing the threat. It's always good to know someone is watching!

"The LORD is in His holy temple, the LORD's throne is in heaven: His eyes behold, His eyelids try, the children of men" (Psalm 11:4). What a thrill to know in these difficult times, it is great to know our Heavenly Father is at the window of Heaven watching all that is happening around us. Nothing surprises Him! He is on guard for the sake of His children! When the bullies of life have you pinned down, don't worry too much ... God has more than a cast iron frying pan!

There was one other thing that Mom looking out of the kitchen window did for me ... I was forced to behave. That occasional gaze from the window kept me in line. I knew if my Mom looked out that window, and I was doing something I was not supposed to be doing, there would be a wooden spoon in my future. I already wrote about the wooden spoon, so I will not dwell on it any more here.

There is something about knowing the authority is looking at you. I noticed when driving if a police officer is spotted sitting in his car on the side of the road, all the drivers immediately slow down. It doesn't even matter if they were obeying the speed limit before they saw him/her, they still slow down to a safer speed! It is the same with God and me. Knowing He is watching me helps me to obey the spiritual "speed limits" He has given me in the Word of God. Today I am both encouraged and challenged to think God is watching everything happening around me. I am encouraged He has a watchful, protective eye on me. I am challenged to think of all the times I fail Him, He sees openly and plainly. I want to please Him today. I need His protection. I will trust Him throughout today!

Well Done – November 5

We often think just because we are Christians, we will hear God say, *"Well done"* to us when we reach Heaven. It might do each of us some good to read Matthew 25:14-30. That greeting is going to be kept for those who have actually invested their lives in the things God thinks are important. This greeting will be reserved for those who have taken what God has given to us, and has used those gifts/abilities to make an impact on the cause of Christ.

There is a story (parable) Jesus was telling to illustrate a fundamental truth He wanted His followers (including us) to understand. A lord had given five talents to a servant. The servant had taken those five talents and had invested them wisely. When the lord returned, the servant presented the lord with ten talents. Here was the response of the lord to this servants efforts: *"His Lord said unto him, 'Well done, thou good and faithful servant: thou hast been faithful over a few things, I will make thee ruler over many things: enter thou into the joy of thy lord'"* (Matthew 25:21).

It touched my heart this morning to think of the many talents, abilities, and gifts God has given me. I immediately thought about the verse that says, *"For of whomsoever much is given, of him shall be much required: and to whom men have committed much, of him they will ask the more"* (Luke 12:48). I have been given much ... you have been given much. The real question is what are we doing with what we have been given to affect the Great Commission? I hope you have read your Bible enough to know the responsibility of taking the whole Gospel to the whole world is the responsibility of every believer!

God originally called the Jews His chosen people. They were called that because it was God's desire for them to make Him known to the whole world. The failure came when they began to look at the other nations they were supposed to be influencing, and adapted their gods and idols in the place of God. Their failure to make God known to the whole world was largely because they were duped into thinking something outside God's plan was better than God's plan. I want you to know we are the people God is depending on today to continue His heartbeat for this world. He still wants the whole world to know about the sacrifice His Son made for each of them. Are you going to do something today to make Him known? Are you going to invest your talent(s) today to affect the spreading of His message? If you are there is a *"Well done"* waiting for you. Don't bury your talent!

The Darkest Time in the History of the World – November 6

There have been many "dark days" in the history of the world. There have been many "dark days" in the history of your country. There have been many "dark days" in your own personal life. But, there has never been a day darker than one that took place over 2,000 years ago. *"Now from the sixth hour there was darkness over all the land unto the ninth hour"* (Matthew 27:45).

During the time when Jesus was dying on the cross of Calvary on that hill called Golgotha, there was absolute darkness for those three hours. Have you ever thought about why? Have you ever considered what caused this darkness? Have you ever thought about what made the sun hide its face for three hours in the time when it normally shined the brightest? There is one simple answer. God Almighty had turned His face from His righteous, Son, Jesus Christ. God had turned His face because the sin of the entire world had been laid on Him! God had placed your personal, disgusting, horrific sins on Jesus Christ.

There is a very important point that this darkness highlighted for us, and one we all need to pay attention to today. The reality is that God cannot co-exist with sin! God cannot even stand the sight of sin. The first words Jesus cried out from the cross were, *"My God, My God, why hast Thou forsaken Me?"* God had turned His face from the Son He called His *"Beloved Son"* more than once. God turned His face because He could not look on your sin that had been placed on Jesus Christ. He could not look at any of our sin.

Jesus Christ literally became sin for us. He was not a sinner, but took on Himself the sin that we would be involved in, so He could offer the one and only perfect sacrifice for sin! Jesus alone had the ability to pay this price! No preacher, pope, pastor, minister, missionary, or political leader could pay this price! Only Jesus Christ is worthy to take the sins of the world, and pay the price for them. The price for sin has always been, and will always be death. Jesus paid the price for you!

The darkness that came for the space of those three hours came because God had turned His face from His Son ... from your sin and mine. How could the sun shine when its Creator was dying with the sin of the world on Him? How can we live in a way that ignores this tremendous sacrifice and continues in sin? God forbid! We ought to desire to live holy lives for Him today. He took on sin for us, it is the least we can do. Shine for Him today!

Serve Enthusiastically – November 7

What a great time to be alive and able to serve the King of all kings! We are so blessed to be able to know God through His Son, Jesus Christ! We have been honored to be a part of a long line of faithful followers of Jesus! I want to encourage you today to live this day with enthusism! There are many today who are always talking about how bad things are, and how bad thing will become; but we who are saved know there is a real place called Heaven awaiting us! An old hymn asked the questions: "*Why should I feel discouraged, why should the shadows come, Why should my heart be lonely, and long for heav'n and home, When Jesus is my portion? My constant Friend is He: His eye is on the sparrow, and I know He watches me.*"

Paul gave us this challenge in Colossians: "*And whatsoever ye do, do it heartily, as to the Lord, and not unto men. Knowing that of the Lord ye shall receive the reward of the inheritance; for ye serve the Lord Christ*" (Colossians 3:23-24). Take heart today, you and I have the opportunity to serve the Lord Christ! What an incredible honor and privilege we have today! We are living in exciting times to serve the Lord Christ. This day you have today will be given to you by the Lord, and the possibilities for service to Him will be scattered all throughout the day. What will you do with this day?

I am amazed at how much Christians have allowed this world to influence our perspective (in general). Yes, I used the word, "our" because I struggle with this too. We have an anchor we must run to on a daily basis. We need not simply read the Bible in the morning to "check off" some duty we have performed. We must read our Bible as though it is the map for our day and then follow it. This Bible is our spiritual and practical GPS for living right before God. Please be encouraged by your Bible. Paul encouraged us to do everything we find in front of us today with enthusism! I might even clean my desk today!

Today I have the opportunity to serve the King of all kings and to lay up rewards in Heaven. I want to make good use of this day, and every day the Lord Christ will give me to serve Him. I want to do it with all the enthusiasm I had when I played sports. I want to do it with all the effort I would to please my earthly boss. I want to do it because my Heavenly Father is worthy of it. Don't look at this day with a depressed view. This is the day the Lord has made ... rejoice and be glad in it!

Life Lessons Devotional

Walk ... Work ... Word – November 8

"LORD, who shall abide in Thy tabernacle? Who shall dwell in Thy holy hill? He that walketh uprightly, and worketh righteousness, and speaketh the truth in his heart" (Psalm 15:1-2). Do you seriously want to spend time with God? Are you committed to making a difference where you go today? Are you ready to show you belong to God today? How can all this happen in a sinner like you? You may be asking these kinds of questions about yourself today. If you're not, you should be. God has placed us on this earth to glorify Him in our lives and actions. He has chosen to advertise a relationship with Him, by displaying it to the world through the actions and attitudes you will show the world.

What does the world around you think about God from the way you WALK? Do the friends and family you know think God has some very bad habits and behavior? I have met many unsaved people who have told me, *"If that's what being a Christian means, I want no part of it!"* That kind of statement always breaks my heart. First, because an unsaved person seems to have been hurt by a believer's testimony; second, because that believer has missed the idea of what the purpose of our walk is. Walking is different from leaping. Walking involves a methodical, day after day consistency. Those around you will be watching the way you walk today. Walk worthy of the Lord all day today. Let you actions show a clean and pure testimony.

What does the world notice about your WORK today? I believe as a Christian I should be the best employee my boss has working for him/her. I think I ought to be going above and beyond what is expected of me when asked to complete a task. I believe I should be known as a person who gives an honest day's work regardless of what others are doing around me. I want the things I put my hand to, to reflect my absolute commitment to excellence ... not for a paycheck ... but for my Heavenly Father. You see, the way you work (or don't work), reflects directly on your relationship with your God! Work hard ... someone is watching you.

While your walk and your work are very important, they are not nearly as powerful when accompanied by your WORDS. Speak up for your God today. You might worry about offending someone ... I have noticed they are not worried about offending you. Someone needs to tell others today about the wonderful Savior we have. After you have walked the walk, and worked the work, tell someone about what Jesus means to you!

328

He is at My Right Side – November 9

"This world is in such a bad way, what am I going to do?" "*I have set the LORD always before me: Because He is at my right hand, I shall not be moved*" (Psalm 16:8).

"I'm not sure my insurance will cover my bills that are upcoming … what am I going to do?" "*I have set the LORD always before me: Because He is at my right hand, I shall not be moved*" (Psalm 16:8).

"My children are getting involved in things that worry me … what am I going to do?" "*I have set the LORD always before me: Because He is at my right hand, I shall not be moved*" (Psalm 16:8).

"I'm not sure I will have a job next year … what am I going to do?" "*I have set the LORD always before me: Because He is at my right hand, I shall not be moved*" (Psalm 16:8).

"I don't know what's going to happen to me after I die … what am I going to do?" "*I have set the LORD always before me: Because He is at my right hand, I shall not be moved*" (Psalm 16:8).

Now, I know some of you think I am so innocent that I don't know what you are going through, and that this verse is not an answer to all the problems you are facing. I would tell you My God is big enough to handle any and all of the challenges you are facing today and will face tomorrow. I know the God I serve parted the Red Sea and allowed the Israelites free access to cross onto the other side. I know my God, even though all the forces of Hell were trying to keep Jesus in the tomb, raised Him on the third day. I know that the resurrection, when applied to my sin-debt, is the conquering force over my sin, my death, and my Hell. I am sure my God is able to do exceedingly, abundantly, above all that I could ever ask or think when it comes to tackling my problems. It does not matter how big my problems may appear at the time. What matters is how much I will trust my God to take me through the problems I face on a daily basis. As for me and my house … "*I have set the LORD always before me: Because He is at my right hand, I shall not be moved*" (Psalm 16:8).

There is an old song that said, "*I don't worry about the future, 'Cause I know what Jesus said, And today I'm gonna walk right beside Him 'Cause He's the One Who knows what is ahead … But I know who holds tomorrow. And I know who holds my hand.*" Hold firmly to His hand today, and trust Him!

Do Right With the Little Things – November 10

There is a great story in the Old Testament of a niece and her uncle. God used these two "normal" people in an extraordinary way to preserve His children while they were in captivity. The story is of Mordecai and his niece, Esther. A wicked man had devised a plan that looked impossible to overturn. Haman was so enraged that Mordecai would not bow to him, that he had tricked the king into signing a law that would allow him to wipe out the entire Jewish population in the Persian Empire. Things looked very grim for the Jews living there. They looked grim until God stepped into the picture.

In reading through this wonderful story, you will notice how God used one simple act by Mordecai to preserve His people in this foreign country. In Esther 2, there is a short section that tells about Mordecai hearing of a plot to kill King Ahasuerus. He quickly informed someone in the king's guard, and the men were caught. It seemed like a very small thing the time. It was forgotten, but not by God. The event was recorded in the book of the chronicles that was at the king's disposal. Later, in perfect timing, the king could not sleep and brought the books of the chronicles out to be read. He heard the recording of Mordecai's act and rewarded him.

God used this simple act of Mordecai to turn the king's heart. Haman was caught in his evil plot by chapter 7. Look at the statement made by a servant of the king when they were deciding what to do with Haman: "… *'Behold also, the gallows fifty cubits high, which Haman had made for Mordecai, **who had spoken good for the king**, standeth in the house of Haman.' Then the king said, 'Hang him thereon'*" (Esther 7:9). The simple testimony of Mordecai … the man *who had spoken good for the king* … not only saved his life, but the lives of thousands of Jews living in the Persian Empire at the time.

What small "good thing" will you do that will turn the tide for someone, somewhere today? Have you thought about the difference just attempting to live righteously in an unrighteous world can make? I'm sure you feel insignificant a good bit of your life. Take heart in this story, and realize there is nothing that is arbitrary about your God! He has a perfect plan for your life today, and if you will surrender to His will, He will use simple little you to make a huge difference in the world you are living. Don't simply pass through your day today without the knowledge that God wants to use you, and he will use you if you surrender to Him.

In Hot Pursuit – November 11

"As the hart panteth after the water brooks, so panteth my soul after Thee, O God" (Psalm 42:1).

Is this true for you? Does your heart yearn for God like a thirsty deer looks for the refreshing water of that mountain stream? Are you searching for it, with a thirst that will not be easily quenched? There ought to be a deep desire within every one of us as believers to know our God and to get to know our Savior. We ought to yearn for the Holy Spirit of God to have free access to our "database" at all times, every day. Sadly, in my own life, my own agenda takes the place of priority too often. I don't come to the place where I am hotly pursuing God's will until all my own options have been exhausted. Shame on me!

Let me ask this a little differently … how easy is it for you to find an excuse not to pray? How easy is it for you to find a reason to put off reading your Bible? How many excuses can you come up with for not responding at an invitation that has truly touched your heart? How many ways have you rationalized your sin away so the conviction does not seem so harsh? If we are honestly pursuing God there will be a cost. If we are going to pursue God, there will need to be some sacrifices made. If we are going to "sell-out" for God, there will need to be a price that is paid on other accounts.

This pursuit of God that David describes here in Psalm 42 is what should become the "norm" for us believers. It should not be seen as some supreme sacrifice for this to happen in our lives daily. Think about it for a moment. How strongly did God pursue a right relationship with you? God gave the "pearl of great price," His only begotten Son, in Whom He was well pleased. God gave His absolute best for you. How much did it cost God to pursue you? It cost Him the life of His Son, as well as the agony of turning His face from that Son in His hour of deepest need. Was it something that happened quickly, or did it demand some time? The redemption of your soul started in the Garden of Eden, and it is still costing God till this day!

The truth of this verse is that we are encouraged to follow the example of the thirsty deer in pursuit of our relationship with God. Don't let up today. Look for ways to be with God today. Look for ways to please God today. Take time for time alone with God in His Word today. Look forward to the time you will spend with Him in prayer today. *"As the hart panteth for the water brooks …"* allow your soul to pant for God today. It will be the greatest chase of your life! Do it all over again tomorrow!

You Can Depend on Him! – November 12

"God is not a man, that He should lie; neither the son of man, that he should repent: hath He said, and shall He not do it? Or hath He spoken, and shall He not make it good" (Numbers 23:19)?

Words are cheap, and promises seem to be cheaper at times. Recently I was in a meeting and I was talking about us making a promise/commitment to God. As I asked if folks were willing to promise God they would follow His will for their lives, a voice was heard from the audience saying, *"Promises can be broken."* In most cases I would agree. However, according to this wonderful verse in Numbers 23, we can totally trust in the promises God makes to us in the Word of God.

If God makes us a promise in His Word, I guarantee you that you can build your life upon it. If God says something will happen, it is as if it has already taken place. What is the difference between the promises we make each other as human beings, and the promises of God? Well, the voice from the crowd that said, *"Promises can be broken ..."* was talking about us, not about God. When another person makes a promise to you, it generally means they will "try their best" to do what they have told you they will do. Making a promise to a friend or family member is always based on our ability to make it happen.

This is where God's promises are totally different than ours. Where we are sometimes limited in our ability to carry out the promise we have made, our God has limitless ability! You may have the best intentions to do what you have promised, but the resources you thought you had, might not be available when the time comes, and you find yourself failing at the promise you have made. God has never had that problem, and He never will. If God makes a promise to us, we can stand firmly on that promise because He has the ultimate power to make it come about.

We live in a world full of promises ... and we all know the disappointment of an unfulfilled promise. You are holding a Bible that is full of promises from God. Every last one of those promises has come true for those who have trusted them in the past, and will come true for those of us who will place our faith and trust in them now and in the future. Be careful not to walk through this life worrying and fretting about things when God has given you a Book full of promises. Those promises were made from a loving Father to his needy children. You can trust your Heavenly Father today. The world will fail you, but He never has, and never will!

Close to the Life-giving Water – November 13

"Blessed is the man that trusteth in the LORD, and whose hope the LORD is. For he shall be as a tree planted by the waters, and that spreadeth out her roots by the river, and shall not see when heat cometh, but her leaf shall be green; and shall not be careful in the year of drought, neither shall cease from yielding fruit" (Jeremiah 17:7-8).

We have a small run off from a pond above our property. We call it a creek, but it is more like a ditch with water in it. I have noticed all along this little "creek" there are trees growing. During the dry stretches of our summers here, those trees still look healthy and strong. What little moisture there is in that "creek" provides them the water they crave. The prophet Jeremiah lived during a time in Israel's history when it seemed all the "creeks" were drying up. However, he knew where the real power came from.

As he kept his heart tender toward his God in Heaven, the Words from God came to him and became all He needed during the spiritual drought his people were experiencing. Where are you getting your nourishment from today? You might not be in as tough a place as Jeremiah found himself, but you still need a place to get your spiritual refreshment from today. Verse seven makes it obvious that the real Source for hope in a seemingly hopeless situation is the Lord. Many have left trusting the Lord and have begun to trust their jobs, or their intelligence, or their bank account, or their good health, or their ...

Don't trust a temporary cistern. A cistern in the Bible days was like a holding tank. They would store water in these tanks so when the drought came, they would have a source of water. The problem with these holding tanks and the problem with us putting our trust in something, or someone other than God is that the water did not remain fresh for very long. The Lord is a constant Source of strength for those who put their trust in Him. The reason is because He is God and He is always going to have fresh answers to the challenges you face, or will face. Your job ... intelligence ... bank ... health ... or any other thing will fail you.

The challenge of these verses today is to stay firmly planted near the Source of all help, the Lord Jesus Christ. Others will fail you; He never will. Others have limitations as to what they can offer; He has no limitations. Don't lean on men today for your help. Trust the all-powerful God to be all you will need for this day and its challenges!

Safe in the Potter's Hands – November 14

"'O house of Israel, cannot I do with you as this potter?' saith the LORD, 'Behold, as the clay is in the potter's hand, so are ye in Mine hand, O house of Israel'" (Jeremiah 18:6). The potter's wheel represents a place of transformation for something as useless as clay. Yesterday morning I helped my cousin put up a fence. All morning, as we moved from one post to the next, I spent time trying to get the mud off the bottom of my shoes. God used an illustration here in the book of Jeremiah to show us what He can do with us.

I don't know about you, but there are many times when I feel God has so little to work with when it comes to using me in any way that might benefit the cause of Christ. I have so many flaws. I have so many weaknesses. I have so many sins that I constantly seem to struggle with on a daily basis. The question often comes to my mind, *"God, how can you use someone … something like me?"* Well, the answer comes here in Jeremiah 18. God does not need much to begin the work. He can use a lump of clay to make a beautiful display of His handiwork.

The beauty of this passage is that it is not the value of the clay, but the life-changing power of the hands that mold it! Don't you see today, if God can use a lump of clay, He can certainly use the things you have to give Him today! You are far more valuable than a lump of clay! God did not send His Son to buy back clay. God sent His Son into this world because YOU are a sinner! He sent His Son into this world to rescue YOU from your sinfulness, and your sinful behavior! He loves YOU!

As flawed as you might be, you are so valuable to the Potter that He gave all He had to get you back on the wheel again. Here is the key to this entire passage … stay on the wheel! Stay in a place where God can gently re-make you. Don't resist the hand of the Potter today. Remember, there is plenty of clay in creek beds today that will never resemble a work of art, because they have remained in the creek bed. There are multitudes of people beyond number, who have tremendous potential, but will never amount to what God wanted them to be, because they never allowed God to put them on the potter's wheel. Don't make that mistake today.

It would be a good thing for each of us to stop right now … to take a moment to surrender all we are and all we have to the hand of the Potter. Ask Him to mold and make your life into that vessel that most resembles His plan for us. You will not regret it!

Be Quiet – November 15

When I was a child, and even into my teenage years, I remember hearing the phrase, "*Be quiet and listen, you might learn something.*" Needless to say, I have always been very eager to share my opinion, and still struggle with this today. I have a friend who I think could be a genius. When I am talking to him, he speaks very deliberately and chooses every word with great caution. To a person like me ... well, let's just say I feel the need to help him out, and fill in the word I think he's looking for. Usually when I do that, he simply replies, "*No, that's not what I was thinking.*" I've come to realize his vocabulary is far more expansive than mine, and my few choices do not do justice to the meaning he is looking for. I am trying to learn to be quiet. It's tough for me.

I find that even when I am praying to my Heavenly Father, I can get into a rut of doing all the talking and as a result, doing very little listening. Before you start to worry about me, I will tell you I have never heard an audible voice of God, but I can tell you that He has touched my heart while in prayer in some very specific ways. I know He has led me that way in the past, and I yearn for that same leading in the future. Look at what God told the church in Thessalonica: "*And that ye study to be quiet, and to do your own business, and to work with your own hands, as we commanded you; That ye may walk honestly toward them that are without, and that ye may have lack of nothing*" (I Thessalonians 4:11-12).

It is interesting to me that God starts by telling them to "*study*" to be quiet. That word has the idea of working hard, making it your aim. You see, God knows we tend to talk first, and then think second. God knows that this does not come naturally to us, but we will need to put some effort into it. He then instructs us to "*do your own business.*" My Mom always said, "*Mind your own business.*" I think it's the same thing here. Don't be so worried about what other people are doing today. Get quiet and focus on what God wants you to do! Do the work that He places in your hands to do. Don't spend any time worrying about what others in the world are doing, or not doing; on what others in the church are doing, or not doing. You quietly do the work God has given you to do and He will take care of the details. We are encouraged simply to "*walk honestly,*" especially in regards to those who are not saved. This is great advice to us. Be quiet ... mind your own business ... work hard with your own hands ... do all of this honestly before the unsaved. They will want what you have. They cannot be quiet, because they are not at peace. Show your relationship with God where you go today.

That Christ May Be Glorified – November 16

"Is my life really important? Is there any way I can make a difference in this huge world I live in? What will it matter if I am faithful to the Word of God when so many other people are not around me? Can I make a difference even in the church I attend, or are we all just going through the motions of Christianity?" These are questions I have asked through my lifetime. I ask these kinds of questions because I understand my insignificance in many ways. However ... I am asking these questions based totally on my own human understanding and reasoning.

The Bible says, *"Wherefore also we pray always for you, that our God would count you worthy of this calling, and fulfill all the good pleasure of His goodness, and the work of faith with power: That the name of our Lord Jesus Christ may be glorified in you, and ye in Him, according to the grace of our God and the Lord Jesus Christ"* (II Thessalonians 1:11-12). According to these verses, I have the possibility of actually bringing glory to the name of Christ with my life! I know, it sounds absolutely impossible to think that ... but let me remind you ...

Ø There was a woman who lived in a town called Samaria where no Jew wanted to be found. She had been married five times before and was considering making a sixth attempt when she met Jesus. I'm sure she thought she was insignificant, and had no chance of bringing glory to the name of Christ. After Jesus changed her from the inside – out, she brought the men of the town to hear Him and revival broke out in Samaria.

Ø There was a man possessed by a legion of demons who lived among the tombs, and cut himself repeatedly. The people of the town had tried to tame him, but it proved to be impossible. Jesus met the man, cast out the demons and transformed this man's life. When Jesus was preparing to leave for another town, the man begged to go with Him. Jesus told him to return to his friends/family and show them the great things that were done. I'm sure this man thought his life would have no impact, and certainly no chance of glorifying God. That was before he met Jesus ...

Ø There was a woman who had been a prostitute until she met Jesus. She later bought a costly bottle of perfume and poured it on the feet of Jesus. Even though criticized, she glorified her Savior. I'm sure she felt she would never be able to do that, but her story is in our Bible.

You and I are here now ... it's our turn ... look for the possibilities today!

What Do You Have? – November 17

"He saith unto them, 'How many loaves have ye'" (Mark 6:38a)? When faced with the challenge of feeding over 5,000 people, Jesus asked this question. This is a question I want you to consider for your own personal service to Jesus Christ. I am sure when you trusted Christ as your personal Savior, God's plan was to simply allow you to be a spectator in the arena of your life. God saves us so we can serve Him. Each of us brings a different set of abilities, likes/dislikes, passions, and goals to achieve. Like a body, each of us is different ... but each of us in important.

This story has always caught my attention. Jesus is planning to do something that would shock the people gathered on this mountainside, and it would be a miracle His disciples would never forget (not to mention a little "lad"). They were facing an impossible situation. There were 5,000 men (not sure how many women and children), and only five loaves and two small fishes to feed them all. It is not possible to feed that many people with those very limited resources.

There are times when you will find yourself in the same situation. God is going to put you in situations where you are asked to do something that is far outside your abilities or resources. I believe God likes to do these kinds of things to us to keep us dependent upon Him for what we will need. I am sure there were thoughts running through the disciples minds, like: "There were only five loaves ... there were 5,000 men ... there was no way these five loaves would meet the need!"

Notice Jesus did not ask the disciples to provide the food for the crowd. He simply asked what was available. The only things available were this meager offering of five loaves and two "small" fish. The important lesson for us to learn, and continue learning was that the thing placed in the hands of Jesus was not what was important. The placing of the thing in the hand of Jesus was all that was needed. The value or ability of the things placed in Jesus hand were not the focal point of this story. What Jesus did with those things was what made headlines!

Your gifts and abilities are far more valuable than five pieces of bread! You may have some worries, but He is able! You may have some apprehension about what might happen, but He is able! You might have doubts that anything good could come out of you, but He is able! You and I just need to place all we have in His hand, and watch the multiplication happen.

Wait ... – November 18

"Show me Thy ways, O LORD; teach me Thy paths. Lead me in Thy truth, and teach me: For Thou art the God of my salvation; on Thee do I wait all the day" (Psalm 25:4-5). Lord, show me ... teach me ... lead me ... teach me ... Is this your heart's desire today? Are you sitting at the feet of your Savior asking for direction today? Or, have you already made your list of plans for the day and you are expecting God to fit in to what you have in mind for your life? If you are normal, you have done the second thing. If you are walking with God, you have done the first.

Obviously, the first plan is the best plan. Why not stop what you're doing right now and ask God to show you what He wants for your life today? We often look so far into the future that we miss what God had for us for this day. We are so consumed with what we will become, and where we will go that we don't accomplish the will of God He has given us for this day. The Bible clearly teaches that our lives are like a vapor ... we see it for a very brief time, and then it is gone. Ask God to show you what He wants you to do with your life today.

Ask the Lord to teach you all throughout this day. Ask Him to help your heart to be open to His plan for you. Keep your eyes open for the lessons God has for you today. If your heart is eager to learn, you will improve. If you think you already have all the answers ... you're stuck with what you presently know. The person that is continually learning is continually growing and making themselves more valuable in the end. Don't miss the learning opportunities God will place in front of you today.

Ask the Lord to lead and guide your steps throughout the pitfalls that await you today. Just like the character, "Christian" in John Bunyan's Pilgrim's Progress, there will be many distractions today for you to follow rather than the will of God. Stay firmly focused on the hand of the Master, so He can easily and quickly move your heart to what you need to be doing. Again, ask God to guard your steps so you avoid any wrong moves.

The last part of these verses contains what might be the hardest of all these things ... wait on God for the answers to your challenges. We love to run ahead and see what's in front of us ... wait. We want to know what is one year and five years ahead. God wants us to wait for Him to open and close doors. He wants us to be totally dependent upon Him. Here is where the ultimate victory comes. Trust your God today, and wait for His salvation! It is just ahead of you!

No Vision Will Cost You – November 19

God promised the Israelites He would lead them out of the bondage of Egypt. They had been there 400+ years, and much of that time as slaves. The focus of all the Jews was the Promised Land that God told them would be theirs ... or was that their focus? I would think if I had been in a strange land for so long, I would not be able to wait to escape! Or, would I? Would I too, become so accustomed to the foods, the customs, and the comforts of that lifestyle that I would be like the Israelites in the wilderness ... complaining of missing the things they had left behind in Egypt?

When the time came, and Moses glimpsed the Promise Land, he sent a man of valor from each of the twelve tribes into the land God had promised. He gave them specific instructions to see what was there and to return with a report. Ten of these men gave a negative report about the impossibilities that faced them in that land. Two of the men had vision, and clearly communicated they thought the land was theirs to be conquered. This lack of vision cost, not only the ten men, but all who were in their families over twenty-years of age.

Today, I read a sad verse in the book of Numbers. After counting the people from the twelve tribes, the Bible says, *"But among these there was not a man of them whom Moses and Aaron the priest numbered when they numbered the children of Israel in the wilderness of Sinai"* (Numbers 26:64). In other words, none of the family members of those ten tribes were about to step into the Promised Land. Why? Their brave spies were men without a vision. God's punishment was that their families over the age of twenty at the time of the first look into the Promised Land had died in the wilderness.

Their lack of vision cost not only them, but their families in a tremendous way. How is you vision of the promises God has made to you in the Bible today? Do you find yourself doubting God's ability to conquer the "giants" and the "walled cities" in front of you? Don't follow the example of these men and their families. Be people of vision today! Trust your God! He is able to conquer any challenge you find in front of you today! He was able to bring Israel into the Promised Land. Think about it ... those same giants and walled cities were still there forty years later! God enabled Israel to take that land then, and He is well able to take care of you today. You are required to have vision enough to trust Him! He is able!

My Hiding Place – November 20

"The LORD is my Light and my Salvation; whom shall I fear? The LORD is the strength of my life; of whom shall I be afraid (Psalm 27:1)?

When the wicked, even mine enemies and my foes, came upon me to eat up my flesh, they stumbled and fell (27:2).

Though a host should encamp against me, my heart shall not fear: Though war should rise against me, in this will I be confident (27:3).

One thing have I desired of the LORD, that will I seek after; that I may dwell in the house of the LORD all the days of my life, to behold the beauty of the LORD, and to inquire in His temple (27:4).

For in the time of trouble He shall hide me in His pavilion: In the secret of His tabernacle shall He hide me; He shall set me up upon a rock (27:5)."

Do you know Him? No, I mean really know Him. Troubles will come to every person in this world. When the troubles come in your life, you will see where you really put your trust. You can tell people to trust God when you are having it good, or easy. It is quite another thing for you to trust God when the troubles pull up at your front door. Do you really know Him?

When difficulties come to you, is God the first Person you turn to for help? Do you depend more on your family, friends, teachers, pastor, or even a stranger for your help? for your counsel? There is only One Person I know Who can change the course of the direction of your life ... it is God Himself. I want to encourage you to get to know this God David wrote about in Psalm 27.

David did not find out God was a good hiding place while living in the palace ... he discovered it while hiding out in the caves while running away from Saul. He realized the truth of it when Saul came into that very cave where he was hiding and fell asleep. David found God to be a resting place in the middle of the battles of life. Instead of complaining today about all the bad things you think are happening to you, why not look for the "resting place" in the midst of all the trouble.

If you will look for it, you are going to find God waiting to help you. If you insist on running to others for comfort and consolation in trouble, you will just find they have a boat-load of trouble of their own, and you will begin to share more trouble. Run to the Rock of your salvation today! Run to the "King of Glory" (Psalm 24:10). Don't throw your hands up and lose hope today. There is a God Who has not moved, and He is ready to help you in your time of need today. Run to Him! He will never fail you!

Use What God Gives You – November 21

"A man's gift maketh room for him, and bringeth him before great men" (Proverbs 18:16).

One of the worst things we can do is to try to get everyone to fit into what we think they ought to do. We love to tell other people what we think they should do, when that is really none of our business. God has uniquely made and gifted each of us to be used in unique ways. If we were all the same, we would be horribly lacking in many areas. Because we are all different, we have the potential of functioning very well when working together. The Apostle Paul used the illustration of us being different body parts in I Corinthians 12. It is a wonderful study, and can explain this far better than I can.

When I read Proverbs 18:16 today, I realized each man has a gift that has been placed in our life. According to this verse, that gift we have been given will make a place for us in the world we are living. It will place us before *"great men."* There are probably times in your daily life when you feel very insignificant, and wonder why you are here on this earth. The answer lies in the gift(s) God has given you. Anything good that can come from your life will be a result of what God has placed within you that He expects you to use for His glory.

Many years ago, God touched my heart with the need for Deaf people to be able to see the Gospel through Sign Language on my hands. I was apprehensive in the beginning years, because I have never been good at learning a foreign language. It is not something that comes easy for me (it still does not). But, I began the process of learning the language and asking God for opportunities to use the language to tell Deaf how to go to Heaven. I praise the Lord, as I look at where we have gone in working with the Deaf, and where we are going ... it simply amazes me! For more than thirteen years, we have been serving the Lord in attempting to reach and teach the Deaf all over the northeastern states of the U.S., in Eastern Canada, and in Ukraine!

How is that possible? The answer is that it has nothing to do with us, and everything to do with us simply taking the gift which has been given to us, and *"making room"* for it in our lives. All the blessings we have experienced after that have been totally of the Lord! We simply praise God for all He has enabled us to do, and then for the opportunities to stand before *"great men"* and use what He has blessed us with! Use what you have for Him!

Thank You God – November 22

"I thank God through Jesus Christ our Lord ..." (Romans 7:25a).

Thanks be to God ... Thank You so much for allowing me to know You God ... Thank You for caring about me, and even the smallest needs no one else knew about ... Thank You for reaching out from Heaven to the pit of my sin to pull me up from the depths of Hell I was headed to ... Thank You for giving me a Bible in my own language ... Thank You for giving me faithful Bible teachers to help me understand the Word You gave me ... Thank You for providing me with a Pastor who loves the Word and faithfully challenges me to follow it ... Thank You for sending Evangelists into my life to push me out of my comfort zone and into the world to share the Gospel ... Thank You for saving people after I have showed them the way to Heaven from Your Word ... Thank you for convicting my heart when I have wandered from the path You have planned for me, and thank You for being patient to draw me back to Yourself ... Thank You for the abilities to see, to hear, to touch, and to taste ... Thank You for allowing me to be around people who do not have these same blessings to help me to appreciate them more ... Thank You for giving me parents who have loved me for my whole life ... Thank You for giving us children and grandchildren who we can love for their whole lives ... Thank You for giving me a warm, dry and safe home to come back to ... Thank You for giving our children the same salvation you offered to us ... Thank You for meeting with me every morning around Your Word ... Thank you for the blessing of knowing the truths from Your heart that You put on the pages of my Bible ... Thank You for the abilities You have blessed me with ... Thank You for the beauty around me and the changing of seasons I have the privilege to witness every year ... Thank You for godly friends who challenge me to walk with you every day, and who have the courage to stand up to me if they see me going the wrong way ... Thank You for a godly wife of thirty-seven years ... Thank You for a godly father and mother-in-law ... Thank You for the ability to speak a language I did not grow up with, with my hands so precious Deaf folks can understand the Word of God and trust You too ... Thank You for clean water and air ... Thank You for providing every need I have had, and my family has had for all these years ... Thank You for touching my heart with the needs of others ... Thank You for allowing me to write a devotional every day with the truths You have touched my heart with that day. God ... it seems small, but I want to say, "Thank You," for all you have done for me! I love you!

Joy in the Morning – November 23

Every person who has ever lived has had to cope with problems. It seems sometimes we wake up facing problems, and then spend our whole day trying to solve them. I'm sure there are times when you just wish you could have a day without anything going wrong; without anyone complaining about what you have done, or are doing. The Bible tells us we are going to have problems in this life. That is not the greatest promise, but the one that follows is. *"Sing unto the LORD, O ye saints of His, and give thanks at the remembrance of His holiness. For His anger endureth but a moment; in His favor is life: Weeping may endure for a night, but joy cometh in the morning"* (Psalm 30:4-5).

If God is getting angry at us, it is because we are allowing the sin He hates to rule in our lives. God is righteous and is justified to have anger when we turn our back to Him. There is a chastening, or a disciplining that comes when we violate the principles of the Word of God. However, as this writer here says, it is only temporary. Let me encourage you today to realize the difficulties you may be facing today, can result in joy for tomorrow if you have the right reaction to them.

I have written before about some of the discipline I received as a young boy. I never liked the discipline then. As a matter of fact, I can remember begging, and making incredible promises that I would live a life of perfection if I could just avoid one spanking. Thankfully, my mother was smarter than me and knew I needed the spanking to help me to experience the joy later. Today I am a father/grandfather and I can tell you with a totally honest heart that I am very thankful my parents paid the price to discipline me as a young boy. Without discipline as a young boy, I hate to think about where I would be today. God has a righteous anger toward sin. We should thank Him that He will share that with us when we walk in opposition to His will.

Oh, I know at the time it is tough, but in the *"morning"* there will be rejoicing if we have the right attitude. Don't fight against the discipline of God in your life. Repent, accept the consequences, and make adjustments so you will do better the next time you face that same temptation. When I coached sports, I told my players there are two kinds of people in the world. The loser makes excuses when scolded; the winner accepts responsibility and then makes adjustments. There can be joy in the morning for you, if you will have the proper reaction to the discipline. Be a winner today!

A Good Thing – November 24

November 24, 1979 God gave me a help-meet. The Bible says when a man finds a wife, he finds a *"good thing."* Now ladies, don't get upset about the word *"thing."* I would argue slightly with the word *"good."* When I was twenty-two I married a girl who was only twenty. Many times in recent years I have wondered what her parents must have been thinking. They had raised this young lady to have a fear of God; to be faithful to her church; to love a Savior Who gave His life for her; and had taught her to love and respect her future husband. I would call that a *"great thing."*

On our wedding day, we claimed a verse that many couples may have claimed as well, but we have never forgotten Psalm 34:3. *"O magnify the LORD with me, and let us exalt His name together."* I will be the first to admit to you we have not always magnified the Lord. There have been failures on both our parts through the years, but like anything else, success will always involve some pitfalls along the way. I praise God that today we celebrate over thirty-five years together ...still holding hands ... still in love ... still reaching for the goal of *"exalting His name together."* Since it is my anniversary, I would like to ask for grace from you to share more than one verse.

"Through wisdom is a house builded; and by understanding it is estab-lished: and by knowledge shall the chambers be filled with all precious and pleasant riches" (Proverbs 24:4-5). When I read these verses this morning, I was reminded that building a house takes a great deal of work and effort. It will involve hitting your thumb a few times with a hammer ... it will involve a few wrong measurements where things need to be started all over again. Building a home is no different. There are far too many people who begin to build a home, but at the first signs of trouble, they stop the building and leave a house unfinished.

I have also noticed a good builder will continue building in spite of bad weather and adverse circumstances. I have seen some incredible things built when the proper materials were not available, and the conditions were not perfect. Follow the example of the Master Builder. God continues to work on us, even though we have faults and flaws. His faithfulness is nev-er-ending. If you and I will build our lives attempting to exalt His name, He will build something that will last through the tests of time. *"If thou faint in the day of adversity, thy strength is small"* (Proverbs 24:11).

Don't Forget – November 25

"Yet did not the chief butler remember Joseph, but forgat him" (Genesis 40:23).

Has someone done something nice for you, or has helped you and you never said, *"Thank you?"* Have you ever done something nice for someone else and had them totally ignore you and not even whisper a short, *"Thanks?"* This is the season for giving thanks. Really, every day we have life is a good day for thanking someone, including God. I often take time to reflect on how good God has been to me over my life time. He allowed me to be born into the home of a saved man and his wife. He allowed me to be raised by these people who loved God and loved me. He gave me a wonderful sister, a good home, a place to run to when the storms of life were brewing. God then gave me a wonderful wife and four wonderful children. He provided saved partners for each of our children, and now we enjoy nine wonderful grandchildren!

We have been blessed with some of the greatest friends anyone could ever want in the world. I am amazed at how many people come running to help Terry and me when we need something. God has placed some of the sweetest, most gifted people in the world within our sphere of friends. We have had, like everyone else, some very difficult times when we really needed our friends. We have seen them run to us while many others were running away from us. We have had the opportunity to run to our friends as well, and this is a great blessing!

We have been blessed with some of the greatest advisors any people could ever have. I'm a bit of a dreamer. God has allowed us to have people to come along side us who know how to make those dreams become reality. As John Maxwell said, *"Teamwork makes the dream work!"* We have experienced that over and over again. There have been many things that were outside my knowledge or ability, and God has drawn just the right person to us to help at the exact right time.

Joseph interpreted the butlers dream, but the butler forgot him (for two years), and forgot to say *"Thank you."* I don't want to be guilty of that today. I thank you for reading this devotional regularly. I thank you for investing in my life and making a difference for me. I thank you for helping me to stay accountable to God in trying to practice in my daily life what I put on these pages each day. I thank God He is working in our lives, and He has given us an inexhaustible book to study together!

Most Important – November 26

When Jesus was asked which commandment was the first of all (meaning the most important), He replied: *"And thou shalt love the Lord thy God with all thy heart, and with all thy soul, and with all thy mind, and with all thy strength; this is the first commandment. And the second is like, namely this, Thou shalt love thy neighbor as thyself. There is none other commandment greater than these"* (Mark 12:30-31).

Your mind might argue that last phrase, *"There is none other command-ment greater than these."* Think about it for a moment or two. If we love the Lord our God with all our heart, soul, mind and strength would we ever consider replacing Him with an idol ... making an idol ... taking His name in vain ... not setting aside a day for focusing on Him ... dishonor our par-ents ... killing someone .... adultery ... stealing ... lying about someone else ... coveting? No!

The simplicity of Scripture has always amazed me! It seems we like to complicate things with details and questions and challenges. If we would simply take the Word of God as it is, in its simplicity, there would be an undeniable spiritual depth to our lives. Think about you reply to this kind of question, if you did not know this passage in the Bible. Your answer might long and complicated. Jesus brought the attention directly where it belonged. Today, as in Jesus' day, the most important thing you and I can do is to love the Lord with all our heart, soul, mind, and strength! Are you doing it today? Is there any part of you that you are holding back from total and absolute surrender to Him today?

Have you come to Him offering your heart? Are the things you are passionate about the same as the things He is passionate about? Have you offered Him your soul – the center of your being? Is your motivation for living today that you will accomplish all He designed you to do? Have you offered Him your mind today? Will your thoughts be in line with His thoughts for you today, or will you allow the clutter of sin and the clamor of the world to replace them? Have you offered your strength to God uncon-ditionally today? Are you willing to put your hand to the plow God has placed before you and work in the field of ministry that is before you; or will you make excuses for sitting of the couch of apathy while others struggle to do the work?

Jesus made it clear that loving God ... and loving those He has put next to us is His priority for our lives today. Serve Him whole-heartedly today!

Undeserved Grace – November 27

In the midst of Job's sufferings, he asked this good question: "*I know it is so of a truth: but how should man be just with God*" (Job 9:2)? Pause to think about that question for a moment. Consider the holiness of God first. He has no sin; has never had a sinful thought; never has done anything motivated by selfishness; never lashed out in anger on an impulse for something we had done against Him … He is perfect! Now consider yourself. You have sin; you have sinful thoughts on a daily basis; you sin every day; you are motivated by your selfishness to get all you can while you can; you react negatively to those who do not do what you would like them to do … you are a sinner.

With all this being known to God, He reached out to you and me. Just as it hit Job in his time of testing, we need to consider the fact that left to ourselves, we have nothing that is redeeming … nothing that is attractive to God … nothing that would earn us a right standing with Him. It is tragic how completely Satan has blinded men to believe they can somehow please God by being a religious person. He has tricked them into thinking if they go to church on a fairly regular basis that they will somehow earn their way into Heaven. What a liar the Devil is!

I realize today there is nothing I can do, say, think, or give that will earn my way into Heaven on my own! I realize today if I am going to touch Heaven, I must have the help of Almighty God to do that! What a joy to realize from the depths of despair … from this unlovely reality I am a sinner to my very core … my sin must be judged, and it separates me from a righteous God … that there is hope. There is hope because of God. 100% because of God … nothing to do with me!

I am thankful today when I came to the place Job described, I found the grace and mercy of God waiting for me. His grace offered a pure sacrifice for my sin in His Son. He offered me what I did not deserve, and could not earn! His mercy offered me a freedom from my debt of sin. Wow! He declared me righteous when I trusted His Son, and with that came a boatload of His mercy that is new every morning for me. Oh, I need mercy so much each day I live. I would love to tell you I have advanced to the place where I do not sin anymore … that would be a lie that you would know for sure as you watch me live. No … I agree with Job. No man can be just with God … but God came to be just with us! Thank God today for Jesus. Thank God for that perfect sacrifice for your sin!

Big Promises – November 28

Have you ever been stirred to make a decision in church and later you never followed through? I can remember walking down the aisle to the altar and pouring my heart out to God with some very serious and great promises. I will tell you right now I was completely serious about the promises I made to God during those times. I can remember promising God I would read my Bible every day of my life when I was a teenager. I must tell you I failed on that promise over and over again. But there is something I want to touch on today that will not follow the path of failure, but of success.

Peter made grandiose promises to Jesus in the last hours just prior to the crucifixion. His deepest promise was this: *"But Peter said unto Him, 'Although all shall be offended, yet will not I'"* (Mark 14:29). Jesus informed Peter his promise would fail before the next morning! Peter followed with this more powerful promise: *"But he spake the more vehemently, 'If I should die with Thee, I will not deny Thee in any wise.' Likewise also said they all"* (Mark 14:31).

Peter is a perfect picture of me and my failed promises. I could dwell on this part of the story for a long time, but I want you to see something I hope will be an encouragement for you today. Jesus knew all that would happen in the hours, and days ahead. He knew full well about the cross. He knew everything about the cost of the crucifixion. He knew about the cold grave His body would be laid in, and the guards who would surround the mouth of it. He also knew about the first day of the next week and the resurrection. He knew the disciples would become apostles, and Peter would be the unofficial leader of the group.

Here's my point for today: Jesus knew about Peter's failure in denials … He also knew what he would learn from those failures, and He knew the memory of those failures would help Peter to stand tall when the time came. God knows when you make a promise to Him and then fail, that that is not the end of the story. You see, we serve a God of the second, and third, and fourth, and infinity chance! We have a God Who has perfected making something out of nothing. Don't stop making promises to God! If you fail in that promise, don't stop trying … He will not stop pulling for you to do what you promised. When I was a teenager, I would never have imagined I would be able to say I have read the Bible through each year for over thirty years! With God's help, all things are possible. Keep promising!

Hold On! – November 29

There is a great deal of pressure on every Christian today to compromise and to "bend" a little when it comes to areas of what we believe. Have you ever noticed those who oppose Christianity are not asked to "bend" or to compromise what they believe? We are given a strong admonition from the Word of God to hold on! As a matter of fact, this challenge was originally given by the Apostle Paul to the younger preacher, Timothy as Paul was nearing the end of his life here on earth. He said these strong words to Timothy then and to us now: "*...I know Whom I have believed, and am persuaded that He is able to keep that which I have committed unto Him against that day. Hold fast the form of sound words, which thou hast heard of me, in faith and love which is in Christ Jesus. That good thing which was committed unto thee keep by the Holy Ghost which abideth in us*" (II Timothy 1:12-14).

There is a great sense of power and triumph in these words Paul spoke to Timothy. He wrote the words from a prison in Rome. That prison would be the last home for Paul on this earth. Despite his imprisonment, and the pressures of his life, he still penned these powerful words of victory. It all stemmed from what he stated in verse twelve. He had a firm knowledge of the Person he has entrusted his eternal destiny to. He was not wavering at all about Jesus' ability to keep him saved. He did not doubt the incredible saving power of the risen Savior. Remember, he had met Jesus on a road to Damascus (as Saul of Tarsus), and he knew the reality of the risen Savior. He was confident God could take care of anything he was facing here on this earth. Do you have that confidence today? Jesus is just as alive and powerful today as he was when Saul met Him on that road to Damascus. Trust Him completely today. Hold on to Him!

Hold on to "*sound words.*" Don't let someone who is slick convince you that what you have learned from your own study of the Word of God is not true. Read your Bible. Ask the Holy Spirit to guide you into the truth of it, and then stand strongly on what He teaches you. Don't allow the cares of this world to push you off what you know the Bible teaches and says today. The Holy Spirit lives within you! He is far superior to the Devil that opposes you from the outside. Don't enter the battle alone. Walk in the Spirit ... trust the Word of God ... don't lean on your understanding, but fully depend on the Word of God. You and I will see the victory Paul had there in that prison in Rome; if we will completely sell out to the God he served! Hold on today! Don't lose your focus! Praise God He is real!

Send Out the Search Party – November 30

"'For I know the thoughts that I think toward you,' saith the LORD, 'thoughts of peace, and not of evil, to give you an expected end. Then shall ye call upon Me and ye shall go and pray unto Me, and I will hearken unto you. And ye shall seek Me, and find Me, when ye shall search for Me with all your heart. And I will be found of you,' saith the LORD" (Jeremiah 29:11-14a).

What an incredible set of verses! If you ever feel you are not important, read these verses again. God tells each of us He thinks about us. He not only thinks about us, but His thoughts for us are for peace and not evil. In other words, the idea that God is some mean and cruel Judge just waiting to "zap" us for any sin against Him is simply not true. His thoughts for us are for peace. He wants us to experience His peace in this world of turmoil.

He wants us to have peace, but we will not have it if we do not do our part. Notice He says in verse twelve we need to "*call*" on Him, and "*pray*" to Him. Verse thirteen says we need to "*seek*" and "*search*" for Him. You see, this peace does not simply come floating down from Heaven and rest upon your shoulders. If we want this peace to be evident and apparent in our lives, we need to get busy in pursuing an active relationship with our God!

Think about how much time you spend in a normal day *calling* on the Lord. We are very quick to pick up our phone and call our friends/family when we have a problem, but how many times do we stop what we are doing and *pray* to our Heavenly Father, asking for His help? God says if we want the peace He can offer, there needs to be a communication between Himself and the believer for it to come to pass. Just yesterday I was thinking about a burden I have for a specific group of people in my life. I was in deep thought about what I could do to help them become more faithful to God when a unique idea hit my mind ... I should pray for them! Wow! How intelligent I am! Not really ... I struggle with just stopping what I am doing and asking God to step in for me.

I also am challenged from these verses to spend more time *seeking* and *searching* for the things my Heavenly Father wants from me. I want to follow Him ... I want to walk so closely to Him that when He stops quickly, I will run into Him ... I want to constantly dig in the Word of God to be able to understand my Father better. I want to be actively involved in *searching* for what God wants me to find. Join me today!

MONTH OF
December

Unquenchable Thirst – December 1

"O God, Thou art my God; early will I seek Thee: my soul thirsteth for Thee, my flesh longeth for Thee in a dry and thirsty land, where no water is" (Psalm 63:1).

I remember many times when I was so thirsty I would have given almost anything for a cold glass of water. There was one summer when we were in Ukraine helping with a Deaf Camp that comes to my mind. The temperature rose above 100 degrees for most of the week we were out at camp. That was not the norm for the area, but we also met with some cultural challenges that week as well. Many Ukrainians don't like fans or air conditioning. We "spoiled Americans" were dreaming of AC when we finally did get to sleep. The other thing that is unique to America is that we like ice in our drinks in the summer. Ukrainians don't follow that line of thinking either. I remember going to town with my missionary friend. We went into the grocery store, and I saw a refrigerator with soda's stacked in them. I quickly ran to the glass door, and opened it ... only to find only the light worked ... there was no refrigeration ... all the sodas were warm. All I wanted was an ice-cold drink of water!

This chapter was written by David when he was in the wilderness of Judah. This is a very dry and arid area of Israel. He wrote about a spiritual thirst that was demonstrated by a physical thirst he was surely experiencing. What about you and me today? David wrote about a thirst for God in a time when the only Scriptures available to him were the writings of Moses and the first five books of the Bible. We have the complete sixty-six book set of the Word of God! There is not a word missing! We have God's heart visible on the pages of our Bibles! Do we have this thirst for His Word today?

I want this verse to be my hearts cry every day of my life! I want to have an insatiable thirst for time with my Heavenly Father. I want His Word to be the thing that quenches the longings of my soul. I want to run to Him for everything I need, and trust Him completely to meet all the needs I have. I want to be like Job in times of challenge, and trust God even when I cannot see or understand His plan for me. I want to do more than write these devotionals, or give a testimony in my church. I actually want to consume the Words of God daily, and I want to be consumed by the Words of God when I read. I want to continue to thirst for more knowledge about my God. I want to be spiritually challenged to become the man He wants me to be!

A Good Testimony – December 2

"I said, 'I will take heed to my ways, that I sin not with my tongue: I will keep my mouth with a bridle, while the wicked is before me" (Psalm 39:1).

I do not think we understand how important our testimony is before those who are without Jesus. I have heard all my life the greatest witnessing tool we have is our own personal testimony. Here the psalmist makes it clear the things we do ... the words we speak have a powerful impact on the "*wicked*" who are in front of us. Today is a new day, with new opportunities, and new challenges. Will you demonstrate godliness before the ungodly today which will impact their lives for Christ?

When I was in Jr. and Sr. High school, I had one guy who was my "best-friend." Truthfully, he was like a brother to me. He spent a great deal of time at my house, and I spent a good bit of time at his house. We were together almost every day of our lives from the ninth grade on. My best-friend was not saved. I remember being so burdened for him I felt compelled to witness to him at every opportunity. We reached a point when he told me he had heard enough about salvation and Christ from me. He told me he knew what I believed, and he did not want to hear any more. I began to pray for him at that point (honoring his wishes, I did not "push" him anymore).

After two years of praying for my friend, I invited him to a concert; he came. There the Gospel was presented and my best-friend became my brother in Christ. He was saved and his life style radically changed. I asked him later what was different that night from all the other times I had told him about the Gospel. I asked him what made him decide that night to trust Christ when he resisted before. His answer was simple ... "I knew the truth before, but when I saw that many people who were so sold out to the Gospel in one place, I knew it was true." Praise God for the power of a testimony.

Be careful not to miss an important part of this verse today. Use your testimony today for the honor and glory of God, but make sure what comes out of your mouth matches the way you live. As powerful as a testimony can be to an unsaved person; if your preaching does not match your practice, you are hurting the testimony of Christ. Your walk and your talk need to match for the power of God to be evident in your testimony. My best-friend became one of the greatest witnesses in our High School after his salvation. The reason was that his walk drastically changed, and others were interested to hear why. Speak up today and live right!

Dividends from Your Bible – December 3

"My son, forget not My law; but let thine heart keep My command-
ments: For length of days, and long life, and peace, shall they add to thee"
(Proverbs 3:1-2).

How much clearer could God make this thing of spending time in your
Bible? He tells us clearly time spent in the Word of God is time well spent.
If you plant the seeds of the Word, you will grow length of days ... long
life ... and peace. Who wouldn't want those things in our world today?
It is funny to me how much the world searches for these things and finds
them to be constantly just outside their reach. Let's consider each of these
individually today.

"Length of days" – we have people who try to fill their days with more
and more "stuff" in order to make more money, or to get more done. If
you will spend a bit of time in the Word of God, I believe it will help you
to make better use of the time you have in each day. You will accomplish
more in a normal day if you will give God some time alone with you in His
Word. If you neglect the Word of God, I believe you will find yourself in
the same "rat race" the rest of the world is in ... running around that wheel
and getting nowhere.

"Long life" – it is amazing to me how many doctors are trying to find
the secret to long life, and failing while they do it. Ponce de Leon searched
for the "Fountain of Youth," and died trying to find it. Men/women have
been searching for it ever since. The answer to having a long life is found
in giving time to the Word of God. I don't believe this means you will live
more days; I believe it means you will accomplish more with the days you
have than you will without the influence of the Word of God.

"Peace" – if there is one united cry around the globe today, it would
be for peace. I have friends in Ukraine who are yearning for peace in their
country. Here in the states, we would love to see peace between the different
races of people who constantly seem to be fighting one another. There will
be a promise of peace from Anti-Christ that will draw many to him during
the seven-year Tribulation period. Men/women are longing for peace today.
Reading your Bible faithfully will give you a peace the world cannot give,
and that Anti-Christ cannot give. God is the Author of peace, and He offers
it to us on the pages of His Bible.

Get into the Word of God – length of days, long life, and peace
await you.

Don't Drop the Baton – December 4

When I was in High School I had the privilege of running on our track team. I ran three different races, but my favorite was called the 880 Relay (today it would be called the 800 meter relay). This was a race that involved four team members. Each runner ran around half of the track (or 220 yards). Each of the four depended on the other three to do their part in the race. Each of us on this team had a goal to beat the other runners we were facing so the other three men on our team had a better chance to win. I recall one race in particular when I was the fourth runner on our team. The first three guys on our team were getting beat pretty bad. I watched as the third leg of the team turned the corner coming towards me. I noticed the other team was leading by about ten yards. Just as the other team was handing the baton between their third and fourth runners, I saw the baton drop and hit the ground. My third runner and I made a clean hand-off and our team won the race that day!

We believers are also in a race in this life. There have been people who have blazed a trail before us. They have given us the path we should run on, and they have passed the baton to us. It is important to them that we hold onto that baton and finish the race in front of us. It is also important to those we will hand the baton off to that we maintain the right course. It is also important we encourage those we will hand off to that they realize the importance of running their leg successfully as well. The Apostle Paul wrote to his young protégé, Timothy these simple, yet powerful words: "*I have fought a good fight, I have finished my course, I have kept the faith*" (II Timothy 4:7). Paul was saying, "*I have run as far as I could; now it is your turn. Don't drop the baton!*" I can't help but think the "*great cloud of witnesses*" spoken of in Hebrews 12:1 are not there watching what we will do today, and cheering for us to hold onto the baton until we can hand it off to the next person. You and I might not feel that important, but I can tell you from experience … every member of the relay team is vital to the success of the other members. One runner cannot complete the course alone. The race demands teamwork for success!

You might be a parent who is responsible to hand the baton to your children. You might be a child who is responsible to accept the baton and run forward into the future. You might be a friend who encourages your other friends to live for God. You might be a student who receives the knowledge from your teacher. You might be the stranger who explains how to get to Heaven. Wherever you are today … don't drop the baton!

Nothing Too Hard for God – December 5

"Ah Lord God! Behold, Thou hast made the heaven and the earth by Thy great power and stretched out arm, and there is nothing too hard for Thee" (Jeremiah 32:17). *"'Behold, I am the LORD, the God of all flesh: Is there anything too hard for Me'"* (Jeremiah 32:27)? In a day when it seems there are multiple things too hard for us to handle, this statement and question in Jeremiah's prophesy is especially comforting to me. There is a story of a group of passengers on a flight across the country. They began to hit some turbulence, and passengers started to become panic-stricken. As the turbulence increased, so did the number of panicked passengers. One lady noticed one little boy remained totally calm through the entire traumatic situation. When she asked him how he could remain so calm, he simply answered; *"My Dad is the pilot."* He was at peace because he had total confidence in the one who was controlling the plane.

Please don't forget our Father is in control no matter how much turbulence this life has in store for us. Storms will come in any life. Hard times will press upon all of us. Difficulties will see insurmountable at times. Take comfort knowing your Heavenly Father is in control. Take comfort there is nothing that will come to your life that is too hard for Him. After all, He is the One Who stretched out His arm and in great power made the universe. He is also the One Who stretched out His arms on the cross to do the impossible. He removed your sin-debt when Jesus died in your place. No religion could accomplish this. No pastor could offer this. No amount of good works can satisfy the righteous demand of God.

The Israelites must have felt they were in a hopeless situation with the Egyptians closing in and the Red Sea on the other side … but we know what God did there. Daniel must have felt a little uneasy as he made his way through the hungry lions in that den … but we know what God did there. Shadrach, Meshach and Abednego must have felt a little tense as they stepped into the fiery furnace … but we know what God did there. David must have felt somewhat uneasy looking at the heavily armored giant in the valley … but we know what God did there. Elijah must have felt outnumbered by the 400 prophets and the 450 priests of Baal on Mt. Carmel … but we know how God brought fire down from Heaven. Are you getting the picture? I could name more, but I'm running out of space. Your story and mine can be added to these if we will simply rest in our God. Trust Him today, and write your own story of success in the face of failure. This is our time to serve God. Depend on Him and live for Him today!

Why Don't You Ever Call? – December 6

Usually when I call one of my friends, the first thing he says to me is something like, "*I had not heard from you for so long that I thought you had died.*" He's exaggerating, but I wonder how many times God feels this way with good reason. How many days can we go without spending some time with God alone in prayer? Communication in any relationship is one of the key parts to having success. In school, if you are understanding the teacher and communicating well, you will have a good grade. In business, if you have open communication and clear exchange of ideas you will also have success in business. In your family, if you communicate well with your husband / wife, you will have a happy home. If parents and children are able to express their hearts to each other there will be harmony in that home.

Your relationship with God is no different. He said, "*Call unto Me, and I will answer thee, and show thee great and mighty things, which thou knowest not*" (Jeremiah 33:3). I can almost hear God begging us to spend time with Him. I was reading an interesting book recently, and the thought was proposed in the book that our time alone with God not only benefits us (which it does), but it also is something God wants from us. Let me explain … Why did God create man? He created Adam for the pleasure of inter-action with him. Everything was going great until sin entered the picture. But, before sin came on the scene, God enjoyed the open and honest communication with Adam and Eve. I am sure when Adam and Eve sinned, it grieved their hearts … but I think it probably grieved the heart of God even more. His fellowship with man was now broken.

God provided His only-begotten Son to build a bridge between you and Him through the salvation by His shed blood. He still wants that communication with you on a daily basis. The time you spend in prayer, is a time for you to express your heart and burdens to God. That time in prayer is also a time for God to communicate His heart and burden with you. In other words, God yearns for that time in prayer with us every day just as much we should. It is a mutually beneficial time – a time that is good for us (which we know), and also a time that is good for God (He seeks that fellowship with you). When I hear my friend's voice on the phone, it brings joy to my heart. When I speak with my friends in a different country over the computer, it brings me joy. Why should my communication with God be any less important to me? Call on Him … He is waiting to hear from you! Let Him know the burdens and joys of your heart … He wants to share in them with you! He loves you!

Obey Him! He Is God! – December 7

"Know therefore this day, and consider it in thing heart, that the LORD He is God in Heaven above, and upon the earth beneath: There is none else. Thou shalt keep therefore His statutes, and His commandments, which I command thee this day, that it may go well with thee, and with thy children after thee, and that thou mayest prolong thy days upon the earth, which the LORD thy God giveth thee, forever" (Deuteronomy 4:39-40).

I think God is the only Person Who can say, *"Because I say so ..."* and it really is true. I remember when our children were younger and in that stage when they were constantly asking *"Why?"* about everything. I would do my best to answer all the questions until I realized there was never going to be an end (that mixed with the fact I did not know the answers), and I would try to cut them short by saying, *"Because I say so."* When I said that, it did not necessarily carry the weight of intelligence and experience needed. When God says it, it's time to stop asking questions.

In the passage written above, I love the phrase that comes at the end of verse thirty-nine. *"There is none else."* In other words, when God speaks, we do not need a second opinion ... or do we? Why is it we question the clear teaching of the Word of God? Why is it when the Bible convicts our soul we try to find an excuse for our behavior, instead of confessing our sin; repenting of it; and forsaking it? Why is it when others speak about our God in condescending ways we allow them to get away with it, without standing up for Him? Why is it when we have the opportunity to tell someone God in Heaven reached down to us with His very own Son, we often balk and miss the opportunities?

Obedience to our God and His Word will result in blessings ... not only for you, but for your children and into the future! Why would we not acknowledge our God in everyday life? Why is it we seem to be far more concerned with what others think about us than we do what God thinks about us? I believe it is time for those of us who are Christians to stand up and begin to serve our God like He is God and there is none else! It's time to stop playing the game of Christianity and begin to live a Spirit-filled life that will demonstrate to those we meet on a daily basis that God is more than a curse word. I think it was the same in the days of Moses. God was depending on Israel to stand for Him and let the world see what He could do for a nation that followed Him. Decide to stand for your God today. Don't allow the world to miss this wonderful God we serve!

God is God – December 8

Of all the relationships we have on this earth, God has the right to expect our whole hearted devotion to Him. After all, He made us ... we turned our back on Him ... He sent His perfect Son to die in our place, and for our sins ... Jesus rose from the dead conquering our sin and death ... He gave everything for us ... the least we can do is love and obey Him. *"For the LORD thy God is a consuming fire, even a jealous God"* (Deuteronomy 4:24).

Many times when I read this verse, I am thinking about those who completely deny God and shake their finger at Him. The reality is this verse was written to the children of Israel, the chosen ones of God. This statement of reminder was to this group of people who had His laws; who carried His name; who were responsible to show a world that was polytheistic (believing in multiple and many gods) there is only One God. This passage was written to a group of people who were supposed to be followers of God. Something happened to them ... even though they had the advantage of having His laws, and seeing His hand leading them, and His protection in battle, they still were being drawn into the false teachings of those around them.

Those of us reading this today have had the advantage of holding the entire sixty-six books of the Bible in our hand; written in our language; with study tools and preachers/teachers to explain all its details to us; and yet, we still play around with the philosophies of the world today. We have set up our church services, our music, the way we dress, the attitudes toward sin ... on what the "demographics" tell us rather than what God says is right and true. Rather than getting on our knees before God to beg Him for wisdom about how to build our churches, and how to most effectively minister to people, we are raising our finger to feel which way the wind is blowing through surveys, and area studies, and statistics.

God is God ... and there is none else! The only One whose opinion really matters is God! It does not matter what my common sense tells me. It does not matter what my neighbor, or politician, or doctor, or teacher, or lawyer, or sports star tells me ... what matters is what God is trying to tell me. If God is a jealous God (and He is), am I listening with both ears open and my hands cupped behind each ear to hear every detail? Or, am I so busy listening to the continual chatter of the world trying to influence me I miss His "still small voice?" Listen to Him today! He is always right!

God in the Middle – December 9

"God is our Refuge and Strength, a very present help in trouble. Therefore will not fear, though the earth be removed, and though the mountains be carried into the midst of the sea; though the waters thereof roar and be troubled, though the mountains shake with the swelling thereof, Selah. There is a river, the streams whereof shall make fat the city of God, the holy place of the tabernacles of the most High. God is in the midst of her; she shall not be moved: God shall help her, and that right early" (Psalm 46:1-5). When God is in the middle of something, there is no reason to fear. When we keep God in the center of our lives and His will as the driving force in our lives, we will be far more likely to stay on the course He wants for us, and we will have His help along the way. When God is in the center of our dreams for the future, the path we are to take will unfold in front of us with a clarity we cannot miss. When God stays in the center of our lives and our finances are under His control, we will experience the blessing of our needs being met, and having money to use for His causes. When God is in the "midst" of our lives, there is nothing He cannot do for us. He can remove the earth; He can put a mountain in the middle of the sea; and He can shake mountains. The key is for us to keep God in the middle of our lives and plans.

When we move God off the center-place of our lives, we become responsible for the drastic changes that need to be made. When we put our desires above God's desires for us, and we take the control for our own will for our lives, we will potentially end up in a ship-wreck. When we make our money more important than the simple principle of tithing the Bible gives us, we will face potential financial disaster. Regardless of what you are facing in your life, you will face potential disaster without God in the center of your plans. One leader after the other throughout the history of mankind has tried to take God off His rightful throne in the center of their lives, and to sit on that throne themselves. The result has always been the same. God allows them to be their own source of strength, and disaster follows. For those who have humbled themselves before God, He has always "moved mountains" to benefit them and their righteous cause.

Even when things look toughest, keep your God in the middle of your plans and life. You will not be sorry for doing that. Any other person or thing that replaces Him cannot promise you the power God brings when He comes to live within you! Don't trust the temporary things around you in this world for help. Trust your God and keep Him central in your plans!

It's Easy to Bend – December 10

"Just have one drink ... it won't kill you." "Just try it, everybody else is doing it. All your friends are doing it. It won't hurt you." "Nobody sees what you're doing, go ahead and try it." The first two set of phrases were actual statements made to me during my formative teenage years of life. The last phrase was what my sin nature has whispered to my soul many times since. Today I read a wonderful story of a group of young men who decided they would not bend to peer pressure, or to that rotten sin-nature within them telling them it's okay to go against the standards and principles of the Word of God.

One family; the children of Jonadab (son of Rechab), had made a promise to their father that they would not drink wine, or build houses. In this account in Jeremiah 35 we read someone told them to sit down and enjoy some wine with them. They refused, stating they had made a commitment to their father not to go against his word. Today we are living in a society where excuses many things the Bible says we should avoid. Jeremiah was so impressed with the conviction of these young men that he wrote their story in the Bible. Not only was Jeremiah impressed with them, but God also was and is. *"And Jeremiah said unto the house of the Rechabites, 'Thus saith the LORD of hosts, the God of Israel; Because ye have obeyed the commandment of Jonadab your father, and kept all his precepts, and done according unto all that he hath commanded you: Therefore thus saith the LORD of hosts, the God of Israel;* **Jonadab the son of Rechab shall not want a man to stand before Me forever**" (Jeremiah 35:18-19).

God is looking for some people who will stand and be counted today. I know it is tough to do what is right when so many other people are doing what is wrong and making seemingly rational excuses for their behavior. I'm thankful I was taught Biblical principles to build my life upon and to understand where to take a stand. This world will always try to entice the believer to "step over the line" from what is right to what is just slightly wrong. Please beware of this trick, and be careful where you step! God is still searching for young and older men and women who will not bend to the pressures of the society around us. Will you be one of them, or will you give in to the deception of the world? God's Word is clear enough about what we should and should not do. God gave the believer the Holy Spirit to witness with our spirit when we are about to do wrong. The ministry of conviction the Holy Spirit gives to you, while not necessarily enjoyable, is needed every day. Don't bend ... please!

For Your Own Good – December 11

I remember when I was a little boy, having to take some very nasty tasting medicine. I've heard horror stories of castor oil (I have a feeling that is the medicine I'm talking about), but I'm not sure if that's what I was taking. I can only tell you that every taste-bud in my mouth, nose, ears and eyes (I know you don't have taste-buds in some of those places, but I'm trying to make a point) revolted as the medicine left the spoon and proceeded down my throat. I can still hear my mom telling me I should take this horrible tasting medicine for my own good.

God has provided some medicine for our lives that tastes much better and I am sure is far superior to whatever medicine that was I was taking years ago. *"And the LORD commanded us to do all these statutes, to fear the LORD our God, for our good always, that He might preserve us alive, as it is at this day"* (Deuteronomy 6:24). God had provided Moses and the children of Israel a road map for success in their lives. He gave us His laws and statutes to help us stay out of the ditches of life, and to stay in the center of His will. All that sounds good to us … until we get nearer the ditch and see something that looks attractive over there. We know better, but for some reason, we are drawn to the ditches.

I love this verse today because it is so true! God gives us a list of guidelines for our lives to be lived successfully. Some may call them "rules," or "laws," or some other word that often makes us feel restricted. However, as this verse says, God's standards are not for restriction, but for freedom! You see, if you step outside God's standards, you will find a pitfall of life. You will wish you had stayed on the right path. The ends of our choices are often destruction and heartache. The greatest joy and freedom we will ever experience is in the center of the will of God. In the center of the path that God desires us to walk upon. The greatest joy in the life of any person on this earth is to accomplish the things God desired us to do when He originally designed us. One day a friend of mine invited me to hunt pheasants with him. He told me he had two "bird-dogs" to help us find the pheasants. I had never hunted with a dog like this before. As we started to walk through the fields, I watched these dogs as they pointed a straight line from the tip of their tail to the tip of their nose … directly where the pheasants were hiding. These dogs were so excited to go with us, because they were doing exactly what God made them to do. Are you following His Word today and being obedient to what you read? You will not find true happiness until you surrender to His Word today. It's for your own good.

From the Cradle to the Cross for You – December 12

Santa Claus and Rudolph and mistletoe and candy canes and tinsel and shopping and ... have crowded our attention with the purpose of replacing the real meaning of Christmas. Today I was reading in the book of Hebrews and was reminded again why we celebrate Christmas. *"Forasmuch then as the children are partakers of flesh and blood, He also Himself likewise took part of the same; that through death He might destroy him that had the power of death, that is, the devil ... Wherefore in all things it behooved Him to be made like unto His brethren, that He might be a merciful and faithful high priest in things pertaining to God, to make reconciliation for the sins of the people. For in that He Himself hath suffered being tempted, He is able to succor them that are tempted"* (Hebrews 2:14, 17-18).

I hope you take the time to read these verses and don't just fly right past them. These verses contain the true meaning of Christmas. You and I (*flesh and blood*) were without hope; separated from a holy God because of our unholiness. God in His great mercy left the absolutely indescribable beauties of Heaven to be made *flesh and blood* so He could destroy the eternal death that was awaiting each of us. He took on this human cloak, and wore it for about thirty-three years without sin, so He could stretch His arms wide on a cross and die for the sins of the entire world. He did all that for you and for me ... amazing love ... how can it be? According to verse eighteen, He did all of this so He could purchase the guarantee of our reconciliation back to a God that demands righteousness.

Now comes the part that totally falls on as our responsibility. Jesus Christ has done all He can to provide this salvation for all mankind; what are you doing to tell them about it? *"How shall we escape, if we neglect so great salvation; which at the first began to be spoken by the Lord, and was confirmed unto us by them that heard Him"* (Hebrews 2:3). I have heard this verse preached that we need to respond to the Gospel when we hear it; and I agree we should. However, this verse is speaking to those who are already saved. The meaning behind this verse, and the meaning I hope you and I will carry all through this Christmas season is that we who are saved already ... we who know the reality of this salvation ... need to be careful we do not neglect to tell others about it. We have already been given the greatest gift of all, but God still has an extended hand to offer that same gift to *"whosoever shall call upon the name of the Lord."* When was the last time you invited someone to accept His gift of Jesus? When will you tell someone? Today looks like a perfect day to do it!

What Will You Leave Behind? – December 13

"A good man leaveth an inheritance to his children's children: and the wealth of the sinner is laid up for the just" (Proverbs 13:22).

Just last week I was talking to our oldest granddaughter about Heaven. She began explaining some specific things about Heaven (thanks to excellent teaching from her dad and mom). During her explanation, she talked about my mother, her Nana. She was talking about my mom and the things she was experiencing in Heaven, and a thought ran through my mind. Rylie never met my mother. My mom graduated to Heaven in September and Rylie was born in November of that year. How does she know so much about her great-grandmother whom she never met face-to-face? Her mom has told her story after story about "her" Nana, so much so, Rylie has come to know her through her mom's stories.

When we think about an *"inheritance,"* like the verse above talks about; we mostly think of money, or possessions that will be coming our way! The reality is, if the only inheritance we pass on to those coming behind us is money and property, they will last only for a very brief time. My mother was raised a little poor girl by parents who were poor. She did not know she was poor, until later in her life. She lived a very "average" life when it came to finances. If we wanted something in our family, we had to work extra to earn the money to buy it ... we did not have a trust fund we could reach into. As the world would view my mother, they would say her life was not that impressive ... they would be wrong.

My mother spent her life leaving behind an inheritance ... not only for my sister and me ... not only for our children ... but now for the children of our children who have never even met her. My mother lived in a way that affords our children the privilege of sharing multiple stories of adventure, and love my mother gave them. I want to give this same kind of inheritance to our children/grandchildren/great-grandchildren (if the Lord tarries His coming). If I want to leave this, I must make the investment of time, energy, love, and yes, even my money.

This is not only true for our family, but I also have this burden for our ministry as well. We want to leave a mark that will remain long after we have touched Heaven. I am hopeful the things I will do today will result in heavenly dividends for the future. I want to make a difference for the generations to come. How about you? What will you do today to make a difference that will far outlive you? Get busy and make a foot-print!

Truth Mixed With Faith – December 14

Just having good information is not enough. Action must be mixed with the information you have. I would say we are living in a time of "information explosion". My family and I watched a movie (a tear-jerker) a couple of years ago about a family who bought a yellow lab puppy. The movie was basically about the life of the family mingled with the life of this dog. The dog became older and eventually the movie dealt with the family having to deal with the death of this treasured pet. When the movie ended, I asked *"I wonder how many dogs it took to film this movie?"* It was just a question of curiosity, and I did not think I would ever learn the answer. In just about three minutes one of our son-in-law's said, *"Eighteen ..."* I had forgotten the question, but he was busy on his phone "googling" the question and giving me the answer. If something that insignificant is found that easily, think of all the "important" information available to us today.

God gave us His Word ... it contains all the truth we need for living right before Him on this earth. Our problem is not a lack of information, but a lack of faith to apply that information. Check out these incredible verses: *"Let us therefore fear, lest, a promise being left us of entering into His rest, any of you should seem to come short of it. For unto us was the Gospel preached, as well as unto them: But the word preached did not profit them, not being mixed with faith in them that heard it"* (Hebrews 4:1-2). Did you catch that last phrase? *"But the word preached did not profit them, not being mixed with faith ..."*

Over the years of my life I have heard many people use the excuse for leaving a church, that they are not being fed. I am all for going to a church that faithfully teaches and preaches the Word of God and feeds its people. However, I am convinced much of our problem (if we are honest) comes from the fact we often hear the Word of God, but we are so filled with skepticism and doubt that we do not benefit from the simple teaching that is being given. Let's not dwell on the negative today, but get the lesson I believe God wanted us to have after reading these verses. Take the Word of God you read, or hear, and mix it with a big dose of faith. The reason is that the information in the Bible is not enough to change your life. Many people own a Bible. Some people actually believe it and the change that faith makes in their life is undeniable! Be one of those people. Don't simply gather spiritual information to be able to debate someone. Take the truths of the Bible as your standard for living and watch what mingling faith with the truth will do in your life!

An Eternal Perspective – December 15

In all of Job's troubles, he cried out to his friends and said, *"Oh that my words were now written! Oh that they were printed in a book! That they were graven with an iron pen and lead in the rock for ever"* (Job 19:23-24)! Little did he know his words would be placed in the Book of the ages, and they would be far more secure than if someone took an iron pen and engraved them on a rock. The rocks of Job's day are buried under the dirt of the ages since his time, but the Word of the Lord is going to endure forever!

What I really wanted you to see are the verses that follow these, because they are the message Job wanted to make sure endured through time. He wrote, *"For I know that my Redeemer liveth, and that He shall stand at the latter day upon the earth: And though after my skin worms destroy this body, yet in my flesh shall I see God"* (Job 19:25-26). The message Job wanted to be sure was engraved for the generations ahead to see is, regardless of what happens to us physically, God is in control, and His Redeemer will live no matter what man thinks of Him.

I want to encourage you who are reading this today with the same thought. What happens to you in your physical body, does not affect the effectiveness of our God! Regardless of good health, poor health, or something in between, God is still God and He will remain faithful all the way through. We have a saying we repeat in our church often. *"God is good all the time ... all the time God is good."* This is so true, and it was exactly the message Job wanted to convey to those who were sitting beside him trying to destroy any hope he had left!

There will always be news that is discouraging ... your Redeemer still lives! There will be tragedy that hits your family ... your Redeemer still lives! There will always be bills that seem insurmountable ... your Redeemer still live! Your health will be good and bad ... your Redeemer still lives! There will be good and bad leaders in your business, country, and church ... your Redeemer still lives!

I'm not sure what is in front of you or me today, but I do know my Redeemer liveth today! I do know there is nothing that will come to me that will be more than I can handle. It may feel that way to you (just like it did for Job), but in the dark moments, just remember your Redeemer still lives and He is in control! There is nothing that will happen today that you and He cannot handle together! Trust Him today for all you will need.

No, Not One – December 16

If we are not careful, the longer we are a believer, the greater the tendency is for us to become self-righteous. *"After all, I've been at this a long time … I think I've got this "Christianity" thing down pretty well by now."* What a dangerous way of thinking! Now I know none of us would actually say those words, but our thoughts and actions prove they are in the heart of many of us "seasoned" believers. Let me give you three verses that will help to shake you out of that comfortable way of spiritual thinking.

"The fool hath said in his heart, 'There is no God.' Corrupt are they, and have done abominable iniquity: There is none that doeth good. God looked down from Heaven upon the children of men, to see if there were any that did understand, that did seek God. Every one of them is gone back: They are altogether become filthy; there is none that doeth good, no, not one" (Psalm 53:1-3).

Adam – created in perfection, ate of the fruit of the one tree he was told not to eat from. Noah – built the ark and lived righteously and got drunk and was a disgrace. Abraham – the father of the Jews, lied twice about his wife being his sister … oh, that's right … that was only a half-lie (she was his half-sister). Jacob – the father of the twelve tribes of Israel stole his brother's birthright and lied throughout his life. Joseph – a man of character, but was filled with some pride as he revealed his dream to his brothers of them bowing down to him. Moses – led Israel out of captivity, but murdered an Egyptian before doing so. Peter – promised allegiance to Christ, but denied Him.

The above list in no way is meant to take away from what these men did in their life-times; it is simply meant to show you and me that the verses from Psalm 53 are absolutely true! The one who penned the words (David), raped a women and murdered her husband. *"There is none that doeth good … Every one of them is gone back … altogether filthy … none that doeth good, no not one."* The sooner we recognize that this describes us, the better chance we have of living a spirit-filled life. You see, when we think we have arrived, in essence we are saying, *"There is no God."* What I mean is, our self-righteous attitudes and actions display that we have not humbled ourselves to the point where God is actually elevated to the throne of our lives. When we act as though we have arrived, and all others are some kind of spiritual peons hoping to attain our level of spirituality, we are in trouble. Thank God for sending Jesus! Humble yourself before Him today!

Milk or Meat? – December 17

On the one-year anniversary of our wedding, we decided we would go to the nicest restaurant in our town to celebrate. We had never been there before, so we invited another couple to join us. I will never forget the meal. I was trying to be the "loving" husband, so I told my lovely wife of one year to order anything she liked on the menu (we had saved our money for some time for this night). Thinking we were doing a great thing, we ordered a Filet Mignon steak (she order the "queen cut" and I ordered the "king cut"). I could not wait to see our steaks. The husband of the other couple also ordered the "king cut." His wife (who weighed about eighty-five pounds with every piece of clothing she owned on) ordered the Prime Rib. When the waiter approached our table, my mouth was watering for that HUGE "king-cut" Filet Mignon steak I was going to enjoy. She sat my plate in front of me, and I was in sheer excitement. The others received their Filet Mignon steaks, and we all three sat in wonder as we watched the Prime Rib being served to the skinniest person in our group. I had never seen a Prime Rib before, and I was thinking it was a little piece of meat hanging on a rib ... the piece of beef not only covered her plate, but hung over the sides. We all sat with our mouths hanging open in shock!

The Bible uses the illustration of milk and meat to describe what we dine on in the spiritual way. *"For when for the time ye ought to be teachers, ye have need that one teach you again which be the first principles of the oracles of God; and are become such as have need of milk, and not of strong meat. For every one that useth milk is unskillful in the word of righteousness: For he is a babe. But strong meat belongeth to them that are of full age, even those who by reason of use have their senses exercised to discern both good and evil"* (Hebrews 5:12-14).

When we first started out in our faith, we were like a baby ... all we needed was some simple truths to excite us (the milk of the Word of God). As we grow up and mature in our walk with God, there ought to be a change in our appetite spiritually. We ought to crave that Prime Rib God has in His Word. It takes more to get a Prime Rib than it does to get a bottle of milk. Be willing to work to find these delicious truths in the Word of God today. Don't settle for the milk ... go for the Prime Rib! I learned my lesson in that restaurant. We returned to that fancy restaurant again for our tenth anniversary ... I ordered the Prime Rib! I don't want any less in my spiritual diet either. I want to study to find the most precious truths in my Bible today! Pull up a chair and enjoy the feast waiting in God's Word!

God's Requirements – December 18

"And now, Israel, what doth the LORD thy God require of thee, but to fear the LORD thy God, to walk in all His ways, and to love Him and to serve the LORD thy God with all thy heart and with all thy soul, to keep the commandments of the LORD, and His statutes, which I command thee this day for thy good" (Deuteronomy 10:12-13).

How can I please God? What does He require from me to be considered successful by Him? We spend too much time in our lives trying to please others. We are all guilty of this. We wear clothing we don't even like in order to please others. We go places we don't really like going to, to please others. We eat things we don't particularly like to please others. What can we do to please God? He makes it clear. There are four things we need to do if we want to be a success in the eyes of our God.

1. Fear the LORD thy God – I have written about this phrase so many times you are probably tired of reading about it, but God includes this as the very first thing we need to please Him. Are you living in a way that shows you have such respect for God that you fear disappointing Him? Or are you trying to live near the edge, and close to the world? I want to fear God enough to stay close to Him and far from the world.

2. Walk in all His ways – This is a deliberate process, not a quick sprint. When you walk with someone, you tend to have time to discuss the things that really touch your heart. Hurry is not involved in this step. We need to spend time, slowing down, listening to what God has to say to our hearts in the quietness of that moment.

3. Love Him and serve Him – This sounds simple, but it is absolutely necessary. When you love someone, you want to do things that show your love for them. You develop a heart of service for them, and you don't mind doing things for them. If we love God, we will do things we know bring delight to His heart. If we love God, we will look for things to do to show Him that love.

4. Keep the commandments and statutes – This sounds simple too, but if we really love God we will not be constantly questioning the principles and truths of His Word, we will simply obey what He has written clearly, and even what is inferred, or suggested in the Bible. Walk honestly before men and God. Follow His Word with all your heart!

Heavenly Hiding Place – December 19

When we were kids, one of our favorite games was "Hide and Seek." One person counted to 100, while the rest of us hid from them. The idea was to find the best hiding place and be the last one who was found, or better yet, to never be found. Every now and then you could find a spot no one else knew about and it became your "sweet spot." When I was six years old I found the best "sweet spot" in the history of mankind. One day, after having broken off my mother's favorite flowers and lying about doing it, I realized I was a sinner and needed a Savior. I found my best "hiding place" in Jesus Christ. What a day that was for me! It is still my fondest memory of all. That day, my sins which still hound me to this day, were covered and removed by my wonderful Lord, Jesus Christ.

We are living in turbulent times and times when we could begin to fear if we are not careful. Let me share some wonderful verses I just read that could give you hope and peace. *"What time I am afraid, I will trust in Thee. In God I will praise His Word, in God I have put my trust; I will not fear what flesh can do unto me"* (Psalm 56:3-4 [verse 4 is repeated again in verses 10-11]). I love this whole chapter. It again and again reminds me where my strength and protection come from. If we are not careful we will begin to trust in our own abilities and wisdom to take care of us. The reality is that our own wisdom gets us into more trouble, and into wrong thinking. I want to trust God! I want to depend on His power, rather than my own, to guide me in this life.

There are a number of lessons I learn from this chapter. First I learn that all of us experience fear at some point in our lives. Even David, the second king of Israel, and one of the fiercest soldiers experienced times of fear. Having fear is not a sign of weakness, or an indication that we are not loving and trusting God. It is a natural emotion we must deal with properly. The second thing I learn is that after the fear comes, I need to run to my Heavenly Father for protection. I hope you noticed the phrase, *"In God"* throughout those two verses. The hope we have for safety is not in our bank account, or our good health, or our friends or family, but in our God! God is able to protect us, to guide us, to care for every need we have (even before we know we have the need), and He alone is the Person we ought to run to. So, as you face the problems and fears of the day today, run to your God! He is waiting to give the help you will need for the challenges of this day and all the days you have to live. I am so thankful for this Heavenly Hiding Place! What a blessing to be a Christian!

Glued to God – December 20

Over thirty years ago the pastor who married my wife and I told us we were to "leave" our parents and to "cleave" to each other. He explained the word, "*cleave*" meant we were to be glued to each other. We discussed then the importance of weathering the storms that life would bring to us, and the importance of staying together. We certainly have had storms, but we have also has the best that more than thirty years can bring a couple! God has been good to us every step of the way.

Today I read "*Ye shall walk after the LORD your God, and fear Him, and keep His commandments, and obey His voice, and ye shall serve Him, and **cleave** unto Him*" (Deuteronomy 13:4). There is that word, "*cleave.*" My mind ran back to earlier this week when I had read, "*Thou shalt fear the LORD thy God; Him shalt thou serve, and to Him shalt thou **cleave**, and swear by His name*" (Deuteronomy 10:20). I think God wants us to get this idea! Any time I see a phrase or a word repeated, it makes me sit up and take notice. When God repeats Himself, I think it is something He wants us to take notice to.

In both of these verses we are encouraged to stay glued to our God. Just as in the days when Moses wrote these words, there are constant pressures from this world to conform to their way of thinking; to their standards; and to their practices. The Israelites were tempted throughout their history to give in to idol-worship. For us today it might not be an idol, but a car, clothing, a house, a position at work, or something like these. It might be to be far looser in our personal standards than we know we should be according to the Bible. It might be to take "just one" drink. It might be to go just once into that place we know we shouldn't. It might be the pressure to laugh at a filthy joke so we don't stick out among our "friends." It could be to cheat just a little on our taxes (after all, everyone else is doing it …).

These two verses tell us the importance of "cleaving" to our God in the day we are living. We ought to stay closely glued to the truths our God has given us in the Bible. We ought to walk with Him on a daily basis, so when He wants to reveal something to us, we have such sensitivity to the Holy Spirit that we hear His voice loud and clear! Walk with Him … fear Him … follow His commandments … obey His voice … serve Him … in short, "*cleave*" to our God! Just as the preacher advised my wife and me to be glued to each other, I am encouraging you today to be glued to your God! He should be the only source for guidance you totally depend on today.

Peculiar People – December 21

"For thou art an holy people unto the LORD thy God, and the LORD hath chosen thee to be a peculiar people unto Himself, above all the nations that are upon the earth" (Deuteronomy 14:2).

God called the believer to be a light to this darkened world. Have you ever thought about this ... light cannot blend with darkness? Light and darkness are total opposites. Why is it we believers try to look and act so much like the world today? We let the television determine how we dress and what we think is normal. Families are a mess on TV and they are a mess in real life because we have developed the world's philosophies on what a real family ought to look like. In case you have not noticed, this world is in a real mess right now. Why would we want to imitate and copy what they think and do?

God called His children in Israel to be a different kind of people. He encouraged them not to conform to this world and its pagan practices. I want to tell you the world around us still practices pagan activities every day. Oh, I know we all wear clothes now (some not so many as others), but our society is involved in incredibly horrific activities ... and we believers, if not careful, will be drawn into thinking all these things are just fine and acceptable.

What ever happened to us being "different?" God was not talking about us being weird, but "peculiar." This word carries the idea of a precious stone, or a treasure. The idea I believe God wanted us to get is this ... you and I are valuable to Him, so we ought not allow ourselves to be drawn down to the world's way of thinking, to their standards. We are precious to Him, and extremely valuable. When you think of the price God paid for our redemption, it ought to cause us to desire to live for Him and walk with Him!

Be careful today not to let the world pull you down to their way of thinking and to their standards. You are a precious jewel in the eyes of your God. Let your light so shine before men today that they will see your good works and give glory to the God Who saved you! Don't let your testimony be tainted by the influences of the world today. God is depending on your living in such a spirit-filled way that those in the world watching you will want what you have. When was the last time your testimony made a difference to someone outside of Christ? It should be our goal for that to happen somewhere along our path today!

Answering Words of Truth – December 22

It is this time of year when people flock to the shopping malls for last minute shopping, and just to be a part of the "event" of Christmas shopping. When I was in my High School years, I went to the mall most Friday nights. Before you judge me, let me explain. I had a youth worker from my local church who went to the mall every Friday night to hand out tracts and to witness to people. He invited me to come with him, and I agreed. We spent many Friday nights arguing and debating issues like reincarnation, and transcendental meditation, and whether there really was a Heaven or Hell. It was a great time of "on the job training" for me.

My fear and frustration came in that I did not know my Bible enough at the time (even though saved for about ten years) to adequately defend or present what I believed. One of the greatest advertisements I can give for reading your Bible every day is that you cannot know it if you are not living in it every day! The writer of Proverbs wrote, *"That I might make thee know the certainty of the words of truth; that thou mightest answer the words of truth to them that send unto thee"* (Proverbs 22:21).

I want this verse to be true of me. First, I want to know the *"certainty"* of the words. There are those around us every day who are telling us the Bible is not true; that it is a book of fables for weak minded people; or it is outdated and not relevant for the days we live in. The people who say those things have never read this Bible. I want to read it and allow the Holy Spirit of God to guide me into its deepest truths so I can know the *"certainty"* of what it is saying. That word means evenly balanced; the actual weight of something; the reality of it. I want to know the realities of Scripture for my own life and the life of those I influence.

The second part of the verse says this knowledge of Scripture is important so I can *"answer the words of truth to them that send unto"* me. There are people with real questions today. There are people who are genuinely searching for the truths we know from the Bible. I want to know my Bible well enough so when they have a question, I will know the answer from my Bible. There have been many times when someone has asked me a question like I am describing and I was without an answer. I silently prayed, asking the Holy Spirit to guide my heart to the right answer. I have seen it happen many times when praying this way when I recall a verse I have read, or a passage that deals with the exact question that has come. We need to be students of the Word so we can answer words of truth!

A Simple Door-keeper – December 23

"For a day in Thy courts is better than a thousand. I had rather be a door-keeper in the house of my God, than to dwell in the tents of wickedness. For the LORD God is a sun and shield: the LORD will give grace and glory: no good thing will He withhold from them that walk uprightly. O LORD of hosts, blessed is the man that trusteth in Thee." (Psalm 84:10-12).

There was an old picture I remember growing up of a farmer riding a mule. In the farmer's hand was a stick with a carrot tied to the end. The farmer had the carrot dangling just over the nose of the mule. The idea of the picture was that the mule moved forward trying to reach the carrot. It is obvious the Devil knows this trick. He has been "dangling" small sins just out of the reach of Christians ever since the Tree of the Knowledge of Good and Evil in the Garden of Eden. He enticed Eve and Adam to take of the fruit that was there, but seemed just out of their reach. He has not changed his plan even today.

The Devil is the master of deception. He will make those things that will destroy our lives seem like they are not really that bad. He has convinced many believers that "just one time will not hurt anything." I love the second phrase in the verses above ... *"I had rather be a door-keeper in the house of my God ..."* I think this is the response we all need to practice for the times when the Devil comes knocking on our hearts door with an option for sin!

The door-keeper does not seem that important on the surface, but think about it for a moment or two. The door-keeper guards those who are inside the building. He is responsible to keep a sharp lookout so when danger approaches, he recognizes it and prevents it from coming in. Today, you need to be a door-keeper over the things you will allow into your heart, mind and body. You also will be called to help those you love to keep the door of their heart pure as well. Now, I know you cannot force someone else to protect their heart, but you can pray for them ... you can advise them when asked ... you can live in a way before them that will encourage them to follow your example.

I may never have some of the things the Devil is dangling in front of me on a regular basis ... but *"I had rather be a door-keeper in the house of my God ..."* with a smile on my face, and a heart that is purely following God. This is a challenge for me and you, but it is something that is altogether possible for us to attain. It is Gods desire for each believer reading this today. He has a wonderful will that will bring joy to our heart if we are faithful!

The Key to Heaven's Door – December 24

A good point is made in Hebrews 10. *"For it is not possible that the blood of bulls and of goats should take away sins"* (Hebrews 10:4). Think about it ... for thousands of years, since Adam and Eve sinned in the Garden of Eden, mankind was looking for the Messiah. They were looking expectantly for the Lamb of God Who would take away the sin of the world. They knew the reality of this verse. They knew the bulls, goats, sheep and pigeons they were sacrificing were not perfect. God requires a perfect sacrifice for sin. This same thing is true today with the substitutes men offer today to replace Jesus Christ. Many people believe if they go to the right church that will satisfy the demands of God. That is not enough! Some feel if they do more good than bad then there is some grand scale in Heaven that will tip their way to allow them to enter. We cannot do enough "good" things to erase the sin of our past! There is no substitute for THE Lamb of God!

How is God ultimately satisfied? *"By the which will we are sanctified through the offering of the body of Jesus Christ once for all"* (Hebrews 10:10). There is the answer for all mankind. It is not found in bowing in a certain direction so many times a day. It is not through taking of communion to wash away our sins. It is not through sitting in a booth confessing your sins to another sinner, expecting him to be able to somehow forgive your sins when he cannot stop sinning himself. It is not through joining a church (of any denomination). It is simply through trusting the sacrifice God made for you. WOW! Read that again ... salvation comes to all men/women simply through trusting the sacrifice God made for you ... not through the sacrifice you make for your sins, or some other person offers for your sin!

I have a horrible habit. I get a key and put it on my key-ring, only to look at that key a few months later and wonder what door it fits. I have done this numerous times. Right now there is a key lying on my desk. I have no idea what it is for. I have walked to my front door and tried the key ... It doesn't fit. If I want to enter Heaven, I need to use the key the Owner has made to get in the door! God gave us all the Key to Heaven. It is none other than His only-begotten Son! There is no other way! The blood of Jesus Christ was God's final answer to the sin problem we face, and the world faces today. The good news is we have the Key. The bad news is we have not told the rest of the world about it like we should! We have the answer! Take the time to tell someone about it today!

What Did God Buy for Christmas? – December 25

Merry Christmas! One of the things I miss the most at Thanksgiving and Christmas is my mom. She lived for this morning! She had a very hard time not giving out gifts as she bought them, because she loved giving so much! I want to divert slightly from what I normally do in writing this devotional to share a story my mom told hundreds of times during her lifetime. I want to honor of her today, the day we honor Jesus' birthday.

There was a little boy who made a beautiful sailboat with his father. They worked on gluing the different parts together. They carefully made the sail, and ran the strings through the correct loops and made sure they were fastened in the right places. They painted the sailboat a dark blue with a white stripe running around the boat. When they were all finished with the boat, the little boy painted his initials at the back of the boat and the date he had finished. He and his father ran to the large lake near their house to sail the boat for the first time. They had attached a string to the boat so they could hold onto it. The wind blew stronger than they imagined, and the ship sailed wonderfully out into the lake. As the string tightened, it snapped, and the ship sailed out further and further into the lake until they could not see it anymore. The ship was gone. They searched the banks around the lake, but could not find the ship. Finally, one day the little boy saw his ship in the window of a local second-hand store. He went in and told the owner of the store that it was his ship he had lost. The owner told him he would need to pay the price to buy it back. The little boy worked and worked, saving his money until he had enough to buy his own boat back.

This boy is a picture of our Savior. He made us. When we had the choice to make, we sailed away from Him in our sin. He was not content with that, and He came here to buy us back with His own blood. This is the Christmas story. Here's how God described it: "*Who **gave Himself for us**, that He might **redeem** us from all iniquity, and purify unto Himself a peculiar people, zealous of good works*" (Titus 2:14). God bought back the people He had made. He purchased our forgiveness with the blood of His only-begotten Son. The message of Christmas is Jesus. The reality is God viewed each of us as so valuable that He sent His Son in order to buy us back! You have worth today! Praise God for His unspeakable gift!

My mother is in Heaven with her Savior on this Christmas day. I am thankful for a mother who told me and thousands of children this story! I'm thankful for the opportunity to tell everyone I meet this same story!

Welcome Home – December 26

When I was in college, I remember hearing a song around Christmas that talked about being home for Christmas. I always loved coming home around the holidays, and especially around Christmas. I remember coming home for Christmas when we lived in Maryland and the rest of our family lived in Pennsylvania. It was so great to come walking down the walk to our house and seeing the lights on inside. The hugs and laughter that followed entering the house were so special to all of us.

There is a story in the Bible I always enjoy reading in Luke 15. There are actually three stories about something that was lost being found, and the joy in Heaven when a sinner repents. I love all the stories, but the third story is about a son who leaves home and then returns. There is one verse in this chapter that always deeply touches my heart. It is the picture of the son that had left, returning home. He is nervous about the reaction of his father to his change of heart and his return. He is returning without any money, with a stench from working with pigs, and with a totally repentant heart. He is planning to ask to become a simple servant in his father's home. The verse that touches my heart every time says, *"And he arose, and came to his father. But **when he was yet a great way off**, his father saw him, and had compassion, and ran, and fell on his neck, and kissed him"* (Luke 15:20).

Anticipating the worst, the returning, repentant son found the best. Before he could ask for restoration, the father granted far more than he could have imagined! Before he could make the long speech asking for forgiveness that he had been practicing over and over during his long trek home from the far country, his father poured love and forgiveness on him. Before he could reach the back door of the house, before he got close to the house, his father ran to meet him!

The father in this story represents my Heavenly Father. The son who had left and turned his back on his father is me. The pig's sty represents anything outside of God's will for me that I thought was a better alternative. The far country is a place that is not so far away from any of us. It's just on the other side of God's plan for our lives, and it will always result in a lack of satisfaction and fulfillment. Why do we go there? Why wander from the joys of the place where all our needs are met? The important part of this story is not the son leaving … it is the reaction of the father at his return! I'm so thankful for my Heavenly Father running to meet me when I turn back toward Him! What a great God we serve! Thank Him today!

For Their Sake – December 27

I must praise God today for all the people who left the comfort of their church building, or their home to reach out to my ancestors with the Gospel of Jesus Christ! We sometimes get so caught up with the things that are happening around us on a daily basis that we forget to look back at the path of blessing God has provided for us and our family. I am here writing to you today as a third generation believer. My spiritual roots may run deeper than that, but to my own understanding, I am sure of three generations past who knew the Gospel and were saved because of it. I am also thrilled to tell you we have two more generations which have come from us. Our children are all believers, and some of our grandchildren have already made a professions of faith in Jesus Christ.

The Bible says of Jesus: "*Wherefore Jesus also, that He might sanctify the people with His own blood, suffered without the gate. Let us go forth therefore unto him without the camp, bearing his reproach*" (Hebrews 13:12-13). Did you catch that phrase, "*suffered without the gate*"? To me that means Jesus willingly left through the gates of pearl that surrounded Heaven to come to this sin-cursed earth to bring us redemption. Jesus, even though equal with God, left that position in Heaven to take on a form that would have no reputation ... that would be like a servant ... that would display humility to the point of the death on a cruel cross (Philippians 2:5-8). He left the security of the gates, to come to die for you and me.

Don't miss the challenge of the second of these verses bring us. Just as Jesus left His place of safety and security, God encouraged us to do the same in this world we are living. We ought to go out where the unsaved are and proclaim the message of hope Jesus brought to us. The first opportunity I had to preach an "official" message, was at the Green Street Rescue Mission in downtown Philadelphia. I remember having a half-hour message that lasted almost five minutes! I was horrible ... but I fell head-over-heels in love with going to the places Jesus would go to preach/teach! I have not gotten over the thrill of preaching/teaching to people who are generally forgotten by Christianity today. I love that I get the chance to preach in places where I know I will never receive any pay. I want to be an ambassador in this foreign land we call "the world." I want to go there and represent my Savior, the King of all kings, and Lord of all lords. Don't hunker down in the safety of your Christian fortress today. Get up and go outside the gate where the needy world lives, and tell them about your Savior! They are dying to hear about Him today!

The Heart of God – December 28

As we near the end of another year, many people will make "New Year's resolutions." These will be goals that are set for the coming year that will be positive and will produce results that will hopefully result in becoming a better person. I have nothing against these for Christians, but I believe our "resolutions" ought to involve a Bible principle. Today I read a good verse that ought to become one of our resolutions for every day we live. The verses I want to share are truly the heart of God for us every day.

"Take heed to yourselves: IF thy brother trespass against thee, rebuke him; and if he repent, forgive him. And if he trespass against thee seven times in a day, and seven times in a day turn again to thee, saying, 'I repent;' thou shalt forgive him" (Luke 17:3-4).

These verses remind me of Peter's question to Jesus about how many times he ought to forgive someone that has offended him. Are you getting the idea that at the heart of God is a forgiving heart? If you have not, you have not read your Bible well. Immediately, I am sure some of you thought there are some people who are habitually sinning that do not deserve the forgiveness of God. There are two things I believe the Bible teaches that might help you.

One of those is found in verse 4 above. There is genuine repentance involved in the asking of forgiveness in these verses. Genuine repentance requires our forgiveness. You might argue that this person returned seven times for the same thing! Is there truly repentance involved? Let me ask you; have you always been successful in completely turning from the sins you have repented of? God knows our wretched condition as sinners. If He can forgive us over and over again for the same sin, I believe we ought to follow His example.

The second thing the Bible teaches clearly is that vengeance is the Lord's, it is not our business. Don't get involved in something that is God's responsibility. We have enough to worry about trying to stay away from sin ourselves. Let's do our part, and honestly and completely forgive and allow the judgment for insincere repentance up to God. It will take all my energy to completely forgive, but it is in this forgiveness I have freedom and peace. Yes, that's right … if I refuse to forgive, and I hold a grudge or bitterness in my heart, then I am the one who will suffer … not the person who offended me. Forgive others today like God has forgiven you. If God can forgive and forget your sins, it is time you follow His heart today!

Do It! – December 29

When my mother was battling cancer, we were always on the look-out for something that would help her ... for something that would give her hope of a solution for the problem. What a tragedy it would have been if we heard about a cure for cancer, but we ignored it. How horrible would it have been if we read all the articles written about the cure, studied it every day, and just ignored all we had read. Are you kidding me? We would have done anything we could to get my mother any treatment we thought would have helped her.

Many of us Christians are guilty of something similar. We have a Bible ... we read the Bible ... we go to church and listen to good Bible teaching/preaching every week ... we attend Bible Study groups ... we memorize verses ... but we don't follow the principles we have read. We go about our normal routines in life just as if we knew nothing of the Bible principles we have read, and our lives show no evidence of having read the Bible. James wrote: *"Wherefore lay apart all filthiness and superfluity of naughtiness, and receive with meekness the engrafted word, which is able to save your souls. But be ye doers of the word, and not hearers only, deceiving your own selves"* (James 1:21-22) (Don't get stuck on the phrase, *"filthiness and superfluity of naughtiness"* – it just means an abundance of bad behavior and hatred).

This verse makes it clear that, to hear the Word of God and do nothing about it means we are really fooling ourselves, and we are not the person we think we are. To listen to all these wonderful truths from the Bible and then to live whatever way we want to afterwards is ... sinful. As a person who wants to be a man of God, I find it daily challenging to surrender to the truths I read each day. I see my flaws, faults and failures every day I read through the pages of my Bible. When I was younger I thought if I just could read my Bible every day I would become a godlier person. I have found for myself that simply reading the words with my eyes and not putting into practice what I have read is of no more value than if I had not read the words at all. I don't want to be a genius in Bible Trivia games, and not live what I have read. I want to be the real deal as a Christian. I want my Heavenly Father to be able to find me ready and willing when He needs something done. If I am going to be that person, I must live out what I read from my Bible each day. If I simply read the pages, but don't transfer the truths to my life, I am simply fooling myself! Let's practice what we read today!

Who Is Propping You Up? – December 30

A verse that has touched my heart for many years took on a special significance to me today. *"But Thou, O LORD, art a shield for me; my glory, and the lifter up of mine head"* (Psalm 3:3). Yesterday I had climbed a tree to hunt deer. As I was preparing to come down the tree (after seeing no deer whatsoever), I fell about fifteen feet to the ground. I landed squarely on my left shoulder in the fall. It knocked the breath from my body. After getting my breath back, I rolled onto my stomach and was very happy to find I could wiggle my hands and could move my feet as well.

To give you the shorter version of a long story, after a trip to the local emergency room ... an EKG ... chest x-rays ... and a CT scan, I was told I have four fractured ribs, and multiple fractures to each rib. Needless to say, it is very difficult to breath, stand, sit, and pretty much everything else! I am praising God today for the reality of Psalm 3:3. I need help doing the most mundane things because if this. There was a point when I found myself asking my dad to help me lift my head up. I thought about this verse.

God certainly was my shield and the lifter up of mine head! Laying there in the woods on my back, I remember looking up toward the sky and thanking God for taking care of me. In hind-sight, I have thought of many things, but there in one central theme I come to each time ... God is good all the time, and all the time, God is good! God shielded me from landing on my head when I fell. He guided me to the ground so I did not break my back. He provided me a cousin close by to come and help me get out of the woods. He has given me two of the best nurses in the history of the world (my precious wife and my dad). He has taken very good care of me, and I am so thankful for it all.

You don't need to fall from a tree to understand this truth. I want to encourage your heart today. I don't know what you are facing as a challenge in your life, but God has promised to be the "lifter up" of your head. I want to tell you to trust Him and His guiding hand. We serve a God Who is paying attention to the things you are facing today. Don't trust the world to provide for your needs, yield yourself to the almighty hand of God today. I think it is appropriate to end this with this thought today ... they say you will always fall in the direction you are leaning in. Lean on the God Who has promised to lift up your head when you need Him the most! Don't lean on your own understanding.

Another Year Passed – December 31

Hard to believe we have come to the last day of another year. I came across a wonderful verse to end the year on. *"And when they saw it, they all murmured, saying, 'That He was gone to be guest with a man that is a sinner'"* (Luke 19:7). What a great thought to end this year! Jesus met this height-challenged tax-collector named Zacchaeus. Those who opposed Jesus thought this was a negative comment about Jesus, but it was the clearest statement about the purpose of Jesus coming to earth. He came for sinners! I hope you find the comfort in this thought that I find. Jesus is a man Who came to save sinners ... and I fit that description perfectly!

As you think about the end of this calendar year, take a few moments to revel in the truth that Jesus humbled Himself to come here for us sinners! There are many people today who spend most of their time to impress others with their religious value. Jesus was unimpressed with this kind of person when He was here on the earth. The criticism He was getting in this verse, was from this very group. I believe it is a good reminder for each of us today; and it is also a good check for us to see if we are really following Jesus Christ today.

If I am going to live my life full out for God, I must give my heart to reaching sinners as well. I want to be sold out for Jesus so much that what He loves is what I love. I want to have a broken heart for the things that broke the heart of Jesus. Think about it ... He left Heaven, not to make a name for Himself, but to reach out to sinners. He left Heaven, not to become popular, or to impress the religious leaders of His day, or ours. He came here for sinners! He came here to become sin for us so we could become the righteousness of God in Him!

As we close out this year, it would be good for us to consider where we are in our walk with the Lord. It is not enough for us to try to impress other believers, we ought to be about our Father's business ... reaching sinners before it's too late! Please consider what you are doing today to make a difference in the lives of sinners who are desperately yearning for forgiveness of sins! I hope when people speak of me and my ministry they say I had a heart for sinners. I want to go where sinners are so I can tell them there is hope regardless of how hopeless they may feel. As we close out these devotionals for another year, let's commit ourselves to doing all we can in the new year to reach sinners for Christ! He has a heart for sinners, and we ought to as well.

CPSIA information can be obtained
at www.ICGtesting.com
Printed in the USA
BVOW08s0439251017
498569BV00001B/1/P